ALSO BY JOE CONASON

*The Hunting of the President: The Ten-Year Campaign to
Destroy Bill Clinton* (with Gene Lyons)

*Big Lies: The Right-wing Propaganda Machine and
How It Distorts the Truth*

*The Raw Deal: How the Bush Republicans Plan to Destroy
Social Security and the Legacy of the New Deal*

It Can Happen Here: Authoritarian Peril in the Age of Bush

MAN OF THE
WORLD

The Further Endeavors of Bill Clinton

JOE CONASON

Simon & Schuster Paperbacks

NEW YORK   LONDON   TORONTO   SYDNEY   NEW DELHI

Simon & Schuster Paperbacks
An Imprint of Simon & Schuster, Inc.
1230 Avenue of the Americas
New York, NY 10020

First Simon & Schuster Paperbacks edition November 2017

SIMON & SCHUSTER PAPERBACKS and colophon are registered trademarks
of Simon & Schuster, Inc.

For information about special discounts for bulk purchases,
please contact Simon & Schuster Special Sales at 1-866-506-1949
or business@simonandschuster.com.

The Simon & Schuster Speakers Bureau can bring authors to your
live event. For more information or to book an event contact the
Simon & Schuster Speakers Bureau at 1-866-248-3049
or visit our website at www.simonspeakers.com.

Interior design by Paul J. Dippolito

Manufactured in the United States of America

10   9   8   7   6   5   4   3   2   1

The Library of Congress has cataloged the hardcover edition as follows:

Names: Conason, Joe, author.
Title: Man of the world : the further endeavors of Bill Clinton / Joe Conason.
Description: First Simon & Schuster hardcover edition. |
New York : Simon & Schuster, 2016. | Includes index.
Identifiers: LCCN 2016031629 (print) | LCCN 2016032161 (ebook) | ISBN
  9781439154106 (hardcover : alk. paper) | ISBN 9781439154113
(trade pbk. : alk. paper) | ISBN 9781439156223 (ebook)
Subjects: LCSH: Clinton, Bill, 1946- | Presidents--United States--Biography.
 | United States--Politics and government--1989-
Classification: LCC E886 .C66 2016 (print) | LCC E886 (ebook) |
DDC 973.929092 [B] --dc23
LC record available at https://lccn.loc.gov/2016031629

ISBN 978-1-4391-5410-6
ISBN 978-1-4391-5411-3 (pbk)
ISBN 978-1-4391-5622-3 (ebook)

For Eleanor and Edward, who already have begun to understand why our common humanity must bring us together. And for their mother, who has taught them so well.

cupied new home. Neither did any of the others standing around in the kitchen with them. But everyone needed caffeine, badly.

"Let's go get some coffee," said Clinton.

The first executive decision of William Jefferson Clinton's post-presidency was to venture into the snowy little town to visit the local delicatessen and bring back some coffee and sandwiches. Pulling on a bright yellow fleece sweatshirt over his T-shirt and jeans, Clinton joined Band in an armored Cadillac limousine, driven by a Secret Service agent, followed by another vehicle with four more agents.

Clinton noticed the first hint of trouble a few minutes later, when they arrived at Lange's Little Shop and Delicatessen on King Street, the town's main drag. The deli's Sunday morning crowd of customers was friendly enough, with a few people shouting "Eight more years!" and "We love you, Bill!" But reporters were milling on the sidewalk, too. When they spied Clinton's small entourage pulling up, a few began to bark questions. At first he could barely hear what they were saying.

"Why did you pardon Marc Rich?"

Alarmed, Doug Band leapt out of the back passenger seat and walked around to the other side of the car, where Clinton already had stepped out. He put an arm around Band's shoulder and whispered softly but firmly: "I'll give you five minutes to clear all this away." He didn't want the armored limousine and all the agents swarming around the closed street. He wanted to arrive in his new hometown more in the style of an ordinary citizen.

Minutes later, Clinton ventured into the crowded deli, where spontaneous applause lit his face with a smile. While Band placed their order, including an egg-salad sandwich for Clinton, he shook hands with his new neighbors, posed for cell phone snapshots, and signed autographs on scraps of paper.

There was no means of escape from the gang of perhaps a dozen or so reporters, which felt to Clinton and Band like a horde of hundreds who suddenly had total access to the former president. Nor did Clinton feel he could simply walk away without answering any of their questions—some friendly, some not so friendly. *New York Times* reporter Adam Nagourney, who had covered both Clintons for years, would later write that the president appeared "in a chatty mood," relaxed and rested as he mingled with neighbors and reporters.

CHAPTER ONE

On the first morning he woke up as a private citizen there was nobody around to serve breakfast to Bill Clinton. For eight years he and Hillary had lived in the White House, where staffers and servants rushed to meet every need; and for ten years before that, they had lived in the Arkansas Governor's Mansion, where similar if not quite equal personal service had always been available at any hour.

It was Sunday, January 21, 2001—and that was all over now.

Both Clintons rose to face their new life somewhat exhausted from the long ordeal of Inauguration Day, which had begun in the White House greeting the new occupants, then continued through the ceremonial investiture of President George W. Bush amid snow and sleet, a protracted farewell with hundreds of friends and staffers at Andrews Air Force Base, and an unusually long journey from Washington to their new home.

Under the foreboding sky, a freezing downpour had grounded the Marine helicopter that was supposed to transport them from the capital, and had later slowed the usual hour's drive from John F. Kennedy Airport to Chappaqua, roughly forty miles north of the city. There they had ended the day dining late at a local restaurant with daughter Chelsea, their close friends Terry McAuliffe and his wife Dorothy, and Douglas Band, a former deputy assistant to the president who had agreed to stay with Clinton into his post-presidency.

Nobody had known just how tired the former president was until he fell fast asleep in the Chevy Suburban that brought them all from Kennedy Airport to Westchester.

When the Clintons came downstairs on that first morning, the former president and first lady realized that not only was there nobody available to prepare breakfast for them, but that they had no idea how to make even a cup of coffee in their sparsely furnished and rarely oc-

"So far it's been wonderful," Clinton said of life after the presidency. On his first night in Chappaqua he had slept "like a rock," he added—and no, he hadn't bothered to read the Sunday papers or turn on the television yet.

With pleasantries out of the way, what ensued was an impromptu press conference. The journalists peppered a wholly unprepared ex-president with inquiries about the scores of pardons and commutations—totaling 177—he had signed during his last day in the White House. Mostly he responded to the questions in generalities, offering a promise to prepare a memo on the "pardon process" for his successor, and a short lecture on compassion toward former sinners.

"The word 'pardon' is somehow almost a misnomer," said Clinton. "You're not saying these people didn't commit the offense. You're saying they paid, they paid in full." In fairness, he suggested, "we ought to be more open-minded" about individuals who have discharged their debt to society.

Perhaps those deserving of compassion included people like Susan McDougal, the Whitewater figure who had refused to implicate the Clintons in wrongdoing and spent miserable years in jail, or Henry Cisneros, the former housing secretary convicted of paying off a mistress with public funds, who had left office in disgrace. He had pardoned both of them. Arguably even a repentant narcotics smuggler who had done serious time might deserve consideration. That "paid in full" category, however, most assuredly did not include Rich, the "fugitive financier" holed up in a luxurious Swiss chateau while refusing to face multiple charges of tax fraud and violating the U.S. embargo against Iran.

Why would you pardon him?

"I spent a lot of time on that case. I think there are very good reasons for it," Clinton replied, and referred further inquiries to Rich's Washington attorney, Jack Quinn, who had formerly worked for him in the White House counsel's office. Quinn could explain the legal theory behind the pardons of Rich and his business partner, Pincus Green, who had faced similar charges, fled to Switzerland with Rich, and received a pardon, too.

At last Clinton said he needed to go home, to continue the weekend's work of unpacking with Hillary, who was thrilled to have a private home again and always loved to organize anything and everything. Sitting in the house were well over a hundred boxes of books alone. He needed time to get himself together, he chuckled, and get some more sleep.

But back on Old House Lane, reporters and TV crews would soon line up on the street, outside the tall white security fence surrounding the Clintons' rambling Dutch colonial residence. Notoriously unfriendly to the press and sensing a media emergency, Band placed a call for help to Howard Wolfson—a tough and loyal pro who had handled press and communications for Hillary's Senate campaign the year before. Wolfson dutifully drove up from the city and, before sundown, Clinton stepped into the chilly air outside for a photo opportunity and a few offhand remarks so that everyone else could finally could go home, too.

The newly sworn junior senator from New York stayed inside all day, wisely insulating herself from even the appearance of entanglement in her husband's latest burgeoning crisis. That afternoon, a familiar atmosphere of tension loomed over the house, a feeling that things might be descending once again from bad into much, much worse.

————

The former president could be excused, perhaps, for mistakenly expecting his departure from Washington to be less dramatic and more cheerful. His approval ratings on leaving office were exceptionally high, matching or exceeding those of such titans as Ronald Reagan and Franklin Delano Roosevelt at the end of their presidencies. Although much of the valedictory discussion had lamented a presidency disrupted by scandal, his administration's long list of accomplishments had not been ignored. Offering an editorial verdict on his "mixed legacy" and his failure to fulfill an innate potential for greatness, his frequent critics on the *New York Times* editorial page nevertheless conceded that he had established an impressive record of progress on the economy, the environment, social justice, equal rights—and acknowledged that his bold engagement with a changing world had enhanced American prestige as well as prosperity.

There had been lingering echoes of the Monica Lewinsky affair, in a last-minute legal settlement that Clinton and his lawyers had signed with Robert Ray, the successor to independent counsel Kenneth Starr. After his impeachment acquittal in 1999, his most determined enemies in Congress had consoled each other with the promise that he would surely be criminally indicted upon leaving office.

But following weeks of negotiations with Clinton's attorneys, Ray agreed not to indict him for perjuring himself before the grand jury investigating the Lewinsky matter, in exchange for his public acknowledgment of making false statements under oath, and acceptance of a five-year suspension of his license to practice law. And now even some of the right-wing Republicans who had voted to remove him expressed relief that the Clinton wars would finally reach an armistice as a new Republican president took office.

So Clinton had left town with the grumbling muted and the cheers of hundreds of admiring friends and staff still ringing in his ears. Here at least was an end to the constant partisan warfare and the opportunity to begin something very different.

Yet that respite was to be measured not in weeks or even days but in mere hours. Scarcely had his successor settled into the Oval Office for the new administration's first day of work, when Clinton's old enemies in the media and on Capitol Hill had returned to full uproar, over the Marc Rich pardon and a thousand other supposed offenses. However much they might sniff and snark about "Clinton fatigue," they never really got tired of kicking him around. And as they quickly discovered, he was an easier, more vulnerable target now.

Unlike the battles of the past, Clinton could no longer turn to a devoted phalanx of presidential assistants, press flacks, personal aides, Democratic Party officials, and congressional allies to shield him. Now he was virtually alone, without protection, as an unrelenting barrage of assaults, insults, complaints, and threats suddenly poured in from every direction.

But a pair of loyal young aides would spend nearly every moment of the next ten years with him: Doug Band, who had earned a law degree from Georgetown while working in the White House and turned down an enticing job offer at Goldman Sachs to continue working for Clinton at Hillary's fervent request, and Justin Cooper, a native of the Philadelphia suburbs who had worked in Oval Office operations after graduating from American University. Their role in shaping and protecting his post-presidential life on many levels—from philanthropy and politics to press guidance—would too often be underestimated.

———

On Monday morning, January 22, Hillary Clinton left Chappaqua early to return to Washington with Dorothy McAuliffe. Chelsea and her boyfriend had gone, too—leaving Band; Cooper; Clinton's military valet Oscar Flores, who had quit the White House to stay with him; the Clintons' brown Labrador retriever, Buddy; and Terry McAuliffe, who understood that this would be a good day for a friend to stay by the former president's side.

Plainly irritated by a crescendo of criticism focusing on the Rich pardon, Clinton was grim and angry. His mood didn't improve that evening, when the network and cable news broadcasts all featured versions of the Rich story that emphasized improper or at least unorthodox procedures—and suspicions of bribery.

"Opponents of the pardon say they think contributions by Rich's ex-wife, Denise, who has given nearly $1 million to Democratic causes during the Clinton era, were also a factor, though Rich's lawyers deny that," reported NBC News White House correspondent Pete Williams. "Lawyers involved in the case today say Clinton never contacted the Justice Department for its views on pardoning Rich. . . . [With] a presidential pardon, Marc Rich is free to come back to the US, no longer facing trial in one of the biggest tax fraud cases ever."

Unpacking books and souvenirs didn't seem to provide much distraction for the former president. As he watched an agitated Clinton stewing all day, McAuliffe decided to stay over in Chappaqua for another night. They stayed up late talking and trying to relax over a couple of beers. By the following morning, the rumblings of outrage over Marc Rich had erupted into a national uproar.

The lead editorial in the *Washington Post* demanded to know "what conceivable justification could there be for former President Clinton, on his last morning in office, to have pardoned fugitive financiers Marc Rich and Pincus Green? Unlike most of those pardoned on Mr. Clinton's last day, Messrs. Rich and Green have never paid a fine, served a day in jail, disgorged a single dollar of allegedly ill-gotten gains or reimbursed US taxpayers the money that is allegedly owed."

The pardons were not only "indefensible," roared the *Post*, but had defined him and his presidency downward: "With his scandalous present to Mr. Rich, Mr. Clinton has diminished the integrity and grandeur of the pardon power just as surely as he diminished the various privileges he abused by invoking them to defend his tawdry conduct in office. What a way to leave."

The *Philadelphia Inquirer* asked even more pointedly: "Did Mr. Rich's pardon have anything to do with the hundreds of thousands of dollars that his ex-wife, songwriter Denise Rich, has given the Democrats? Or could it relate to Mr. Rich's choice of Jack Quinn, a former White House counsel, as his lawyer? . . . This was simply a perversion of justice."

And on ABC News, former Clinton aide George Stephanopoulos had furiously denounced his old boss. "He pardoned a man named Marc Rich. You may not remember Marc Rich but he was a banker, a commodities trader, who was trading with Iran when they were holding terrorists and trading with South Africa under the apartheid regime. . . . Instead of facing trial he went on the lam, lived in Switzerland for seventeen years. His ex-wife has given $600,000 almost, over $500,000 to the Democratic Party over the last two years. This is outrageous!"

Many of the newspaper stories on the pardons quoted Rudolph Giuliani, the New York mayor and former federal prosecutor, who had originally indicted Rich and Green. On cable television and the networks, too, Giuliani was urging Congress to "investigate" Clinton's pardons, insinuating corruption of the worst kind. The U.S. attorney in Manhattan, Mary Jo White, a Clinton appointee, had let the world know that she was equally furious because nobody had asked her about the Rich pardon before it was granted.

Later, McAuliffe would recall again and again how Clinton had looked during those two gray, awful days: "Just like a deer in the headlights." As the Rich furor exploded around him, literally nobody was publicly uttering a word in his defense. Indeed, sometime on that Sunday afternoon, both he and McAuliffe noticed that none of the articles or broadcasts quoted Jack Quinn, who seemed to be hiding from the press. It was not long before McAuliffe, in anguish, picked up the telephone and called Quinn.

"Jack, the president is hanging out here," he remembered muttering to Rich's lawyer, not wanting Clinton to overhear the conversation. "You did this to him, and you're not saying anything to defend him. You did it, and he's out here all alone."

But Quinn was no longer the president's lawyer, and apparently felt no responsibility to protect Clinton. With the possibility of a congressional investigation on the horizon, or worse, he was protecting himself.

"Well, Terry, my lawyers say I can't talk," he replied coolly.

"Your lawyers should just go fuck themselves, Jack." The usually amiable McAuliffe's voice was rising quickly. "This is *your* deal and you've got to get *your* ass out there and defend the president."

That Tuesday evening, Clinton ventured out in public for the first time since his Sunday morning trip to the deli. He dragged a reluctant McAuliffe and Band with him to the Metropolitan Opera at Manhattan's Lincoln Center, where they were to attend a performance of Verdi's *Aida*, starring Luciano Pavarotti, with Chelsea and her current beau, an Oberlin College music student and aspiring opera singer. It was a high-profile event, with the presidential party seated in the main box overlooking the stage for nearly five hours of heavily costumed singing—an endurance test for Clinton and his companions, none having even the slightest taste for opera, with other matters weighing on their minds.

What were they doing at the Met, McAuliffe asked himself, with a media firestorm developing around them? But it was Chelsea's evening and he said nothing.

After the opera's tragic finale—in which both hero and heroine are sealed up to perish together in an Egyptian tomb—the Clinton party made an obligatory visit backstage to meet the cast, shake hands, take pictures, and trade back-slapping jokes with Pavarotti. Though the great tenor was suffering from a severe cold, he seemed delighted to see the former president. Clinton smiled and laughed, too, still determined, as he had so often proved during the years of turmoil in the White House, to push trouble aside and live in the moment.

The long evening concluded with Clinton and McAuliffe driven back to Chappaqua, where they again sat up late drinking beer and fretting over the latest barrage of attacks. While they were out on what McAuliffe sarcastically described as a "double date" with Chelsea and her boyfriend, a fresh cascade of damaging tales had gained traction in the national media. The pardon scandal seemed to be metastasizing.

On CNBC's *Hardball* that night, host Chris Matthews—a strident and persistent Clinton critic—summed up the Rich pardon as a straightforward bribe. "This guy [Rich] took $50 million from the US government. He gets—his wife kicks in a million to the Democratic Party. The mathematics is perfect. It only costs a million to make up for $50 million."

Then with a mixture of glee and disgust, Matthews and his guests delved into new accusations that Clinton staffers had vandalized or even "looted" the White House and Air Force One before departing on January 20—and that the Clintons had taken hundreds of thousands of dollars' worth of artwork and furnishings from the executive mansion that didn't really belong to them.

The initial stories about the items supposedly misappropriated by the Clintons were based on a mandatory, publicly available document that they had filed with the White House Gift Office before leaving: essentially, a long list with estimated dollar values of what were, at least in their view, personal gifts from friends.

Coverage of this mundane matter began innocently enough with a brief Inauguration Day story about the list in the New York *Daily News*, which noted that the Clintons had accepted roughly $200,000 in gifts—mostly household and decorative items given by various intimates and acquaintances, including two sofas, an easy chair, and an ottoman valued at $19,900 from a New York businessman; china worth $4,920 from director Steven Spielberg and his wife, Kate Capshaw; and nearly $5,000 worth of flatware from actors Ted Danson and Mary Steenburgen. The official list released by the White House also disclosed receipt of a pair of coffee tables with chairs, estimated at more than $7,000—given by none other than Denise Rich.

Stories quoting anonymous sources swiftly followed, suggesting that Hillary had requested specific items she hoped friends would buy for her new Washington house in various stores, almost like a bridal shower or a wedding registry. Many of the same stories indicated that the Clintons had appropriated furniture, artworks, and other items that ought to have remained in the White House. Aside from soliciting expensive gifts from their rich friends, hardly proper conduct for an incoming U.S. senator and her presidential spouse, both Clintons stood accused of absconding with White House furnishings that didn't belong to them at all. In fact, Clinton had meticulously catalogued every item, including those for which he would have to pay.

Tabloids quoted former Reagan social secretary Sheila Tate—whose friends Ron and Nancy had accepted the gift of a two-million-dollar home—clucking in shocked disapproval. "Now we know why they had to have such a big house. . . . These are not the kind of gifts you take with you. It's usually a silver bowl with your name on it."

Daily News columnist Michael Kramer groused: "Most First Families view the gifts they get as the nation's property—and leave town without them. . . . But the Clintons—naturally—are in a league of their own. They walked off with close to $200,000 in furniture, china, flatware, TVs, sculpture and assorted other 'necessities.' "

A week after the first gift story, the *Daily News* followed up with a story showing that there had been no registry-style Hillary Clinton gift list—but the rest of the media simply ignored that explanatory footnote. By then the press corps had moved on to the thrilling tales of vandalism, an irresistible metaphor for many of the capital's loudest voices, figures such as Chris Matthews and Maureen Dowd, who felt that the Clintons had somehow escaped proper punishment for all the scandals and sins that the public seemed so determined to dismiss.

Here was evidence that the Clinton White House was nothing but a gang of hooligans that had seriously damaged White House offices and other public property to vent displeasure with the incoming Bush administration.

What had started as mildly amusing rumors about an alleged frat-boy prank—removing the letter "W," a nickname and symbol of the new president, from White House typewriter and computer keyboards—quickly expanded into far more troubling tales. NBC News reported "phone lines cut, drawers filled with glue, door locks jimmied so that arriving Bush staff got locked inside their new offices, obscene messages left behind on copying machine paper," and more, as well as "glasses and hand towels pilfered" from the presidential airplane.

An early version of these charges popped up on the *Drudge Report*, the notorious website whose status as a Washington tip-sheet (especially on Clinton) had continued to swell ever since proprietor Matt

Drudge broke the news of the Monica Lewinsky affair in February 1998. And they seemed to be emanating directly from the Bush White House staff, in particular the new press secretary, Ari Fleischer.

On January 24, Drudge quoted White House sources in an exclusive: "The Bush Administration has quietly launched an investigation into apparent acts of vandalism and destruction of federal property—after incoming Bush staffers discover widespread sabotage of White House office equipment and lewd messages left behind by previous tenants! Harriet Miers, 55, Assistant to President Bush and staff secretary, will be investigating possible legal ramifications of the White House trashing and possible theft, the DRUDGE REPORT has learned."

According to a "well-placed source," wrote Drudge, "Miers is just beginning her investigation," adding, "The level of the trashing is very troubling, this is not just 'W' keys missing from keyboards." He quoted a "close Bush adviser" claiming that the "damage left by departing Clintonites goes 'way beyond pranks, to vandalism.'" Finally Drudge warned, "photographic and audio evidence is being collected—as the full scope of the damage becomes clear. Bush's staff has been cautioned not to go public with the extent of the damage and the worst is being closely held among very top staffers for fear of leaks."

That night the same stories came up on CNN's *Crossfire*, with the *Washington Post*'s Mike Allen, a reliable sounding board of capital insiders, on set to discuss the missing "W"—a sign that the Clinton "scandals" were dominating Washington chatter and would spread rapidly through the national media. It was all erupting just in time to spoil Hillary Clinton's first historic opportunity to preside over the Senate the next day, and it wasn't about to subside anytime soon.

———

To Hillary, McAuliffe, Band, and others close to Clinton—not to mention the former president himself—it seemed obvious that the Bush White House was playing a very cynical double game. On the press podium in the briefing room, Fleischer pretended to downplay the "vandalism" story while keeping it alive; privately, White House aides were leaking ugly, unproven allegations about the trashing of the White House, the Old Executive Office Building next door, and the presidential airplane. Nearly every story on the subject featured a "close Bush adviser," a "high-level Bush staffer," or some similarly unnamed source talking about the awful destruction perpetrated by those Clinton people.

To come under this kind of sustained attack by the White House was a signal of how far and how suddenly Clinton had fallen. Only days before, the vast communications operation of the presidency would have served and protected him. Now he could rely on nothing even resembling that mighty bureaucratic apparatus—only a tiny temporary office that sat, ironically enough, across the street from the White House in a townhouse on Jackson Place.

Directed by Karen Tramontano, who had served as a special assistant to the president, the Clinton "transition office" consisted mainly of a few aides on six-month stipends from the federal government. Still on hand was Betty Currie, who had famously endured crisis after crisis, and more than one grand jury appearance, as Clinton's personal secretary, along with Laura Graham, who had worked on the White House scheduling team, Mary Morrison, who had helped to run Oval Office operations, and former White House social secretary Capricia Marshall, a Hillary confidante who served more as a consultant than a full-time employee—plus several employees who continued as they had before, handling correspondence from the tens of thousands of people on the Clintons' various lists.

A highly competent executive originally recruited from a top position in the labor movement by White House chief of staff John Podesta, Tramontano had never overseen media relations, let alone a full-blown crisis. Receiving phone calls every few minutes from reporters who had managed to find her, demanding responses on the Rich pardon, vandalism in the White House, and Hillary's gift registry, she lacked the skills and experience to respond effectively.

In the final weeks before the end of his presidency, Clinton had remained busy and preoccupied, with very little time devoted to what might come after. He and Podesta had hastily assembled the transition office, approaching Tramontano to run it less than a month before Clinton left the White House. They hadn't anticipated the need for a press secretary—let alone a war room. Now Clinton sat isolated in Chappaqua, hundreds of miles from the transition office, and nobody there could begin to help him cope with a burgeoning public relations disaster.

Tramontano did what she could under the circumstances. She knew how to pick up the phone and reach officials in the White House, and within a day or so after the vandalism stories broke, she placed an irritated call to Andrew Card, Bush's chief of staff. She had been in the White House during those final days; she knew that the trashing tales were wholly fabricated or at most terribly exaggerated. It was also obvious to her that whatever Fleischer might say, those stories emanated directly from the highest levels of Bush's staff.

But rather than return her call, Card told his deputy Joseph Hagin to ring Tramontano back—and a "senior Bush official" instantly leaked word of the exchange to a CNN White House reporter. Then Fleischer described the conversation between Tramontano and Hagin to the White House press corps, complete with yet more insinuations of serious misconduct.

According to Fleischer, Hagin described "plural incidents" of vandalism to the Clinton aide, although he would not say what those incidents were. A "senior Bush aide" confirmed to CNN that the incidents had occurred mostly in the Eisenhower Executive Office Building, but that some also took place in the West Wing. Yet while his colleagues kept whispering poison, Fleischer primly remarked that the White House had tried to minimize the entire flap from the beginning and "move forward."

———

Through the final days of January, massive waves of negative coverage were washing over Clinton and his meager staff, leaving them virtually drowned and demoralized. Former Clinton press secretaries would clock in for temporary duty on what they all privately called "the shitshow," but they had other commitments and were hardly in any position to push back effectively. When Jack Quinn finally appeared in the press to defend the Rich pardon on legal grounds—including an op-ed essay under his byline in the *Washington Post*—scarcely anyone noticed, and almost nobody cared.

What drew far more attention was the spectacle promised by the House Republicans who had seized upon the Rich case, apparently still eager to vindicate impeachment. Representative Dan Burton, chair of the House Government Reform Committee, announced on January 25 that he would soon open an investigation of the Rich case, because the former president "has not given an adequate explanation as to why Mr. Rich deserved a pardon." Burton released a letter he had sent to the Justice Department seeking documents and promised to subpoena "a host of different groups that may have played some kind of a part in this pardon."

Burton's announcements excited the Washington press corps, many of whom had once ridiculed his committee's clownish and ineffectual probes of Democratic fundraising and other alleged scandals. The Indiana Republican was probably best known for inviting reporters to his own backyard, where he had blasted a watermelon with a pistol to dramatize his suspicions about the death of Vincent Foster, the White House counsel whose 1993 suicide aroused right-wing conspiracy theorists.

Suddenly, Burton was a figure to reckon with again in Washington, where the network news and cable shows all wanted him to discuss the pardon investigation, and in certain circles he even became a potential hero. "I just wish one of these times you would catch them, Congressman," cried Chris Matthews when he interviewed the eccentric Burton on *Hardball*. "You've been in pursuit. You've been like Smokey the Bear trying to catch this guy," meaning Clinton, as if Burton were a dogged state trooper tirelessly hunting a career criminal.

Unwilling to cede the glaring scandal spotlight to the House, Senator Orrin Hatch, chair of the Senate Judiciary Committee, soon announced that he, too, would convene pardon hearings—evidently with the eager support of Senate Democrats, several of whom had publicly denounced Clinton's pardon of Rich, including their leader, Senator Tom Daschle.

Among the most voluble grandstanders, rather predictably, was Senator Joe Lieberman, the Connecticut Democrat and longtime Clinton friend from Yale days, who had vaulted onto the Democratic presidential ticket in 2000 because of his moralistic scourging of Clinton during the impeachment crisis. Lieberman had even pushed himself forward to comment on the White House vandalism, while admitting that he had no idea what had actually happened.

But Lieberman's irrepressible urge to promote himself was merely the least attractive expression of a basic Washington reality: Almost every prominent Democrat felt obliged to express disappointment if not disgust over the Rich pardon. Those who had always disliked Clinton could barely conceal their satisfaction, while those who had been close sought a safe distance from him, sadly shaking their heads.

In those early days, Clinton rarely left the house in Chappaqua. When Hillary came up from Washington on weekends, she saw that he was "out of sorts" and angry, indeed often "madder than hell." What made him especially furious were the stories about the furniture that he and Hillary had supposedly purloined, portraying him and his wife as some kind of low-class thieves.

Worried friends noticed that no matter how many times they urged him to turn off the TV and stop reading the newspapers, he couldn't help himself. He would promise to stop, and then get on the phone with friends and ask whether they had seen the latest cable TV slurs against him.

"You've got to stop it!" McAuliffe told him. "Stop reading this stuff and stop watching this junk on TV! You're going to drive yourself nuts." But he couldn't help himself. He watched constantly.

———

As January ended, a few small signs appeared of possible relief from the cable-driven scandal storm. After the Clintons voluntarily returned several items of furniture to the White House, the gift stories started to recede. The vandalism stories began evaporating, too, because Fleischer could never produce the "list" of damage incidents that he had said the Bush staffers were compiling; there was never a single photograph of any trashed office, or even a missing W. (Eventually Mark Lindsay, Clinton's former assistant for management and administration, who had forcefully denied the vandalism charges at every step, would be vindicated by a General Accounting Office investigation that found no basis for them.)

Nor had the missing champagne glasses on Air Force One been stolen. A White House photographer, on board for Clinton's final flight as president, had smashed them accidentally. When the steward came out of the galley carrying the glasses, the photographer had turned and, with her telephoto lens, hit and knocked over about ten of the tall flutes. Shards of glass falling into a celebratory cake had left it inedible.

But revulsion against the Rich pardon showed no sign of fading away—just the opposite. Both the Senate and House investigating committees were preparing to subpoena witnesses, including several top Clinton aides, Denise Rich, and the prosecutors who believed that Clinton had made a corrupt bargain to vacate their case against Rich. Worse still, rumors were circulating that the Justice Department, under a new Republican attorney general named John Ashcroft, who had voted to convict Clinton in the Senate, would open a criminal investigation of the pardon.

The prospect of a criminal investigation, with a grand jury calling witnesses under penalty of perjury, revived chilling memories of the very worst days of the Starr investigation. For anyone who had ever worked for Clinton, this was a nightmare déjà vu.

As for the Clintons themselves, the idea that they would again have to hire lawyers to defend themselves was utterly depressing. They were still deeply in debt to David Kendall and the other attorneys who had handled their defense in Whitewater and all the other fizzled scandals that Starr had investigated, plus the Lewinsky case, with unpaid bills that still totaled somewhere north of $11 million. To pay off that obligation, as Hillary told friends, her husband would have to earn at least $25 million before taxes. Now there would be more debt, not less.

While the roar of contemptuous media coverage, bipartisan congressional probes, and prosecutorial threats continued, Band and Tramontano had the satisfaction of knowing that at least a few important goals had been achieved. Most significant was the contract she had helped to negotiate with Don Walker, a prominent and highly respected booking agent whose agency would set up lucrative speaking engagements for the former president both in the United States and abroad. He paid a significant sum up front that helped the Clintons to retire their mortgage.

Walker had gotten off to a rapid and successful start, inking contracts for a heavy schedule of appearances, mostly at corporate events, that would pay no less than $100,000—and as much as $250,000—for what usually amounted to no more than a few hours of travel, talking, and face time. Having declined to join any corporate boards, as so many of his predecessors had done, paid speeches and book deals looked to Clinton like his only hopes for erasing the burden of debt hanging over him and Hillary and paying for the costs of two big homes. He was working on a speech that would be worth the money.

Every week or so, Tramontano would come up from Washington for a meeting with Clinton. She would board an Amtrak train for the three-hour trip to New York's Penn Station, then walk over to Grand Central Terminal and board a Metro-North commuter train for another hour's to Chappaqua. This time, on the last day of January, she had news that she didn't want to discuss over the telephone.

Tramontano called Oscar to make sure that nobody except for Band and Cooper was there. "How is he?" she asked. "Can I come up to see him?"

She wanted to tell Clinton in person what Walker had told her the day before. Almost all of the corporations, trade groups, and venues that had lined up to book Clinton speeches were withdrawing those commitments—with as many as five or six canceled in a single day.

"These bookings are just going away," the gentle agent had told her sadly. "I'm not sure what to do, not sure what the president will want to do." He paused. "I know this isn't going to last. They're going to come back."

When Tramontano arrived at the house in Chappaqua, she hung around the kitchen until Clinton came downstairs. They sat down in the living room, making small talk at first. "Mr. President," she finally said. "I just talked to Don Walker. He had thought most of these speeches would hold, that they would stay with us. But sir, they're not."

The next day, news broke of Clinton's first scheduled speech at a Morgan Stanley bond sales conference in the posh Florida coastal enclave of Boca Raton, with a reported fee of $100,000, scheduled for February 5. That date had not been canceled, and Clinton looked forward to combining a lucrative speech with a short vacation at the Biltmore in Coral Gables, where he could escape New York's freezing weather, play golf, and rest.

The bond traders and the Boca residents were friendly and welcoming. So were the Florida Democrats with whom he mingled at the Biltmore. The speech went well and his hosts thanked him warmly.

But even before Clinton spoke, the financial firm's branch switchboards across the country began lighting up with calls from furious clients, threatening to pull their money out. The protests grew so loud and angry that Morgan Stanley president Philip Purcell felt he had to do something to quell the growing panic in his company.

"I fully understand why you are upset that former President Clinton spoke at one of our conferences," said Purcell in a message released three days later to all of the firm's clients and the public. "We clearly made a mistake. . . . We should have thought twice before the speaking invitation was extended. Our failure to do so was particularly unfortunate in light of Mr. Clinton's actions in leaving the White House."

By the end of that week, almost every speech scheduled for Clinton in the United States was gone.

CHAPTER TWO

With the nationwide explosion of fury over the Marc Rich pardon, Clinton's adversaries in politics and the media realized how much they still enjoyed lashing him, regardless of his physical exit from the capital. If anything, the compulsion to pursue their old quarry seemed to be swelling, now that he was no longer the leader of the free world but just another defenseless citizen.

Almost overnight, his poll ratings declined by more than 20 points, with the Gallup poll showing his personal approval dipping below 40 percent—the lowest ebb since he began his national career. Suddenly there was no jeopardy in attacking him, and plenty of opportunities to continue the hunt.

Both Clinton and his staff had yet to comprehend how persistently the enmity toward him still festered, and how their own seemingly innocuous decisions could flare into nasty complications. Choosing an office space might have seemed uncontroversial, for instance, but quickly became the latest public relations debacle. Like the pardons and the gifts, Clinton's decision to locate on Manhattan's swanky West 57th Street fed persistent media narratives about his grasping, high-handed, and presumptuous attitude.

Toward the end of January, word had leaked to the *New York Post* and the *Daily News* that the former president was seeking to lease premium luxury office space in Midtown to house his post-presidential operations. Clinton's post-presidential office, led by Karen Tramontano, was talking with Rockrose, one of the largest real estate firms in the city, about renting an entire floor near the top of Carnegie Tower, a marble-and-glass palace on West 57th Street, with magnificent views northward of Central Park.

That same floor had housed *Talk* magazine—an ill-fated print venture edited by the legendary Tina Brown, British-born queen of media-mad Manhattan, and bankrolled by Miramax Pictures chief

Harvey Weinstein, a longtime Clinton donor and personal friend. Still whirling through the tower's glass doors and into its supercharged elevators were the likes of entertainment mogul Barry Diller, former Universal Studios president Frank Biondi, directors and producers such as Robert Benton and Stanley Jaffe, America Online chief Bob Pittman, and entertainment lawyer Allen Grubman. Not to mention Jerry Seinfeld, then at the pinnacle of sitcom stardom—"and a huge Clinton fan," according to his publicist—who was reportedly bidding for offices just one floor below the space coveted by the former president.

Many of the other potentates of 57th Street were huge fans as well, buzzing over Clinton's anticipated arrival on their rarefied and luxurious turf. It was easy to imagine him ensconced comfortably among them; his attraction to the world of showbiz had always been mutual. Visiting the building a few weeks earlier, on a visit to Manhattan with Hillary, he had said: "I'm kind of tickled. . . . Here I am in New York, where all the writers, artists, and athletes are above average, and everyone gets their vote counted."

Not everybody would be quite so tickled by the pending Midtown lease as Clinton and his prospective neighbors were, however—or at least not for the same reasons.

The editors of the *New York Post*, flagship tabloid of Rupert Murdoch's right-wing media empire, knew exactly what to do when they learned that Clinton was seeking to rent big fancy offices in midtown at taxpayers' expense. While the United States Treasury is required by law to pay for office space for every living former president in the location of his choosing, leasing the fifty-sixth floor of Carnegie Tower would cost no less than $600,000 a year and possibly much more.

On the morning of January 28, the *Post* splashed an embarrassing headline across its front page: "'CADILLAC' BILL'S $665G DIGS: OFFICE COSTS MORE THAN OTHER 'EXES' COMBINED." The story inside explained that the rental cost of the Carnegie Tower office space would exceed what the federal government's real estate arm, the General Services Administration, was paying for the offices of Gerald Ford, Jimmy Carter, Ronald Reagan, and George Herbert Walker Bush, which altogether amounted to less than $625,000 a year. Although sources familiar with the lease negotiations between the federal agency and Rockrose whispered that the price was actually "a steal" at $80 per square foot—when the going rate in that class of Manhattan building ran closer to $100—that argument sank beneath a torrent of outrage.

At first, the chairman of the House appropriations subcommittee that oversees funding for former presidents—a hard-core ultraconservative Republican representative from Oklahoma named Ernest Istook—responded rather mildly to the *Post* exposé. "If the [former] president chooses to have his office in his newfound state rather than his home of 50 years, that is his prerogative," said Istook. "But obviously, it's going to cost the taxpayers a lot more money." Taxpayer and public interest groups across the ideological spectrum swiftly condemned the proposed lease as an unjustified extravagance, demonstrating how little residual goodwill toward Clinton remained.

The "Cadillac" headline quoted a quip from the president of the National Taxpayers Union. Expanding on the same theme, Thomas Schatz, president of the conservative Citizens Against Government Waste, said: "The Clintons have always treated public money with a sense of entitlement, but this takes the cake. . . . Once again, Mr. Clinton has displayed his narcissism, his spendthrift habits, and willingness to squeeze the maximum benefit out of every loophole."

Then Charles Lewis, executive director of the liberal Center for Public Integrity, chimed in with a reminder of Clinton's waning popularity. "After his pardons and his gifts," said Lewis, "I think we should give him a pup tent in Central Park." A spokesman for the Congressional Accountability Project, founded by consumer advocate and 2000 presidential protest candidate Ralph Nader, eagerly joined the chorus of disapproval: "There's no question that it's arrogant, it's a slap at the taxpayers. It shows tremendous disrespect for the taxpayers."

In Clinton's adopted hometown, the Carnegie Tower story provoked snark and snobbish gossip, if not so much fiscal indignation. As a Manhattan real estate broker told the *New York Observer*: "That building fits him like a glove. It's a building for currently successful scoundrels. You have to have the money, but it's not really high class."

Emboldened by this broad upwelling of public anger, Istook announced that he would oppose the Carnegie Tower lease and sent a letter to GSA officials warning that they would be "extremely unwise" to proceed. "Congress appropriated every penny that former President Clinton asked for his transitional expense, and in specific, the rental expense at a rate equivalent to $228,000 for his office space," he wrote. "Unfortunately, we're being told now that the former president wants to spend about three times as much as he asked for and as we budgeted and appropriated for the purpose."

The weakness of Clinton's position could be gauged by the response of Jake Siewert, the last of his presidential press secretaries, who had stepped temporarily into the breach at Band's request to mount a defense.

"This president should not have to pay some penalty because he chose to live in New York. Every New Yorker knows it's expensive to live here, but it's worth it," he said. "We'll work with the money that government appropriates for us."

———

Affable but sharp, even Siewert—who privately bemoaned the handling of Clinton's early post-presidency—didn't find Carnegie Tower easy to justify. By that point neither did Karen Tramontano, whose efforts to secure the luxury space seemed to be doing her boss far more harm than good. Seeing pictures of the dark glass skyscraper in the press and on television, over and over again, had begun to make her feel physically ill.

Acting to put the gifts controversy behind them, the Clintons decided to personally pay for the furniture and other presents, mostly from personal friends, that they had taken with them from the White House. Contrary to the screaming headlines, tut-tutting editorials, and lacerating columns, the fact was that nearly all of the gifts had been donated during the course of Clinton's eight years in office, rather than during 2000. Most of the financial value of the gifts was accounted for by two Dale Chihuly glass sculptures—one donated by the acclaimed artist himself, another given by the president's Georgetown classmates. In short, there was no substantive ethical issue, just a poisonous cloud of misinterpretation.

Nevertheless, Hillary Clinton's new Senate press secretary, James Kennedy, told reporters that they would write checks totaling roughly $86,000 to Steven Spielberg, Ted Danson, and Mary Steenburgen, and about two dozen other friends who had given fine china, flatware, and other furnishings (including the table and chairs from Denise Rich).

They would still keep other presents received before 2000, valued at over $100,000—noting in a statement that, like other presidential families, they had "received gifts over the course of our eight years in the White House and followed all the gift rules."

At least one of the gift-givers was disappointed to learn that he would receive a check from the Clintons. Said Paul Goldenberg, owner of Paul's TV, a big discount electronics retailer in Los Angeles, "I think it's too bad. I feel they've done a good job for the country, and I was more than happy to give them something for their new home." When a reporter asked what he had hoped to get in return—what was his "agenda"?—Goldenberg replied tartly: "How could there be an agenda? I'm just a guy who owns a television store."

To Clinton critics in Washington, however, this latest gesture only confirmed the couple's essential guilt. Why would they pay up if they did nothing wrong? Indeed, every attempt to put the bad press to rest looked more and more futile, with still worse stories looming.

On Capitol Hill, both the Senate Judiciary Committee and the House Government Reform Committee had announced public hearings on the pardons, focusing on Rich, to be held back-to-back on February 7 and February 8. The subpoenas that began to arrive at the William J. Clinton Foundation office were passed on to David Kendall, the Williams & Connolly partner who had served as personal counsel to both Clintons for almost two decades.

With the tide of public opinion running so powerfully against him, and with so few resources at his disposal, the best defense that Clinton still had resided in Kendall—a loyal, dependable, and exceptionally capable attorney who had shouldered the legal weight of every Clinton scandal, real or phony, from the beginning. An Indiana native, calm but tough, Kendall was a veteran of the civil rights movement—he had been arrested several times in Mississippi during the 1964 "Freedom Summer" campaign to register black voters—and met Clinton at Oxford in 1968 when both were Rhodes Scholars. Like the Clintons, Kendall had later graduated from Yale Law School. When the Whitewater controversy first erupted in 1993, they had turned to him.

Over the years, Kendall's wide-ranging career had included libel defense work on behalf of the *National Enquirer*. The tabloid's editor Steve Coz once said that profiles of the smooth, immaculately attired lawyer always portrayed him as "a Quaker choir boy," but "in reality he is a street fighter, a polished version of James Carville."

Anticipating a circus on Capitol Hill, Kendall briefly attempted to resist a subpoena from the House committee demanding the name of every foundation donor. A grandstanding Senator Arlen Specter, chair of the Senate committee (and at that time still a Republican), told the *New York Post* that he might subpoena Clinton himself to testify—an unprecedented indignity for a former president. (President Gerald Ford had testified about his pardon of Richard Nixon in 1974 but appeared voluntarily.)

In the end, Burton issued no subpoena to Clinton. Although he never testified before Burton's committee, the former president promised to cooperate fully with the investigation—and ultimately he did, waiving all executive privilege claims and allowing three of his top aides to testify at length about their private conversations with him concerning the pardons of Rich and Green.

Specter also announced that he would seek testimony from Denise Rich, in pursuit of evidence that the pardon of her former husband represented a "quid pro quo," as he put it—a Clinton favor in return for the many hundreds of thousands of dollars she had donated in previous years to Democratic political campaigns and to the Clinton foundation. The Pennsylvania Republican wondered aloud whether she had served as a conduit for funds flowing from Marc Rich in his Swiss hideaway to the Clintons, insinuating a series of indirect payoffs from the fugitive. "I don't know the source of the money, but I think it's a fair question," he added.

Basking in unusually favorable coverage from right-wing media outlets, Specter told reporters a few days later that, as a constitutional matter, Clinton could be vulnerable to a new impeachment proceeding, even though he was no longer in office. While the "second impeachment" was a characteristically eccentric proposal—swiftly quashed by House speaker Dennis Hastert and Senate majority leader Trent Lott—Specter was reflecting a real desire in certain Washington quarters. Some in the capital cherished the prospect of "impeaching" Clinton again, if not in Congress then in public opinion, feeling certain that this time he would not escape.

With that vengeful enterprise under way, media coverage during the week leading up to the hearings was relentlessly scorching, provoking scarcely any substantive response from the Clinton camp. Seemingly bored by the nascent Bush administration, which offered nothing as titillating as a Clinton scandal, the Washington press corps returned to a scandal frenzy, offering up abundant rumors, tangents, and of course, copious leaks.

Perhaps the most intriguing leak, which almost nobody bothered to follow up, appeared to emanate from the House Government Reform Committee, which was reportedly planning "to look into the question of whether financier Marc Rich . . . may have been involved in spying during his flight from U.S. authorities." The *New York Post*, obsessed with Clinton and working its own sources in Jerusalem and Tel Aviv, reported suggestively—without any further pertinent detail—that Rich "had a relationship with the Israeli Mossad intelligence agency."

"The government of Israel considered Rich a critical ally and the president took that seriously when he considered the pardon request," Siewert told the *Post*. But attention swiftly turned from the Mossad to Jack Quinn, the Rich lawyer who answered a subpoena from the House committee by turning over documents concerning his communications about the pardon with Deputy Attorney General Eric Holder at the Justice Department—and simultaneously released them to the press.

According to Quinn, his notes proved that he had indeed consulted Holder about Rich and the Swiss fugitive's business partner, Pincus Green, contrary to the assertion that he had bypassed the usual pardon process. But if he was trying to help Clinton—after Terry McAuliffe's profane admonishment two weeks earlier—Quinn only raised new questions about Holder, who appeared more aware (and supportive) of the pardons than he had acknowledged. Evidently Holder had also discussed with Quinn his desire to be appointed attorney general, should Al Gore win the presidency.

On the day before the hearings, a lawyer for Denise Rich told Congress that his client would claim her Fifth Amendment privilege, refusing to testify lest her words incriminate her. This announcement only inflamed suspicions that the songwriting socialite and her money had played a dubious role in the pardon process.

If Republicans on Capitol Hill and in the White House were gleefully exploiting the Rich pardon and all of Clinton's other troubles, the

Democrats now felt exhausted by him. Having fought back day after day against impeachment, Whitewater, and the assorted other scandals, real or mostly invented, that plagued the Clinton White House during two presidential terms, figures like Rep. Henry Waxman of California, ranking Democrat on the House Government Reform Committee, had little energy left for this renewed battle. Even had they roused themselves to support Clinton again, what was there to say in defense of the Rich pardon, which looked so much like an unjustified favor for an arrogant, well-connected criminal on the lam?

"The Rich pardon is a bad precedent. It appears to set a double standard for the wealthy and powerful," said Waxman at the hearing. "And it is an end run around the judicial process."

"It's indefensible, they all know that," said a Republican committee staffer, referring to the chastened Democrats. Rep. Christopher Shays, a moderate Connecticut Republican and longtime Clinton antagonist, summed up the tenor of the hearing: "Everything about [the Rich pardon] seems sleazy."

Veteran Clinton critics in the Washington press corps could scarcely contain themselves—or confine their copy to mere facts. Among the most unrestrained was Dowd, whose *Times* column so faithfully echoed the hostile tone of the capital's establishment toward the former first family. That the paper would publish her accusations of criminality verging on treason was a signal of Clinton's perceived weakness.

"Oh heck, let's just impeach him again," she began, continuing:

Beyond Denise Rich's $3 million fund-raising lunch and personal donations—$450,000 to the Clinton library, more than $1 million to Democrats, $10,000 to the Clinton legal defense fund, $7,375 for Clinton furniture—let's hope Bill Clinton has a Swiss bank account set up by Marc Rich.

Otherwise, it would not be worth sliming the Constitution, his legacy and his party.

Bill and Hill are tornadoes, as James McDougal memorably observed, twisting through people's lives and blithely moving on.

But this time, they may not dance away from the wreckage. The egg may have hit the fan, as Congressman Steven LaTourette put it at the Congressional hearing on the Rich pardon.

This time, maybe the user was used. Bill Clinton was manipu-
lated by a man who made billions manipulating foreign markets.
Marc Rich bought a pardon with the money he made betraying
America.

Dowd's column was extreme but not exceptional. Despite the torrent of speculation and suspicion aroused by the pardons' circumstances, however, nothing emerged during hours of droning testimony
to suggest, let alone prove, that Clinton had granted them in exchange
for Denise Rich's generous campaign and foundation contributions—
all of which she had given months and years before she approached
him on behalf of her ex-husband.

While the first round of congressional hearings found no evidence of bribery or corruption, they certainly showed that the vetting of Clinton's last-minute pardons had been haphazard at best. At
least forty-seven pardons, or more than a third of all those granted
by the president during his final days in office, had not gone through
the usual review procedures at the Justice Department and were instead brought directly to his office. Most of those seeking clemency
had never even filed a petition with Justice; others fell outside the legal
parameters of that system; and a few had already seen earlier pleas rejected by Clinton.

His grant of clemency to four Hasidic Jewish men from upstate
New York—serving time for defrauding the government of $40 mil-
lion—also provoked distrust, because their hometown of New Square
had delivered nearly all its 1,369 votes to Hillary in her Senate campaign. But if Clinton was selling pardons, or merely doling them out as
favors to his friends and supporters, he had rebuffed at least two generous donors who had done much more for him and the Democratic
Party than the former Mrs. Rich or the New Square rabbis.

In the first instance, Clinton had rejected a clemency application
from Leonard Peltier, the Native American militant long imprisoned
for the 1975 murder of two FBI agents on the Pine Ridge Reservation in
North Dakota. Peltier's campaign had become a cause célèbre in Hollywood circles led by movie mogul David Geffen, who along with his
DreamWorks partners had given well over a million dollars toward the
Clinton library and hundreds of thousands more to Democratic can-

didates and causes. (Years later, a "disillusioned" Geffen would cite the rejection of Peltier as a major reason for shifting his allegiance from Hillary Clinton to Barack Obama, as the 2008 presidential campaign approached.)

In the second case, Clinton had refused to grant a pardon to Michael Milken, the legendary junk bond financier and convicted fraudster, who had served twenty-two months of a ten-year sentence before his 1993 release. He had turned down Milken's application, even though its outspoken supporters included Rudolph Giuliani, who had sent Milken to prison as a federal prosecutor—and despite a fervent request from Ron Burkle, a personal friend with whom Clinton would soon enter a business relationship. By then Burkle already had given at least $4.5 million to the foundation and other Clinton causes.

Still, eliminating the checks and balances of the normal process had left Clinton vulnerable to charges of abuse, especially in the case of Rich and Green. Testimony from former White House counsel Beth Nolan, former White House chief of staff John Podesta, and Bruce Lindsey, the presidential lawyer and confidant who headed the Clinton Foundation, revealed that they had all bluntly opposed pardoning the fugitives in Switzerland. And until the last minute of the last day, all three of those close advisers said, they had been certain that Clinton ultimately would deny a pardon to Rich and Green.

———

In Clinton's Washington transition office, Karen Tramontano and her colleagues worried that the reputation of the former president might never fully recover from the incessant incoming attacks. Tramontano knew she could do nothing about the pardons furor. Nobody in the press cared about the nuances and complications of the Rich case, which hinged on arcane tax law. But the impasse with Congress over high-priced Manhattan office space just might be resolved, if only she could persuade Clinton to choose a different location, somewhere less costly and controversial.

On a cold February morning, she steeled herself and called the house in Chappaqua. "How is he today?" she asked Oscar Flores. "He's OK," replied Flores, who handed the phone to the former president.

For a few moments, she and Clinton made small talk, which turned quickly toward the continuing torrent of ugly publicity over the pardons, the gifts, and the Carnegie Tower offices. There would be no good time to bring up her new agenda with him, but this sounded like an opening—a chance to suggest constructive action.

"Certain things . . . we can't do anything about," she began, a bit gingerly. "But let's get out of this lease."

"How can you do that?" he replied angrily. "You're giving in!" He hung up the phone.

Tramontano ignored his outburst of temper and went up to New York on the train to meet with an executive representing Rockrose Development, the building's owners. Having benefited from the publicity surrounding Clinton's potential tenancy, Rockrose no longer cared whether the lease was ever signed. It was true that they had given the former president a break on the cost; the market rent for his premium floor had only risen. "No worries," the executive laughed, when she asked whether it was too late to cancel. "Do you realize what I can rent that space for?"

In the ensuing days, Tramontano talked with John Sexton, the New York University president, who had known the Clintons well since the 1980s, when his wife, Lisa Goldberg, became a close Hillary friend. As Clinton's exit from the White House had approached, Sexton had broached the possibility of creating a global policy institute at NYU as a home for Clinton and the foundation. He was sure that he could find decent office space somewhere on or around the university's vast Manhattan territories for them.

But then Tramontano took a call from Representative Charles Rangel, the Democrat from upper Manhattan, who had first pitched the idea of Hillary's Senate candidacy. "Karen!" roared his familiar voice over the wire, gravelly yet piercing. "He should come to Harlem! Have him call me."

To Tramontano, this idea was at least intuitively appealing. But was there adequate modern office space in Harlem to accommodate Clinton and his operations? A few days later, Rangel personally escorted her to visit a nondescript glass-fronted building at 55 West 125th Street, just east of Lenox Avenue. The top floor, fourteen stories up, offered a majestic view looking downtown over Central Park, but not much else. The space wasn't attractive—"the ugliest place," she later admitted—and further inquiry revealed that there might not be enough water pressure to flush the toilets. Ultimately she was persuaded that all these problems could and surely would be fixed for a prized tenant like the former president.

Tramontano called Clinton at home again. "This is a very good option," she told him. He grumbled, but agreed to talk with Rangel.

Not many days later, Clinton called back to tell her about a great new idea: They could move the offices to Harlem! Talking about all the things he could do in and for the neighborhood, and what it would mean to be there, he was clearly excited. On February 13, after touring the space with Hillary and their close friend, Washington attorney and civil rights veteran Vernon Jordan, he emerged from behind the glass doors onto Harlem's busiest street to greet jostling reporters and camera crews. "I have decided to locate my office in this building. *If* we can work it out." A crowd of jubilant residents who had stopped to listen began cheering.

In Harlem, nobody cared about Marc Rich.

——————

With the congressional pardon probe bearing down and the strong chance of a criminal investigation by the U.S. Attorney's Office in Manhattan—where the Marc Rich prosecution had originated under Rudolph Giuliani—Clinton was talking with Kendall almost every day. He told the lawyer that he wanted to write an op-ed essay for the *New York Times*, laying out the best case for the Rich pardon without equivocation. It was important to make that case for the record, and to clearly reject the accusations of criminal misconduct.

The *Times* editorial page editors quickly agreed to give Clinton plenty of space to explain himself. As he wrote and rewrote, plowing through dozens of drafts that he handed over to Kendall and others for comment, the newspaper of record found opportunities to express a subtle satisfaction over the former president's political fall, which had only justified the negative assessments of his character long nurtured by its editors and columnists. More than a hint of institutional schadenfreude could be detected between the lines of Adam Nagourney's "Political Memo" column on February 14, a mocking Valentine to Clinton. Soon to be appointed the paper's chief political correspondent, Nagourney outlined the tribulations that had beset the former president since his arrival in New York, depicting him as enfeebled, unprepared, and perhaps ruined:

> Until recently, when Mr. Clinton's former aides lumbered back to life, the same Democrats who had reliably come to his aid over the last eight years were notable for their silence. Part of that was because, as one of Mr. Clinton's strongest advocates said yesterday, the defense of his presidential pardons was a daunting task for even the most devout Clinton supporters.
>
> But it also was clear evidence that former presidents do not have the clout of sitting ones, and that there is little price to be paid for being silent.
>
> Mr. Clinton was described yesterday as increasingly concerned about how he was being perceived and irritated at coverage that some of his advisers described as unfair. And he and his advisers were beginning, if belatedly, to try to help Mr. Clinton through a period that some of his own supporters acknowledged had permanently stained his reputation.

The next day, as if to confirm that judgment, U.S. Attorney Mary Jo White, the chief federal prosecutor for the Southern District of New York—and appointed by Clinton in 1993 as the first woman to hold that prestigious post—announced that she had opened a criminal probe into the pardons.

"The seriousness of the crimes is diminished, and the fact and the appearance of evenhanded justice is compromised," she had said when the pardons first became public. Now she would make her displeasure felt.

The media bombshells began to explode shortly after dawn, when the network morning shows all led with Clinton's latest embarrassment. On ABC News' *Good Morning America,* the assignment fell to correspondent Jackie Judd, whose professional hostility toward Clinton dated back to the Whitewater investigation. Although Judd reported the story straight, she made sure to air tape of Senator Jefferson Beauregard Sessions, Republican of Mississippi, explaining his theory of the case.

"If a person takes a thing of value for themself [*sic*] or for another person that influences their decision in a matter of their official capacity," he explained, "then that could be a criminal offense." The irony of such a remark coming from a man who had accepted millions of dollars in campaign donations from lobbyists, banks, insurance companies, agricultural interests, and defense contractors was not remarked upon.

Closer to the mark was *Good Morning America* anchor Charlie Gibson's colloquy with ABC correspondent and former top Clinton aide George Stephanopoulos. It would be difficult for White to prove that Clinton had knowingly taken money from Denise Rich as a payment on a pardon for her ex-husband—especially, although neither Gibson nor Stephanopoulos said so, because she had not even been asked to support his pardon application until many months after she had made those donations.

But how would Clinton ever prove that he *hadn't* taken a payoff? Gibson wondered. "What does he do now to get this cloud off, if he can?"

Replied Stephanopoulos, "The big question is, does he go public with his explanation in some kind of an interview and really lay out this case and say, 'Listen, you guys may disagree with my decision, but I did not do it—it wasn't a trade for campaign contributions.' He's got to lay out the reasons for this decision in a clear way."

On CNN, the morning anchors displayed the front pages of the *New York Times* and the *Washington Post*, with the pardon probe news splashed in bold headlines above the fold—the prelude to a report by correspondents Frank Sesno and Daryn Kagan on Bill and Hillary Clinton that described them as unpopular "losers" and pariahs in their own Democratic Party.

"They are distancing themselves thoroughly from Bill Clinton," remarked Sesno. "As one Democratic strategist commented to me today, 'he's not our responsibility anymore.' And you're not seeing any Democratic senators or others rush to his defense; quite the contrary."

On February 18, three days after White's announcement, the *Times* published Clinton's op-ed, titled "My Reasons for the Pardons." At nearly 1,600 words, the final product of many hours of rewriting provided a detailed legal rationale for his decision on Rich and Green, citing the opinions of top tax attorneys and prominent Republican lawyers, including Vice President Dick Cheney's chief of staff, Lewis "Scooter" Libby.

Clinton explained why he believed that the original prosecution of Rich had overreached, applying criminal statutes to business practices that had resulted in mere civil fines for other oil companies. Rich and Green had paid nearly $200 million in fines and penalties already, he noted—and he had required them to waive "any and all defenses" against further civil litigation by the government as a condition of the pardons. He acknowledged that he ought to have consulted directly with the United States attorney and that he had proceeded with excessive haste in discussions with the Justice Department. Finally, he expressed the pain that the accusations of corruption had caused him.

Firmly denying any quid pro quo in any of the pardons he had granted, Clinton concluded: "I want every American to know that, while you may disagree with this decision, I made it on the merits as I saw them, and I take full responsibility for it."

The prose was competent, the reasoning was lucid, and yet the op-ed fell flat, with no discernible impact. It was simply too late, too dry, too emotionless, and above all, too reticent in detailing the real diplomatic context of the pardon decision. By the time that context finally began to emerge, Clinton's enemies had set the narrative of sleaze in concrete.

The House committee continued to drag out its investigation, eventually diverting attention to other pardons when the Rich case turned into a dead end. Committee staff delved into clemency applications pushed by Hugh Rodham, Hillary Clinton's brother, and Bill Clinton's brother, Roger, in hopes of earning large fees. Rodham, a lawyer and public defender in Miami, had received roughly $200,000 each from Glenn Braswell, a businessman convicted of mail fraud in connection with the sale of a baldness remedy, and Carlos Vignali, a convicted cocaine trafficker with family connections to Democratic politicians in California.

Clinton had rejected the pardon promoted by his brother, and had been unaware of the fees collected by Rodham—which he and Hillary angrily (and successfully) urged her brother to refund after learning of them. Staying in Washington at Hillary's residence when he learned that the Rodham story was about to come out, Clinton had jumped abruptly into a van with two Secret Service agents and driven himself home to Chappaqua in the middle of the night. He didn't want to be in the capital when the next round of gloating began.

While the House committee probe went on for months, the evidence that emerged substantiated none of the suspicions voiced by the chairman—and in fact came close to proving the opposite. Ultimately, what Burton's machinations revealed was not a corruption conspiracy, but the unfolding diplomatic and political relationship that had impelled Clinton to issue the risky pardon.

When Clinton waived executive privilege to allow the testimony of Podesta, Bruce Lindsey, and Nolan, he simultaneously opened his administration's archives—under the control of Bush White House lawyers—to the Burton committee investigators. Among the many Israeli officials and former officials who had contacted the White House on behalf of Marc Rich, as the press had already noted, was Ehud Barak, then Israel's prime minister. Barak had reportedly discussed Rich with Clinton on at least two and perhaps three occasions. Armed with that scant knowledge, the Burton staffers made an unprecedented demand: They wanted the transcripts of notes recording the conversations between the two heads of state that had been taken down by stenographers in the Oval Office.

While all such discussions between the president and other heads of state are recorded in that manner, virtually no documents in the White House would be considered more sensitive—especially involving the prime minister of Israel, and even more especially during a period of critical negotiations between the Jewish state and the Palestinian Authority. Transcripts of private conversations between the president and foreign heads of state are not routinely provided to congressional committees or anyone else, particularly not when the conversations had occurred only months earlier.

It was difficult to imagine a more blatant breach of the discretion expected by world leaders when they are on the telephone with the president of the United States.

Yet the Bush White House bowed to the committee's request swiftly and even eagerly. Alberto Gonzales, the White House counsel, ensured that the written notes of three Clinton-Barak conversations concerning Rich—which had occurred on December 11, 2000; January 8, 2001; and

January 19, 2001—were declassified, redacted, and released to Burton "at warp speed," as one lawyer put it. (As a shining example of transparent government, this contrasted sharply with the obsessive secrecy that shrouded the following eight years of the Bush presidency.)

The extraordinary alacrity of Gonzales in releasing the transcripts to Burton troubled David Kendall, who assumed that the Bush White House wanted nothing more than to discredit his client. Kendall and Clinton had repeatedly discussed those conversations with Barak, which the former president recalled very clearly. During three lengthy calls with the Israeli leader about the complications of the peace talks with the Palestinians—which had reached an impasse that required further Israeli concessions to revive any chance of success—Barak had raised the subject of the Rich pardon request, according to Clinton. The justification offered by Barak was Rich's many services to the Israeli state and the Jewish people, whom the Swiss-based oilman had assisted even while trading with hostile regimes in Iran, Iraq, Yemen, Lebanon, and Syria.

Now Clinton told Kendall again that those conversations, if released, would confirm the "foreign policy" rationale for the Rich pardon. But like any wise defense lawyer, even one whose client has a memory renowned for near-photographic accuracy and detail, Kendall fretted that the documents might somehow contradict or undermine Clinton.

———

The Israeli prime minister's intervention on behalf of Rich had been anything but casual. Months earlier, at the beginning of the quiet pardon campaign mounted by Rich's legal and public relations team, a man named Avner Azulay had reached out to the prime minister in Jerusalem. A former Mossad operative, Azulay headed Rich's private foundation, which had given millions to charities in Israel and Europe. He had also once served as an Israel Defense Forces captain alongside Barak—who would become the most decorated soldier in Israel's history—when both were young officers in the intelligence corps. So when he contacted the prime minister's office, Barak had agreed to see him.

Azulay told Barak that Rich had been serving as a covert instrument of Israeli policy for nearly a quarter of a century—dating back at least to the fall of the Shah of Iran, who had supplied most of Israel's oil needs until his overthrow by Shiite Islamist militants. Rich had been doing business with the Shah, and yet somehow continued to work with the regime that followed under Ayatollah Khomeini, serving as a middleman for the continued flow of Iranian oil to Israel.

But Rich had done much more than provide petroleum, explained Azulay. Beginning in the early 1980s, Rich had used his connections with various regimes in Africa and the Middle East to negotiate the safe exit of Jewish families from places hostile to them. The first covert operation had involved Ethiopia, where Rich assisted Jerusalem in negotiating the exit of the Falasha Jews from that country, ravaged by famine and civil war under Mengistu Haile Mariam, a Soviet-backed dictator. Rich's firm oversaw construction of an emergency medical clinic as part of a deal with Mengistu to release thousands of Jewish Ethiopians to emigrate to Israel.

Rich also maintained connections with the regime in Yemen, where hundreds of Jewish families remained after most had emigrated, and were under the constant threat of anti-Semitic attacks. Again, he was able to make deals with Yemeni officials who would never have talked with the Israelis, helping to bring dozens of Jews to safety in Israel. Over the next two decades he conducted similar operations—quietly spiriting endangered Jewish families out of the tiny remaining communities in Iraq, Syria, and Iran. In all those places, he had done business with officials who could be persuaded to look the other way.

Rich had also regularly allowed his firm's offices in many of those countries to serve as safe havens for intelligence officers and their local sources. As a high-ranking Israeli official explained, the cover of Rich's company was often used "just to allow access to a place, like when someone is active in some country in Africa, for example—to go visit certain places where you can't go otherwise." On some occasions, a Rich employee, or Rich himself, had carried messages from Jerusalem to a leader in Yemen or Libya or Syria or Iran, whose government had no official or any other kind of relations with Israel.

What Barak might have considered even more convincing at the time was Rich's willingness to provide financial assistance to the Palestinians as part of the peace process—a favor he had already done on a small scale at the behest of Israeli president Shimon Peres.

Barak listened carefully to his old army buddy, and promised to consider Azulay's plea that he carry the pardon request to Clinton. Later, the prime minister made some discreet inquiries among people he trusted in the Israeli intelligence community to check what Azulay had told him. He quickly learned that the story was true: Rich was not a Mossad agent but was instead what the spy agency calls in Hebrew a "sayan"—a helper, or in American parlance, an asset. Without delving too deeply into sensitive details, Barak established to his own satisfaction that Rich and his company had been exceptionally helpful to Israel and the West.

The declassified "telcon" notes released to Burton by Gonzales showed that on the evening of December 11, Barak had reached Clinton in the White House residence, where they had spoken about other matters ("redacted") before the Israeli brought up the subject of Rich. They were talking often in those days, as the president mulled his final and most ambitious effort to revive the Mideast peace talks that had imploded at Camp David during the summer of 2000. Acknowledging that Rich, this "American Jewish businessman," had "violated some rules of the game" under U.S. law, Barak nevertheless asked Clinton to "consider his case" because of Rich's philanthropic activities.

"I know about that case because I know his ex-wife," replied Clinton. "She wants to help him, too. If your ex-wife wants to help you, that's good," he quipped.

On the evening of January 8, the president and prime minister spoke again for about twenty minutes. During the first eighteen minutes or so, they discussed Clinton's effusive remarks about Barak the night before, in a speech to the Israel Policy Forum, a liberal Jewish organization, held at the Waldorf-Astoria hotel in Manhattan.

Of Barak's decision to pursue the peace process, with substantial concessions and at no small political sacrifice, Clinton had declared:

No dilemma I have ever faced approximates in difficulty or comes close to the choice that Prime Minister Barak had to make when he took office. . . . He knew nine things could go wrong and only one thing could go right. But he promised himself that he would have to try. And as long as he knew Israel in the end could defend itself and maintain its security, he would keep taking risks. And that's what he's done, down to these days. There may be those who disagree with him, but he has demonstrated as much bravery in the office of Prime Minister as he ever did on the field of battle and no one should ever question that.

Indeed, by repeatedly engaging a recalcitrant Yasir Arafat and offering the Palestinian leader a series of fresh concessions on territorial division, the final status of Jerusalem, the "right of return" for Palestinian refugees, and other issues, Barak had consciously placed his own political career upon the altar of peace. Even as he continued to pursue those negotiations—hoping for a breakthrough agreement that to many observers seemed painfully close during those final days—the Israeli prime minister was looking at polls that showed him trailing far behind the Likud Party's Ariel Sharon in the forthcoming national election, scheduled for April.

From Clinton's perspective, Barak had done nearly everything he had asked, unselfishly and without complaint. Now he was asking for something that was very much within Clinton's power to grant, and that conceivably might be justified on the merits as well. It was Barak's final plea on January 19, when he and Clinton spoke again, that seemed to tip the balance in favor of Rich.

"Might it move forward?" Barak had asked, referring to the pardon.

"I'm working on that but I'm not sure," Clinton had replied. "I'm glad you asked me about that. When I finish these calls I will go back into the meeting on that, but I'm glad you raised it. Here's the only problem with Rich; there's almost no precedent in American history. There's nothing illegal about [a pardon], but there's no precedent. He was overseas when he was indicted and never came home. The question is not whether he should get it or not, but whether he should get it without coming back here. That's the dilemma I'm working through. I'm working on it."

"OK," Barak had said.

That final call preceded by only two days the scheduled opening of the last round of serious peace talks in the Sinai Peninsula resort of Taba, Egypt, following many weeks of preparation by Clinton and his diplomatic team. While those negotiations ultimately failed, they came closer to achieving a workable settlement than any before or since. And for that possibility, even before the talks began, Clinton would always feel deeply indebted to Barak. Clinton's aides later testified to their surprise when he signed the Rich pardon request on January 20. But given Barak's pressure and the intertwining of the pardon and the peace talks, perhaps they should not have been.

When the Taba talks faltered weeks later—and after Barak fell, as predicted, in the April 1 election against Sharon—Clinton became even less inclined to "kick him while he's down." In the *New York Times* op-ed, he noted the urgings of "many present and former high-ranking Israeli officials of both major political parties" as "importantly" influencing his decision. But he would never specifically mention Rich in the same breath with Barak, a man he genuinely liked and admired.

For his part, Barak and those around him sought to downplay his role in the Rich pardon. Not wishing the prime minister to be blamed for what had become an embarrassment to Israel in the United States, Barak's staff would tell any reporter who listened that his conversations with Clinton included only one "marginal telephone mention" on behalf of the fugitive oilman. Surely, they whispered, that couldn't be why the pardon had been granted.

Yet to someone who understood the full diplomatic context—someone like Hillary Clinton, whose first weeks in the Senate were cast into unflattering shadow by the Rich controversy—the only real question that remained was not why President Clinton had signed the pardon in the end, but why he had not clearly and publicly explained his compelling *raison d'état*. In private, sometimes intense conversations with her husband, Hillary came to realize that he would never seek to shift any responsibility onto Barak for what he had, after all, chosen to do himself—and she agreed.

———

Neither the Burton committee's continuing endeavors nor the U.S. attorney's investigation would achieve much of substance—aside from the political damage inflicted on the Clintons—although the lawyers involved kept themselves busy for many months. Upon close examination, there had never been any evidence to sustain the notion of a bribery conspiracy in the Rich matter, and as time wore on both probes began to appear punitive rather than principled. Burton's partisan purposes had always been obvious, along with his loony demeanor. But the media uproar over the pardons had allowed the Indiana Republican to run roughshod over all the cowed Democrats on his committee, at least for the first few months.

The motives of U.S. Attorney White and her senior staff weren't partisan but professional. Angered as they were by Clinton's decision and his lack of concern for their opinion, they were also too smart to believe that they would find any criminal conduct.

In Kendall's view, they behaved fully within the bounds of propriety; unlike the Starr investigation, which had brazenly used Washington journalists as its promotional agents, White's office did not leak. But her investigators continued to demand the Clinton Foundation lists and then call the donors, long after any purpose had evaporated. She and her staff made Clinton pay heavily for a decision they hated, until her Republican successor, James Comey, cleared him in 2002.

In late August, Clinton received a small measure of vindication on the Rich pardon when reporter Michael Isikoff published the transcripts of the Barak-Clinton conversations in *Newsweek*. Although Burton refused to release the transcripts to Kendall, who had been forced to obtain them from the National Archives and Records Administration, someone had seen fit to give them to a magazine that had often maligned Clinton throughout his presidency. (It was Isikoff, after all, who had broken the story of the Lewinsky affair.)

The *Newsweek* story provided no diplomatic or political context— and wrongly described Rich's pardon as "unconditional"—but its appearance nevertheless gratified both Clinton and Kendall, who was relieved to see that the documents confirmed his client's recollection. In a follow-up story, the *New York Times* obtusely observed that the conversations with Barak "do not appear to shed any light on Mr. Clinton's motivations."

Most of the ensuing coverage was similarly witless and poorly informed. The mythological narrative depicting the Rich pardon as a corrupt quid pro quo would endure. But the release of the Barak transcripts marked an unofficial conclusion to the pardon scandal. When the Burton committee finally released its two-volume, 1,500-page report on the pardons several months later, rehashing all the same material, most media outlets paid little attention.

———

Not only had the Rich pardon badly tarnished Clinton's reputation, but its fallout continued to hinder the most urgent tasks he faced during the first year of his post-presidency. By raising taxes, reducing spending, and most of all by fostering economic growth, he had erased the perennial deficit and come close to eliminating the national debt—but rather ironically, he and Hillary had left the White House carrying enormous personal and institutional indebtedness. Estimates of what they owed to lawyers alone, following the years of investigations and impeachment, ranged from $12 million to $20 million. They also had owed mortgages on two expensive homes, in Chappaqua and Washington, D.C., where Hillary lived in a $3 million house on Whitehaven Street, near Embassy Row.

Meanwhile the Clinton Foundation, established in 1997 to build his presidential library in Little Rock, still needed to raise more than $125 million to complete construction. Despite all the noise over supposedly illicit donations to the library from friends like Denise Rich, the truth was that much of the money raised so far had come in small donations via direct mail solicitations. In 2000, the entire amount raised for the library had amounted to less than $3 million. At that rate, it wouldn't be paid off until the middle of the century.

Having enjoyed free public accommodation—housing, meals, security, and transportation—for more than two decades, Clinton was haunted by the specter of debt. He had grown up in very straitened circumstances, if not quite poverty; he had never made much money or invested successfully; and he had scoffed when friends insisted that he would almost certainly become a wealthy man after leaving the presidency.

"Financially, you just don't ever have to worry ever again," the reliably cheerful Terry McAuliffe had assured him more than once. "Listen, you're going to . . . at a minimum, sir, you're going to write a book, you're going to have speeches. You know, you're going to get paid a lot of money to give speeches. You're going to be fine."

"All right, Mack, if you say so," Clinton would reply skeptically and somewhat glumly. "I guess so."

But in the months following his tumultuous departure from the

White House, as the speaking engagements dried up, McAuliffe's insistent optimism seemed more and more dubious. Even if the speech bookings eventually returned, the library was starting to look like a much more persistent problem. Fundraising from larger donors was rendered nearly impossible after the Burton committee and the United States attorney had demanded the lists of all the library donors and started issuing subpoenas to the individuals whose names appeared on them.

Knowing what might happen if Burton's staff got the donor records, Kendall had initially resisted the congressional subpoena, citing privacy concerns. But by the end of February, with additional subpoenas arriving from White's grand jury in New York, he and Clinton had realized that they could no longer withhold the records. Every month or so, the library's temporary office in Little Rock, then overseen by Skip Rutherford, a longtime friend and campaign aide, would receive a fresh subpoena from New York.

When donors who had given more than $5,000 or so began to receive calls from the U.S. attorney's FBI investigators, asking questions about exactly why they had given money to the Clinton library, fundraising at that level became nearly impossible. Nobody with enough money to write a big check wanted to attract the scrutiny of law enforcement or the media attention that might follow.

The immediate effect was crippling. As Clinton and his staff knew, the year after a president leaves office usually opens the most lucrative window for library fundraising. Four years earlier, the foundation had started with about a million dollars in seed money left over from the second inauguration. Then in 1998 and 1999, mostly through direct mail and small donations, the foundation staff in Little Rock had raised about $3 million a year, with another $8 million in large and small donations in 2000. Donations were on track to raise roughly $8 million or so in 2001—all of which added up to a significant amount, except when considered against the eventual cost of construction, which would exceed the original estimate of $165 million.

Those numbers represented an emotional burden weighing on both Bill and Hillary Clinton that they rarely expressed. "It was hard," she would say, years later—not only because the levels of expense and debt were so daunting, but even more because of the sudden, hurtful coolness of many old friends and allies who might have been expected to help. As a United States senator, wary of ethical missteps, she could do nothing but watch as her husband struggled.

To Hillary, Bill had always resembled "the small boy digging through the manure because he thinks there must be a pony there." In her eyes, he was almost too eager to look for the positive side in people, even amid disappointment, to give everyone the benefit of the doubt. Yet during the period since they had left the White House, she noticed a subtle change in him. The loneliness and frustration of the first post-presidential months had not extinguished but certainly had tempered the relentlessly sunny side of his personality, she thought.

The former president was truly surprised, in a way she found poignant, to discover that quite a few people whose reputations and careers he had fostered, if not entirely created, were avoiding him. They wouldn't take his phone calls. They wouldn't meet with him. It saddened and upset Hillary to see him treated in a fashion "that he would never treat anybody, ever, that he had any relationship with—and certainly not anybody he thought he owed something to."

CHAPTER THREE

In the long aftermath of the pardon debacle, Bill Clinton was often surprised—and hurt—by the disdainful attitude of old friends and allies. Amplifying the negative media coverage, which he seemed unable to ignore, their withdrawal represented a judgment that sometimes seemed universal. More loyal friends worried that he was moody, sometimes angry, and worse still, distracted from thinking seriously about his own future.

Visiting him in Chappaqua, former White House chief of staff John Podesta—a calm and trustworthy figure to whom Clinton often turned at times of difficulty—left feeling concerned. Podesta always thought of his former boss and old friend as "a guy who never stays down." But that winter, Clinton struck him as downcast, "stuck in a negative cycle."

Nor did Clinton's mood improve when he called a meeting of longtime aides and friends to advise him on "what to do next" at Hillary's Washington home, situated among the capital's fanciest embassies and residences. Podesta, Band, and Tramontano were present, as were pollster and strategist Mark Penn, former national security adviser Sandy Berger, and Hillary, who had been enduring her own bout of bad publicity. She sat with her husband and listened as they told him bluntly, "You need to stand down for now. You are damaged goods."

So much reputational damage had been sustained, they advised, that he should stay out of sight for the coming six months, perhaps as long as a year, focusing quietly on his library and his memoirs. This moment of unanimous, undiluted candor left their former boss "very pissed off," as one observer later noted. But even as the advisers spoke, they all knew that hiding away for an extended period was not really to be expected of him. Even if he had wanted to do so, finding shelter from the deluge of public scorn during the first year of his new life would not be easy.

Whatever he had lost, however, Clinton still possessed an unusual capacity to "compartmentalize," as Podesta liked to put it—to turn his mind away from his own troubles, and focus his attention elsewhere, at least temporarily. Soon he and his staff came to realize that however diminished his popularity might be in his native land, much of the rest of the world was ready to welcome and even celebrate him. And he was more than ready to extend himself to an emerging global community.

Actually, the first opportunity had materialized just four days after he arrived in Chappaqua. Late on the evening of January 25, news outlets began to report an incredibly destructive earthquake in the province of Gujarat, India. The massive temblor measured 7.7 on the Richter scale, far stronger than the Northridge or Loma Prieta earthquakes in California, and with far greater casualties: Tens of thousands believed dead, hundreds of thousands more injured, perhaps a million or more homeless, and untold billions of dollars in property damage.

As president, Clinton had been proud of improving America's relationship with India, which had declined for many years as a consequence of Cold War politics. His outreach to Delhi had been strategically valuable in South Asia and paid political dividends at home, encouraging successful members of the Indian American diaspora, many of them in the financial and technology industries, to befriend the Clintons and contribute generously to them.

Over the years, Clinton had become particularly close to a few Indian American businessmen, notably Vinod Gupta, who had built infoUSA, a leading information brokerage firm that was probably worth a billion dollars, and Sant Singh Chatwal, a Sikh hospitality entrepreneur whose far-flung properties included Manhattan's Bombay Palace restaurant. Both men had visited the White House; Gupta had played golf with Clinton and even slept once in the Lincoln Bedroom. Occasionally Chatwal still sent some of Clinton's favorite menu items—butter chicken, lentil dal, kebabs, and fish curry—up to Chappaqua.

During the days that followed the earthquake, Clinton began calling Chatwal, Gupta, and other members of his Indian American circle, including Raj Gupta (no relation to Vin), a managing director at McKinsey & Company, the international management consulting firm, and Victor Menezes, a senior vice chairman at Citigroup.

"Now is the time for you and everybody who has done well in your community to step up" and organize aid to the flattened villages of Gujarat, he told Menezes. "And I will do everything in my power to help."

Clinton sent the same message to a friend in New Delhi—Atal Bihari Vajpayee, the prime minister whom he had gotten to know while touring India as president in March 2000. The first trip by an American president to the subcontinent since Jimmy Carter's visit in 1978, Clinton's warmly received visit had been widely regarded as inaugurating a new partnership between the two countries. Now, Vajpayee's staff arranged a telephone call between the Indian leader and the former president for the evening of February 1. During that call, Vajpayee officially requested Clinton's assistance for the earthquake victims. They set a short-term funding goal of $1 million, but Clinton knew that his Indian American team would be good for much more.

The next day, Victor Menezes hosted a meeting in a conference room on one of the upper floors of the imposing aluminum-sheathed Citigroup Center in Manhattan, where Clinton presided over the creation of the American India Foundation. Chosen unanimously as the new group's honorary chairman, he would oversee a coast-to-coast fundraising sweep.

Within two weeks, the AIF publicly announced its founding in a press release that led with a quote from Clinton: "The Gujarat earthquake in India has brought about tremendous human suffering. It is important to harness the management skills, financial resources and entrepreneurship that reside in the Indian community in the U.S. and use these to benefit India in its hour of need." Its board included Menezes, Chatwal, the two Guptas, along with a score of other financial, business, and technology leaders—and just for an extra touch of glitz, the bestselling wellness guru Deepak Chopra.

All this frenetic philanthropic activism went on well beneath the radar of the mainstream media, too preoccupied then with pardons and other embarrassments to take notice of any good works. But that scarcely deterred Clinton, who was well aware that he would accomplish nothing if he had to depend on positive press clippings. His staff regarded the Gujarat initiative as properly presidential in scope and, beyond that, highly therapeutic for him at a time of depressing daily abuse.

Collaborating with the Indian American CEOs and academics,

Clinton felt refreshed and energized. Every conversation and meeting about Gujarat pulled him out of his claustrophobic existence as a media target. Unlike other friends, they weren't going to dump him over the pardons or worry whether his bad press might be contagious. When he was with them, he remembered how it felt to be recognized for qualities he liked in himself—his compassion, his intelligence, his openness to the world, his concentration on problems and solutions, his capacity to bring people together for a constructive purpose.

———

Yet wherever he went, in the United States, at least, the controversies and enmities of his presidency pursued him. Not long after the debut of the American India Foundation, Clinton flew to San Jose for a major fundraising event to aid Gujarat, where he appeared onstage alongside Deepak Chopra and M.C. Hammer, the rap-star-turned-preacher, at the city's biggest evangelical church.

Raising more than $2 million in a single evening, that event sparked a lively controversy within the evangelical community, whose strongly conservative and Republican orientation included powerful feelings of hostility toward Clinton. During his presidency, the evangelical right's assessment of him had ranged from merely "immoral" to "anti-Christ." Perhaps unsurprisingly, Dick Bernal, the founder and minister of Jubilee Christian Center, which hosted the Gujarat fundraiser, had endured a barrage of criticism from many of his own twelve-thousand-strong flock as well as other local pastors and congregations since the announcement of Clinton's participation.

Five families quit Bernal's church, and he received no fewer than six hundred "hate letters," including death threats and dark predictions that he and his family would be "blown up" when God passed judgment on them.

"They wanted to know if he was bringing Monica Lewinsky with him," the bemused pastor later recalled. "They wanted to know if Clinton was going to come here and violate women in the church."

Responding to the unexpectedly severe backlash, Bernal placed a large advertisement in the *San Jose Mercury News* a week later, apologizing for Clinton's appearance at the church. This act of contrition irritated the local Indian American businessmen who had sponsored the event. "Some of the most sophisticated people in the Silicon Valley were there that night," complained Kailash Joshi, a tech entrepreneur and Clinton friend who had organized the event. "Although there is no anger here, I think the apology he put in the newspaper was an insult."

Yet while Bernal might have appeared to disavow Clinton, his own opinion of the former president was more complicated. Both the pastor and his wife had felt a surge of empathy for the former president while they watched him that evening. To her, Clinton had "looked sad," while he observed that Clinton "doesn't get invited to a lot of churches." Later, Bernal told the evangelical magazine *Charisma* that he believed Clinton had repented his sins—and that God still had "great plans" for him.

Confiding what a "well-known televangelist" had told him of a prophecy for Clinton, Bernal said, "The word was, God's hand is on him for a higher purpose than even being president. And God will never remove His hand from him." Within that enigmatic prediction lay the question that Clinton still had not answered. Aside from paying off his debts and building his library, exactly what was he supposed to do with his energy and talent?

————

While Clinton certainly felt gratified by the appreciation of the Indian American community, moving toward a global presence made very practical sense for him as well. Morgan Stanley and other American organizations had backed away from him and even canceled his speech bookings, yet the same reaction had not occurred overseas—a difference reflected in his schedule, which would send him far from home during much of that difficult initial year.

By early March, he was preparing to fly across the Atlantic for his first post-presidential trip abroad. Don Walker had booked a series of well-compensated speeches in the Netherlands, Denmark, and Germany, where Clinton would also confer informally but publicly with several heads of state. None showed any sign of wishing to shun him.

Releasing news of the trip, his new spokeswoman Julia Payne assured the New York *Daily News* that Clinton "really could be booked every day this year. He is the most sought-after speaker in the history of the lecture circuit." Payne, a former White House staffer brought on to handle the press, didn't mention that bookings in the United States had not recovered yet; cancellations were still occurring. But those losses were offset by the demand in other countries, where tickets for his appearances—priced from $200 and up, and as high as $10,000 to sit with him at dinner—quickly sold out. Speeches were booked in cities large and small, from Norway, Poland, and Ireland to China, Brazil, Argentina, and Australia. More than a thousand tickets for a hospital fundraiser in Hamilton, Ontario, sold out in a single day. Certain that they could attract many more paying guests, the organizers seriously considered moving to a venue that would accommodate 3,500 seats. On the global platform, "Bill Clinton" was a stellar brand.

Karen Tramontano had hired a speechwriting team, including Jeff Shesol and Paul Orzulak, former Clinton White House staff wordsmiths who had formed a company called West Wing Writers after leaving government. They came up to Chappaqua several times with her to discuss the tone, frame the subjects—settling, very broadly, on globalization and the future of humanity—and begin crafting a draft. The speech, which would be delivered in slightly varying forms over the coming months to many audiences, "had to be tops," she told them. They all knew from years of experience how Clinton would rework their prose until it could not be regarded as belonging to anyone but him. Ultimately he used little of the speechwriters' work at all, building a speech informally titled "Our Common Humanity," arguing why what binds people together is more important than what divides them. He would use and adapt the same basic text, with appropriate introductions and fresh wonkish digressions, for well over a decade in most of his paid appearances.

Before leaving for Europe, he conferred by telephone with both Sandy Berger and former secretary of state Madeleine Albright. They agreed that as an ex-president, he should be careful in his remarks and conversations not to step too hard on his successor in the White House. Already Bush was becoming widely disliked in Europe for his administration's abrupt decision to kill the Kyoto treaty on reducing carbon pollution, without consulting America's allies, among other offenses of substance and style.

Especially sensitive on this trip would be Clinton's visit to Germany, where he was scheduled to deliver the keynote address at an event honoring Chancellor Gerhard Schroeder. As president, he had enjoyed a close relationship with Schroeder, a Social Democratic reformer sometimes known as "the German Clinton." But the U.S. relationship with Germany was changing under Bush, owing to strong disagreements over climate change, missile defense, and relations with Russia.

Just before he departed New York on a private jet, Clinton's staff let the organizers of his European speeches know that they were imposing one final requirement: No reporters or photographers would be admitted to any of his appearances on the continent. That demand proved extremely awkward, since members of the press had already received invitations to attend his talks in The Hague and Copenhagen.

The decision to bar the media was more than slightly ironic, because the sponsor of the Danish event was *Børsen*, that country's premier financial daily, while the sponsor of the German event—where Schroeder would receive the German Media Award—was a marketing research company that polled the nation's editors-in-chief to select the annual winner. Having received the German Media Development Award in 2000 at the White House, Clinton had been invited by media executive Karlheinz Kögel to attend the luncheon for Schroeder as the guest of honor.

Awkward or not, the contracts for his speeches clearly gave him the right to control any media presence on the premises. So the embarrassed sponsors dutifully dispatched messages to scores of journalists who had signed up to attend, officially disinviting them. "We did everything we could to create a workable situation for the press," said the sheepish letter sent out by the Dutch public relations firm handling Clinton's speech. "Unfortunately that didn't work." Leo van der Kant, director of the Assemblee Speakers Bureau that brought the former president to the Netherlands, explained frankly that the speech had been closed to the press due to the "uproar over Clinton's pardon of fugitive financier Marc Rich."

Apart from the squall over press access, however—which didn't at all trouble Clinton or his staff, who tended to hold journalists in dim regard—the three-day European tour was a success, setting a pattern for his peripatetic career as the world's best-paid public speaker. Don Walker, president of the legendary Harry Walker Agency that booked all his speeches, would tell any reporter who asked: "This is our 55th year in business, and Clinton is the most sought-after speaker ever in the lecture industry."

In The Hague, he sat down for lunch before the speech with a group of a dozen or so high-rolling businessmen, each of whom had reportedly paid as much as $10,000 for the privilege. (A ticket for the speech itself, held in the auditorium of the capital's Crowne Plaza hotel, was priced at a mere $1,000.) Relaxed and casual, he chatted about life after the presidency—he was getting much more sleep, he confided—as well as U.S. relations with Europe, his disapproval of Bush's tax cuts, and the future condition of the American economy. After lunch, he posed for a photograph with each guest.

Somewhat predictably, perhaps, Clinton's speech betokened a bright future for the West, with the rapid development of the Internet and electronic commerce. But he went on to remind several hundred well-heeled listeners that in the rest of the world, most people still could not afford reliable electric power. Unless Western firms invested in developing countries, acknowledging both a moral duty and economic necessity, he warned, the promise of the twenty-first century would never be fulfilled. If the content sounded slightly bland, the force of Clinton's personality and intellect left his paying audiences gratified.

"He's certainly very charismatic," said the founder of the discount European airline Easyjet, who attended the speech, "and his knowledge of foreign policy is formidable."

From the hotel, he went on to an afternoon tea with Queen Beatrix, then to a brief, cordial meeting with another old Social Democratic ally and friend, the Dutch prime minister Wim Kok. That night, Clinton flew to Baden-Baden, the famed German spa town, where his speech was scheduled at lunchtime the following day. His last visit to the Federal Republic had occurred less than a year earlier, in June 2000, when Schroeder had given him the Charlemagne Prize for promoting "European unity and values" at the ancient cathedral in the city of Aachen.

When he arrived at the awards luncheon in Baden-Baden, the Germans had arranged a musical greeting by a band of high school saxophonists, playing Elvis Presley's "Don't Be Cruel." Touched by this gesture, Clinton quickly wiped away a tear. On this occasion reporters were present, and he opened his remarks with a joking jab at the press.

"I really wanted to come here because everyone in America found it astonishing that anyone in the media anywhere would give me a prize for anything," he said as the audience laughed. "Although at home they might give me a prize for having survived them."

The remainder of the speech outlined the opportunities and perils of globalization, again appealing to the Europeans to provide more aid and investment to developing nations. Such an admonition might have offended any listener who understood that Europe provides far more in foreign aid per capita than the United States, but somehow Clinton could say it without provoking any complaint. Walking back to his hotel along the resort town's streets, he was "mobbed by people wanting to get close to him," according to Myron Cherry, a Chicago lawyer and Clinton friend present at the luncheon, who later said, "I felt like I was in a Fellini movie and I was walking along with Mick Jagger."

The next day, Clinton flew into Copenhagen to address the six hundred members of a businessmen's club sponsored by *Børsen*, a daily newspaper whose name means "stock exchange," at a beautiful, century-old theater in the city's center. Before departing for home he stopped by Marienborg, the eighteenth-century residence of Prime Minister Poul Nyrup Rasmussen, for a pleasant lunch with Rasmussen, the U.S. ambassador, and their wives. For those few hours in Denmark, he was paid $125,000. All told, his two weeks crossing the continent would net well over a million dollars.

The European jaunt had been ideal from his point of view, with plenty of appreciative citizens in his audiences and seeking his autograph on the streets, not to mention the lucrative fees—and no pestering questions from journalists. He didn't mind the frequent flying or the grueling pace. He valued the meetings with world leaders. He took great joy in his newfound freedom to walk around Europe's cities, many of them places he had visited in his youth, without a presidential schedule. And of course he loved to talk and talk, whether at a podium or a dinner table. But he knew that his post-presidential existence could not be defined by a banal, mercenary routine of speechifying. He needed to *do something*.

———

In Gujarat, he had found a compelling cause—with donors so enthusiastic and generous that the American India Foundation increased its fundraising goal to $50 million and scheduled a weeklong visit to the subcontinent, led by Clinton, primarily to assess conditions in the desolated western region. His experience as governor and president had afforded him considerable expertise in dealing with disasters, both natural and man-made.

Returning to India little more than a year after his historic March 2000 state visit, Clinton's itinerary included a couple of days touring the damage in Gujarat state, a morning at the late Mother Teresa's orphanage in Calcutta, and a banquet hosted by the prime minister in New Delhi. No paid speeches were on the schedule. With a far smaller entourage (including a dozen AIF leaders) and a humanitarian rather than geopolitical agenda, the trip established a post-presidential style that would serve as the template for many of his foreign tours. Usually he would enjoy all the perquisites and comforts due a visiting head of state: traveling via sleek private aircraft, staying in the very finest hotel suites, eating at the best tables in the best restaurants, riding in black Chevy Suburban SUVs with his Secret Service detail, flanked by local police vehicles and motorcycles. His staff made a valiant effort to uphold that standard, as did his hosts. It wasn't always possible.

When Clinton stepped off the Indian Airlines plane that had taken him from New Delhi to Bhuj, one of the largest and most heavily damaged cities in the state of Gujarat, the temperature under the glaring sun was 41 degrees Celsius—or just under 106 Fahrenheit. Wearing only a dark green T-shirt and khaki slacks, he jumped into a blue Jeep with Doug Band, joining a slow crawl of two dozen vehicles—somehow without air-conditioning or bottled water—that were packed with members of the AIF contingent and local dignitaries. The perspiring convoy headed out from Bhuj's airport for the towns of Ratnal and Anjar, a trip of less than thirty miles that would take nearly two hours to complete. Along the roads, thousands of men, women, and children had lined up to greet the motorcade, applauding loudly and crying "Clinton! Clinton!" as it arrived an hour late.

What they found in the flattened villages left Clinton and his companions stunned, stricken, overwhelmed. There simply wasn't much left of those places, their small stone houses and concrete storefronts all tumbled into a jagged rubble of rocks, broken red roof tiles, and smashed wood beams, all strewn amid streets that nobody had cleared, two months after the quake. Yet the people of the towns, furious that the government had so far failed to restore their villages or homes, were nevertheless thrilled to see the tall white-haired man from America, an important man whose presence would, they hoped, draw fresh attention to their dismal living conditions. Dozens of young women and children greeted him with tossed rice and flower petals, as an elderly woman anointed his forehead with a reddish dot of blessing. Their energy lifted Clinton as he spoke.

"Today I have come to look, listen, learn, ask questions, see what we can do to help," he said. "The people of this place have lived through an unimaginable tragedy. The most important thing is to see whether this can be rebuilt." He said the world had not forgotten them, and promised that soon much more help would be forthcoming, a message he repeated at every stop. "He's a big personality in the world," a dazzled truck driver told the *New York Times*. "Something good will come of his visit, though we don't know what it will be." (The *Times* headline on the trip, featured on page one, treated him like a down-market showbiz personality: "Whatever Happened to Bill Clinton? He's Playing India.")

———

Gujarat state officials handed out a glossy brochure in every town Clinton visited, which claimed that following the earthquake, "the state government immediately swung into action and mobilized all available resources. . . . The entire machinery of the state responded to the calamity with fortitude and determination." That blatantly aggrandizing message contrasted distinctly with what the survivors told Clinton and his friends. Government at all levels had failed them so far, providing little more than a $40 stipend along with some sheet-metal shelters and plastic tents. After two months, many thousands remained destitute and homeless.

"Nothing has been done, and nothing is going to be done. This is all for show," complained a teacher, as he waited to see the former president. "If Clinton stayed here a month, maybe then we would get some proper help."

Reaching Anjar, their main destination, the visitors from America went straight to a street where one of the most horrific incidents had occurred. More than two hundred elementary school students were parading on the morning of January 26 to celebrate Republic Day, a national holiday, when the temblor suddenly toppled buildings from both sides of the narrow lane and killed all of them. He was supposed to unveil a memorial plaque there, but that plan—like the relief efforts in general—had gone wrong. The memorial assemblage had been placed mistakenly on private property whose owner, irritated because the authorities had not first asked whether his land could be used, had removed the plaque, leaving only the modest stone pedestal.

Rotting garbage and ponds of sewage surrounded the area, a situation that local workers had tried to remedy by hastily covering the ponds with dirt and broken stones. The smell combined with the heat was almost overpowering. In remembrance of the dead children, Clinton set a bouquet of roses down on the stone pedestal and bowed his head for a moment of silence.

There were no words adequate to this tragedy, but he had to try. "We will raise funds to help the people of Anjar to confront their loss," he promised. "We have a plan to see if money can be given to people to rebuild their lives. We are interested in seeing results."

Sweat running down their faces and soaking their clothes, Clinton and his companions piled into their cars for the long, hot drive back to Bhuj, where the International Red Cross was operating a makeshift medical clinic to replace the city's badly damaged Jubilee Hospital. A CNN reporter at the clinic described Clinton as "visibly shaken" by what he had seen already. At the Red Cross site, located on the ruined hospital premises, he held a news conference with a crowd of mostly Indian reporters.

Saying that much of the money raised for disaster relief had not been deployed "very well" in years past, Clinton explained that the AIF planned to collaborate with other nongovernmental organizations and the Indian government on focused action to restore jobs, education, and housing to Gujarat. They would develop a program based largely on what he and his colleagues had witnessed. In the years ahead, Clinton would try repeatedly to improve the world's response to the desolation and trauma of such vast disasters.

Now, his voice quavering slightly with emotion, he mentioned the March 2000 state visit. "I will never forget it. I have always wanted to come back, but this sad event has brought me back earlier than expected." Before climbing into his Jeep, Clinton made another vow that he repeated at every stop: "I intend to come back to India for the rest of my life."

He met with relief officials from the Red Cross and other agencies the next morning in Ahmedabad, to discuss what they needed in Gujarat and how the AIF could be most helpful. By then, the scale of the destruction and suffering that they had witnessed was spurring him and his AIF companions toward more and more ambitious plans. Later that day, they announced that AIF had raised its fundraising goal for Gujarat to $100 million, with tentative plans to adopt one hundred villages for reconstruction.

In his meeting with the relief agencies, Clinton seemed to be grasping at larger aspirations for himself as well. According to Vimala Ramalingam, the secretary general of the Indian Red Cross, he expressed a desire in that meeting to support other humanitarian work across India—particularly to prevent the spread of HIV/AIDS. He also talked about discovering new ways to solve problems in Gujarat that could improve the lives of people in poor villages around the world.

"One of the things I am interested in," he later told reporters, "is coming up with a model which will be helpful in developing other villages in India or Africa or Latin America, that may not have had natural disasters, but would like to build a different future."

During the afternoon he toured Akshardham, a ten-story, hand-built, pink sandstone edifice in Gandhinagar that is one of Gujarat's largest Hindu temples. He was received with a big garland of crimson and white flowers hung around his neck, as women devotees chanted a peace prayer. Standing before the great temple he looked up, marveling that such an enormous building still stood perfectly intact, without any support from steel or concrete. "The earthquake has not damaged Akshardham?" he asked Pramukh Swami Maharaj, the guru of the modern Swaminarayan sect, which emphasizes service and tolerance. It had not. The swami walked him through the complex, trailed by monks swathed in orange robes, and Secret Service agents, perspiring heavily in polo shirts.

Despite the torrid air, again over 100 degrees Fahrenheit, Clinton noticed that he felt surprisingly calm and comfortable. Scheduled for fifteen minutes, the tour stretched into an hour as the swami and the former president ventured beyond the temple into a garden, filled with statues and carved stones, including a life-sized likeness of Gandhi. Then Clinton's glance fell upon an extraordinary artwork—the figure of a man, sculpting himself with a hammer and chisel from a giant block of yellow stone. "What an amazing, incredible idea," he blurted. "So powerful!" The swami smiled.

The sculptor's metaphor of self-realization intrigued Clinton, who stood and gazed at it for minutes. At last, someone reminded him that they had fallen behind schedule—and that some of his companions were almost fainting in the heat. Before he left, Pramukh Swami introduced him to temple volunteers working in the earthquake relief effort—and to a Muslim man who told Clinton that although there was not a single Hindu family in his village, Akshardham had sent workers, construction materials, and food to aid the people there every day since the quake.

In the visitor's book, he wrote:

> *April 5, 2001*
>
> *Thank you—*
> *for welcoming me.*
> *for making me feel at home.*
> *for reaching out to all God's children.*
> *for helping the people hurt by the earthquake.*
> *for working for peace and reconciliation.*
>
> *—Bill Clinton*

The seven days in India were sometimes exhilarating, sometimes sad, and often grueling for Clinton, who felt like he was spending more days on the road than at home—and was booked on excursions to every continent on earth before the year's end. In mid-April, he and Hillary took six days off for spring vacation in Punta Cana, the Dominican Republic resort owned by a group that included their friend, fashion designer Oscar de la Renta. Within days of returning to New York, however, he was leaving again on a seventeen-hour flight to South Africa.

No matter how tired Clinton felt, Nelson Mandela's request that he deliver a talk at a "civil society forum" in Johannesburg—free of any honorarium—was an undertaking he would have been most reluctant to refuse. The eighty-two-year-old Mandela had stepped down from his country's presidency just a year before Clinton. Both were now members of the fraternity of former heads of state. But their connection went much deeper.

Over the years, the friendship between the two leaders had grown increasingly intimate, like that between a loving father and son; it was the kind of relationship that both men had struggled with in their own families, years earlier. Having lost his biological father three months before he was born, Clinton had fought repeatedly with the abusive, alcoholic stepfather whose surname he carried. Some friends thought he had looked for a caring dad ever since. The stoical Mandela, imprisoned for decades after two wives had given him six children, knew all too well that he had missed the chance to serve as a proper father to them. And some of Mandela's children later voiced their resentment over his absence.

None of those troubles shadowed the affinity that they felt toward each other, cemented forever after Mandela spoke out publicly for Clinton when impeachment loomed. On September 21, 1998, the same day that American television broadcast Clinton's four painful hours of grand jury testimony on the Lewinsky matter, he addressed the opening of the U.N. General Assembly. At the end, the gathered heads of state rose as one, clapping for a memorable six minutes. All agreed they were applauding the man more than his speech about fighting terrorism.

The following day, Mandela flew down to Washington for a White House reception in his honor hosted by the Clintons, with African American ministers, civil rights activists, and members of the Congressional Black Caucus present. When his turn came to speak, Mandela was blunt.

"We are aware of the national debate that is taking place in this country about the President, and it is not our business to interfere in this matter," he began, then proceeded to do precisely that.

"But we do wish to say that President Clinton is a friend of South Africa and Africa, and I believe the friend of the great mass of black people, and the minorities, and the disabled of the United States. . . .

"We have often said that our morality does not allow us to desert our friends. And we have got to say tonight, we are thinking of you in this difficult and uncertain time in your life. . . .

"I repeat that I will not interfere in the domestic affairs of this country." His face broke into that incomparable smile as his audience laughed. "But you should have seen the way he was received by the General Assembly of the United Nations," as if they had missed it. "The applause was spontaneous and overwhelming. All of us rose to our feet when he came in. It was the same after he delivered his speech. That sent a strong message as to what the world thinks on this matter. . . . If you judge from the reaction of the General Assembly, the United States is completely isolated on this question." News outlets across the world quickly reported Mandela's provocative remarks, with several stories noting that Clinton appeared to wipe away a tear as he listened.

In Johannesburg three years later, again standing beside Mandela, Clinton's mission involved more than delivering a speech on civil society. Among those joining him on the trip was Eli Segal, the longtime Democratic activist and successful corporate entrepreneur who had served as chief of staff of Clinton's 1992 campaign—and who had later organized and directed AmeriCorps, Clinton's signature domestic Peace Corps program. The former president still considered its creation to be among his proudest achievements.

At Mandela's urging, Clinton had brought over Segal and a group of twenty enthusiastic alumni from AmeriCorps and its largest affiliate, City Year, which pays young men and women a small stipend to live and work in urban and rural communities on every variety of local problem, from disaster relief, housing for the homeless, and improving schools to delivering food and services for poor HIV/AIDS patients. They had all come to encourage South African political and community leaders to consider the possibility of starting a South African affiliate of City Year, with promises of American assistance and funding.

"Just before I left to come to South Africa," Clinton explained to the hundreds of civic leaders and students at the conference, "I saw television coverage of the terrible flooding along the Mississippi River in the United States, and there were pictures of people in a small community in Iowa packing sandbags against the rising waters, and in the midst of them were young people with AmeriCorps emblems on their shirts, working with people who formerly would have been strangers to them, to build the bonds of community.

"These young people embody the vision that drove me to run for president and serve. I wanted to build a country where there was opportunity for every responsible citizen, a national community that celebrates our incredible diversity while reaffirming our common humanity." Gesturing toward the AmeriCorps and City Year veterans, he said, "That's what they do every day."

The second leg of his Africa trip took Clinton to Abuja, the Nigerian capital, where he was invited to address a major three-day conference on HIV/AIDS called by the Organization of African Unity (soon to be reorganized and renamed the African Union)—the largest event of its kind in the continent's history. At the "Extraordinary OAU Summit," as it was billed, he would share the spotlight with U.N. Secretary-General Kofi Annan, as a high-ranking audience of African heads of state, health ministers, officials from donor countries and medical NGOs, including the American mega-philanthropist Bill Gates, grappled with the worsening health crisis.

Only eight months earlier, in August 2001, Clinton had visited Nigeria as president, shaking up the country with a televised appearance during which he physically embraced several AIDS patients—an act that violated taboos and elicited "a very powerful response in Nigeria and the rest of Africa," according to a local AIDS activist. Among the country's 110 million people, an estimated 15 million were infected, driven into hiding by the pervasive stigma. Discrimination and fear were so strong that a judge suspended the trial of a woman with HIV/AIDS because he viewed her presence in his courtroom as a threat to public health.

"In every country, in any culture, it is difficult, painful, at the very least embarrassing to talk about the issues involved with AIDS," he had told the Nigerians. "But is it harder to talk about these things than to watch a child die of AIDS who could have lived if the rest of us had done our part?" Based on his own administration's decision to support exclusive patents on AIDS medications and to oppose production of cheaper generic alternatives, he might well have been talking about himself.

Now he was in Nigeria again where, despite his attempt to break down prejudice against people suffering with HIV/AIDS, the virus continued to spread. For both the OAU and the U.N., the chief purpose of the Abuja conference was to formulate a consensus plan for fighting an epidemic that, as Clinton noted in his speech, might kill as many as

100 million Africans in the coming decade. By putting together a credible plan with U.N. backing, including major contributions from their own governments, the African leaders hoped that they could attract more support from the West. Specifically, Annan and the OAU leaders wanted to mobilize vast new resources from the developed nations to begin providing antiretroviral drugs to sick Africans.

Until then the Western consensus had been clear and chilling, if usually left unsaid. Antiretroviral medications or ARVs, the only known treatment for HIV/AIDS, were simply far too costly for most citizens of the developing world to afford. Long struggles over patent protection for the European and American pharmaceutical companies that produced the drugs—with the Clinton administration mostly advocating the narrow interest of those U.S. corporations—had left millions of people to die, even though generic versions might have saved at least some of them. Western governments preferred to promote prevention rather than treatment, as the more feasible and cheaper alternative. It was easier not to talk about the real consequences of that choice.

But on April 19, just days before the conference opened, a consortium of thirty-nine international pharmaceutical companies abruptly dropped a lawsuit against the government of South Africa over its attempts to purchase and produce generic medications. Under growing international pressure, the drug manufacturers had abandoned their effort to overturn a law signed by Mandela, which empowered the South African health minister to import generic drugs without regard to patent protection. Announcing their decision, the firms claimed that South Africa had promised to recognize their rights and consult them in implementing the law.

This sudden legal victory shot a powerful tremor of hope through the Abuja conference. Branded medications that cost $10,000 to $15,000 a year per patient in the developed world might soon cost as little as $700 a year in generic form—still too expensive for most patients or governments, but far closer to affordable. With legal obstacles removed, the possibility of effective action and the moral imperative to act were at the top of the conference agenda.

Annan's keynote address to the conference urged the creation of a global war chest of up to $10 billion annually, raised from governments, corporations, foundations, and individual donors, to provide

AIDS medications in the developing world "at the lowest possible price," in cooperation with manufacturers. He pledged that if money was forthcoming, as he expected, the U.N. would take the lead in coordinating financial assistance with strategic planning in this proposed "Marshall Plan."

Following Annan, Clinton endorsed the secretary-general's call for funding and action, warning that although Africa was currently the "epicenter" of the disease, other major nations such as "India, China, or even Russia" could take its place in the future if the world failed to act. He had a warning for the three dozen African heads of state who were present, too: Unless they began to establish national systems in their countries to ensure effective use of the global funding, the additional money would accomplish little. "You still need to get enough medicine distributed," he emphasized, "and educate your people on how to take the medicine."

The obvious question for Clinton himself was what he could do, besides delivering speeches, to advance the cause. It was good to hug an AIDS patient on TV, so that the stigma surrounding the disease might diminish. But however warm and sincere his embrace might be, he knew that this gesture alone would save no lives. Without treatment, every person—every little child—that Clinton hugged would die, as would millions more.

He could not expect to sway U.S. government policy, which was at best equivocal toward the U.N. effort. Annan wanted the United States to pay up to $3 billion annually toward his global war chest, but word from Washington indicated skepticism in the White House toward any program overseen by the United Nations. "There are still a lot of questions to be answered," said a Bush administration official on the eve of the conference.

Privately, the distrust ran in both directions. Angered by Secretary of State Colin Powell's decision to send a lower-level delegation to the conference—rather than attend in person—the organizers responded by removing the new secretary of state's "message of hope" from the opening ceremony schedule. Only a forceful intervention by U.S. embassy officials persuaded Nigerian and OAU officials to put Powell's message on the program at all.

The conference concluded with the approval of a "framework for action," requiring African leaders to fund primary health care in their countries and create "sustainable mechanisms" to fund HIV prevention and treatment, especially to protect vulnerable women and children. The heads of state also signed an "Abuja Declaration," taking personal responsibility for leadership in their own countries against the pandemic, and committing a "target allocation" of 15 percent of national budgets for "improvement of the health sector" as well as HIV/AIDS prevention. Not surprisingly, the declaration also pleaded for increased foreign assistance and debt forgiveness.

For the moment, Clinton was obliged to place a higher priority on his own problems—completing the transition to the new office in Harlem, shopping a book deal for his memoirs, and raising as much as a hundred million dollars for his presidential library in Little Rock. But on the list of useful functions he might still serve, leadership in the fight against the AIDS pandemic appealed to all his instincts. He instructed his staff to respond positively whenever the international community of scientists and activists requested him to appear.

When Clinton visited China a few weeks later to speak at business events in Hong Kong and Shanghai, he talked at length about AIDS in Africa and the threat posed by the pandemic to a globalizing world. Meeting for over an hour in Hong Kong with Jiang Zemin, he tried to draw out the Chinese premier on the topic of HIV and AIDS on the mainland.

While on Chinese territory, Clinton also sought to improve his relationship with the Bush administration and to ameliorate tensions between the U.S. and China—which had risen sharply after the midair collision between an American spy plane and a Chinese fighter jet over Hainan Island on April 1. Although the Chinese government had released the American plane's pilot and crew, it was still refusing to release the downed U-2.

On the day after Jiang appeared at a forum sponsored by *Fortune* magazine, Clinton urged his listeners not to assume that present tensions would always define the relationship between China and the United States. "The world will be a better place over the next 50 years," he said, "if we are partners." Acknowledging the "difficulties and bumps in the road" that are inevitable between two great powers with differing cultures, he added, "The recent incident involving the airplane and—in my time—the terrible accident in which the American plane bombed the Chinese Embassy in Belgrade" during the 1999 Balkans war "is something I still profoundly regret." More to the point, he echoed Jiang's call for the World Trade Organization to admit the People's Republic as a member: "It is imperative to complete China's accession to the WTO at the earliest possible date."

Well before departing for Hong Kong, Clinton had contacted Condoleezza Rice at the National Security Council to let the administration know about his plans and the likelihood that he would encounter Jiang, whom he considered a personal friend. Would President Bush prefer that he cancel the meetings and stay away from China for the moment? Or did the president and his advisers wish to send a quiet word to the Chinese at the highest level?

The White House approved Clinton's trip and let him carry a straightforward message: If the Chinese wanted to prevent a further deterioration of relations, they should return the U-2 forthwith. According to Sandy Berger—and with Berger's counsel—his former boss "strongly encouraged [Jiang] to give the plane back." Jiang's response and the content of their talks remained private. But by early July, after further bilateral negotiations, the spy craft was dismantled and shipped back in parts via Russia's Polet airline.

———

At home, many Clinton critics—writers like Andrew Sullivan and outlets like the *New York Post*—continued to complain that Clinton wouldn't go away, proving only that they could not bear to lose him as a target. Having shown little constraint while he was president, they now seemed to feel liberated in their attacks. In a June article headlined "Bubba Eyes Big Bucks," the *Post* quoted an unnamed "celebrity booker," who supposedly told the paper that the money-grubbing Clinton was "unlike any other former president. He's the only one who might show up at your bar mitzvah if you paid him."

And in an essay titled "Bill's Big Bucks," on the occasion of Clinton's paid appearance at the Hay-on-Wye literary festival in Wales, Sullivan complained, inaccurately, that he had sat down with the Chinese president and talked diplomacy "without consulting his government. . . . These are the actions of someone who still, somewhere in the back of his mind, thinks he is president—or ought to be." Reiterating the old "Clinton fatigue" theme perennially proclaimed by his critics, Sullivan concluded: "Forgive America if it sighs a little as it sees his charm exude exponentially elsewhere—for the moment at least. After eight long years, it's time for someone else to take the strain."

Despite the persistent sarcasm and cynicism of media coverage, Clinton could detect signs by summer that the chill surrounding him in his homeland had finally started to thaw. He and Hillary celebrated Chelsea's graduation from Stanford in late June, blowing kisses to her from the stands while she and 1,600 classmates danced and cavorted in the traditional "wacky walk" as they filed into the university's stadium. She had earned a bachelor's in history with highest honors, avoided the drinking and drugs that made so many other politicians' children prey for supermarket tabloids—and in the fall planned to leave for Oxford, where her father was once a Rhodes Scholar, to study international relations. Even the *New York Times* carried no negative comment about the joyous occasion. "We're going to parties and dinners with her friends and their families, attending her graduation events and whatever else she wants to do," Clinton told the paper. Invited to lunch at the Palo Alto home of Steve Jobs, the Clintons were among the first to see Apple's new iPod, which would debut officially in October.

Back in New York, Karen Tramontano had been preparing the new premises in Harlem, with a big, comfortable office for Clinton that featured sweeping views of Central Park and Midtown Manhattan from its oversized south-facing windows. On August 1, the official opening date, with bands playing and residents literally dancing in the street, his new neighborhood exploded with celebration. Thousands of people filled 125th Street, waiting hours in the sun to welcome him. State and local politicians crowded onto the dais erected on a plaza nearby, where a state official presented Clinton with a proclamation from New York's Republican governor, George Pataki, marking "William Jefferson Clinton Day" in the Harlem community.

To many Harlem residents, Clinton was still "the first black president"—a Southern white politician who had somehow come to represent their outlook and aspirations. In remarks from the stage, he spoke of his lifelong love of African American culture and recalled how, as a young saxophone player in Arkansas, he had yearned to visit the legendary Apollo Theater. "I dreamed that one day I might be like Louis Armstrong and Ella Fitzgerald. Well, I never made it, to play at the Apollo. But I ain't dead yet. I may play there yet!"

Somewhat vaguely, he promised to be a good neighbor. "You were always there for me and I will try to be there for you." When he finished speaking, the Benny King jazz group struck up "Stand by Me," and he sang along with feeling.

In New York, he was no longer a social pariah. As a counterpoint to the Harlem street celebration, a reporter for the *Los Angeles Times* quoted David Patrick Columbia, whose *New York Social Diary* website chronicles Manhattan society, predicting that Clinton would soon be making the rounds of the city's most exclusive tables. "I think he's going to charm the birds right out of the trees," said the blogger, who confided, "I know certain unnamed hostesses are giving him dinners in September. I know they're hot tickets."

The summer's most significant affirmation came a week later, when publisher Alfred A. Knopf announced that it had acquired Clinton's autobiography. On August 6, Knopf president and editor-in-chief Sonny Mehta issued a brief statement that confirmed earlier leaks: "President Clinton is one of the dominant figures on the global stage. He has lived an extraordinary life, and he has a great story to tell."

Represented by Washington attorney Robert Barnett—a partner of David Kendall at Williams & Connolly, whose literary clients included Prince Charles, Barbra Streisand, Hillary Clinton, and many other political and showbiz celebrities—the former president had not shopped his book around, despite expressions of interest from many publishers around the world. Nor had he put together a written proposal of any kind. Instead he had simply outlined his ideas for a personal and political memoir in a series of discussions with Mehta and other editors at Knopf.

Although neither Barnett nor Mehta spoke publicly about money, Clinton was reported to have gotten an advance of no less than $10 million, and as much as $12 million. Either of the reported figures would have made Clinton's the largest book advance in the history of publishing, a record previously held by Pope John Paul II at $8.5 million. In return, according to Knopf, he had agreed to produce "a thorough and candid telling of his life, with a primary focus on the White House years"—although as every reporter apparently felt obliged to mention, that description left unclear how much he would reveal about his disastrous romance with Monica Lewinsky.

In a *Newsweek* column, Jonathan Alter fretted that Clinton's book was likely to be as "boring" as most presidential memoirs. According to Alter, Clinton was telling friends that the book "may not be as mean as some people want it to be. This shouldn't be about settling scores but setting the record straight." The only way to avoid the "memoir curse" of predictable dullness, urged the columnist, would be a searching self-examination of his failures in and out of office. Vulnerability and candor would lend credibility to any boasting about his accomplishments.

"I don't want a book that's either turgid and boring or unduly defensive," he quoted Clinton telling friends privately. "I want to explain to people who I am and what I tried to do in public life—the good things we did and the mistakes I made. And I want to make it come alive." That was the least he could do for $15 million—the actual price paid by Knopf for all rights, foreign and domestic.

By the first week of September, with summer fading, Clinton was up in the air again—soaring toward a week of speeches, dinners, and golf in Australia. The round of events began with a major Saturday evening gala in Sydney to benefit a children's hospital, pulled together by friends of the moderately left-wing Australian Labor Party—and a more intimate dinner on the same evening with a group of forty-four business executives that reportedly netted more than $1.5 million for the party. Two nights later, he was in Melbourne for a speaking event overseen by Liberal Party stalwarts and chaired by Andrew Peacock, who had served as Australia's ambassador to the United States during Clinton's presidency. His earnings in the two Australian cities came to nearly half a million dollars.

At the luncheon speech in Melbourne on September 10, Clinton took questions from the audience of business leaders, as he often did at small gatherings. Asked about international terrorism, he brought up the name of Osama bin Laden, describing the al Qaeda chief as "a very smart guy," before continuing.

"I spent a lot of time thinking about him. And I nearly got him once.

I nearly got him. And I could have killed him," the former president went on, "but I would have had to destroy a little town called Kandahar in Afghanistan, and kill 300 innocent women and children, and then I would have been no better than him. And so I didn't do it."

Before midnight, he boarded a jet in Melbourne that took him, Band, Justin Cooper, and his Secret Service contingent to Cairns Airport—the jumping-off point for the little town of Port Douglas and the Great Barrier Reef. He had longed to return there ever since he and Hillary had visited in 1996, as he told the crowd waiting to greet him at the hangar.

"I've got two friends with me who have never been to Australia before, so I told them they had to go to Port Douglas, they had to go to the reef." For the next couple of days, Clinton had nothing on his agenda except snorkeling, eating crayfish, and playing golf.

Relaxing in a Pacific time zone, fourteen hours ahead of New York City, Clinton and his companions were spared the shocking sight of the fall of the Twin Towers until very late on the evening of September 11. They had been relaxing in a pub, celebrating Cooper's birthday and Band's passing the bar exam in Florida, his home state.

———

In Clinton's suite at the Sheraton Mirage, a luxurious hotel surrounded by palm trees, he turned on the television to see the nightmarish images that would soon become a historic symbol of horror for Americans. Across the bottom of the screen, a crawling ticker listed the names of passengers on the four flights hijacked by the al Qaeda terrorist teams. Suddenly, Clinton saw the name of a friend, someone who had worked with him for years, a man with a family of his own. "Oh my God," he breathed.

He knew Chelsea was in New York City, visiting a friend before her scheduled departure for England. Now he had to find out exactly where she was and who was with her, but nobody had been able to find her yet. When Hillary finally got through to his room, she pretended to know already that their daughter was safe, hoping to calm him—even though she felt inwardly frantic as her Senate staff continued to try to locate their daughter.

By her own account, Chelsea had been watching television at her friend's apartment in Union Square when the second plane hit, and quickly tried to call her mother in Washington—but as she spoke with an aide in Hillary's office, overburdened phone lines went dead. In a panic, she left the apartment and headed downtown, searching desperately for a pay phone to reach Hillary's Senate office again. She was standing in line at a pay phone, about twelve blocks from the disaster scene, when she heard the deafening roar of the second tower collapsing. She headed back toward Union Square, eventually found her friend, and they walked uptown, like thousands of other New Yorkers. When she found a working phone and reached Hillary, her mother burst into tears of relief.

At Clinton's office in Harlem, Karen Tramontano and members of the foundation staff were meeting in a conference room with a panoramic southward view when they saw the first plane. Someone came running into the room and suddenly they were watching the catastrophe on television. Tramontano picked up a phone immediately, trying to reach Band in Australia.

With all flights into the United States canceled, the Clinton entourage was stranded in Australia. After talking with Band, Tramontano placed a call to Condoleezza Rice to ask for help. After some wrangling that involved more calls from Band to the Secret Service and to Transportation Secretary Norman Mineta, the Pentagon dispatched a military aircraft to pick them up at Cairns Airport in Port Douglas. "It won't be very comfortable," Rice warned, "but it's the only plane we have available out there right away."

It wasn't comfortable at all aboard the C-130 cargo plane and the trip took almost twenty-four hours. There were no seats, there was no food, and at thirty thousand feet, the interior of the plane was cold—very, very cold. They stopped in Guam and switched to a refueling plane, which was no better. Band had tried to scrounge some sweaters and other warm clothing at the hotel, but they were all bone-chilled, starved, and exhausted when the plane finally landed at Stewart Airport, a New York National Guard airbase about fifty miles north of Chappaqua. Almost immediately they departed for Manhattan, where they headed to Union Square.

Despite their ordeal, Clinton was grateful to have gotten home, unlike thousands of Americans left overseas with no way to return until the airports reopened. Among them was Al Gore, who had been in Vienna when the terrorists struck, giving a speech to an Austrian Internet forum.

Evidently the Bush White House was not prepared to provide military transportation for the former vice president, who could find no way to get back except via Gander Airport, a tiny facility in Newfoundland. From there, he and an aide would have to drive southward across the Canadian border.

While seeking help with their predicament, a former Gore aide—who had also worked in the Clinton White House—called the Harlem office. Gore and Clinton had exchanged messages within the first hours after the terrorist attack, but had not spoken yet. Distant as relations between their bosses had become, the staffers remained friendly. When Gore's aide reached Tramontano, they talked casually about "the crap that's gone on for far too long" between Gore and Clinton—who literally had not spoken since a bitter two-hour argument about who was to blame for the disastrous outcome of the 2000 election. She suggested that on the long drive down from the Canadian border, Gore might stop in Chappaqua.

When Tramontano reached Clinton to discuss the proposed sleepover, she wasn't surprised by his enthusiasm. That evening around 8 p.m., the former vice president picked up his cell phone to speak with the former president for the first time in many months.

"Why don't you come down here, and then we'll fly down together Friday morning?" Clinton asked. An Air Force jet provided by the White House would take them to the capital for the special memorial service on September 14 at the National Cathedral.

Hours after midnight, driving a rented car, Gore arrived at the five-bedroom colonial on Old House Lane. Clinton was waiting for them in the living room, where he had been napping on and off, and got up to greet Gore.

As he climbed the steps to the front porch, the former vice president noticed a refrigerator, sitting where it had been moved while the kitchen was undergoing renovation—a tableau that struck him as more hillbilly Ozarks than chic Westchester. Eyeing the fridge, he cracked, one Southerner to another: "Well, you've really come a long way, haven't you?" At the door, Clinton roared with laughter.

They stayed up almost until dawn, talking mostly about the 9/11 attacks, their own efforts to deal with terrorism, and the murky times ahead. Chelsea met them in the morning at Westchester Airport to fly to Washington. On the flight down, Gore invited the Clintons to join his family after the memorial service for lunch at his home in Arlington, Virginia.

At the cathedral, a century-old Gothic Revival structure on the northern outskirts of the capital, Clinton sat in a front pew alongside President Bush and the other living former presidents, Gerald Ford, Jimmy Carter, and George H. W. Bush. He listened as the president delivered words of compassion for the bereaved and a warning to the enemy. He was speaking out forcefully in support of Bush at every opportunity, starting with his departure from Australia. He had canceled all of his speaking engagements abroad to remain in Manhattan, spending hours at local vigils and especially at the Armory on Park Avenue, where he tried to comfort families whose loved ones were missing and presumed dead.

"They cheered, they wept, they hugged him," wrote a reporter for London's *Daily Mirror*. "All around him, New Yorkers gathered, some to pass on their thanks that he had rushed to their side, others to grab his hand and use him as an emotional crutch. . . . All felt lifted to be in the presence of the man they had looked to for most of the past decade when their country was in its hour of need."

The *Mirror* correspondent was not alone in contrasting Clinton's instinctive leadership with the unsteadiness displayed by his successor in the early hours following the attack, although Bush soon righted himself and took command. America and the world had turned a page, moving beyond the petty controversies that had almost consumed Clinton in the days after he left office. Gaunt, somber, and worried, he and his fellow Americans now found themselves in a very different world.

Not everyone was willing to leave old habits behind, however, especially among Clinton's most rigid detractors on the right. Even as Bush and congressional leaders prayed for the nation to unite, the habitual haters simply could not resist a fresh opportunity to target him.

Nothing mattered more than proving (or at least asserting) that the terrorist attacks of September 11 should be blamed not on the current president, but the one who preceded him. Before long a writer for *National Review* warned, only half-jokingly: "If we members of the Vast Right-Wing Conspiracy don't get back to our daily routine of obsessive Clinton-bashing, then the terrorists will have won."

CHAPTER FOUR

For years afterward, many commentators on American life would refer to 9/11 as "the day everything changed," a phrase meant to mark that stunning moment when the nation awoke from its debilitating obsession with trivia and confronted existential threats. The act of terror, followed by war, and all that came thundering in their wake, instantly overshadowed the "scandal" mentality that had long dominated news coverage, political analysis, and commentary. Suddenly, the sustained hysteria over such banal concerns as the Whitewater land deal and the Monica Lewinsky affair seemed shamefully misguided. Even a few leading figures in the Washington press corps were glimpsed briefly flagellating themselves for those sins.

The national mood of reflection and humility did not linger too long, however, especially concerning the subject of William Jefferson Clinton. Scarcely taking breath after the terrorist attacks, while the rest of the country mourned, Clinton's dedicated adversaries seized upon 9/11 as an opportunity to resume their pursuit of "the politics of personal destruction" that blighted public discourse during his eight years in the White House. With a powerful impulse to blame someone in authority—at a moment when nobody dared to scrutinize the actions of George W. Bush, commander-in-chief—the former president became an irresistible target.

Representative Dana Rohrabacher, a Republican from Laguna Beach, California, literally couldn't resist for more than a few hours. At a news conference on September 11, Rohrabacher explained that the disaster's underlying cause was simple: "We had Bill Clinton backing off, letting the Taliban go, over and over again." The right-wing congressman may have hoped that if blame fell on Clinton, nobody would remember how Rohrabacher had once welcomed the Taliban's seizure of power, praising the Islamist movement's determination to "establish a disciplined, moral society" that would emphasize "stability."

Others on the right swiftly joined the chorus of condemnation, from Newt Gingrich, who denounced Clinton's "pathetically weak, ineffective ability to focus" on the terrorist threat, through an assortment of pundits and politicians—almost none of whom had paid much attention to terrorism, al Qaeda, or Osama bin Laden before September 12, 2001. Nearly all of them had been far too preoccupied during the previous nine years with the so-called Clinton scandals and peccadilloes that led to his impeachment. Many had opposed and even mocked Clinton administration initiatives against al Qaeda and other terrorist organizations.

By early October, perennial gadflies such as Paul Greenberg of the *Arkansas Democrat-Gazette* were regularly stinging Clinton, saying he had "mainly only talked about terrorism" while pursuing a policy that was "showy but pitiful." The *Washington Times* editorial board opined that "much of the time Mr. Clinton spent fighting to save his own political hide would have been far better spent fighting the bin Ladens of the world." Rush Limbaugh weighed in with a *Wall Street Journal* essay that held Clinton "culpable for not doing enough when he was commander-in-chief to combat the terrorists who wound up attacking the World Trade Center and Pentagon."

Although little noted for his national security expertise, Limbaugh had made an obvious point: The success of the attackers meant, by definition, that Clinton had not done enough to protect the United States from al Qaeda before September 11. The question of whether Clinton's successor had "done enough" in the eight months before the attack—or done anything at all—would not be addressed for years to come, and then only in the face of a concerted cover-up by George W. Bush and his administration. As Bush prepared to invade Afghanistan, with the support of well over 90 percent of the American public, he enjoyed an extraordinary exemption from criticism by the national press corps, Democrats on Capitol Hill—and Clinton himself.

In *USA Today*, the verdict on whether Clinton "could have done more to stop bin Laden" lacked "black-and-white clarity," but reporter Susan Page emphasized that "fighting terrorism wasn't his highest priority." When bin Laden emerged as "the mastermind of plots against Americans" during his second term, Clinton was "enmeshed in the Monica Lewinsky scandal and impeachment." Page didn't examine whether fighting terrorism had been a top priority for Bush and Cheney during the months before 9/11.

While the *Washington Post* noted that a "particularly acrid" debate had commenced over responsibility for 9/11, "the outcome of which could weigh heavily on Clinton's legacy," the argument remained rather lopsided. As the national media examined the history of U.S. counter-terrorism efforts, Clinton critics seized upon every purported lapse, while erasing every nuance, detail, and doubt to renew their public arraignment of him.

Having rarely underestimated the bitterness of his enemies, Clinton was nevertheless stunned by the right-wing effort, in the wake of a national catastrophe, to mount a show trial of him. Angered and shocked by their lack of restraint, even in the face of an event as grave as 9/11, he could only vent privately. If he or Al Gore had been in the Oval Office on that day, he told friends, Republicans would "never have offered me the support that Democrats have given President Bush."

It amazed him to read that some of his most cynical assailants were blaming him for the first assault on the World Trade Center in February 1993. When that attack occurred nobody, least of all Clinton himself, had thought to blame George Herbert Walker Bush, the former president who had departed the Oval Office only six weeks earlier—despite the national intelligence shortcomings that had allowed a group of Islamist terrorists to plot for three years, undetected, the detonation of a truck-bomb in the basement of the complex.

But in the months following 9/11, the sheer volume of vilification from the right overwhelmed the halting defense of Clinton mounted by Democrats, including the former president and his aides. Sandy Berger, his former national security adviser, assured the *Washington Post* that counterterrorism "was an urgent priority for the Clinton administration, and the intelligence community specifically engaged in an intensive effort directed at bin Laden [and al Qaeda] across a range of fronts." But as the *Post*'s John Harris observed in the same article, while conservatives were loudly denouncing Clinton, "there has been no corresponding effort on the Democratic side to argue opposing points—such as the successful quashing of terrorist attacks planned for the 2000 New Year."

In a speech at Harvard University on November 20, Clinton accepted broad responsibility for his administration's failure to build closer ties with Muslim nations generally, and more specifically with Afghanistan after the Soviet occupation ended. "There is a war raging within Islam today about what they think about the modern world in general and the United States in particular," he said. "We all have to change. The world's poor cannot be led by people like Mr. bin Laden who think they can find their redemption in our destruction. But the world's rich cannot be led by people who play to our shortsighted selfishness." On that occasion he didn't comment on the lengthy indictment compiled (and largely fabricated) by conservatives to demonstrate his "criminal negligence."

Among the most damaging and deceptive accusations was the claim that Clinton had repeatedly ignored opportunities to capture or kill Osama bin Laden. "The Sudanese government offered to hand over bin Laden to the United States," wrote Andrew Sullivan, the former *New Republic* editor turned blogger. "Astonishingly, the Clinton administration turned the offer down." This charge was based on a widely quoted (and misquoted) article published in the *Washington Post* on October 3—which said that Khartoum had offered to consider turning bin Laden over to the Saudi authorities, but only if Washington lifted sanctions on the Sudanese regime, designed to punish its genocidal campaign against Christians in its southern provinces. According to the *Post*, both the White House and the State Department sought to induce the Saudis to accept custody of bin Laden, a request that Riyadh adamantly rejected.

Nowhere did the carefully worded *Post* story suggest that Sudan agreed to deliver bin Laden into American custody, because that had never happened (except possibly in Sullivan's imagination). Insisting on Clinton's culpability, Sullivan and others claimed that he had allowed bin Laden to escape repeatedly—or had simply never tried to bring down the al Qaeda chief.

Explaining his alleged inattention to the terrorist threat, many of those same critics sneeringly cited his extramarital affair with Monica Lewinsky—and its aftermath, leading to his 1999 impeachment—as a self-inflicted distraction from the nation's defense. Of course, when one of several attempts to kill bin Laden became public in August 1998, the same Republican critics insinuated that those famous cruise missile strikes were launched to deflect public attention from his personal scandal. It never seemed to occur to those worthies that they were smearing not only the president but also several high-ranking intelligence and military officers, including General Anthony Zinni, who had urged the missile assault (and later joined the Bush administration as Mideast envoy). Earlier that year, in fact, Clinton had authorized an intensive, ongoing campaign to destroy al Qaeda and seize or assassinate bin Laden in a secret National Security Decision Directive. Later, he signed an executive order freezing $254 million in Taliban assets in the United States, while the State Department worked to maintain the regime's international isolation.

That Clinton never succeeded in killing bin Laden was a problem of luck rather than will. The al Qaeda chieftain had escaped every one of several painstaking attempts on his life mounted by the CIA. Clinton had lacked the congressional and international support to order an invasion of Afghanistan, even if he had considered such action prudent. And as Bush later discovered—when U.S. forces invaded that country under his command—even with tens of thousands of American soldiers on the ground, including crack Special Forces units, rolling up the al Qaeda and Taliban leadership in hostile terrain was nearly impossible; both bin Laden and Taliban leader Mullah Omar escaped.

Echoing the right-wing chorus, Sullivan complained that Clinton "did little that was effective" against terrorism and "simply refused to do anything serious about the threat." Leaving aside the secret campaign against bin Laden, however, the Clinton administration had in fact pursued several serious initiatives against terrorism, while his political adversaries directed their attention elsewhere. The former president's first crime bill, submitted to Congress within months after the February 1993 attack on the World Trade Center, had included stringent new antiterrorism provisions—notably including stronger deportation authority and a federal death penalty for terrorists.

When Clinton sought to expand those protections in 1995, after the bombing of the federal building in Oklahoma City, a coalition of civil libertarians and antigovernment conservatives argued that this "overreaction" posed a threat to constitutional rights and helped to defeat his bill. Then, at the urging of industry lobbyists, the Republican leadership rebuffed administration proposals to improve airport security screening, to tighten controls on encryption software, and to close loopholes in offshore money-laundering laws. Any or all of those measures might have helped to prevent the 9/11 attacks.

Indeed, during a period when the public, the mainstream media, and most political leaders were paying little attention to terrorism, Clinton initiated or expanded several key programs to address the likelihood of a disastrous attack. From 1996 to 2001, federal spending on counterterrorism increased dramatically, to more than $12 billion annually. The FBI's counterterrorism budget rose even more sharply, from $78 million in 1996 to $609 million in 2000, tripling the number of assigned special agents and creating a new counterterrorism center at the bureau's Washington headquarters. Seemingly obsessed with the prospect of a biological attack, Clinton had increased spending on "domestic preparedness" programs from $42.6 million in 1997 to more than $1.2 billion in 2000.

In December 2000, a month before Clinton left office—and a year after his administration had thwarted the "Millennium Plot," a major terrorist attack on the Los Angeles airport scheduled for New Year's Eve 2000—the former ambassador for counterterrorism in the Reagan State Department, a career diplomat named Robert Oakley, had praised the Democratic president's operations and programs. "Overall I give them very high marks," Oakley told the *Washington Post.* "The only major criticism I have is the obsession with Osama, which has made him stronger." Paul Bremer, who had succeeded Oakley in the same position under Reagan and later chaired the National Commission on Terrorism, mostly agreed—except that Bremer thought Clinton had "correctly focused on bin Laden."

Had Clinton felt free to defend himself, he might have mentioned a number of those salient facts in public. He might have revealed, as he finally did years later, the highly personal, face-to-face warning about the looming menace of al Qaeda that he delivered to George W. Bush in the White House residence early in January 2001, with national security advisers to both men present, during the traditional "exit interview." For reasons of post-presidential decorum and wartime solidarity, he didn't feel at liberty to say anything that could be interpreted as a direct criticism of his successor. The complete account of their contrasting records concerning terrorism—before "everything changed"—

would unfold slowly over the coming years. That painful reckoning would not begin until Americans became ready to confront hard questions about the competence, character, and motives of the Bush administration.

———

As Clinton's presidential legacy came under withering criticism from the right, those responsible for preserving and defending his place in history felt the pressure to respond—and to do so in a way that was literally concrete. There was yet no end in sight to fundraising for the Clinton Presidential Center (whose estimated cost was nearing $200 million), but the architectural and landscaping plans were complete and the foundation had enough money banked to start construction. Unless building commenced soon, there would be little hope of opening as scheduled in 2004.

By late 2001, in fact, the project already was almost a year behind schedule. The foundation had hoped to break ground on the twenty-eight-acre site along the Arkansas River, just a few blocks east of the city's revitalized downtown River Market district, in December 2000. The most durable obstacle was a long-running lawsuit against the project, filed by a local landowner named Eugene Pfeifer III. According to Pfeifer, who had commenced legal action against the city of Little Rock not long after Clinton selected the riverfront site in 1997, the use of eminent domain to obtain his two-acres-plus parcel was unlawful—even though the city had offered compensation of $400,000, a price he agreed was fair.

Pfeifer believed that the use of bonding authority to pay for the land, with $11.5 million in revenues pledged from the city's zoo and parks, was both unlawful and unfair. "Why shouldn't the Clinton Foundation just raise the money and pay for the land?" he had demanded repeatedly, arguing that the presidential center didn't satisfy the statutory definition of a "park," invalidating the city's use of revenue bonds to finance the land acquisition. Rebuffed by judges at every level, he had appealed all the way up to the Arkansas Supreme Court.

A local gadfly whose family had operated businesses in Little Rock for more than a century, Pfeifer was not alone in opposing the library—or at least the expenditure of city funds to purchase the land. Sniping at the overall project as well as the bonding scheme had been led by the *Arkansas Democrat-Gazette*, a staunchly Republican daily newspaper whose editorial-page editor, Paul Greenberg, had long since developed a national profile as the city's most bitter opponent of all things Clinton. (A single Greenberg line captures the theme of hundreds of his editorials and signed columns: "Before this President's tenure is mercifully concluded, one suspects that Warren G. Harding is going to start looking like a poor misunderstood saint.")

But opinion polls indicated that most residents of Little Rock—and most citizens of Arkansas—were still excited by the prospect of a presidential library honoring the state's most famous son.

Plans for the Clinton Presidential Center would transform the designated area, a "weed-choked, rundown warehouse district," into a world-class tourist attraction with a large new city park, a restored natural riverfront, a newly refurbished pedestrian bridge across the river to North Little Rock, as well as the University of Arkansas's new Clinton School of Public Service, located in the old Choctaw Station railway depot next door. The center was expected to attract tens of millions of dollars annually in new construction, discretionary spending, and tax revenues. To the city's leaders, dedicating a portion of park revenues to debt service seemed a small price for such a massive investment in the city's future.

On November 1, almost exactly a year after Pfeifer filed his appeal, six justices of the Arkansas Supreme Court unanimously ruled against him and upheld the city's authority to move forward. (The seventh justice, a distant relative of the former president, abstained.) The court found that Pfeifer had failed to prove his contention that the presidential center would not qualify as a park under state law. "I'm shocked," he told the Associated Press. "This is truly disappointing news."

The Supreme Court decision was exhilarating news to Skip Rutherford, the Clinton Foundation president overseeing the project. Within two hours after the court announced its ruling, Rutherford was on the phone with Clinton, selecting a date to break ground. They chose December 5, rushing to avoid the oncoming holiday season and put down a symbolic stake before the New Year. Like so many events across America that autumn, it was a moment shadowed by 9/11, yet a celebration of an ambitious plan that now seemed to be on the brink of fulfillment.

Ambitious may be too modest a term to describe the vision that the Clintons had nurtured during years of development stretching back to 1997 when, as president, Bill had announced that the library would be located in Little Rock. Two years later, following a lengthy selection process that involved both Hillary and Chelsea, he had picked the New York architecture firm led by James Stewart Polshek to design the project's buildings and park.

The sixty-seven-year-old Polshek was by then one of the most accomplished architects in America, if not the most critically venerated—and he was on the verge of popular acclaim with the opening of the Rose Earth and Space Center, a new planetarium shaped as a giant orb-within-cube, at the American Museum of Natural History in Manhattan. But that hadn't happened yet and nobody had expected Polshek, lacking the flash of more famous competitors, to win the library commission. Aside from the personal rapport that he developed with the Clintons, however, he possessed qualities that the most flamboyant names seemed to lack: a sophisticated political awareness and a strong social conscience.

The son of a politically progressive businessman from Ohio, Polshek often expressed his conviction that the work of architects needed to be more than clever, original, or visually arresting; he believed firmly that buildings, especially public structures, ought to serve society's broader goals as well as the needs of a particular client. Self-effacing and even shy when compared with the outsized personalities populating the upper reaches of his profession, Polshek didn't hesitate to identify himself forthrightly as a liberal Democrat. On one occasion, he even declared that he could never design a library for a Republican president. "Architecture and politics will always be connected," he later explained in an interview. "I like to think that there's a certain coherence between one's idealistic beliefs about the world and the clients one works for."

The distressed Little Rock site, the library's dimensions and purposes, the overwhelming need for exhibit and special storage space—not to mention the highly opinionated client himself—presented special challenges to Polshek and his partner, Richard Olcott. Clinton's library required the largest archival capacity of any of the eleven presidential repositories administered by the National Archives and Records Administration, to cope with over 80 million pages of documents and two million photographs comprising nearly 36,000 cubic feet of space, along with thousands upon thousands of artifacts, gifts, and curios. (The records of Franklin D. Roosevelt, who served as president for twelve years, took up less than 9,000 cubic feet at Hyde Park in upstate New York.)

Permanently preserving those records and artifacts required careful protection from excessive light and changes in temperature, but Clinton insisted that the library's interior spaces must be suffused with natural light, potentially ruinous to those objects. He wanted the library building and exhibition space to embrace the Arkansas River flowing by on its northern side, while opening up to Little Rock's downtown on the west.

Having initially situated the library on an east–west axis that would afford a river view from within its galleries, Olcott and Polshek turned the building 90 degrees so that its entrance faced the river and its long, glass-enclosed sides would admit natural light from east and west— using special glass that blocked the most damaging spectrum. (Most of the papers and artifacts would be stored inside huge basement vaults in an adjacent, climate-controlled archive building.) Visitors would enjoy the riverfront scenery while strolling through the park—landscaped with native trees, plants, and flowers—or over the restored railroad bridge that would bring them across the river from North Little Rock.

That uplifting vision was still no more than an architectural model on December 5, when a hastily assembled crowd of about two thousand friends and supporters showed up at the site. Many were unable to attend on short notice, but among those who did were Terry McAuliffe and David Kendall, as well as former White House chief of staff Thomas "Mack" McLarty, former White House political aide Craig Smith, and former White House advisers Bruce Reed and Tom Freedman. Their reward was a mountainous luncheon plate—including an entire barbecued chicken, a turkey leg, a pork sandwich, a few sausage links, and a portion of beef brisket, all courtesy of a locally renowned businessman and philanthropist named Jennings Osborne.

From the former president—after the benediction by a local rabbi and a quick introduction by Skip Rutherford, who noted that Hillary had been detained in Washington by pressing Senate votes—the audience heard an unusually concise and circumspect speech.

Clinton began by recalling "the very first groundbreaking of a presidential library, by our neighbors in Missouri," in May 1955, when construction started on Harry Truman's library. He paused for timing. "At the time, they commented on the astonishing sum—$1,750,000," he said, as the audience roared.

He went on to speak briefly about the achievements of his administration, which he described as eight years of "peace, prosperity, social justice, and social progress," but noted the failures too, particularly the defeat of universal health care. He talked about his belief in public service, the dangerous world that America would confront after 9/11, and the "bridge to the 21st century" that had served as the theme of his re-election campaign and had since been adopted by Polshek and Olcott as the reigning metaphor for the library design.

And then he read from one of the documents that would someday be displayed there—a letter, he said, written by a grieving young widow, following the sudden death of her husband in an automobile accident.

"It seemed almost unbearable at the time," wrote Virginia Blythe, the president's late mother, to a friend in Chicago. "But you see, I am six months pregnant, and the thought of our baby keeps me going and really gives me the whole world before me." With a hand wiping his eyes, Clinton said he hoped that he hadn't "let her down."

In the next day's *Washington Post*, reporter John Harris perceived a "jab" in Clinton's speech at his successor, when the former president promised that visitors to his library would be able to peruse documents pertinent to presidential decisions "when the classification period ends—and at this library, it will end." That remark seemed to refer to the Presidential Records Act Executive Order, issued by George W. Bush a month earlier, which allowed former presidents the right to extend the period during which documents remain under seal. Historians and journalists had protested the order, amid speculation that Bush was trying to protect his father from unwanted revelations about his conduct during the first Bush presidency and the Reagan years.

For Clinton, with his legacy under fire, the legitimacy of the library's portrayal of his presidency—and its scholarly acceptance—would concern him as much as its architectural quality and popular success. At the groundbreaking, Bruce Reed told the *Post*: "George Orwell was right. He who controls the past controls the future."

Unable to control the past in Orwellian style, Clinton still hoped to influence the future. When he concluded his speech, he picked up a gold-painted shovel and dug into the earth. The library would be built and he could turn toward his own future.

———

With the advent of 2002 came a new regime in Clinton's office. After nearly a year of building out the human and physical infrastructure of the foundation—and exhausting herself in the process—chief of staff Karen Tramontano had departed to pursue her own ideas for an international nonprofit and consulting work. She was replaced by Margaret "Maggie" Williams, another trusted colleague who had endured the administration's very worst times, following the suicide of White House counsel Vincent Foster, during which her role as an adviser to both Clintons had led to threats of indictment, awful press coverage, and more than $300,000 in personal legal expenses. After that searing experience, it was not at all clear why Maggie Williams should ever want to return to work for Bill Clinton—especially when she already had a plum job in Washington as president of Fenton Communications, the largest progressive public relations firm in the capital.

Before Clinton left office, she had been approached by Bruce Lindsey to work in the post-presidential apparatus, and she had said no. But when Tramontano finally had to be replaced, Lindsey had approached Williams again for help in finding a new chief of staff—and she had gone to see her former boss to discuss the possibilities.

At a meeting in his spacious but still unfinished office on 125th Street, Williams had listened in captivated silence as Clinton energetically held forth—for nearly two hours—on the lives of some of the men who had preceded him as post-presidents.

Leaning back in his chair, he conjured stories of John Quincy Adams, whose crusade against the slave trade after leaving the White House proved more consequential than anything he had done as president; of Teddy Roosevelt, whose action-packed post-presidency had included a bird-and-game collecting expedition in Africa, an extremely perilous exploration of the Amazon rain forest that almost killed him, a triumphal tour of European capitals, and a second presidential campaign as the founder of a new political party; and of Jimmy Carter, whose successes in overcoming the tropical disease known as river blindness, overseeing democratic elections abroad, and speaking out for the dispossessed Palestinians in the Holy Land, seemed most likely to serve as some kind of model for Clinton.

"We'll have some fun!" he concluded, with a mischievous smile, perhaps sensing that she was hooked in spite of herself.

When Williams returned home to Paris, she told her husband, William Barrett—a professional diplomat who had been working for Ambassador Felix Rohatyn at the U.S. embassy—that they might soon be moving to New York. Trying to explain, she described the former president's lecture on post-presidencies as "one of the most incredible journeys I've ever taken. He was telling the story straight, yet it was so visual and so fascinating. There is just so much he could do."

What made Clinton's historical recital thrilling, as she came to understand, was that every one of the successful post-presidents had found a higher purpose to pursue with passion. Now, a full year after leaving the White House, Clinton was still groping toward that kind of galvanizing mission.

———

When Williams showed up in Harlem to take over the stewardship of Clinton's post-presidency, she saw her own mission as "professionalizing" his office. She instantly understood the need for a highly skilled public relations professional, the critical missing element during the early firestorm over the last-minute pardons. She wanted a foreign policy professional to oversee Clinton's relationships with foreign governments and leaders, which she regarded as "integral to his brand." And she wanted to make sure that the correspondence and communications functions would continue to function at a presidential level, which she regarded as essential to preserving the Clinton "brand."

Yet even the most skillful branding wouldn't mean much—and would diminish rapidly over time—unless it came to stand for something active and substantive. Clinton and his advisers had mulled this problem rather fitfully for months, without reaching any firm conclusion, even as he continued to make speeches and pull in money for the library in Little Rock.

In the meantime, just as Williams arrived in Harlem, Clinton once again became a target of convenience in the Washington scandal culture.

For months, the ongoing financial implosion of the Enron Corporation—a freewheeling energy conglomerate based in Houston with more than $60 billion in assets—had threatened to pull major political figures, including President George W. Bush and his advisers, into the maelstrom of the largest corporate bankruptcy in history. Replete with complicated bogus accounting schemes, executive corruption, massive exploitation of consumers, and cynical manipulation of federal agencies and elected officials, the Enron affair was a growing source of embarrassment to the White House and Republicans in Congress. Bush and Enron chief Kenneth Lay, who had donated enormous sums to the GOP, were on intimate terms—the president was known to refer to Lay as "Kenny Boy" on their frequent golf outings in Texas.

Fearing the scandal's potential consequences in the 2002 midterm elections, Republican operatives were busily seeking to lay at least a share of blame upon the Democrats, by proving that both parties benefited from Enron's political largesse. The raw numbers showed otherwise, but that wouldn't matter if Republicans gained control of the media narrative. What they needed was another partisan scapegoat, preferably with a familiar face.

On January 11, the *Drudge Report*—which had broken the Monica Lewinsky scandal online almost exactly four years earlier—ran a short item designed to prove that the Clintons, not the Bushes, were the true stooges of Enron. According to Drudge, "[Ken] Lay also played golf with President Bill Clinton and slept in the Clinton White House." Matt Drudge refused to disclose the source of this allegation, saying only, "Lay's direct ties to Clinton are well documented."

Drudge's power to steer mainstream coverage was considerable; within two days, the *Chicago Tribune*'s Washington bureau produced an article detailing Enron's bipartisan favor seeking in the capital. "Lay was no stranger to the Clinton White House," wrote the *Tribune* correspondent, "playing golf with the president and staying overnight in the Lincoln Bedroom."

From there the tale migrated overnight to Fox News, where *Weekly Standard* editor Fred Barnes declared that Enron wasn't really a Republican scandal at all, because "Ken Lay not only played golf with

Clinton, he spent a night in the Lincoln Bedroom." Within moments, a Republican consultant made the same claim on CNN, telling viewers that "Ken Lay slept in the Lincoln Bedroom," hosted by Clinton. During the weeks that followed, the story appeared in numerous other publications, from New York, Washington, and Arkansas to South Korea, Australia, and England, where the *Times* of London reprinted a version. Meanwhile Fox continued to repeat the allegation, over and over.

Actually, Lay had not set foot in the White House while Clinton was president, nor had they ever played golf together—as Gene Lyons reported in the *Arkansas Democrat-Gazette*. To Clinton's intense frustration, almost nobody picked up the Lyons column or his own denials for weeks. But eventually, under pressure from readers protesting the falsehood, the *Chicago Tribune* issued a retraction, as did several other papers. Frank James, the *Tribune* reporter whose byline had appeared on the original erroneous article, explained with surprising candor that he had transposed the memory of a Lay sleepover in the White House during the first Bush administration into a Clinton event. James hadn't bothered to call anyone to check before committing his flawed recollection to print.

And the Bush White House, eager to draw moral contrasts with Clinton from the beginning, had again showed its willingness to blot his reputation for political convenience. Beneath the surface pleasantries, a state of cold war still prevailed between the former president and his successor. And Clinton, still scarred by the impeachment and pardons, remained vulnerable to almost any smear.

———

Not long after Maggie Williams arrived, she and Clinton agreed on an idea that had percolated in his mind for several months: The foundation should spearhead a program to assist small businesses in Harlem, as a gesture toward fulfilling the former president's promise to be a "good neighbor." Helping local restaurants and beauty parlors would scarcely transform the neighborhood, which was already beginning to change thanks to the historic drop in urban crime and rising rents across the city. What it might do is mitigate the gentrifying impact of Clinton's own presence on 125th Street, which had already drawn sporadic protests despite his local popularity.

To oversee the program, Maggie Williams brought in another former Clinton White House veteran named Clyde Williams—no relation to her—whose energy and ambition had impressed the president as he rose from a position on the domestic policy staff to deputy chief of staff in the Department of Agriculture.

Clyde Williams had grown up in the tough Southeast quadrant of the District of Columbia, pretty much on his own since adolescence, and had then worked his way through Howard University by waiting tables. He had moved to a stylish brownstone in Harlem with his wife, Mona Sutphen, a former National Security Council staffer, near Marcus Garvey Park. She worked for the Swiss bank UBS and although both were African American, they might be viewed as emblematic of the community's gentrification dilemma.

The proposal that Clyde Williams devised over the first few months of 2002 was straightforward in conception but ambitious in the details. Business specialists from Booz Allen Hamilton, the management consulting giant, and New York University's Stern School of Business would be asked to provide counseling to ten small Harlem enterprises as a pilot project. Some of the businesses would be well established, some would be recent start-ups, but no franchises, no fast-food joints, and no chain stores would be accepted. Williams also brought in the Greater Harlem Chamber of Commerce, the Harlem Business Alliance, and the National Black MBA Association as partners to give the project—quickly dubbed the Harlem Small Business Initiative—an additional layer of acceptance and authenticity.

Both Clinton and Maggie Williams found this plan appealing because, as she later said, bringing the highest-priced consultants in the country to the people of Harlem "showed such respect."

Within a few months, Clyde Williams and the team from Booz Allen had settled on selection criteria. For the first round, they chose firms that represented community values, including the Heaven's Hat Boutique on Adam Clayton Powell Junior Boulevard, where Evetta Petty designed and sold hundreds of varieties of stylish millinery, many of them made-to-order; the Pan Pan Restaurant, a landmark soul-food diner serving chicken and waffles for more than three decades, where Clinton had lunched several times; Dee's Card and Wedding Services, a purveyor of handmade black-themed greeting cards, artisan crafts, and gift items; a fancy new florist on Malcolm X Boulevard; and a video store, an independent insurance agency, a pharmacist, a plumber, and a dentist.

The challenges faced by the initiative's volunteer advisers were substantial. Few of the Harlem businesses were equipped with computers at all, let alone current technology; none were able to communicate electronically with their customers, or reach out to new ones. Most of them had no way to keep abreast of inventory, track and analyze expenses, or evaluate product sales—in other words, to run their businesses like the large chain competitors that were invading their neighborhood and driving them out of business.

With technical assistance provided by the program partners—eventually involving more than a hundred advisers with expertise in marketing, finance, computerization, and inventory management—Clinton hoped to establish a record that would attract many more community businesses, and encourage new entrepreneurs.

"Everyone," he told Clyde Williams, "deserves an opportunity to succeed."

———

On a chilly morning in January 2002, Ira Magaziner picked up the telephone in the office of his small consulting firm, known as SJS Advisors, in Quincy, Massachusetts, a suburb just south of Boston. Standing at his desk, the tall, thin, angular Magaziner realized that he hadn't seen or spoken with Maggie Williams for at least five years, since she and then he had both left the Clinton White House. Now she was on the phone, back with Clinton, asking his advice: Would he help them to decide what the former president should do now?

Magaziner was soft-spoken, almost diffident, but his manner concealed a steely temperament. He had done very well since leaving government and he didn't hesitate. His children were grown, he had money and time—and he still carried many of the same ambitions that had driven him as an idealistic young activist, when he and Clinton had first met at Oxford. Yes, he told Williams, his business success would allow him to take time away from his firm, and he wanted to do "something of value. . . . I want to help the Senator and the President, if I can."

The urgency of finding a post-presidential purpose—beyond the endless speechmaking and fundraising—was growing as Clinton faced the first anniversary of his departure from the White House. He needed something bigger than himself, bigger than his library, bigger than the small business program for his Harlem neighbors. A few months earlier, joining with his former 1996 adversary, retired Kansas senator Bob Dole, Clinton had agreed to raise another $100 million to finance college scholarships for the children of the 9/11 dead. That sounded like a huge undertaking, and would require some of his time, but he needed to do more than that, too—something more substantive than soliciting for a charitable cause, no matter how worthy. Without that, he would end up looking like a glorified pitchman.

But to focus his attention on a single issue would be difficult, as Williams knew. Both she and Doug Band, with whom she shared responsibility for booking and planning Clinton's time, were preoccupied with trying to keep him from appearing on behalf of organizations and causes they considered distracting, unworthy, or beneath his stature, simply because someone had approached him at an event or a party. Rarely would Clinton himself say no.

Talking with Magaziner, Williams explained that they had at least narrowed the list of potential projects down to a few broad categories, based on guidelines the former president had articulated. Whatever Clinton did should be connected in some way to the Millennium Development Goals, eight key priorities set forth by the United Nations in 2000, which ranged from eradicating extreme poverty to achieving universal primary education, reducing infant mortality, and promoting gender equality. Whatever project he undertook should be located mainly or entirely outside the United States, said Williams, since any domestic enterprise might be perceived as violating the unwritten protocol for former presidents not to get in the way of their successors.

Clinton was considering a foray into education, an issue with which he had long been associated, dating back to his stint as Arkansas governor. Many developing countries still required families to pay school fees, a backward policy that harmed children and hindered progress. He was also thinking about economic development, a signature issue on which he also possessed substantive credibility. It would not be hard to advocate economic or educational reform, and to notch a victory here and there.

What preoccupied him more and more, however, were the enormous global consequences of the AIDS pandemic, sweeping lethally through the poorest countries on every continent like a postmodern plague. Curtailing the ravages of the incurable virus was also among the Millennium Development Goals, although nobody had been able to provide a persuasive plan.

Taking on AIDS as a cause would be far riskier than many other global issues. The potential for a public failure was much higher. Moreover, the Clinton administration record on HIV and AIDS remained highly controversial. While he and Al Gore had devoted far greater attention—and federal money—to fighting AIDS than previous administrations, scornful activists still said they had never done enough.

When the topic came up in interviews, Clinton's tone sometimes turned defensive. At those moments, he would blame the xenophobic (and homophobic) Republicans in control of Congress for blocking broader action; he would contrast his legislative and budgetary activism with the utter passivity of the Reagan-Bush years; he would point out that they had tripled overseas aid funding against the pandemic; and then, he would finally agree that indeed, he still had not done enough.

Among the people who shared that mixed opinion—and whose views mattered most to Clinton—was his daughter. The previous autumn, Chelsea had enrolled at University College, Oxford, where her father read politics on a Rhodes scholarship in 1968, and where she would pursue a master's degree in international relations. For her thesis topic, she had chosen the sensitive but acutely relevant history of global efforts against pandemic disease, specifically the creation of the Global Fund to Fight AIDS, Tuberculosis and Malaria—the massive health financing organization created by the World Health Organization, the G-8 countries, and other nations, along with private-sector funders in 2001, which would eventually raise and disburse as much as $30 billion. While she had scarcely begun working on her research, she had spoken with her father about her choice of topic, and what she might learn from looking at his role.

Whatever Chelsea might discover—and whoever ultimately might share blame for the world's failure to act—Clinton knew that his best efforts during the final years of his presidency had been inadequate to the crisis. He was also aware that the pandemic was raging out of control across the less developed countries in a way that most Americans did not begin to comprehend.

Since leaving the White House he had become increasingly voluble about the impending catastrophe of AIDS, addressing far-flung audiences in a tone that sought to balance the terrible reality with a measure of optimism. He had brought essentially the same message to Rev. Jesse Jackson's PUSH convention in Chicago, to the United Nations AIDS Summit in Abuja, Nigeria, to the National AIDS Trust in London, where he gave a speech in memory of Princess Diana. More than 40 million people were infected, and more than 100 million could be infected within a few years, he said. AIDS, the equivalent of the European plagues of centuries past, threatened both developing and advanced nations far more than al Qaeda—yet much less money had been committed to ending that threat.

World leaders already knew what needed to be done, he went on, pointing to the only developing country where both prevention and treatment were available to the entire population. Without available treatment, prevention programs that relied on widespread testing were unlikely ever to work.

"They did a study in Brazil," he told the well-heeled London audience, "and found that it was cheaper to give people the drugs than bury them when they die and pay for their last few weeks in hospital—so it would be morally wrong and economically stupid" to end the program. Within three years, the number of deaths from AIDS in Brazil had been cut in half, and the rate of hospitalization had been reduced by 80 percent. In the rest of the developing world, the number of HIV-positive patients receiving effective treatment was no more than seventy thousand; at least three million were dying every year.

"This is not rocket science," said Clinton. "It is about money, organization, and will."

Invariably, these speeches elicited enthusiastic responses from his listeners—and conveyed the passion he had come to feel about the AIDS crisis. Even a columnist for London's *Sunday Telegraph*, a Tory newspaper deeply and eternally hostile to the Clintons, admitted that he couldn't stop himself from applauding loudly when he heard the former president give a speech about AIDS in Ireland, blaming the famous "charm, hugginess, and irresistible downhome Arkansas sincerity." But the thrust of his column depicted Clinton as an international "con artist" spewing "rubbish" and "pigswill."

Clinton's ideas about confronting AIDS were unworkable and unaffordable, complained the *Telegraph*; what he urged was plainly fraudulent, in fact, just like the man himself: "Clinton isn't looking for a cure for AIDS, but glory, creating morally approving communities wherever he goes, helped somewhat by his fee, pounds 100,000 a pop." It was a bellowing denunciation, extreme and angry, yet it reflected the corrosive skepticism that speechifying alone was certain to provoke, eventually.

As Magaziner listened intently, Williams expressed her boss's own dissatisfaction with talking rather than doing, even as still another major AIDS speech loomed on his calendar. He had agreed to participate in the 14th International Conference on AIDS in Barcelona, she explained, and to speak, along with Nelson Mandela, at the closing ceremony there on July 12.

Six months left ample time to write a rousing oration, but very little time to create a meaningful program of action. Clinton wanted Magaziner to determine what the foundation might be able to contribute concretely to the struggle against the pandemic, without duplicating, or complicating, the efforts of those already in the field.

Magaziner agreed to canvass the relevant players in order to determine what could and should be done. He would reach out to American organizations fighting AIDS, leading public health authorities in the United States, and several African leaders, whose views would influence Clinton's decision about whether and how to move forward. And he would do all this at his own expense, on his own time, living off his savings, because the foundation had no money at all to pay for any of it yet.

What Magaziner learned during his travels confirmed Clinton's most apocalyptic rhetoric about the impact of the pandemic. Conferring at the presidential palace in Dar-es-Salaam with the president of Tanzania, Benjamin Mkapa, whom he had met years before in the White House, he explained that President Clinton was considering how his foundation could advance African development—in education, the economy, health . . . and what would His Excellency advise?

A short, round, blunt man who had earned a master's degree in international affairs from Columbia and spoke perfect English, Mkapa didn't hesitate. "Look," he said, "I'm happy to talk about education. But I can't educate teachers fast enough to replace the number of teachers dying of AIDS. If I don't solve the AIDS problem it's going to undermine my ability to provide any education at all."

From Dar-es-Salaam, Magaziner flew south to Maputo, capital of Mozambique, where he had an appointment with Prime Minister Pascoal Mocumbi, another old acquaintance. A medical doctor and former revolutionary leader in his country's revolt against Portuguese colonial rule, Mocumbi was as plainspoken as Mkapa. "You know, Ira," he said, "we're hiring two people for every one job, because I've got so many people dying from AIDS now." Nothing in his country could move forward—indeed, everything was moving backward—under the relentless stress of the pandemic.

But when Magaziner returned home and quietly tried to float a new proposal to provide AIDS treatment in the developing world, most of the public health experts and Western government officials whom he consulted told him that they would not participate under any circumstances. Among the skeptics was the dean of Harvard University's School of Public Health, who sat in his office with Magaziner and patiently explained why he—and everyone else of any stature in the field—believed there could be no successful treatment campaign in poor countries.

It was sad, terribly sad, but true.

"AIDS treatment is not going to work in those places," said the Harvard dean dismissively. "It's really too hard to do, because you can't just give people pills. You've got to monitor them, test them, do the outreach." None of those countries had the resources, doctors, nurses, clinics, or equipment to complete these tasks properly.

In London, where he met with the head of the United Kingdom's foreign aid agency, Magaziner heard the same argument, warning him against any such foolish undertaking. "We'll continue to support prevention measures, but we're not going to support treatment. We don't think it can be done effectively and we're not going to waste money on it."

They were wrong, he thought, and despite their good intentions, they were insisting on an immoral policy that would condemn millions

to death. He felt certain they were wrong because he had seen successful AIDS treatment delivered in the poorest country in the Western
Hemisphere.

On another trip that spring, Magaziner had visited Haiti, where a
thin, bespectacled Boston doctor named Paul Farmer demonstrated
how his organization, Partners in Health, was successfully treating
AIDS patients on the impoverished island. The scale of Farmer's project was very small, numbering only in the hundreds of patients, but its
effectiveness was undeniable. Dying patients in an extremely poor district, far from any city hospital, had been saved and restored to health.
Although author Tracy Kidder would soon immortalize the young doctor in a gripping bestseller—*Mountains Beyond Mountains: The Quest
of Dr. Paul Farmer, A Man Who Would Cure the World*—he was a radical voice of dissent from the public health consensus, which he frankly
regarded as genocidal in result if not intent.

He was also an eloquent essayist whose most recent work, titled *Infections and Inequalities: The Modern Plagues*, argued forcefully that
relying on AIDS prevention alone in "resource-poor settings" like Haiti
and Africa had failed dramatically. It was neither moral nor practical to
reserve treatment solely for wealthy countries, while allowing people in
the poorer nations to sicken and die by the millions. Only a fresh global
commitment to health equity, and the creation of structures supporting that commitment, could begin to stem the pandemic, by pursuing
treatment and prevention as elements of a single, integrated "platform
to halt AIDS."

Public health authorities steadfastly denied treatment to those
resource-poor nations as "not sustainable," meaning too expensive,
he wrote, pointing a finger at the pharmaceutical sector—"an industry that, as noted, has consistently had among the highest margins of
profit." Institutions of "neoliberalism" such as the World Bank were
likewise to blame, he charged, and so were the skewed priorities of
Western governments, especially the United States.

In that essay, Farmer specifically mocked the extravagance of
the $10 billion crash program that Clinton had proposed in 1999 to
counter potential bioterrorist attacks, describing the president's message to Congress on the plan as "almost incomprehensible" and epito-
mizing "a sort of officially blessed paranoia."

Yet there in Farmer's tiny office stood Ira Magaziner, the representative of Bill Clinton, telling him that the former president wanted to do something to help, although exactly what that might be remained unclear. Farmer could scarcely be blamed for thinking that this seemed much too little, much too late. No longer president, with no discernible influence on the current president or anyone else in power, no political constituency, no capacity to pass legislation, no budgetary authority, and no money to spend, even with the best intentions—what could Clinton possibly do now?

CHAPTER FIVE

No matter what Bill Clinton hoped to do with the rest of his life, as he began his second year out of the White House, he knew the controversies that haunted his presidency might never quite be put to rest—except perhaps in the matter of Whitewater.

Almost exactly a decade after the "Whitewater scandal" had commenced with a confusing front-page headline in the *New York Times*, it finally concluded on March 21, 2002, with the release of a five-volume, two-thousand-page-plus report from the Office of Independent Counsel. That massive document represented seven years of exhaustive legal investigation, still captioned under the anodyne title *In re: Madison Guaranty Savings and Loan Association*, the tiny thrift institution that had financed the Clintons' ill-fated rural real estate partnership with James McDougal—their colorful old friend from Arkadelphia, Arkansas, who turned out to be an angry, dangerous, mentally unstable con man.

Preparation of the final OIC report had been overseen for many months by Robert Ray—a New Jersey Republican named to succeed Kenneth Starr as independent counsel after Clinton's acquittal in the 1999 Senate impeachment trial. In describing the final report, the national headlines, or at least some of the national headlines, reflected reality. Unlike all the "scandal" coverage of years past, however, these acknowledgments of ultimate exoneration were buried deep inside the newspapers. "Final Word on Whitewater Probe Clears Clintons," announced the *Washington Post*. "Report Caps Whitewater Saga," according to *Newsday*, "Finds No Link Between Clintons and Misdeeds." Relegated to page 30, the *New York Times* headline—"Final Report by Prosecutor on Clintons Is Released"—didn't reveal much, but the story's first two paragraphs did:

In a final report that ends the Whitewater investigation that sprawled across a range of subjects and vexed President Bill Clinton and Hillary Rodham Clinton for most of his two terms in the White House, the independent counsel's office said today that there was insufficient evidence to show that either committed any crimes.

Robert W. Ray, the last occupant of the office of independent counsel for Whitewater matters, said in the 2,090-page report that the Clintons' principal business partner in the Whitewater land development scheme in Arkansas, James B. McDougal, had committed several acts of fraud, but that there was no credible evidence that the Clintons either knew of or participated in those acts.

Ray, having begun an effort to secure the Republican U.S. Senate nomination in his home state, deliberately sought to cast suspicion on the Clintons, repeatedly claiming that the probe had been stymied by "insufficient evidence"—and insisting that Hillary Clinton's testimony on her law firm's relationship with McDougal was not fully accurate. Perhaps he believed this would enhance his popularity among his fellow partisans in New Jersey. (It didn't help, and Ray soon abandoned his quest for the Senate seat.)

Whatever his motives, the independent counsel had tried to admit failure without fully exonerating his quarry. Perusing the thousands of pages of turgid prose produced by the OIC—at $73 million, or more than $33,000 per page, probably the costliest single publication in human history—showed just how stubbornly the prosecutors had evaded the moral obligation to admit that their primary targets were in fact innocent. Instead, the report repeatedly complained of "insufficient available evidence to establish [guilt] beyond a reasonable doubt."

By March 2002, it was safe to assume that most Americans had forgotten what, exactly, Kenneth Starr, his persistent associates, and his successor, Ray, had hoped to prove. The Whitewater allegations were vague and constantly shifting, as each headlined accusation quietly evaporated. The few clear and pertinent questions about the defunct development deal were answered with finality by 1995, roughly a year after Starr began his probe.

Had the Clintons abused Bill's political authority as governor to help McDougal keep afloat Madison Guaranty, his insolvent savings and loan, as the original *Times* article had suggested? The investigation had swiftly proved that then-Governor Clinton ordered his appointees to treat McDougal no differently than anyone else. Then, did the Clintons profit illicitly from McDougal's manipulations? Within months after the probe began, investigators determined that McDougal swindled the Clintons, who had lost around $40,000 on the deal. Finally, did Bill Clinton help McDougal to obtain an illegal loan from the crooked businessman and former municipal judge David Hale? The only evidence to that effect came from the unsupported testimony of Hale and McDougal—both sources who had changed their stories repeatedly, sought leniency deals with the OIC, and were bereft of credibility.

Throughout the decade of investigation, no one had mounted a plausible theory, let alone proved, that the Clintons ever committed a single illegal act, or that they even had the slightest inkling of the frauds perpetrated by McDougal. The footnotes to the final report showed that the OIC failed to uncover any significant information about Whitewater beyond what the lawyers at Pillsbury, Madison & Sutro found when they completed an exhaustive (and exculpatory) report late in 1995 for the Resolution Trust Corporation on the Whitewater land deal "and related matters."

When they realized that the Whitewater deal itself would never yield an indictment against either of the Clintons, Starr and his zealous associates decided to rake through the files of the Rose Law Firm, in pursuit of any potential violation of law by Hillary Clinton or any of her former partners. Rose had represented Madison, which sounded suspicious, or could be made to sound suspicious. And the Starr prosecutors did find that Webster Hubbell, a Clinton friend and former Rose partner appointed to a high position in the Justice Department, had committed multiple frauds, mostly against his own firm. From the prosecution viewpoint, however, the problem was that Hillary Clinton, instead of being complicit in Hubbell's crimes, had been among his victims.

As the final report showed, Starr's prosecutors had then tried proving that Mrs. Clinton once lied about or concealed something—and to them the actual significance of the supposed lie didn't matter much. The OIC spent years attempting to show that she had testified falsely about who had first arranged for the Rose Law Firm to represent Madison Guaranty, and whether Jim McDougal had or had not paid his legal bills on time. Had she correctly remembered a brief conversation that occurred eight or ten or twelve years earlier? Could she recall, with perfect accuracy, every minute she had billed any client connected to Madison from that bygone era?

Taking up hundreds of pages of small print, Ray's account of that phase of the investigation seemed numbingly pointless. Hillary Clinton's version of various events differed in minor detail from testimony offered by her former partners and associates—but then none of them agreed precisely with each other. The notion that anyone might face criminal charges over such minutiae would have seemed hilarious if it weren't so sinister. Nobody at the news organizations that had pursued Whitewater as if it were Watergate ever bothered to ask Starr why he considered such endless parsing of trivia to be a mission of national importance.

The final report also contained a tantalizing reference to the missing Rose billing records that caused all of Washington to swoon in January 1996, when those records were found in the White House. Evidently, Starr's theory was that Hillary had concealed her billing records because they would prove that she had guilty knowledge of swindles by McDougal and others. But the records proved the opposite, confirming her testimony (and reaffirming information previously available in other copies of the same documents). She had no conceivable reason to hide the billing records, and even less motive for producing them suddenly at the beginning of an election year.

But Ray could not resist the impulse to impugn the former first lady's reputation one last time, by noting that three witnesses claimed to have seen her carrying a box of what "could have been" a "rolled-up sheaf" of billing records in the White House, sometime in July 1995. Actually, only two of these individuals said they saw her carrying any papers, and none explained how they would have guessed what the billing records looked like. One of the supposed witnesses saw a box but not its contents, another saw "something that could have been a rolled-up sheaf of billing records," while the third thought Hillary might have been carrying some "engineering or technical drawings."

To call that kind of testimony "insufficient evidence" was to put it very mildly. As Clinton attorney David Kendall complained in a twenty-six-page letter responding to the report, there was little basis for Ray's insinuations of wrongdoing. He wrote that "when fairly and carefully read, [the Final Report] lends no support to such an innuendo. One might say with equal justification that the Office of Independent Counsel has uncovered no evidence from which a jury might infer beyond a reasonable doubt that the Clintons had pilfered Powerball tickets, trapped fur-bearing mammals out of season, or sold nuclear secrets to Liechtenstein."

Kendall sardonically noted the "extraordinary" similarity between the OIC report's conclusions, revealing nothing new, and the March 1992 report compiled by attorney James Lyons and issued by the Clinton presidential campaign ("which cost $25,000 and was done in three weeks"). Both reports found that the Clintons had lost money in Whitewater and that Jim McDougal had swindled them.

With all of its lengthy discussion of obstruction and concealment, its massive size and complexity, featuring thousands of footnotes, the OIC's Final Report nevertheless read as if it had been conceived mainly to obscure one fundamental truth: The Whitewater case was dead as early as July 1995, when the Clintons were cleared by the Pillsbury report—still a comparative bargain at only $3.5 million—and no later than January 1997, when Starr made his first abortive attempt to resign in frustration, just as Clinton prepared to celebrate his second inaugural.

There was never a "Whitewater case" in the normal sense, as Ray finally acknowledged with the utmost reluctance. There was only a political prosecution, eventually reshaped from a failed financial investigation into a successful sexual inquisition, encouraged by a Washington media elite that ought to have exposed rather than applauded a gross abuse of prosecutorial power.

Over the years, a measure of very rough justice had been achieved, at an enormous cost to the Clintons and their friends, some of whose most onerous legal expenses they had personally defrayed. Hillary Clinton had gone on to win a United States Senate seat. Jim McDougal had died in prison. David Hale had served more than two years in state prison on multiple state fraud charges, suffering two heart attacks before Arkansas governor Mike Huckabee commuted his sentence. Ken

Starr had forfeited his lifelong dream of a seat on the U.S. Supreme Court, which had seemed within his reach someday when the Whitewater saga began. (Years later, the trustees of Baylor University would remove him, in disgrace, as the school's president for covering up sexual assaults by members of its football team.)

To friends, Clinton privately confided a lingering Whitewater regret. He had pardoned McDougal's ex-wife, Susan—an exceptional woman who bravely refused to deliver false testimony against the Clintons, despite her imprisonment by Starr on contempt charges—but had not pardoned Webb Hubbell or Jim Guy Tucker, the Arkansas governor convicted by the independent counsel on a thin set of fraud charges unrelated to Whitewater.

And Starr would be the last independent counsel. His performance had proved sufficiently appalling in expense and consequence—like those of three other independent counsels appointed during the Clinton years—that Congress had quietly allowed the Independent Counsel statute to expire without renewal.

Despite its shortcomings, the Final Report represented a satisfying denouement upon which Clinton could meditate as he began to consider the outline of his memoirs. And the report's release underlined once more that his past, with all its triumphs and tribulations, could no longer be changed, while his future remained to be written.

Years later, Clinton would say casually that he and his foundation "just sort of fell into . . . the actual things we ended up doing," by which he meant that there had been no master plan or singular objective when he left the White House. Among the first to importune him was Sandra Thurman, a health policy expert from Atlanta who had served as the "AIDS czar" in the second Clinton-Gore administration. It was Sandy Thurman who asked Clinton to cochair an international effort aimed at raising more government money for AIDS—and, together with Nelson Mandela, he had agreed to deliver the closing remarks at the next World AIDS conference in Barcelona, Spain, scheduled in July 2002.

He and Mandela were happy to perform a "dog-and-pony show," as Clinton described it, to raise the visibility of the AIDS crisis. If their exhortations improved the morale of the thousands of health workers, advocates, and officials gathered in Barcelona that would be worthwhile, too. But he was well aware that corrosive tensions were growing between the advanced industrial countries—the "donor nations"—and the developing countries, over not only money but policy. In the absence of a concerted global campaign to fund and provide treatment for the tens of millions who would otherwise be left to die, the entire exercise was beginning to seem pointless. Prevention would fail; the pandemic would continue for decades; hundreds of millions more would be infected; and development would essentially cease across much of the world. To Clinton, this would be an unacceptable, indeed unthinkable catastrophe.

In late May, Ira Magaziner returned to the foundation's Harlem offices to discuss his findings with Clinton and Maggie Williams. Given the dimensions of the problem, there were two very different paths that the former president might take.

"Look, here's the situation. I think as a moral matter, and as a matter of taking something on that fits your stature . . ." he began, then stopped. "You know, you could go out there and do a lot of small things, and check the box that you're doing something charitable—but if you really want to take advantage of Bill Clinton and his global reputation, you ought to take on something big. And that means it will be hard and risky, and something that other people can't do easily."

Both Williams and Clinton already knew what "something" meant. In preparation for this meeting, he had delivered a confidential seven-page memorandum, addressed to Williams and captioned "President Clinton and the AIDS Crisis," outlining how Clinton "can best play a leadership role going forward in the global struggle to stop the spread of AIDS . . . a unique leadership role that . . . will help fill the most significant gap that now exists."

Magaziner's months of research had led him to believe that with enough money and proper organization, "the AIDS crisis can be contained." That was, as the introduction to his memo suggested, "the good news." The unsurprising bad news was that "many of the developing countries that have been hardest hit by AIDS lack sufficient funds and organizational capacity to succeed."

Looking forward, he continued, the United Nations, aid agencies in the developed countries, and several large international foundations soon would increase the overall funding available to support the fight against AIDS in those countries. That funding would still fall short of the needed amount by as much as $7 billion annually, he estimated, but Clinton should not focus on fundraising because of political obstacles.

In a prophetic passage, Magaziner warned: "The U.N. will defer to the US government in the selection of any American to play a leadership role in these organizations and I do not believe that the current [Bush] administration would look favorably on President Clinton in such a role. . . . However, I believe that President Clinton is uniquely placed to help overcome perhaps the most serious impediment to successfully reversing the AIDS epidemic."

That impediment was "the lack of organizational capacity" in the nations suffering the worst outbreaks of the disease. While a few countries like Senegal and Uganda had implemented early and effective programs that kept infection rates relatively low—between 2 and 8 percent of their populations—other countries, including South Africa, Zimbabwe, and Malawi, had not.

In a staggering single-page appendix, he had listed the rates of infection for the hardest-hit countries in Africa, from Botswana, with 35.8 percent of citizens between the ages of fifteen and fifty HIV-positive, to Ethiopia, where 10.6 percent were infected. In South Africa, 19.9 percent in that age cohort were infected. Nigeria had five million infected adults; Congo and Mozambique each had more than six million.

In essence, explained Magaziner, the afflicted countries needed three kinds of programs if they were to have any hope of stanching the damage done by AIDS: prevention, treatment, and assistance to the millions of children orphaned by dead or extremely sick parents.

Prevention meant education, testing, screening, and condom distribution that could "reach into every community and school," as well as programs to reduce the incidence of all sexually transmitted diseases. Sex workers in particular would have to be tested and monitored. But none of these prevention programs could function effectively without treatment.

Treatment required much more than simply handing out pills in a paper cup. Administration of drugs would have to be preceded and followed up by rigorous testing, nursing assistance to reduce the onset of other, related fatal illnesses, and special care for infected pregnant women to lessen the likelihood of disease transmission to their infants.

Moreover, to implement any of these complex protocols meant "significant training of doctors, nurses, allied health workers, patients, and their families," along with the establishment of community health centers equipped to provide all the testing, counseling, and pharmaceutical supplies. To care for the AIDS orphans properly would require "the extension of existing welfare networks to address the psychological, educational, and physical needs of these children," while encouraging acceptance of them in fearful communities.

Although most of the afflicted countries had drafted a plan or strategy on paper to combat HIV/AIDS, usually with the assistance of the United Nations, and while many were hosting individual programs funded by international nonprofit or religious agencies, there was little coordination in reality. On the whole, most efforts in these countries were too small and too poorly organized to achieve much as the pandemic continued to surge.

To grasp the mind-bending complexity of this situation on a global scale would challenge anyone, even Clinton; to grapple with it successfully would be exponentially more difficult still. At a minimum, the necessary elements included money, knowledge, and skills of many kinds. But Magaziner's memo suggested that the truly essential factor was trust. Bringing together the leaders and governments of the developing world with the policy bureaucrats, medical experts, and health professionals of the developed world demanded a trusted figure in leadership—someone esteemed in both the wealthy north and the impoverished south.

He had a candidate for this difficult mission:

President Clinton has extremely good relations with many African and Caribbean leaders who are confronting AIDS crises in their countries. He is also widely admired among people in many nations in Africa and the Caribbean. He has a credibility that not many western political leaders possess in that part of the world. As a result, an organization that is associated with him would be potentially welcomed and trusted by government leaders and by those running programs to fight AIDS in many countries. . . .

[He] would also be able to attract many groups of doctors, nurses, and experts from developed countries to mobilize resources. . . . Finally, President Clinton is widely respected by groups like the Irish, Swedish, and Canadian aid agencies who will be providing funds for AIDS-related projects in these countries.

The role that Magaziner envisioned for Clinton and the foundation was to "coordinate resources" and "galvanize cooperation" among the various private organizations and governments fighting AIDS, in each country and across continents. By establishing a personal base in several nations and delivering real programs, he could not only make a significant contribution to solving the crisis, but create a "credible platform from which to assert international leadership in global forums on the issue, whether negotiating with drug companies or pressing for greater financial commitments."

Without substantive work on the ground, he warned, "I fear that President Clinton's efforts in this arena will be viewed as increasingly hollow. The United Nations will want to follow the wishes of the government in power in the United States on the deployment of any Americans to leadership positions in its various activities. This means that President Clinton may be excluded from playing a leadership role in areas like fundraising and administration [of AIDS programs]. . . . And since many current and former world leaders are now looking to become identified with this issue, there will be many of them making speeches at international meetings. Absent any real action on the issue, President Clinton's credibility as a speaker would eventually fade."

In short, Clinton needed to put up, or, ultimately, he might as well shut up.

Magaziner's memo briefly outlined the first steps toward implementing his ambitious plan, employing mostly volunteers at first, drawn from the "many doctor, nurse, public health and social service groups allied with us on health reform" as well as "groups in the business and legal community" that might fund some staff on a pro bono basis. Within three or four months, he estimated, a core team could be brought together to plan and initiate a foundation-based AIDS program.

Then Clinton could choose a few countries where the program

might best be launched, based on his own relationships and consultation with leaders and groups already involved in those places, a process that would require another few months. Over a period of roughly two years, Magaziner projected the establishment of programs in as many as ten countries.

"Well," said Clinton, gazing out over the cityscape, "put together, what exactly would that look like?" Magaziner replied that the real need was to "scale up"—to seize upon the successful practices of small local clinics established by a few of the international medical charities, such as Paul Farmer's Partners in Health and the French-based Doctors Without Borders, and bring them to national scale by working with government authorities.

"If we're going to really scale up and get major numbers of people in treatment and save lives, we have to work with the governments, we should work with the governments," Magaziner urged. "And you can do that. They'll respect and trust you."

"OK, Ira. Prepare me a plan on how we do this."

Several days later, Williams called Magaziner to discuss two specific questions that Clinton had raised following their meeting: What would be the actual structure of the "on-the-ground initiative" that he had described? And what was the current state of negotiations between governments and pharmaceutical companies over providing AIDS medications in the developing world at affordable prices?

On June 11, Magaziner dispatched a second memo, attempting to answer Clinton's inquiries. Either under the auspices of the Clinton Foundation alone, or in partnership with the International AIDS Trust and possibly other major organizations, the initiative would be headquartered in the United States with a lean staff—an executive director, an associate director overseeing work in developing countries, and another managing partnerships and fundraising in the developed world, along with directors of finance and research. In each country, a country manager would oversee a staff combining "donated international personnel" and local leaders—with much of the in-country staff donated by partner organizations and consisting of people who would agree to spend at least a year, perhaps two, working as part of a team.

What Magaziner really wanted—and what would distinguish this initiative from so many others in the developing world—was a corps of country managers "with a management background, preferably with experience in the public and private sectors." Better still, these managers should have worked in developing countries, to prepare them for the rigors of places where many systems—communications, transportation, utilities, public safety—function intermittently, if at all.

Without being asked, he also answered the question that had to occur immediately to Clinton: Who was going to pay for all this stuff? There would be substantial expenses for travel, rent, utilities, food, and water, to mention only the barest necessities, even if most of the in-country staff began as volunteers.

"I believe that organizations like the major business consulting firms"—such as McKinsey & Company, and the Boston Consulting Group, where Magaziner had once rubbed shoulders with the likes of Mitt Romney—"would be willing to donate people," as would some major corporations that he had advised. "I also believe that many medical organizations could be prevailed upon to finance members to participate," he added. Aside from the in-kind assistance, he wrote, "I think it would be possible to raise funds from some foreign aid organizations, some foundations, and some corporations to provide the baseline funding for the effort."

Among those early volunteers, Magaziner nominated himself: "I would be happy to devote considerable time to helping recruit these potential funding sources, potential partner organizations, and the executive teams. I would also be prepared to donate one or two people [from SJS, his consulting firm based in Quincy] to help get the effort started."

———

Magaziner understood that Clinton's question about the pharmaceutical industry raised one of the most sensitive issues of the last years of his presidency: the defense of patents for costly HIV/AIDS drugs produced by major drug companies, against international demands for the production of cheaper, generic versions of the same medicines that might have saved many lives. In places like Brazil and South Africa, governments approved local laws to encourage the procurement of generic versions of the antiretroviral medicines that had done so much to reduce mortality from AIDS in the United States during the 1990s. The pharmaceutical manufacturers, American and European, took every possible step to stymie those efforts, fully backed by the Clinton-Gore administration.

That international dispute had erupted, momentarily but dramatically, on June 16, 1999, in Carthage, Tennessee, where Al Gore was announcing his presidential candidacy in his hometown. Protesters from AIDS activist groups such as ACT-UP and the Health Gap Coalition interrupted his speech with loud chants of "Gore's Greed Kills!"

Ushered away by security guards, the activists would continue to chase Gore into 2000. As vice president, he had fiercely enforced administration policy by bringing heavy pressure on nations seeking to loosen patent restrictions on AIDS medications, notably South Africa and Brazil, with threats of trade lawsuits, sanctions, and reductions in U.S. aid. Even though the administration had tried to soften its stance on generics by 2000, the shift came too late to spare Gore a severe embarrassment.

The administration's threat to punish developing countries that sought to provide affordable medicine for infected citizens quickly became a favorite theme for Ralph Nader, as the consumer activist prepared his own candidacy for president on a third-party ticket in 2000. He accused Gore of "ignoring" the pleas of AIDS activists.

As a legal matter, the Clinton-Gore administration had believed its objections to any attempt to evade or vacate the patents were valid under the World Trade Organization's rules on intellectual property—known by the acronym TRIPS, for Trade-Related Aspects of Intellectual Property Rights. Before the advent of TRIPS in 1994, many nations didn't recognize pharmaceutical patents at all, costing manufacturers billions of dollars in lost revenues and, in their view, constricting their ability to recover the enormous costs of creating and testing new drugs.

The voluminous TRIPS regulations required all WTO member states to restrict the manufacture or importation of patent-protected drugs, including the antiretroviral formulas that had been developed to slow the debilitating, deadly effects of AIDS. Like most national leaders, Clinton saw the safeguarding of U.S. patents and products as one of his central responsibilities in overseeing international trade. Not only Gore, but also the U.S. trade representatives appointed by the president had carried out that duty for years, with a tough approach and Clinton's enthusiastic backing.

But in human terms, the White House insistence on adhering to protective patents on AIDS drugs, while millions of people suffered and perished, had been inexcusable. Moreover, Article 27 of the TRIPS rules permitted member states to make exceptions when "necessary to protect *ordre public* . . . including to protect human, animal, or plant life or health." Any member state that sought to exercise that clause, however, at least with respect to pharmaceuticals, came under severe pressure from the United States government.

In hindsight, Clinton regarded that policy as a moral and political mistake that had become a huge problem for his administration. He faulted himself for failing to step forward to resolve the issue directly, since it involved a conflict between his trade representative and his "AIDS czar."

Years later, he would admit, "Oh, I should have been much harder for the generic options for AIDS . . . but the trade office thought their job was to protect American patents . . . and I think I should have been more aggressive there." Whether lifting patent protections would have made a real difference was an open question, because even at lower prices there was little funding available at the time for treatment of AIDS in developing countries—a factor that Clinton blamed on congressional Republicans, who had rejected his requests for more money.

Even before Clinton returned to private life, worldwide outrage had exploded over the pharmaceutical industry's self-serving behavior and his administration's support for it. Worried by the rapid erosion of their global image, the major drug companies agreed to discuss providing medicine at discounted prices in the developing world with the United Nations.

Under the umbrella of the International Federation of Pharmaceutical Manufacturers & Associations, or IFPMA—a global counterpart of PhRMA, the American drug lobby—executives from big brands such as Merck, Pfizer, GlaxoSmithKline, and Hoffmann-LaRoche sat down in May 2000 with delegates from the World Health Organization, UN-AIDS, and several African countries, including South Africa, Nigeria, and Kenya, as well as an aide to then-Secretary-General Kofi Annan. These discussions were grandly titled the "Accelerating Access to HIV/AIDS Care, Treatment, and Support Initiative."

The negotiations went on fruitlessly for well over a year. The U.N.

representatives asked for drastically reduced prices in developing countries, with free medicine for some selected groups, and the easing of patent restrictions to permit generic production by Indian, Egyptian, Brazilian, and other local manufacturers. The representatives of IFPMA warned that patents embody the incentive to produce new treatments and cures—and moreover, that simply doling out drugs would be ineffective and even harmful in the absence of functioning health systems to test, monitor, and care for patients.

The drug companies also continued to argue that "prevention" rather than treatment should be the primary objective of health authorities in the developing countries.

After several meetings between the drug manufacturers and the U.N.-led coalition in Amsterdam and Geneva, they had jointly announced a deal in the autumn of 2001. The drug companies promised to provide AIDS medications at considerably lower prices, while the World Health Organization and the African states vowed to build the infrastructure needed to safely deliver treatment—and not to permit those drugs to be resold outside their borders. Yet their agreement, signed by all parties in December 2001, had not resulted in the delivery of a single bottle of medicine six months later.

Or, as Magaziner summed up the situation in his memorandum to Clinton and Williams: "So far nothing has come of this."

Nevertheless, the World Health Organization continued to function as if something might come of its efforts. It had issued a detailed set of guidelines to be used by the developing countries in purchasing, testing, and distributing treatments for AIDS. Specifically, the WHO recommended the use of "triple-therapy cocktails," combining three antiretroviral medications into a single pill, and indicated which particular combinations ought to be tried first with any patient. Use of the triple-therapy technique had reduced AIDS deaths in the United States by 70 percent, as Magaziner's memo noted.

The WHO had also urged that, at minimum, any health center established to dispense anti-AIDS drugs should maintain equipment to conduct HIV tests as well as hematocrit tests to measure red blood cell count. WHO officials had also inspected and certified several generic pharmaceutical factories in India, and one in South Africa, to produce the needed drugs.

With all of those agreements, recommendations, and certifications in place, according to Magaziner, there still remained three gigantic barriers to widespread HIV/AIDS treatment in sub-Saharan Africa—where he estimated that only 36,000 of the approximately six million in need were getting any medicine or care at all. First, regardless of the drug companies' concessions, prices remained too high. Second, the available funding for treatment remained too low. And finally, "the most vexing issues relate to how to organize the distribution and testing efforts within most countries and how to garner and use funds efficiently." There were no health systems in place that could use the money and the drugs effectively even if both fell from the sky.

The conclusion of Magaziner's memo was rather dry. Headed to South Africa on other business in late June, he wanted to know whether Clinton "has any interest in exploring further the approach I have suggested in my memo. . . . I will be making decisions soon on how to allocate my own time and the time of people working for me for the next year. . . . I do believe there is a very valuable role that he can play on this very important issue, and I would be happy to pull this together for him if he wishes to do it."

———

Although Magaziner's proposal intrigued Clinton—who had no illusions about the magnitude of the AIDS crisis—he didn't tell his old friend to move forward immediately. The prospects for success in such an endeavor were extremely uncertain; indeed, failure seemed far more likely. He was still raising money for his library and his own legal debts, and felt reluctant to commit without an independent source of funding. While Clinton considered the proposal, he drew Magaziner into the preparations for his forthcoming appearance at the International AIDS Conference in Barcelona on July 12, when he and Mandela would deliver closing remarks.

For Clinton, the conference represented as much a challenge as an opportunity. Activists from around the world who attended these events would have little patience for the rhetorical mush so often spooned out by speakers on the international stage. They were sure to be acutely aware of the vexed record of the Clinton administration on generic pharmaceuticals. Whatever he might tell them now about the vast increase in funding and attention that he had overseen as president, they would want to know what he had done lately—and what he intended to do now, besides giving more speeches.

Clinton invited Magaziner to join the small entourage going to Barcelona, which would include Sandy Thurman, who had served as Clinton's top AIDS adviser in the White House; Bruce Lindsey; Doug Band; and Magaziner's daughter, Sarah. (The invitation didn't include airfare or hotel accommodations for her or her father, who paid their way from his own funds.)

Upon arriving in Spain on July 10, Magaziner was hardly surprised to learn that Clinton was still working on his speech, although Thurman had prepared a draft for him.

That same evening, he and Clinton held a private meeting with several of the African leaders whom Magaziner had consulted during his spring journeys researching the AIDS crisis—notably Mozambican prime minister Pascoal Mocumbi and Rwandan president Paul Kagame, as well as Denzil L. Douglas, prime minister of the small Caribbean archipelago of St. Kitts and Nevis, who chaired the Organization of Eastern Caribbean States and happened to be a medical doctor. They told Clinton what they had told Magaziner when he visited them months earlier—that their countries were facing a health catastrophe that they could not possibly overcome on their own.

"Look, we don't have a denial problem in the Caribbean," said Douglas, who had organized a group of leaders seeking to cope with AIDS in the region, which had the second-fastest growing rate of HIV infection in the world. "We don't have much of a stigma problem. Our problem is money and organization."

He looked directly at Clinton, who said, "What would you like me to do about it, Denzil?"

"I want you to fix it."

"Okay," Clinton replied. "I'll do it."

———

Sometime that night, Magaziner typed an uncharacteristically passionate and personal note on his laptop, printed it out, and delivered it to Clinton the next morning.

   In keeping with his habit that so offended Band, the note was addressed to "Bill":

> After yesterday's discussion with the government officials, I am more than ever convinced that we should move forward with the AIDS project. Prime Minister Mocumbi, Prime Minister Douglas, President Kagame and the others all clearly are desperate to move forward on AIDS care and treatment but lack the capabilities and resources to do so. . . .
>
>   I will volunteer my time to lead this and I am confident that I can pull together enough volunteers to get it moving successfully. . . . I know that you do not have the funds to support this and that you must direct your fundraising to your library and other matters the next few years, but I believe I can put together sufficient funds to bankroll the travel and other expenses that would be necessary to support the volunteers. I will put in a million dollars myself to get this started.

   He believed that he could persuade his friend David Sainsbury, the British supermarket magnate, liberal philanthropist, and minister in Tony Blair's government, to "put in another million," along with some smaller donors. He would also donate the time of several employees of his consulting firm and the use of its suburban Boston offices.

> I do not know for sure how successful we will be, but I feel like we have to try. You have a tremendous global reputation and are respected by leaders around the world. We should use that reputation and your contacts for something big. If we succeed at this, we can help save millions of lives. If we are not so successful, we still might help save tens of thousands of lives, which would not be so bad.
>
>   As we were discussing last night before the dinner, we cannot stand on the side lines while millions of people are dying each year and the means are available to help save their lives. Let's make the decision and go for it.
>   Thanks
>
>   *Ira*

———

Late in the afternoon of July 12, Clinton walked slowly out onto the huge stage of Barcelona's Palau Sant Jordi, a stadium built for the Summer Olympics in 1992, with the eighty-four-year-old Mandela—who held a cane in one hand and Clinton's arm with the other. Together they looked out over an audience of roughly ten thousand scientists, health officials, and activists, who had been waiting patiently during a long delay before the closing ceremonies finally began. This was essentially the same audience that had literally booed U.S. secretary of health and human services Tommy Thompson off the stage during one of the earlier conference sessions, whistling and shouting while he tried to persuade them that the United States was doing more to combat AIDS than any other country.

But now, even before Mandela or Clinton said a word, they were cheering. Much of what Clinton said in this speech he had said before. Future generations would never understand why the world had allowed a lethal but preventable disease to infect as many as 40 million people, a number that could shortly grow to 100 million, he said. National leaders should "move aggressively to remove stigma and denial. There are still people who think people living with HIV/AIDS are people who are different. Yes, they are sex workers, and poor and often gay men . . . but they are also our friends."

He apologized in passing for the shortcomings of his own administration, confessing that he had been wrong to oppose needle exchange—allowing heroin addicts to turn in old "works" for new, uninfected syringes, a practice shown to reduce that vector of spreading HIV. And then he cast aside his own administration's defense of pharmaceutical patents, urging the drug companies to make more and better deals to reduce prices in developing countries—and failing that, he said, those countries should be allowed and encouraged to purchase cheaper generic drugs from India and Brazil.

"Developing countries have to work out how much they can pay and send the rest of us the bill for the difference," he went on, urging the United States to lead the world in appropriating billions of additional dollars toward a global fund of at least $10 billion for treatment.

"Before the year is out," he vowed, "I will go to Africa and India to lend visibility and support" to the battle against AIDS, to seek "more money, more action, and more understanding. I pledge that in every speech I make and in every meeting I have, I will raise this and I ask you both to hold me accountable to that pledge and to tell me what more I can do."

Introducing Mandela, Clinton intoned, "Only very rarely does the world respect someone as much as we love and respect him." Then he listened as his old friend told the crowd that everyone suffering from HIV and AIDS should receive treatment, "no matter where they live or whether they can afford to pay." Standing beside the iconic South African, Clinton seemed to endorse his position—at once the most radical and the most practical proposal to begin to reverse the pandemic, before a wave of death engulfed the future.

When the applause subsided, the two former presidents walked hand in hand to a backstage room where their aides and associates waited. As Magaziner stood listening, Mandela turned to Clinton and said, "You told me that you would do something for Africa when you left office." He paused. "This is what you should do, focus on AIDS."

That dramatic encounter, like hearing the voice of God, later became the source of a legend that Clinton had commenced his work against AIDS at Mandela's command—a wonderful story, if not precisely accurate. Already Clinton and Magaziner had decided to begin working on what they then called the "AIDS Project." But there was no denying that the direct injunction from Mandela deeply impressed both of them.

Or as Magaziner later put it, "In my mind, that was that."

———

Within two days after their return from Barcelona, Magaziner quickly drafted a six-page memo to Clinton and Maggie Williams titled "AIDS Project—Next Steps." The first three pages again outlined the scope of the problem—six million people in need of treatment within the next twelve to twenty-four months, 37 million more infected with HIV across the world who would need treatment soon, and another 50 million-plus projected to join the infected ranks in years to come "if current trends continue"—and what Clinton could do to reverse the crisis.

What fitted the former president to play a "unique role," Magaziner argued, was his status as "probably the most credible and recogniz-able global leader in the world today. He has credibility in most parts of the developing world as well as in the developed world, a rarity for an American leader. . . . I say this not to flatter him. I have known him too long and have been through too much grief in his service that I have no need to nor interest in flattering him.

"I say these things because they are true and because they give him an ability to play a unique role in this struggle. He has the trust of many of the leaders of developing countries that are confronting this cri-sis and he has the credibility to mobilize resources in the developed world in support of efforts to help the developing countries confront the issue."

He even seemed to suggest that the most radical AIDS activists would be receptive to a Clinton intervention, if that meant more than just talk. Recalling the events of the previous few days, he reminded Clinton that "the world AIDS conference audience was a skeptical one who had been hostile to many speakers during the week. Yet the re-ception for President Clinton was enthusiastic. Even some of the rad-ical activists I talked with after his speech valued the fact that he was expressing a willingness to help. Some expressed the wish that he had done more on issues like needle exchange and drug-company patents while he was in office. And some were still skeptical about whether he would back his words with real actions. But all were still appreciative and hopeful that he would provide leadership for the movement."

World leaders and U.N. officials alike, he wrote, "recognize the value of what [Clinton] could bring, and they want to associate their activities with him as much as possible."

The memo outlined three distinct roles for Clinton: promoting and expanding the new International AIDS Trust, pulling together a group of world leaders to speak out and raise awareness—especially in places like South and Central Asia, Eastern Europe, Russia, and "possibly even China," where entire societies as well as political leaders remained in de-nial about the crisis; raising funds from the public, through the founda-tion in cooperation with other organizations; and, most important by far, "rolling out treatment programs around the world that will save lives."

A massive effort to promote treatment in developing countries was the crux of the program that Magaziner hoped Clinton could launch.

He had accepted Paul Farmer's critique of the emphasis on prevention insisted upon by Western governments, public health agencies, and academic experts, describing the focus on prevention as "easier politically," because most AIDS victims were seen as "homosexuals, drug addicts, sex workers, or poor Black people in remote corners of Africa," which made them "not a priority for many middle class and rich people in the developed world."

Of course Clinton should advocate and promote prevention wherever he went, Magaziner acknowledged—but successful prevention was much more difficult without treatment.

"And where both you and I hang our moral hats, all human life is valuable and all of the victims of this disease deserve our help in any event. Letting people die when they can be saved is simply wrong."

———

No matter how large a program Clinton and Magaziner envisioned, it would be impossible to begin at scale. But they would have to begin somewhere—and the most promising opportunity appeared to be in the Caribbean, a region close to the United States both in proximity and political disposition. Despite the rapidly mounting rate of HIV/AIDS infection among the island nations, they had so far received little attention from Western donors and aid organizations. But under Douglas's leadership, the Caribbean states had banded together to negotiate a preliminary agreement with major drug companies to make medicine available at reduced prices. As Douglas had told Clinton in Barcelona, what they still lacked was the funding and systems to deliver treatment on a mass scale.

Eager to get moving, Magaziner already had followed up with Douglas. Within the next week or two, he suggested, the foundation might send a small team to meet with Caribbean leaders in Basseterre, the capital of St. Kitts and Nevis, to establish a working group on the ground. Over the coming months, their first goal should be to create a detailed "business plan," with very specific budgets and schedules for each Caribbean country to implement credible treatment and prevention programs. With such a plan in hand, Magaziner believed, Clinton could approach major donor governments with the assurance that their money would not be squandered.

To Clinton's delight, the Caribbean initiative jumped to a very rapid start. At Magaziner's instigation, he and Williams had traveled down to St. Kitts to meet with Douglas at the end of July. During their discussions, Douglas had urged them to get in touch with Perry Christie, the new prime minister of the Bahamas, who was trying to provide AIDS treatment to afflicted Bahamians by purchasing cheaper generic drugs—but the cost was still far too high to care for more than a small fraction of the islands' infected population. After his first conversation with the Bahamian health authorities, Magaziner excitedly phoned Clinton in New York.

"You're not going to believe this," he told the former president. "The government here is treating about one-sixth of the people who need it, or maybe less. But they're paying $3,500 [annual cost per patient] for this $500 medicine."

Clinton was flabbergasted. "Why?" he asked.

"The market is so disorganized," said Magaziner, "they're going through two different agents, and both are taking huge markups, and that plus the transportation cost is getting them to $3,500 per." The next day, Magaziner was on the phone with the generic manufacturers in India, dropping Clinton's name to persuade them to sell the medicines directly to the Bahamas government—and obtaining a price cut, during the program's first week, from $3,500 to $500.

"So overnight, for the same amount of money," Clinton later recalled, "they could treat—not quite seven times, because there are other costs, but six times as many people for the same amount of money." He was, as he would put it, tickled.

Once the relationship between the foundation and the Caribbean states was established in July, Magaziner embarked on a series of long trips to Africa, returning to the same places he had visited the previous spring. As he promised Clinton, he had put up a million dollars of his own money and persuaded David Sainsbury, the British supermarket magnate and philanthropist, to put in another million. With that funding in hand, he was able to tell the African leaders that Clinton had established a program that would help them. Before the end of August, he had secured agreements with the governments of Mozambique, Tanzania, and Rwanda to join with Clinton in bringing AIDS treatment to their citizens in need.

Clinton was scheduled to visit Africa in September, including his second visit to Rwanda since leaving the White House. He considered the Rwandan genocide—which had occurred on his watch without significant intervention from the West—to be the most damning stain on his presidency, far worse than impeachment. He had told Magaziner that the small Central African state must be among the very first that they brought into the program.

In late September, Clinton alighted in Kigali, Rwanda, with a pair of celebrities in tow—Oscar-winning actor Kevin Spacey, one of Clinton's closest Hollywood friends, and comic Chris Tucker, with whom he had recently gotten acquainted. Nothing helped to raise American awareness of a social problem, as Clinton well knew, like famous entertainers urging them to pay attention.

It was Spacey's first trip to Africa, but he wasn't shy about telling reporters why he was there. "HIV/AIDS is the single most important issue facing the world today," he said at an AIDS treatment center the trio visited. "If we don't begin to tackle this one, then it doesn't much matter what else we try to do, because we are going to be faced with a devastating plague that would wipe out generations." While Spacey talked, Clinton waded into a crowd of patients, embracing them and shaking hands. He was thrilled to find that the Rwandans, far from shunning or blaming him, were greeting him joyously.

At the presidential palace in Kigali, with Magaziner standing beside him and Band nearby, Clinton signed a "memorandum of understanding" with President Paul Kagame, outlining the steps to be taken by the government of Rwanda and the Clinton Foundation in a new program of treatment and prevention. A few days later, he signed a similar MOU with Prime Minister Pascoal Mocumbi at an AIDS counseling and testing facility in Maputo, the Mozambican capital, where the foundation planned to begin treatment.

Those ceremonies marked the end of a weeklong sojourn through Africa, during which Clinton and his party enjoyed the convenience and comfort of free transportation aboard a Boeing 727 aircraft owned by Jeffrey Epstein. A wealthy new friend of Clinton, Epstein was a tall, graying bachelor in his late forties, who had risen from teaching at the Dalton School to overseeing $15 billion in assets for investors like Leslie Wexner, chairman of The Limited.

Clinton's staff knew little about him, except that he seemed to be acquainted with everyone in Manhattan and Palm Beach, liked to "collect" outstanding scientists and political figures, and was sometimes willing to spend millions of dollars on their projects. He joined the trip to Africa but remained mostly in the background; although he usually shunned publicity, his sudden appearance alongside the former president began to draw the attention of magazines like *New York* and *Vanity Fair*—which both assigned profiles of the reclusive Epstein soon after the Clinton entourage returned. (In June 2008, after a highly publicized, two-year police investigation in Palm Beach, Epstein pleaded guilty to a single count of soliciting prostitution from an underage girl. He served thirteen months in jail and is a registered sex offender.)

————

During that fall, as Magaziner began to recruit volunteers and partners, Clinton met in his office with a group of AIDS experts and activists to discuss what would be known as the Clinton HIV/AIDS Initiative, or CHAI (which happens to be the Hebrew word for "life"). The tone was friendly, not hostile, but the more outspoken AIDS leaders wanted to test the intentions of the former president. They refused to pose for any pictures—their way of letting him know that they wanted no part in any photo-op announcements.

Perhaps to answer such concerns—and to introduce CHAI as a new, leading force against the scourge of AIDS—Clinton published an op-ed in the *New York Times* on December 1, his second since leaving the White House. Titled "AIDS Is Not a Death Sentence," the 1,200-word essay outlined the true grim dimensions of the pandemic, briskly rebutted the excuses for prevention over treatment, and declared that "historians of the future" would judge human civilization's failure to treat its victims as "medieval, like bloodletting."

The only moral and practical way forward, he declared, was a worldwide effort by governments, citizens, and international organizations to provide proper care and medicine to all the pandemic's victims. Letting everyone know that the disease need not be fatal would reduce the associated stigma and discrimination, encourage widespread testing, and enable prevention and education to succeed. Only then would the world have a chance to escape the worst consequences of a global plague.

To prove his case, Clinton cited the example of Brazil, where nearly every AIDS patient was afforded access to "life-saving generic drugs manufactured in that country." The Brazilian experiment already had saved more than $400 million in annual hospitalization expenses, rapidly reduced death rates from AIDS and related diseases, and cut new infection rates by half.

This success can be replicated across the globe. To promote the development of AIDS treatment programs in places where they are most needed, my foundation has begun signing agreements with developing nations, including Rwanda, Mozambique and the 15 states in the Caribbean Community. We are putting teams of expert volunteers in these countries to help governments and health-care institutions develop strategies to establish large-scale testing and treatment programs for their citizens.

These are small, grass-roots efforts. But if they succeed, they will save many lives and provide a model to the rest of the world. And the International AIDS Trust, which I lead with Nelson Mandela, is helping to mobilize the resources and leadership needed to focus on treatment and wage a real war on AIDS.

It would be a war of attrition, stretching much longer and reaching much further than any military campaign, requiring strange new alliances and arcane management strategies—and to wage it, Clinton would put his personal reputation on the line in dozens of countries, rich and poor.

CHAPTER SIX

With his reputation gradually recovering from the pardons controversy, Clinton felt increasingly drawn back into the arena of politics and diplomacy. He felt the pull of politics despite conventional strictures on ex-presidents, who were still expected to remain silent on such matters. But for him, the urge to engage, to speak out, and to intervene posed a special problem: the inevitable tension between his accustomed role in politics and his new vocation in philanthropy.

During the final weeks of February 2003, while he pondered how he would stand up and finance his new HIV/AIDS initiative—as well as the approaching deadline for his $15 million memoir—an urgent request arrived in Harlem from the office of the British prime minister. Rather suddenly, Tony Blair's staff asked the former president to fly over for a late winter weekend at Chequers, the magnificent sixteenth-century country residence used by the prime minister and his family.

It was not a social invitation. Blair wanted Clinton to come over from New York soon, and their offices quickly agreed that the visit would take place over the weekend of March 8.

As president, Clinton had stayed with Tony and Cherie Blair at Chequers more than once, including an official visit during his last weeks in the White House. He was there on the December night when Al Gore conceded the 2000 presidential election to George W. Bush, issuing a statement from the baronial estate in Buckinghamshire that urged Americans to accept the result of the Supreme Court's decision favoring Bush without further rancor.

Now with Clinton out of office, this surprising summons from the British leader carried more than a hint of stress, coming at a moment when Blair faced what loomed as his most fateful decision. In the struggle between Washington and Europe over war in Iraq—with London in the middle—which side would he choose?

While Blair would strive to present himself as a resolute warrior,

Clinton realized that his friend actually hoped to avoid that difficult choice, if at all possible. Widely caricatured in Europe by then as "Bush's poodle," a sobriquet that would endure, Blair felt much less enthusiasm for the prospect of war than he would later profess, or so Clinton believed. Under intense and unrelenting pressure from the Bush White House to join its crusade against Saddam Hussein, the British leader desperately wished to maintain the traditional "special relationship" between the United States and the United Kingdom, and yet to do so without alienating his neighbors in Europe, where many politicians and most citizens firmly opposed the American drive to war.

To finesse this worsening conflict, the prime minister felt he needed advice from Clinton—a sympathetic friend, a political mentor, and a statesman whose skillful maneuvering across partisan and ideological frontiers Blair had long admired. And in fact, he wanted more than advice.

By the weekend when Clinton arrived at Chequers, Blair had almost played out his hand. The Bush White House counted him as its principal ally, sincere if not absolutely reliable due to antiwar sentiment among the British public, in Parliament, and among the ranks of his own Labour Party ministers. The trajectory toward war had been clear for many months, in communications between the two nations' intelligence and defense bureaucracies as well as private conversations between president and prime minister.

Already the breach between the United States and Europe had been fully exposed at the United Nations Security Council, where France and Germany were leading international opposition to any endorsement of the threatened U.S. invasion. Positions on both sides were hardening, even as U.N. weapons inspection teams—led by the Swedish diplomat Hans Blix—raced to complete the difficult, painstaking process of tracking down scientists, sites, warehouses, and laboratories for any trace of the chemical and biological weapons that Saddam had certainly once possessed.

Yet somehow Blair still believed he might be able to forge a compromise uniting the Europeans, the U.S., and the rest of the Security Council members—including Mexico, Chile, China, Russia, and several Francophone West African countries—around another resolution. The new resolution would set a deadline for Blix to complete the inspections and report his group's findings. If Saddam interfered with inspections or refused to disarm, the new resolution would authorize military action.

While Blair and Clinton had met and discussed what to do about Iraq on at least two previous occasions, the March 8 visit to Chequers marked the beginning of the endgame.

"Look, our only chance to work this out, short of war, is to try and get an extension of the U.N. resolution with a deadline," the prime minister told him. Speaking of Bush, Blair speculated hopefully, "I think that George will take what Blix says he needs. I think he'll take three weeks." In exchange for a resolution endorsing military action should Saddam curtail the inspections, he thought Bush might agree to a final deadline set by Blix for his inspectors to report. The earliest possible completion date, according to Blix, was three weeks beyond the vague deadline in late March when Pentagon war planners anticipated invading Iraq.

What the U.S. president might be willing to accept, however, would matter very little unless Blair could recruit other Security Council members to support a new resolution. In that endeavor, he believed that Clinton's powers of persuasion and personal relationships might make a difference. Unless Clinton could bring over the Mexicans and the Chileans, Blair's gambit was dead.

Listening to his friend's argument, Clinton was inclined to agree—and to help, even in the face of political risk.

The etiquette of the American presidency is exceedingly clear on the question of former chief executives meddling in policy after they leave office—especially concerning foreign affairs, war, and diplomacy: They aren't supposed to do that. Whatever any of them might wish to say about a successor's decisions, they should say only to the president, and only when asked.

Certainly that was the way most former presidents had interpreted the unwritten rules, aside from Theodore Roosevelt, who had actually turned around and run for president in 1912 against his own chosen successor and close friend, William Howard Taft. Even T.R. had often refused public comment about Taft's presidency on many occasions, however, before breaking with him completely. In the decades since, most ex-presidents had faded into the background, saying little or nothing publicly that might embarrass the newest member of their fraternity.

Jimmy Carter was the contemporary exception. He rarely hesitated to create difficulties for any of his successors as a matter of principle, and was consequently disliked by all of them, despite his highly successful, quietly effective work to eradicate tropical diseases and promote democratic reform in the developing world.

Constrained by the conventions of the American presidency, and seeking to cultivate bipartisan credibility as a philanthropic leader, Clinton had usually demurred from criticizing George W. Bush. He was well aware that Bush's father—his own predecessor whom he had defeated in a bitter election—had never criticized him, although there had been many tempting opportunities. But well before the end of 2002 Clinton began to chafe against those limits.

While campaigning for his party's doomed congressional and senatorial candidates that fall, Clinton had felt outraged by commercials and speeches questioning the patriotism of the same Democrats who had staunchly supported Bush after 9/11—in approving war against the Taliban in Afghanistan, in the swift approval of national security legislation such as the draconian Patriot Act and the establishment of the Department of Homeland Security, and, in general, refraining from any wartime criticism of the commander-in-chief.

Many of those Democrats, including his wife Hillary, the junior senator from New York, had voted for the Authorization for Use of Military Force against Saddam Hussein in October 2002, despite strong misgivings about Bush's intentions. Their reward was a Republican campaign—overseen by White House political boss Karl Rove—deriding Democrats as weak, fearful, unfit to fight terrorism.

Among the incidents that most outraged Clinton was a series of attack ads in the Georgia Senate race, where a Republican named Saxby Chambliss unseated Senator Max Cleland, the former secretary of veterans affairs in the Carter administration. Decorated with a Silver Star for gallantry in the battle of Khe Sanh, Cleland had later lost both legs and one arm in Vietnam when he picked up a grenade dropped by another soldier. He had bravely reclaimed his life, going on to serve in government, enter politics in his home state, and win election to the Senate in 1996 during Clinton's reelection campaign.

By contrast, Chambliss was a "chicken-hawk" who had avoided the war with various draft deferments. But the three-term congressman nevertheless ran ads charging that Cleland lacked "the courage to lead" against the nation's foes, with stark photos of Saddam Hussein and Osama bin Laden. When questioned about this accusation, Chambliss cited Cleland's vote against a Republican attempt to strip collective bargaining rights from federal employees in the new Department of Homeland Security. The demagogic attacks were effective—and despite Clinton's strenuous efforts on his behalf, Cleland was ousted.

The smashing defeat suffered by the Democrats in the fall of 2002 had left Clinton appalled, frustrated, and angry, not only with the Republicans, but with his own hapless party. During that campaign and in the months that followed, he had started to speak out more forthrightly against Bush's domestic policies, especially on taxation and the environment. But as the deadline for the Iraq invasion approached, he had said nothing critical about administration policy. What comments he had offered were encouraging, as when he told CNN anchor Larry King that he thought Bush was doing "the right thing" to push for Iraq's disarmament.

But privately, neither of the Clintons was so sure. In later years, Hillary's Iraq vote would return to haunt her again and again, eventually forcing her to admit that she had made "a mistake, plain and simple." But according to Clinton, she had been reluctant to support Bush's authorization to use military force—and he had advised her to vote "yea."

"I just don't trust Bush," her husband recalled her complaining privately in the days before the vote. "He's not being serious about these inspections. Maybe I should just vote no."

Clinton shared her concern about Bush's sincerity in promising to respect the findings of the U.N. weapons inspectors. While he, too, suspected that the administration meant to invade Iraq and overthrow Saddam, regardless of the inspection results, he also worried about the risks of dangerous weapons—possibly including chemical and biological toxins—under the control of the Iraqi dictator. Nobody was certain what might remain in his hidden arsenal.

"But Hillary," he recalled replying, "we don't want to leave Saddam with that stuff"—meaning chemical and biological weapons—"if he's got it. He will never use it, but he might transfer it to the people we're worried about"—meaning terrorist enemies such as al Qaeda.

Only the threat of military force would open Iraq up to the inspectors, whose expulsion by the Iraqi government in 1998 had provoked Clinton to order an extensive U.S. bombing campaign against identified weapons storage facilities. He believed those raids had destroyed the vast bulk of Saddam's chemical and biological weapons left over from his country's horrific war against Iran, but perhaps not all. He agreed with Blix, whose "attitude was if [Saddam] doesn't think there are any [military] consequences, he'll lie, cheat, steal." And Clinton had undertaken that bombing campaign without explicit permission from the Security Council, relying legally on previous resolutions requiring Iraq to disarm.

Owing to Clinton's doubts that war would only be "a last resort," as promised by Bush—and despite his utter disdain for "the neocon theories," which he regarded as "a bunch of crap"—he hoped that completion of the weapons inspections might ultimately prevent war. "If they were completed, and Blix gave a clean bill of health, it would be hard as hell for [Bush] to go to war."

Indeed, although in 1998 he had endorsed "regime change" in Iraq as U.S. policy, Clinton didn't believe that war could be justified five years later unless Saddam "was hoarding stuff that could be used." He didn't believe that "America had the resources to go after Osama bin Laden in Afghanistan, or just across the border in Pakistan, and . . . do what we needed to do, replacing the Taliban . . . when the whole damn world supported what we were doing back then in Afghanistan, and open a second front in Iraq. That just didn't make any sense to me."

So when Blair asked him in March 2003 to promote a second Security Council resolution, in the hope of providing Blix enough time to complete the inspections and avoid war, he overlooked the inherent risks to his own reputation if his secret diplomacy were to be exposed. Clinton agreed with the prime minister's assessment of the political balance on the Security Council: the West African Francophone countries—Guinea and Cameroon—were most likely to support France's position against a second resolution, as were permanent members Germany, Russia, and China.

Blair couldn't depend on support for any resolution backed by the United States and the United Kingdom from any other members except Spain and Bulgaria. Passage required nine votes out of fifteen, so they would need to line up Pakistan, Syria, Angola, Chile, and Mexico—a very challenging roster, although they hoped to argue that extended inspections represented the best means to avoid war.

In Clinton's estimation, enough other countries just might support the second resolution if Chile and Mexico did—and he happened to enjoy good relationships with Ricardo Lagos of Chile and Vicente Fox of Mexico. A modernizing socialist president, Lagos had established a friendship with Clinton, whom he regarded as a fellow man of the left. Clinton's rapport with President Fox, a wealthy conservative, was more complicated politically but nevertheless warm. He would find discreet ways to approach both men, he assured Blair.

Three days after returning from England, Clinton was scheduled to address the annual convention of the Communications Workers of America in Washington. In tone and substance, his speech indicated a shift in attitude toward Bush's drive toward invasion.

"I'm not so sure we can't still avoid war and disarm Saddam Hussein, but we've all got to be together. We can't waive the option of using force, but we ought to do this in a way that brings the world together, not divides it," Clinton told the labor leaders gathered at the capital's Convention Center, scarcely more than a mile from the White House.

Clinton was careful to take Bush at his word about seeking U.N. approval. "It's obvious to me that the administration really does want the U.N. to support them," he said. "The question is, do they want the support bad enough to let Mr. Blix finish his work?" Even as the Bush administration was routinely disparaging Blix as an incompetent dupe of the Iraqis, Clinton praised the chief weapons inspector, urging for the first time that Blix alone should declare a final deadline for Iraq's disarmament.

"What I think you should be for, as Americans," he said, "is getting the U.N. to adopt a resolution that is not political on either side—that just asks Hans Blix, an honest, competent man, 'How long it will take you to verify that Iraq has or has not done these five things that are in Prime Minister Blair's resolution?' Then I would hope the United States would agree to that length of time, whatever it is."

Privately, Clinton arranged a discreet contact with Chilean president Lagos through a back channel arranged by his former White House chief of staff, Thomas "Mack" McLarty, who was acquainted with the Chilean interior minister, José Miguel Insulza. Not wishing to appear to intervene in matters between heads of state, Clinton asked McLarty to pass a message to Lagos via Insulza. Please call Clinton on the telephone, and inquire how the former president is doing.

A few days later, the call came from La Moneda, the presidential palace in Santiago.

"How are you, Bill?"

Following the ritual pleasantries, Clinton was direct. "Look, Ricardo, I think it might be useful to know that there is one last opportunity for a resolution, it seems"—that is, a last chance to prevent war. Lagos agreed, but in order to publicly join that final effort, the Chilean leader first wanted the support of the Mexicans. Over the following days, Clinton reached out to Fox, whose early days in office had overlapped with the end of Clinton's second term; their relationship was friendly and candid.

But Fox and other Mexican officials contacted by Clinton told him that they were wary of any resolution that might somehow be interpreted as supporting a war that nearly everyone in their country opposed. If a resolution passed that gave Blix three more weeks, and then he came back and asked for additional time, they asked, wouldn't Bush invade anyway? By voting for a three-week resolution, the Mexicans feared they would appear to have ratified Bush's war.

Prodded by his conversation with Clinton, however, Lagos kept working on an alternative resolution with several other countries, if only to buy more time. When the Chilean president announced the text of their proposed alternative on March 13—giving Iraq an additional thirty days to comply with inspections, among other conditions—the U.S. instantly condemned it. Other countries on the Security Council quickly backed away, including the United Kingdom. With Bush pushing back hard, Blair's final initiative had failed from both directions, and he abandoned it.

Six days later the U.S. invasion began, with unforeseen results that included an estimated cost of three trillion dollars, thousands of Americans and hundreds of thousands of Iraqis dead and wounded, and immeasurable damage to the prestige and credibility of the United States—as well as the enhancement of Iranian power in the region, and the eventual emergence of the Islamic State jihadist army.

In keeping with a tradition of alerting former presidents when American military forces engage in action, Bill Clinton learned of the invasion shortly before the rest of the world on March 19. Hillary Clinton, on record in support of Bush's war resolution, would shoulder a substantial share of blame for its catastrophic consequences. It would not matter that her husband, who urged her to vote for the resolution, had tried to prevent the war.

For Clinton himself, the repercussions of his attempted intervention were never fully clear. Regardless of his efforts to conceal his unorthodox role, there is little doubt that Bush learned about it, possibly in real time. Clinton had traveled to Chequers with his Secret Service detail, and he had engaged in several conversations about Iraq with foreign diplomats on ordinary telephone lines. Those talks had surely been picked up, during those final days and weeks of international negotiation, by the National Security Agency—which was spying intently on the Security Council and its member delegations, especially Mexico and Chile.

Initially reported by the *Guardian* newspaper in early March, the NSA's U.N. surveillance operation devoted special attention to all six nations—Pakistan, Guinea, Angola, and Cameroon, as well as Chile and Mexico—seen as uncommitted on a final resolution. The wiretaps ranged from the delegations' embassies in New York City to the homes and offices of a wide range of individuals whose communications might include "anything useful related to Security Council deliberations," according to a memo circulated by NSA official Frank Koza and leaked to the press by a lower-level employee of Britain's surveillance agency, the Government Communications Headquarters or GCHQ. Eventually, the NSA surveillance of foreign governments was revealed to extend to the personal telephones of heads of state—including Vicente Fox.

Whatever Bush knew about Clinton's attempted intervention over Iraq, the former president's violation of presidential protocol brought no immediate repercussions. Ever since the flap in January 2001 over alleged vandalism by Clinton's staff in the White House and Air Force One, the relationship between former and current presidents had remained quietly tense.

Rarely did the White House bother to respond to Clinton's occasional public criticisms of presidential policy. The usual voices in the conservative media and a few elected officials, like Senator John Mc-Cain, rebuked him. Complaining that "former presidents can do damage," McCain had at least once urged Clinton to "Shut up!" Soon, however, there would be unmistakable signs of renewed hostility from the Bush administration.

————

Only days before he left for England, Clinton had taped a short video appearance for CBS's *60 Minutes* that was intended to mark a new phase of his post-presidential career as a television personality. Despite the controversies that marred his exit from office, or perhaps because of them, many producers wanted his face and his voice on their programs—or wanted him to star in a program of his own—and offered large sums of money to attract his interest.

Doug Band had argued against all of these opportunities as undignified and "un-presidential." When Don Hewitt, the legendary *60 Minutes* creator and executive producer, asked to see him at the Harlem office in August 2002, Clinton agreed to listen. Hewitt hoped to re-create one of the signature segments that had established the Sunday night broadcast: a highly literate and ideologically impassioned verbal confrontation between liberal Shana Alexander and conservative James J. Kilpatrick called "Point-Counterpoint."

Although Hewitt had put an end to "Point-Counterpoint" in 1979, its confrontational style, edgy for that era, had been immortalized in a regular *Saturday Night Live* parody by Jane Curtin and Dan Aykroyd that always featured him barking, "Jane, you ignorant slut!" and her snarling response: "Dan, you pompous ass."

But what Hewitt hoped would stimulate ratings, more than twenty years later, was no such Punch-and-Judy routine. His new idea paired the former president with his 1996 Republican opponent, the retired Senate majority leader Bob Dole, whom Clinton had defeated easily in a campaign that became angry and bitter toward the end. Before Clinton's second term commenced, however, the two men had begun to reconcile. On the eve of his second inauguration in January 1997, only two months after the election, Clinton had bestowed the Medal of Freedom on Dole in a poignant White House ceremony.

Rather than "Point-Counterpoint," Hewitt said the new debates would be called "Clinton-Dole" and "Dole-Clinton" on alternating weeks, with a trial run of ten weeks to the end of the 2003 TV season. For a total of twenty minutes on air, the network would pay Clinton $1 million.

"We can be firm and provocative without being nasty," promised Dole in a promotional appearance with his former rival on CBS's *Early Show*. "We're doing *60 Minutes* because we're too old for *Survivor* and *Star Search*," Clinton joked. The real purpose, he said, was to help people "understand the choices clearly," or as Dole put it, to make them "stop and think."

The first segment aired on Sunday, March 9, ten days before the invasion of Iraq, while Clinton was still visiting Chequers. The topic was whether Bush should go to war in Iraq without raising taxes to cover the invasion's cost, with Clinton arguing the negative and Dole, somewhat out of character, arguing the affirmative. The 150-second debate was neither nasty nor provocative; rather than making people think, the segment made them bored. It was, in the words of one newspaper critic, "must-sleep TV."

Even Hewitt admitted publicly that the first episode was dull. "We're going to make sure it looks like more of a confrontation next time," he told the *New York Post* the next day. But the requisite chemistry was impossible to achieve, in part because, owing to Clinton's demanding travel schedule, the two stars could never be taped together in the same studio. Although a few of the ensuing episodes were more compelling, "Clinton-Dole" never achieved enough telegenic power to develop any buzz at all, let alone lift the show's flat ratings. By the end of the season, everyone quietly agreed that this experiment had failed. Cancellation was expected long before CBS announced its fall lineup without the two politicians.

Among the network's executives there was broad agreement that Clinton had performed well, despite a variety of handicaps that included the choice of topics, the country's mood in a time of war, and awkwardness of Dole. Other television offers would continue to come his way, with promises of substantial income—and Doug Band would keep pushing back against such proposals as shabby, lowbrow, and very risky for the former president's stature.

———

One morning in early August 2001, Ted Widmer picked up the *New York Times* and saw that Bill Clinton had signed a record-breaking book deal with the Knopf division of Random House for his memoirs. An hour or so later, Widmer picked up the ringing telephone in his office at Washington College, the small liberal arts school on Maryland's Eastern Shore, where he worked as an assistant professor of history. On the line was Doug Band, asking Widmer to come visit Clinton that same day at Whitehaven, Senator Clinton's residence in Washington.

During the last six months of his presidency, Clinton had given Widmer an important and demanding assignment: to oversee the gathering of documents, data, and oral histories about his eight years in office from every cabinet department. Until then the soft-spoken, unassuming young academic—the only historian in the speechwriting shop—had crafted speeches on diplomatic and security matters from a tiny cubicle in the National Security Council, as one of hundreds of staffers who saw the president from time to time.

For a president concerned with his legacy, the collection of vast troves of words and numbers that would be used someday to describe what he had done—and left undone—was among the most vital tasks of those final months. It required the collection of hundreds of oral histories and millions of pieces of paper—an experience he described as "some fun" but also a bureaucratic "nightmare." He attended cabinet meetings with the president and dealt directly with top officials in every department.

Widmer's archival work supplemented the crucial documentation by Janis Kearney, the first presidential "diarist" and an Arkansan whose Clinton ties dated back to the statehouse in Little Rock. From 1995 forward, Kearney had kept a detailed daily account of all Clinton's meetings, press conferences, and public events to create a "living history" of his presidency that proved invaluable to his memoir research.

Once he got started, Widmer had reported to Clinton personally and regularly on his progress, and they had developed a much closer relationship. Behind his modest demeanor and quick smile was a very sharp, expansive mind with a wealth of historical knowledge. Clinton and many others in the White House had come to know him well and to appreciate his industriousness, diligence, and sensitivity.

When he arrived at Whitehaven on that August afternoon, Widmer and his old boss went out to the backyard and perched on lawn chairs, as Clinton engaged him in an animated discussion about history, books, and especially books Clinton had loved. How could he write a meaningful work of history about himself? Well before the end of their conversation, when Clinton invited him to come up to New York, Widmer realized that he had been invited to help with the memoir due in early 2004. And when they talked again in Harlem a few weeks later, Widmer realized that Clinton's expectations for this book were formidable.

"He had this great story to tell, really a classic American story of his rise from nowhere to the pinnacle of political power, the legacy of a generation," according to Widmer, "and he wanted to write a great book."

In describing his own ambitions for the book, Clinton had told publisher Sonny Mehta, "I am going to try to write the presidential years, so that people realize how crazy the days are, how everything happens at once, and how it looks when you're president, and you're having to deal with all these things at once." He didn't believe that any previous president had written a great memoir. Many of them he had found boring. Even the vaunted two-volume *Personal Memoirs of Ulysses S. Grant*, which Clinton greatly admired and which Mark Twain himself praised as the best memoir "of any general since Caesar," fell short in a crucial way.

"I looked at all these other presidential memoirs, and most of them are quite wooden—and the one everybody thinks is the greatest, Grant's, doesn't have anything to do with him being president. It's all about the Civil War and the Mexican War." Indeed, Grant's memoir concludes with the surrender of Robert E. Lee at Appomattox.

To tell the complicated story of his presidency, Clinton—although often criticized as perpetually disorganized and unprepared—had spent years in preparation, with the secret assistance of Taylor Branch. The journalist and historian, author of a landmark three-volume biography of Martin Luther King, Jr., and an old friend of Bill and Hillary Clinton dating back to the early 1970s, had met quietly and secretly with the president nearly eighty times in the White House, usually very late at night, collecting his thoughts and recollections on tape for the historical record. Clinton had contacted Branch, whom he had not seen for twenty years, shortly after winning the 1992 election, and asked him to help preserve the contemporaneous recollections that would be in-valuable to historians. As it turned out, those tapes would also form the core of his memoir.

Not many besides Hillary knew what her husband and Branch were up to, because Clinton feared that if news of their midnight tap-ing sessions leaked, either Kenneth Starr's Whitewater prosecutors or a congressional investigating committee, or both, would instantly issue subpoenas. They had successfully avoided any such inconvenience by maintaining tight confidentiality for more than eight years.

The assistance that Clinton wanted from Widmer was much more confessional than literary. He took pride in his own writing skill and didn't need a ghostwriter. Unlike many other subjects of autobiogra-phy, he would write every word of his own. But he needed someone to help evoke and explore his memories—just as Branch had done, from the very first day of his first term to the very last day of his second.

No secrecy or drama attended Clinton's meetings with Widmer. He started to come up to Harlem and then to Chappaqua during the fall, bringing a notepad filled with questions and two microcassette record-ers as a fail-safe. He knew that Clinton planned to rely heavily on the Kearney diaries and on transcripts of the Branch recordings to stimu-late and inform the later chapters about his presidency, and expected that their sessions would develop the same kind of raw material for the earlier chapters leading up to the 1992 campaign.

During the weeks between their meetings, the young historian would return to Washington College, where he continued to teach while conducting background research—on Arkansas politics, on Hot Springs and Hope, where Clinton grew up, on the upheavals of the 1960s, and dozens of other relevant topics. As is so often the case with Clinton, however, the words and memories flowed without excessive prompting. Not only was his capacity to recall events and people stun-ningly clear and detailed, but he had hoarded boxes upon boxes of per-sonal records for decades.

"Hell, I had a report I did on England in the *fifth grade*! I mean, my mother and I, we saved everything. I had every letter my mother ever wrote me. And she had every letter I ever wrote her. I had all the letters that my college girlfriend wrote me. I had everything. I just saved everything."

For several hours, Clinton sat with Widmer in his Harlem office or the big, comfortably furnished living room of the Chappaqua residence. Their intense conversations, he said, "got me to just talk about all of it and it was extremely helpful because, first of all, it got me to thinking about it again."

Just talking helped him to pinpoint important things that he might not otherwise have remembered—and to conjure another era, fifty years gone, when American life and politics were utterly different. At times, talking about his late mother, his grandfather, and other deceased relatives and friends, Clinton became quite emotional.

Transported by his voice, Widmer felt that the former president "was very, very open . . . completely, sometimes painfully honest . . . and held nothing back. It was *gold*. Sometimes we laughed so hard we cried. He told me hard-hitting stories about being a very poor kid. It was a classic Horatio Alger story—no father, and not the kind of household you'd expect a President of the United States to come from. He talked about the hurt of a child wondering where his mom was, where his dad was. . . .

"It was like traveling back in time to those days when he was growing up in Arkansas, an era when people sat on their porches and talked and talked."

Most days, when Widmer wasn't there—and when Clinton wasn't traveling for paid speeches or foundation work—he would sit down to write. Working from the transcriptions of their talks, which eventually amounted to almost six hundred double-spaced typed pages, he would draft pages in longhand, using spiral notebooks. Most of those days he spent with Justin Cooper, whose role as principal researcher, editorial assistant, and sounding board would prove essential to all Clinton's books.

Together Clinton and Cooper would sit at a large table in a converted barn behind the Chappaqua house that served as Clinton's home office, gymnasium, and repository for thousands of books and dozens of souvenirs, paintings, objets d'art, collectibles, and other mementos that were not already on display in his Harlem office. On days when

Clinton traveled—roughly half of any month—Cooper was always with him, and they often worked on the book while airborne.

Every page that Clinton finished, he would turn over to Cooper to type into his laptop, noting facts that required further checking. Later Clinton would review and rewrite, making handwritten revisions on the pages Cooper had typed and retyped, creating second, third, and fourth drafts of nearly every page; some were revised as many as seven times.

With fall turning into winter, and the publisher's deadline drawing closer, Clinton sent the first 150 pages that he had completed to Robert Gottlieb, the admired former *New Yorker* editor who was handling his book at Knopf. A few days later, Gottlieb called him and said, "This is a hell of a story. How much of this did you make up?"

"It's all true," Clinton laughed.

"First of all," replied Gottlieb, "nobody knows that many crazy people."

"Yes they do," said Clinton. "They just don't pay attention."

"Secondly, nobody can remember the names of every teacher they had in grade school, and what their junior high school teachers said."

"Yeah. If you're paying attention, you can," Clinton insisted. "That's what I was raised to do. Keep in mind, I'm the last of the pre-television kids."

As work on the book progressed, the sessions with Ted Widmer came to an end. There was no more time for lingering hours of conversation, with only months left to finish a draft that would reach 1,500 pages plus. Instead, Clinton spent days and eventually many nights with Cooper, whose typing and retyping of the handwritten pages in more than twenty notebooks kept him on daily duty in Chappaqua for more than a year. Living in Manhattan, he would drive back and forth every day, often well after midnight—until Hillary Clinton found out what was going on and ordered him to stay in the guest bedroom. She hated the idea of his driving back to his apartment in the middle of the night after a grueling day's toil at the computer.

Like most authors, Clinton felt oppressed by the publisher's deadline. But he appreciated Bob Gottlieb's insistence on clarity and precision, and "persnickety" attention to detail. "He wouldn't miss things, like if I said, 'There were over 200 people there,' he'd always mark out and put 'more than.' He'd never let me get away with any little slip like that."

Even more than that, he valued the editor's candor: "Gottlieb was most valuable when he'd say this just doesn't make any sense. You ought to take it out." At Gottlieb's urging, Clinton took out thirty pages about his college years at Georgetown that were "just not relevant." Clinton felt many more pages needed to come out and Gottlieb evidently agreed. But more editing and cutting would require more time.

Over the winter, Clinton proposed a solution. Why not publish the book in two volumes? Then he would have more time to polish the second book about his presidency, while the first book, covering events before 1992, would be published on schedule. But the publishers feared that any such strategy would hurt overall sales. They insisted on maintaining a schedule that would get *My Life* into bookstores by mid-June 2004. With the help of a corps of volunteer fact-checkers, led by chief researcher Meg Thompson and Caitlin Klevorick, Clinton and Cooper pushed through to finish the gigantic manuscript, still adding material and making revisions until the very last possible minute.

———

While Clinton conspired to influence the U.N. Security Council's final deliberations over Iraq, Bush was preparing to join the global struggle to contain AIDS. The former president had only begun to assemble the elements of his foundation's Clinton HIV/AIDS Initiative, led by Ira Magaziner, when the current president announced a major new U.S. government program to fight the epidemic.

In his State of the Union address on January 29, 2003, even while warning the nation that "crucial hours may lie ahead in the Middle East," Bush reminded Americans that "our calling, as a blessed country, is to make the world better."

"Today, on the continent of Africa," he continued, "nearly 30 million people have the AIDS virus, including three million children under the age of 15. There are whole countries in Africa where more than one-third of the adult population carries the infection. More than four million require immediate drug treatment. Yet across that continent, only 50,000 AIDS victims—only 50,000—are receiving the medicine they need. Because the AIDS diagnosis is considered a death sentence, many do not seek treatment. Almost all who do are turned away."

But the cost of antiretroviral drugs had dropped drastically, said Bush, "which places a tremendous possibility within our grasp. Ladies and gentlemen, seldom has history offered a greater opportunity to do so much for so many. We have confronted, and will continue to confront, HIV/AIDS in our own country. And to meet a severe and urgent crisis abroad, tonight I propose the Emergency Plan for AIDS Relief, a work of mercy beyond all current international efforts to help the people of Africa."

To finance what would soon become known as the President's Emergency Plan for AIDS Relief, Bush proposed to devote $15 billion over the next five years—a tripling of U.S. funding—"to turn the tide against AIDS in the most afflicted nations of Africa and the Caribbean," by preventing seven million new cases, providing medicine for "at least two million people," and "humane care for people suffering from AIDS and for children orphaned by AIDS."

It was a stunning proposal—and a vast increase over Clinton's own final budget for international AIDS assistance in 2001, which had amounted to roughly $600 million across all federal departments, including the Pentagon.

The boldness of Bush's new multibillion-dollar plan could be measured by the fact that the United States contribution to global AIDS relief under Clinton, inadequate as it was, represented not only the biggest commitment of any donor but about half of the entire annual financing provided by all the developed countries. The U.S. contribution had been growing, along with contributions from Japan, the European Union, and Scandinavia, but remained far below the estimated $9 billion needed annually to curtail the spread of the disease.

Now Bush was promising a figure that for the first time would—with increased contributions from other governments and private donors such as the Bill and Melinda Gates Foundation—begin to approach the scale of the problem. Moreover, his plan would provide treatment as well as prevention, just as Clinton had demanded in his *New York Times* essay only weeks earlier. It was not merely the most worthwhile program of Bush's presidency—which might not mean much—but one of the boldest humanitarian actions any president had undertaken in the modern era.

On many occasions since leaving the White House, Clinton had publicly acknowledged that his administration's funding for international AIDS programs was far less than needed—while arguing, with equal accuracy, that he had greatly increased funding despite resistance from Republicans in Congress. Many of those same obdurate Republicans, urged on by evangelical Christian leaders, were now supporting the Bush plan.

During the months that led up to the unveiling of PEPFAR (the President's Emergency Plan for AIDS Relief), Clinton had spent hours in unsparing conversation with his daughter about the AIDS crisis, and specifically what his administration had and had not done. Chelsea had chosen to examine the global response to the crisis as the topic of her thesis at Oxford, where she was close to finishing her master's in international relations.

At some point in their discussions, wondering about her verdict on his presidency, he had asked, "How do I come out?"

"'You didn't do near enough,'" he quoted her telling him. "'But you did more than anybody else in the whole world, so you come out OK.'" When he told that story to reporters he would laugh, but the subtext was serious.

Now his successor, with whom his relationship was at best lukewarm, was proposing to do far more, much closer to "near enough" than Clinton had done.

Within days after Bush's address, Clinton appeared on CNN's *Larry King Live,* where the host asked whether he was "surprised" when the president devoted so much attention to AIDS in the State of the Union. His answer was defensive.

"Well, first let me say that I was pleased. When I was president we tripled overseas aid to [combat] AIDS and by the time I left office, America was providing about half the money that the governments of the world were spending on this, but it's nowhere near enough. So I was very pleased and I'm very glad."

He quickly noted that his foundation was already working in "16 countries in the Caribbean" and "two in Africa, soon to be three and maybe four," setting up national health systems to cope with AIDS, tuberculosis, and malaria.

And then he hinted at the conflicts soon to come with the pharmaceutical lobby and its friends in the Bush administration.

"But we need—there's still, unbelievably . . . there are still efforts to stop affordable drugs getting out there. Now we've got drugs that stop mother to child transmission [of HIV] when the mother's infected, and the baby's born free of AIDS, 98 percent of the time. We've got drugs that make AIDS from a death sentence into a chronic illness for healthy people, if they can get them."

If they can get them—which seemed certain by no means to Clinton unless someone cleared away the obstacles posed by the Western drug manufacturers, as he had just started to do in the Bahamas.

"This is a global problem and I welcome the president's financing. The Congress needs to pass it," he went on. But the real issue would be the cost of medicines and the systems to distribute them and ensure that they would be used properly.

"If we can get [medicines] out there in these countries for $500, $300, then $1,000 can pay for care *and* medicine. That's going to be the key. That's why I say the government of the United States can have a huge impact in talking to the drug companies and making sure we clear out all of the roadblocks to either getting these drugs out at an affordable price or setting up the facilities like in South Africa, as they do in India, Thailand and other places to produce the drugs. We've got to get the medicine out there."

But Clinton had no way of knowing how Bush intended to proceed, beyond his promise to spend billions. Like nearly all the significant leaders and activists in the global campaign against AIDS, Clinton and Magaziner had been excluded from the secretive planning process in the Bush White House in the months leading up to the PEPFAR announcement. Unlike many of those leaders and activists, they concealed their skepticism about the ideological and corporate imperatives that might undermine PEPFAR's effectiveness, no matter how sincere Bush himself might be.

In a Republican administration, Clinton knew that the power of those imperatives should not be underestimated. The pharmaceutical manufacturers would exert great pressure to protect their patents and markets, just as they had done so successfully when he was president. The evangelical right, despite its refreshing determination to help AIDS victims, would insist on "abstinence education" in PEPFAR's budget, no matter how useless. All those potential disputes could only be exacerbated by the deeply rooted animus against Clinton himself in the Bush White House.

Still, neither he nor Magaziner foresaw the ugly confrontation that would erupt before long.

CHAPTER SEVEN

What Bill Clinton could accomplish with a meeting, or even a telephone call, was remarkable. While the American media still tended to describe his reputation as tarnished, the shine seemed to reappear almost magically whenever he ventured abroad, whether physically or electronically. His sterling international image proved to be worth not just millions but hundreds of millions of dollars for the cause he had taken up.

Having publicly demanded, as a moral imperative, that the world provide treatment to the millions suffering with AIDS across the global south, from the Caribbean to Africa to Southeast Asia, Clinton began to pull together the elements of a strategy to accomplish that objective, devised by him and Ira Magaziner. It would require moving forward on at least three fronts simultaneously, starting out with scant resources.

With the overnight success of CHAI's debut in the Bahamas—where a few direct inquiries to suppliers had reduced the government's cost to purchase AIDS medications by seven-fold immediately—the fledgling initiative had signed on to assist fifteen states in the Caribbean, along with Mozambique, Rwanda, and Tanzania. The combined total of all the AIDS patients receiving treatment in those countries at the time was under two thousand.

To secure sustained funding from Western governments, as Clinton and Magaziner surmised, each country would need to present a detailed and feasible plan to create the physical and human infrastructure for effective treatment. Urban and rural facilities would have to be built or rebuilt, equipped, and accredited; doctors, nurses, and clinic workers would have to be trained; and supply chains for affordable medication would have to be established, all in countries that barely possessed any functioning health care systems. Moving forward on those plans, Magaziner needed to recruit skilled people, willing to spend time in backward and sometimes dangerous places—and he would have to attract them with scarcely any budgeted funding.

The second element was the notion of an international "buying club" for AIDS medications, designed to encourage drug manufacturers to reduce prices in exchange for greatly increased sales volumes. If they could order for two million patients instead of two thousand, Clinton and Magaziner believed they would drive down the unit price of each dose of antiretroviral medicines like azidothymidine or AZT, a first-line treatment for AIDS. Magaziner estimated that the annual cost per patient could be pushed much lower than $500, the level they had achieved in the Bahamas (which as the richest Caribbean country could afford prices that were still too high for other developing nations).

But there could be no promise to expand the market for AZT, and use volume sales to bring down prices, without the availability—or at least the promise—of very large sums, soaring into the hundreds of millions and eventually billions of dollars. The third element was money: Without it, their ideas would remain mere projections.

Magaziner had put in a million dollars of his own money and had raised another $1.2 million from David Sainsbury and other wealthy friends. Although insignificant compared with what would be needed to launch treatment programs at scale, that war chest was enough for him to get started on the ground. From his consulting office in suburban Quincy, Massachusetts, he and his staff began to recruit volunteers. At the beginning, everyone, including Magaziner himself, would volunteer. To conserve funds, CHAI would pay only travel expenses—coach seats, cheap hotel rooms, and a meal allowance.

He approached friends in the public health field, at places like the Harvard AIDS Institute and Columbia University's Mailman School of Public Health, who were intrigued by the idea of Clinton becoming more deeply involved in the AIDS crisis, but still wondered whether his involvement would extend much beyond speeches and press releases.

"No," Magaziner told them in his low, grave voice. "We're seriously going to try" to bring treatment to millions in Africa and across the developing world. They were intrigued, but very skeptical, so he brought a dozen of the top medical experts in the field—including Paul Farmer and Jim Kim of Haiti's Partners in Health, Richard Marlink and Bruce

Walker of the Harvard AIDS Institute, and the University of California's Eric Goosby—to meet with Clinton in Harlem, where the former
president convinced them that he meant to act rather than just talk.
Seeing Clinton move so quickly to obtain signed agreements with several governments helped to persuade them that CHAI was real.

At the same time, Magaziner started calling old friends in the business world, mostly "serial entrepreneurs" who had made money and
were seeking to do something different and socially valuable, like him.
Some were between start-ups, while others were about to retire. He
wound down almost all of the contracts then held by his own firm, SJS
Consultants, and assigned his employees to start working on CHAI.
And he asked former colleagues at the Boston Consulting Group and
at McKinsey & Company to lend him some young employees who were
"on the beach" because they didn't have enough work.

One of his earliest contacts was Dr. Allan Rosenfield, dean of the
Mailman School at Columbia, a legendary figure in the field of international health, and one of very few who had spoken out forcefully in
favor of full funding of AIDS treatment, as opposed to mere prevention, in developing countries. Rosenfield agreed to encourage some
young Columbia doctors to volunteer, but he had one question.

"Ira, there's something I don't understand. Why are you bringing in
all these business people who don't know anything about AIDS? What
can they contribute?" They would bring an understanding of systems
and management, Magaziner replied, making treatment both effective
and efficient while conserving very scarce resources. "OK," said Rosenfield, scratching his head. "Maybe."

When Magaziner brought several dozen of these medical and business professionals to Harlem to meet the president, Maggie Williams
was astonished. She had never quite believed that he would be able to
recruit an entire staff of volunteers to launch this project.

Before long, Magaziner was bringing teams of doctors, nurses, executives, and management specialists into Mozambique, Rwanda,
and Tanzania, where they would meet, often for the first time, on the
ground. They would sit down with officials of the host governments,
"trying to figure out what to do." And then they would spend weeks and
weeks trying to determine what could be done and how best to do it.

How could countries in the developing world organize and manage AIDS treatment without the advantages of modern health systems? Many leaders of the global health community—in the West, at least—doubted the possibility, which was why they had been reluctant to support any expansion of treatment. To answer such doubts, Magaziner and his mixed teams of medical doctors and business executives determined that several steps had to be completed in order to build a successful treatment program in any country.

First, people would have to be brought in for initial testing, despite the lingering stigma attached to AIDS in most parts of the world; second, medicines would have to be purchased and then sent out, while preserving their quality, in a supply chain to both urban and rural centers; third, doctors and nurses would need training to administer tests and drugs; and all of these steps would require support from local and national governments. To bring the new treatment systems "to scale," as Magaziner told his teams, "we have to do it in a way that is institutionalized in the health system that exists, and in the political system that exists."

For Magaziner and Clinton, that institutional fabric included the enormous existing nonprofit sector across all of Africa as well. They had pledged not to duplicate what other organizations were doing to fight AIDS, so they sought out partnerships instead. If Doctors Without Borders or Médecins Du Monde or any other competent medical group had established a clinic in a rural village in Tanzania, then CHAI would work with them on training and supplies. But where nobody was already setting up a supply chain, or arranging laboratory testing, or building relationships with government, CHAI would seek to fill those gaps.

As Magaziner and his teams traversed the rural terrain in Mozambique and Tanzania, where a few clinics operated by Doctors Without Borders were providing treatment at a very small scale, they confirmed the most important assumption of CHAI's plan: If life-saving treatment is available, people will diligently take their medicine. In refusing to consider treatment in poor countries for years, the global health authorities had assumed the opposite.

"If you educate people about how to take these medications, they will follow the protocols. People don't want to be sick," remarked Magaziner dryly.

The other critical assumption that departed from conventional wisdom—and the accustomed practice of many charitable groups operating in less developed countries—was that governments must be respected as equal partners at all times. That injunction reflected a core tenet of CHAI's mission and values. Both Clinton and Magaziner felt intense disdain for the "neocolonialist attitude out there," and communicated that viewpoint powerfully to everyone on CHAI's staff. They understood that they were asking the volunteers and later the paid staffers to undertake difficult and risky work; lots of mistakes were inevitable.

But there was one kind of mistake that Magaziner wouldn't tolerate. He issued a clear warning that to disrespect the project's government partners meant swift dismissal. "There's too much neocolonialism," he would say, "with people sitting around in the capital city in expensive hotels."

If CHAI staffers happened to be in a capital city rather than in a town or rural village, they were usually to be found in a Ministry of Health office, where they had been assigned to train government employees to oversee the new HIV/AIDS treatment program. Working side by side with one official—a method known as "twinning"—the CHAI staffer would essentially direct the program as the government staffer gradually learned enough to take over, in a process of developing systems and logistics that might require as long as two years. The ultimate aim, as Magaziner emphasized repeatedly, was "to work ourselves out of a job."

To him, the emphasis on governments as partners meant that everywhere CHAI worked, "we basically had the government in the lead." His people remained in the background, never seeking publicity for the organization—no big crowds running around in CHAI T-shirts, no big signs on clinics featuring Clinton's name. Their presence wasn't secret and they accepted some credit in newspaper articles or broadcasts, but not too much. When Clinton himself visited, that was a different matter, because government leaders and officials invariably wanted to be seen with him in media coverage.

Embracing national governments was central to Clinton's evolving vision of what his philanthropy should accomplish. While bringing medicine to the neglected millions was primary and immediate, he wanted CHAI to establish competent, self-reliant systems that would someday make his foundation redundant. For him, it would not be enough to parachute in, deliver medicine, and foster a culture of dependency.

In later years, Magaziner would find it difficult to describe what he had witnessed in those early weeks and months—the desperation of government officials, of the people in towns and villages, "dying all over the place, with nobody coming to do anything about it." Slowly, much too slowly, with too little tolerance of any political risk, the United Nations and the Western governments were moving to put financing in place for treatment, through such mechanisms as PEPFAR and the Global Fund to Fight AIDS, Tuberculosis and Malaria. Yet those organizations were far from ready to deliver medicine—and nobody in the affected countries even knew they existed.

When CHAI suddenly appeared—under the auspices of Bill Clinton, following up with local officials and ministries of health week after week, stationing experts on the ground—Magaziner could sense glimmers of hope and inspiration. Being present was not much more than a promise, however, and without money CHAI wasn't quite ready to deliver. But Clinton and Magaziner didn't let that hold them back.

———

Not long after Clinton agreed to proceed with the foundation's HIV/AIDS initiative, Magaziner started to contact the American and European drug manufacturers that produced antiretroviral medications in the hope that—if guaranteed much higher volumes of sales in the developing world—they would lower unit prices accordingly. He got nowhere fast, despite the terrible publicity endured by the pharmaceutical manufacturers over accusations that they were letting millions die.

Leaders of major firms, notably Jean-Pierre Garnier of GlaxoSmith-Kline, had responded by calling for much higher spending on HIV/AIDS treatment globally, with Garnier even demanding a "Marshall Plan" to turn back the pandemic. Garnier was the human face of Big Pharma, the sort of high-minded international businessman honored at dinners for the Sabin Vaccine Institute and the United Nations Association. But Magaziner couldn't even get a meeting with him.

In private conversations with Magaziner, who was known to some of them as a business consultant, other pharmaceutical executives spoke plainly. They felt that their companies had done enough already by providing limited quantities of drugs and dropping a patent infringement case against South Africa in April 2001. Under constant pressure from advocates and governments to lower their prices in poor countries, stop enforcing drug patents, and license generic manufacturers to produce versions of their drugs, the branded pharmaceutical companies had acceded to some of those demands.

"We're not insensitive to public opinion. That is a factor in our decision-making," Garnier had explained to reporters when Glaxo-SmithKline and three dozen other major pharmaceutical companies dropped their case against the South Africans in a settlement that he had personally negotiated. "We don't want the public to misunderstand the issues. We have never been opposed to wider access [to AIDS treatment]. We have discounted our drugs. We've done everything we could."

The branded-drug manufacturers feared that lower-priced versions of their products sold abroad would somehow turn up in gray markets at home—a potentially costly outcome even for companies that were, like GSK, earning profits as high as $30 million a day. Selling their antiretroviral drugs at cost, they argued, the price would still be unaffordable in Africa, Asia, and the Caribbean.

And there they seemed to have a point: Although various pilot programs and tiered pricing schemes had reduced the prices of branded medicines considerably, from a high of $12,000 per patient per year (PPPY) to as low as $2,000, that price remained unattainable for all but the most affluent citizens in poor countries. After more than two years, the concessions wrung from the drug giants had resulted in very little expansion of treatment.

Clinton had no greater success attracting interest from U.S. and European industry leaders. For several months, Magaziner tried in vain to draw pharmaceutical executives into a discussion of tiered pricing for poorer countries and other distribution schemes. In the spring of 2003, when he and Clinton encountered Garnier by chance at an event in Dublin, the former president tried to engage the GSK boss on that sensitive subject. Garnier politely agreed to sit down for a conversation, but he barely seemed to hear what Clinton was saying during the ten minutes or so they spent together.

"It will destroy our business in the United States," he replied, before he stood up to leave.

The only alternative sources of medicine were the generic pharmaceutical makers located in the developing world. Generic firms were already producing antiretroviral medications in places like Brazil, Thailand, India, and South Africa, though not in quantities anywhere close to what the world needed. To Magaziner's eye, even the generic prices still seemed high, measured not only against what poor countries could afford but what he, as a former consultant to the pharmaceutical industry, estimated as their inherent cost. The persistently high pricing of AIDS medications represented a classic market failure, with demand far outpacing supply for a decade—and no obvious path toward balance through reduced costs.

The dysfunctional market might be improved dramatically, Magaziner believed, if CHAI could pull together a "buying club," guaranteeing higher sales volumes and reliable payment over a longer time horizon. Western pharmaceutical manufacturers had rejected any such notion as uneconomic and dangerous to their profits. But would any of the overseas generics manufacturers lower their prices to win a far larger market?

At an early meeting in Harlem to discuss where the money might be found for their vision of a big new market for AIDS medications, Magaziner had asked, "Who do you know who does this?" Clinton understood the shorthand: Among the many heads of state that the former president counted as friends, who had large budgets to spend on global AIDS relief—and might be willing to entrust that money to Clinton?

"Well," said Clinton, ruminating, "my best friends still in office, who have big development budgets, besides Tony Blair, are Jean Chrétien," the Canadian prime minister, "and Bertie Ahern," the Irish prime minister, known in Gaelic as the Taoiseach. In the spring of 2003, he placed a phone call to Chrétien—a feisty Liberal then near the end of his term, who devoted much of his attention during his final year in office to the AIDS crisis. The Canadian leader didn't require too much persuading, as Clinton later recalled, once he had explained what he and Magaziner were trying to accomplish. With information provided by Magaziner,

Chrétien's staff had already briefed him on the outlines of the CHAI plan.

"Look Jean, all these people are dying like flies," Clinton told him. "We've got a limited amount of money, but we're paying too much for this medicine." The market was "disorganized," he went on, dominated by middlemen and agents who charged enormous, unjustified fees. "What we need to do is get this money, let the governments sort it direct, and have the delivery direct from the manufacturers. And I think we can get the cost down."

Chrétien agreed informally to a commitment of $20 million a year for five years, with the understanding that the Canadians could select the countries they most wanted to support, and that a portion of the money would be used for staffing clinics and overseeing care. But the deal would only be announced several months later, after more painstaking negotiations with Canada's foreign aid agency.

Meanwhile in early July 2003, during a trip to Northern Ireland—where he continued to enjoy the overwhelming popularity earned as a peacemaker during his presidency—Clinton also scheduled a call on the Taoiseach at his Dublin office. Again, Magaziner had helped to prepare the way. Years earlier he had worked as an economic consultant to the Irish government, which had opened the door for a sympathetic hearing at Irish Aid, the republic's overseas development agency.

But Magaziner had no illusions about the weight that Clinton brought to their dealings with sovereign governments. An impending visit with the head of state created a strong impetus for discussions with other government officials and staff, as they talked over the request that Clinton would make and prepare briefing papers. Given Clinton's popularity in the republic, the Taoiseach would want a successful meeting—and just as important, he would want to express confidence in Clinton's substantive ability to get something done about this intractable problem. The energy of Clinton's persona organized these systems around his agenda.

His July 2003 appearance in the North was one of many made by the former president after leaving the White House to encourage the process of reconciliation and power sharing between Catholics and Protestants, which was then wearing thin. A year earlier the local elections had been called off, which frankly concerned Clinton. He chose the weekend of Drumcree Sunday, an annual occasion when members of the Protestant militant Orange Order march through Catholic nationalist neighborhoods en masse, often provoking violence. But on that Sunday, as Clinton noted in a press interview afterward, the march occurred without incident.

"It was a pretty good Sunday, yesterday, Drumcree Sunday. So good, I felt able to go to Royal County Down and play golf," he quipped, referring to the venerated links at Newcastle, site of many important tournaments and rated one of the best courses in the world. Earlier in the day, he had delivered a lecture at a Northern Ireland college in honor of John Hume, the Social Democratic politician from Derry who boasted a Nobel Peace Prize for his work with Clinton and Blair on the Good Friday accords.

Expressing optimism about the North's future stability, Clinton had urged leaders on both sides, listening in the audience at the Hume event, to persevere despite setbacks. "When the Middle East peace fell apart, when the future looked uncertain in Bosnia, when Africa was still reeling from losing ten percent of the people in Rwanda and two million died in the Congo, I could always point to the Good Friday accord. You need to think a long time before you give that up," he said. "I ask you to stay the course and lead the world by your example."

Upon his arrival in central Dublin the next day, the Taoiseach greeted Clinton effusively. "From all parts of the world he keeps in touch," Ahern told the reporters assembled. "He has earned a special place in our history and our hearts." Clinton went into Ahern's private office, paneled in light Irish oak, with Doug Band and Eric Nonacs, a young foreign policy specialist brought onto the foundation staff by Maggie Williams.

When they emerged an hour or so later, Clinton had a five-year, $110 million commitment for CHAI from Irish Aid, the republic's overseas development agency. Most of the money would be used to provide AIDS treatment to as many as half a million patients in Mozambique, where only a few hundred were currently receiving medicine. In a stroke, the agreement made Ireland the third-largest purchaser of AIDS medications in the world. As years passed, despite the retirement of Bertie Ahern and the crashing of the Irish economy—and regardless of negative political commentary concerning "foreign donations" to the

Clinton Foundation—Dublin didn't waver from its pledge to support his work.

Meanwhile, Magaziner also approached the government of Sweden, where he had consulted on industrial policy decades earlier. The daughter of a Swedish official he had known well back then, Annika Söder, now held a top position at the Ministry of Foreign Affairs. As state secretary for international development cooperation, she oversaw SIDA, the agency responsible for running Sweden's international health programs. Söder introduced Magaziner in turn to the Nordic nation's recently appointed "AIDS ambassador."

At the time, Sweden belonged to an informal group of development agencies in Northern Europe known as "the like-minded group," which also included the United Kingdom, the Netherlands, Norway, and Denmark—all of which had decided together that their funding would be used only for HIV/AIDS prevention because treatment was too difficult, expensive, and risky. But after several meetings with Magaziner over a period of months—and a strategic phone call from Clinton to the Swedish prime minister—the Swedes agreed to help fund Tanzania's CHAI treatment plan. The Dutch and the Germans had turned Magaziner down—as had the British early on, despite numerous conversations between Clinton and Blair—but the Swedish decision was a break. The next country to move would be Norway.

As the first U.S. president ever to visit longtime NATO ally Norway, Clinton had established close ties with Prime Minister Kjell Magne Bondevik, who was still in office four years later. So when Clinton returned to Oslo in November 2003—after weeks of discussion between Magaziner and Norwegian aid officials—he sealed an agreement with Bondevik for the Norwegians to provide at least $25 million over five years to support CHAI programs in Tanzania and Mozambique.

Smashing through the objections to treatment among the Western governments, as symbolized by the substantial budget commitments from Ireland, Canada, Norway, and Sweden, was tremendously gratifying. But Clinton and Magaziner had taken a real gamble on those funds coming through, by approaching the generic manufacturers well before any of that money had been guaranteed. Magaziner had bet on Clinton, and Clinton had bet on his prominent friends. Still, there was one big bet that had yet to pay off.

———

Well before Clinton approved the project that became CHAI, a brilliant Indian chemist named Yusuf Hamied had told the world that he would provide life-saving AIDS medications at a per-patient/per-year cost of no more than $350, selling to groups that served indigent people in the developing world. As the Western-educated chairman of Cipla, a generics manufacturing giant founded by his father in 1935, Hamied possessed the scientific credibility as well as the industrial capacity to deliver drugs at this new "humanitarian price," which he had announced at a February 2001 meeting in Brussels.

The son of a Muslim father and Jewish mother, Hamied was a maverick billionaire who had fought the branded drug manufacturers for decades. In the AIDS crisis he saw an opportunity not only to do good but to best his old adversaries. But the flood of orders that Hamied expected after his announcement didn't materialize, even though other generic firms in India soon followed his pricing initiative with reductions of their own.

The institutional barriers to reforming the market for antiretroviral drugs were formidable. Despite Hamied's good intentions, the countries that needed his products were chronically disorganized, plagued with corruption, and lacked sufficient funding and health infrastructure. The orders didn't come in, and the generic companies didn't seek them out. There was no prospect of sufficient volumes or timely payment from those governments, so the generic firms simply didn't pursue their business.

The Indian manufacturers, notably including Hamied, soon received personal letters from Clinton introducing CHAI and urging them to talk with his representatives about a new regime for sales of antiretroviral drugs in developing countries. No doubt his restoration of good diplomatic relations with India as president and subsequent work with Indian American business moguls on disaster relief there were helpful. But as he later said, "They got it. These guys got it . . . That's what generics are about, is volume. Once they realized that I could organize volume for them and get them paid on time, then they were interested in our plan." If anyone had the credibility to engage the Indian manufacturers, it was Clinton—and he was going to ask them to take some risks.

Among Magaziner's newest recruits was Kate Condliffe, almost fresh out of college, who had worked for a couple of years at A. T. Kearney, another global management consulting firm. Impressed by her willingness to volunteer, he hired her to run CHAI's Drug Access Program. With Condliffe overseeing a small group of young analysts from McKinsey, Magaziner entered into a long series of visits, negotiations, and consultations at Cipla's headquarters in Bombay— and simultaneously made contact with its Indian competitors Ranbaxy Laboratories, Ltd., and Matrix Laboratories, Ltd., and with Aspen Pharmacare Holdings, Ltd., in South Africa.

Yusuf Hamied and his colleagues were intrigued because, as he later explained, "This is the first time a group has come forward with predictable volumes." He got along well with the respectful Magaziner and welcomed the CHAI team into his factories and laboratories.

What ensued was an extraordinary process of mutual education and cooperation that had few parallels in corporate business and especially in the secretive sphere of drug manufacturing—where ingredients, methods, costs, contracts, and commercial relationships are traditionally held very closely. At Cipla as well as the other companies, executives taught Magaziner and his colleagues about the manufacturing of the most widely used AIDS medications, such as nevirapine and AZT, revealing vast troves of information, both chemical and financial, that would normally be kept secret.

Over a period of nearly six months, Condliffe and a few other CHAI business volunteers traveled back and forth to India, visiting plants operated by Cipla, Ranbaxy, and Matrix to learn the details of the making of AIDS drugs. Their purpose was to understand and analyze the cost structure and variables so that they could make recommendations for savings and determine a reasonable pricing schedule.

Looking at the process in the simplest terms, making large volumes of drugs could mean significant savings. If the vessels used to heat pharmaceutical ingredients were larger and needed to be washed out less often between cycles, for example, that would reduce the cost per capsule produced. So would simpler packaging, and a host of other small improvements that added up. None of this was news to Hamied and the other generic executives. But it helped Magaziner to model a new, high-volume approach to pricing.

"Making a pharmaceutical, you're heating stuff, you're cooling stuff, you're mixing stuff," he explained years later. "The economics are very scale-intensive. If you have a large enough volume, you have a dedicated production line for one drug and save a fortune."

Hamied also urged Magaziner to approach the chemical manufacturing companies, mostly located in China, that produced the "active pharmaceutical ingredients," or API, in the AIDS medications. (To ensure stability and add bulk, the manufacturers combined the API with other inactive ingredients, known as excipients or fillers.) Those chemicals, derived from both natural and synthetic sources, accounted for most of the cost of making AIDS drugs, he said. Again, Hamied disclosed what would otherwise be considered the most sensitive trade secrets, putting Magaziner and his team in direct contact with the Chinese chemical firms. As one of the generic manufacturers told him, their formulations only accounted for 20 percent of the value added in the AIDS medications. The key to making a deal was to persuade the suppliers of APIs to agree to volume discounts.

The CHAI team moved on to China and Korea, bringing the same promise of higher volumes to those companies—all of which stood to increase profits if their Indian clients bought much greater quantities of their chemicals. At sufficient volumes, two of the API suppliers agreed to discounts of up to 50 percent.

The promise of the plan outlined by Magaziner was enticing for the generics companies, but they had heard similar promises in the recent past, when the World Health Organization and the Global Fund had talked about pooling demand from poor countries ravaged by AIDS— and nothing had happened. To enter negotiations with CHAI required them to take what more than one generics executive later described as "a leap of faith."

"If we had been the Joe Smith Foundation coming in to have these discussions, [the generics manufacturers] would have been leery of that," said Magaziner with typical understatement. "But it was Clinton, so they thought there might be something there."

By late summer 2003, Magaziner was again commuting between India and Africa, immersed in quiet negotiations with executives at the four generic companies. For several weeks they worked on the draft of a pathbreaking agreement that promised drastic price reductions for five of the most widely used AIDS medications, including the "triple cock-tail" of nevirapine and AZT. The agreement would set a ceiling price on the drugs based on "dynamic costing" and "forward pricing." Under this agreement, the buyers group of African and Caribbean countries organized by CHAI would issue "tenders," or requests for bids—and any of the generic firms could bid on any contract, so long as they offered terms at or below the ceiling price.

At $139 per patient per year, that new price was far lower than the current lowest cost of $500.

When Clinton announced the agreement in Harlem, it made worldwide headlines. The story broke in the *Wall Street Journal* on October 23, 2003, with a front-page story by Mark Schoofs, a correspondent based in Johannesburg who had won a Pulitzer Prize for his reporting on AIDS in Africa:

> Former President Bill Clinton announced Thursday a landmark program that attacks two of the toughest obstacles to treating AIDS in the developing world: high drug prices and low-quality health infrastructures.
>
> The Clinton Foundation HIV/AIDS Initiative has clinched a deal with four generic-drug companies, including one in South Africa, to slash the price of antiretroviral AIDS medicine.
>
> Engineered by longtime Clinton adviser Ira Magaziner, the agreement will cut the price of a commonly used triple-drug regimen by almost a third, to about 38 cents a day per patient from an already cut-rate generic price of about 55 cents. The lowest available price for the same regimen using patented versions of the drugs in developing nations is $1.54. For a key drug, nevirapine, the price will be cut by almost half. . . .
>
> Under the supervision of Mr. Magaziner, the Clinton Foundation HIV/AIDS Initiative also helped several Caribbean states and three African countries prepare detailed government-approved plans for rolling out the drugs nationwide, instead of just in selected regions. The plans aim to improve the entire health-care system by preparing budgets for hiring and training nurses and doctors, building and upgrading laboratories and clinics, develop-

ing patient-information systems, and improving drug warehous-
ing and delivery. . . .

The *Journal* article emphasized two aspects of this heartening story
that had eluded most other news outlets. Schoofs pointed out that the
South African government had recently named CHAI as "its main advisory group on HIV treatment," despite past resistance by the government of President Thabo Mbeki to deal with the overwhelming impact
of AIDS in his country, the very epicenter of the pandemic.

And in an almost casual aside, Schoofs noted: "Mr. Clinton vehemently denies any partisan motivation, but his efforts threaten to steal
some thunder from President Bush. Months after Mr. Clinton began
working on his initiative, Mr. Bush called for $15 billion over five years
to fight AIDS in poor nations. That proposal still hasn't cleared the
congressional budget-authorization process."

Indeed, nine months after Bush proposed PEPFAR, the program remained in limbo on Capitol Hill, belying the urgency of his State of the
Union message. Without a budget, the White House appointees running PEPFAR couldn't accomplish much, even as Clinton moved forward to launch his ambitious treatment plan. But the Bush officials at
PEPFAR were watching CHAI—and evidently they didn't much like
what they saw.

———

Within weeks after the leaders of Tanzania, Rwanda, and Mozambique
each signed a "memorandum of understanding" to work with CHAI,
Magaziner and Clinton agreed that they should next approach South
Africa, which was estimated to have more AIDS victims than any other
country in the world—and whose government was notoriously reluctant to act on their behalf.

President Thabo Mbeki, the leader of the African National Congress and successor to Nelson Mandela, had publicly expressed
personal doubts that the disease was caused by the human immuno-
deficiency virus, or HIV, and had encouraged the proliferation of conspiracy theories about its true origins, even in official investigations by
his government. His Moscow-educated minister of health, Mantomba-

zana Tshabalala-Msimang, went even further than Mbeki, telling anyone who would listen that AIDS was in fact the consequence of plotting by the Central Intelligence Agency and the multinational drug companies. She also advocated consumption of garlic, potatoes, olive oil, and lemon juice as effective AIDS therapy.

In policy terms, these delusions paralyzed the Pretoria government and left hundreds of thousands of people to die without care, even as Mbeki and his minister mused about "alternative" treatments for the pandemic. Although Mbeki's cabinet voted in 2002 to affirm the scientific fact that HIV causes AIDS, curtailing any further speculation on the matter by the president or his subordinates, the health ministry continued to take no positive action to obtain effective medications or to seek financial assistance for treatment. By early 2003, after more than three years of such official malfeasance and neglect, fury was simmering across South Africa, with growing incidents of protest and civil disobedience campaigns by advocates against the government's "genocidal" failures to act.

Even the loyal Mandela repeatedly stated his open disagreement and questioned Mbeki and his policies within the ANC. Quietly, he had also turned to Clinton for help. On several occasions since the Barcelona AIDS conference, Mandela and Clinton had discussed the medical implications of Mbeki's peculiar denialism, and the possibility of providing treatment to the millions infected in South Africa. Those discussions had pushed Mandela to demand meetings with the minister of health and closer to confrontation with Mbeki over AIDS.

When Clinton himself finally called Mbeki in January 2003, the South African president warily agreed to let Magaziner see Tshabalala-Msimang to discuss ways that the Clinton Foundation might help. But when Magaziner met with her in the capital, she obstinately insisted that AIDS was nothing more than "a capitalist plot." In private discussions with members of her staff, he discovered that they fully understood why her ideas were bizarre and ruinous, but feared her too much to speak out. She was a powerful figure in South African politics, having risen steadily within the ANC since joining as a young student in the early 1960s. Her husband was the party treasurer.

Magaziner left Pretoria disappointed, but he and Clinton continued to push for an opening in South Africa, knowing that the pandemic could never be contained, let alone ended, without concerted action there. No matter how successful their treatment plan proved to be, the disease would keep spreading so long as the continent's biggest country remained a hotbed of infection. Nor could they ignore Mandela's pleas for help and leave the innocent victims of Mbeki's mania to their fate.

Maneuvering around the hostile minister of health, Magaziner made contact with Mbeki's legal counsel, a tall, elegantly attired woman named Mojanku Gumbi, who had become the South African president's most influential adviser. Unlike many in his circle, she was said to be able to speak to the president with absolute candor. And despite her reputation as a hardline African nationalist, Gumbi was open to help from Clinton.

In July, Clinton traveled to South Africa with Hillary and Chelsea to join a week of national celebrations as Mandela marked his eighty-fifth birthday. Discouraged as many South Africans felt by the persistence of poverty, illness, inequality, and other ills in the aftermath of apartheid, they cherished him even more. The father of the nation, known everywhere by his clan name, "Madiba," remained a source of international pride, in sharp contrast with the embarrassments of Mbeki's misrule.

Among the many events marking the occasion, Mandela's friends and staff planned a huge black-tie party at the convention center in downtown Johannesburg, with an array of celebrity guests including Oprah Winfrey, Sir Richard Branson, Bono, Robert De Niro, Coretta Scott King, and Naomi Campbell. Seated on Mandela's right was the former American president, whom he continued to treat as an adopted son. They spent much of the evening laughing and gossiping.

But in a quiet moment, Clinton stepped into a private room for a short meeting with Mbeki, Magaziner, Band, and Mbeki's chief of staff, hastily arranged by Mojanku Gumbi. Band felt they were practically begging Mbeki to meet with Clinton, and angrily told Magaziner that the situation demeaned their boss.

The Americans listened as the South African president enumerated his misgivings about the AIDS treatment program they had been asking him to consider for months. Rather than muttering about conspiracies and superstitions, he talked about practical and legal worries that Magaziner had to admit were legitimate. The South African constitution required any health care benefits or programs to be distributed equally around the country, in both townships and rural districts, he explained, but the expense and complexity of AIDS treatment were simply too burdensome to achieve that constitutional standard.

Under Mandela, he continued, the global health authorities had persuaded South Africa's Ministry of Health to embark on a massive, nationwide campaign against tuberculosis. But inadequate medical facilities in the countryside had meant that many rural patients hadn't received the full course of TB medication, with disastrous, deadly consequences: a terrible epidemic of multi-drug-resistant tuberculosis that had killed thousands more. The health system hadn't improved much since then, if at all, and Mbeki feared a similar result if AIDS treatment couldn't be provided in every community. He was also deeply worried about the ballooning budgetary expense of AIDS drugs, even at generic prices, which would inevitably limit the reach and equity of treatment.

When Clinton responded, he was blunt. "You should let us come in to work with your people on a plan to address the issues you've raised, just as we've done in Mozambique, Tanzania, and Rwanda. We're working on ways to reduce the cost of the antiretroviral drugs by purchasing them together, in bulk." He warned Mbeki that the South African government would be embarrassed again, should other countries start to provide treatment while Pretoria did nothing. When he concluded, Mbeki was silent for a moment. Then he told Clinton and Magaziner that he would let them try to put together an acceptable plan, with his government's cooperation.

They all shook hands and returned to Mandela's party. The entire meeting took fifteen minutes.

———

The next morning, Magaziner flew home to Boston for one day to fulfill a family obligation. The day after that, he boarded a plane back to South Africa, after contacting several of the top experts on AIDS and public health with the momentous news that CHAI had knocked down the political barrier to progress there.

In Pretoria he continued to evade Tshabalala-Msimang, the minister of health, and instead spent a week in meetings with the ministry's director general, Ayanda Ntsaluba, who didn't share the minister's prejudices, and an internal ministry group working on the AIDS problem under his guidance. Together, Magaziner and Ntsaluba drafted a letter to Mbeki's cabinet, recommending the appointment of a special task force to formulate a plan for nationwide treatment that would be ready within three months.

Presented with the letter, which specifically addressed the concerns he had raised with Clinton, Mbeki bypassed the health minister. At a meeting in August, the cabinet approved Ntsaluba's recommendation and officially invited CHAI to work with the new AIDS task force. By September Magaziner hoped to return with a contingent of more than two dozen experts to create a national treatment program within two months.

Among those who agreed to return with him were Harvard's Bruce Walker, one of the most prominent infectious disease specialists in the world; Eric Goosby, a former White House adviser on HIV/AIDS who would later become the U.N. special envoy on AIDS; and Joep Lange, a Dutch clinician who served as president of the International AIDS Society (and later died in the Malaysian Airlines plane shot down by Russian-allied forces over Ukraine in 2014).

But before the project got under way, Magaziner received a series of urgent calls and messages from several of the doctors and public health experts who had planned to join him. They had heard from a young official at the U.S. Department of Health and Human Services named Bill Steiger. His title was special assistant to the secretary of HHS for international affairs and director of the Office of Global Health Affairs in HHS—which meant that he served as liaison for the Bush administration to the Global Fund to Fight AIDS, Tuberculosis and Malaria, and was overseeing the rollout of PEPFAR, Bush's new global AIDS commitment. As Magaziner traveled between Africa and India setting up CHAI's first programs, Steiger was traveling between Washington and Africa, visiting U.S. embassies to pave the way for PEPFAR.

Neither a physician nor a public health expert, the thirty-three-year-old Steiger held a PhD in Latin American history and no obvious qualifications for his powerful position in government. But he also happened to be the son of the late William Steiger, once an influential Republican member of Congress from Wisconsin who had given Vice President Dick Cheney his first job on Capitol Hill. He was also the godson of George Herbert Walker Bush. And he was ideologically attuned to the Republican verities that seemed to be paramount at PEPFAR as it began: Sexual abstinence as preached by faith-based programs was to be upheld as the primary means of preventing disease transmission, and branded pharmaceuticals were to be strongly preferred over generics for treatment.

For the Bush White House to prefer branded drugs over generics came as no surprise to AIDS advocates, who had suspected from the beginning that PEPFAR might serve as little more than a multi-billion-dollar subsidy to the pharmaceutical giants—and a stumbling block to the effort to provide universal treatment with generic drugs. But what surprised Magaziner was the brazen aggression of Steiger in seeking to block his efforts.

The young HHS official had sent a clear warning to the AIDS experts preparing to leave for South Africa. Anyone who worked with CHAI would risk losing the federal grants from the National Institutes of Health that made their research possible.

Magaziner heard a similar story from Sharon Wilkinson, the Clinton-appointed ambassador to Mozambique whom he had known since college days at Brown University. The word had come down from Washington before Wilkinson, a career Foreign Service officer, retired from her post in July 2003. Nobody receiving assistance from the United States, and nobody who hoped to receive money from PEPFAR, should be working with CHAI.

When Magaziner told Clinton that the Bush White House was trying to shut down his new project, the former president sputtered a string of obscene expletives.

"That's just who they are," he said. "There's not a damn thing we can do about it."

CHAPTER EIGHT

Even for Bill Clinton—whose schedule sent him into the stratosphere for a hundred hours or more nearly every month on excursions to speaking venues, foundation events, and conferences—the trip he began in the middle of January 2004 was formidable. But at least he had an entertaining assortment of companions on the luxuriously appointed Boeing 767 hurtling through the night sky toward Saudi Arabia.

At the invitation of Saudi Crown Prince Abdullah bin Abdul-Aziz Saud, the big jet's owner, and Amr al-Dabbagh, a prominent Saudi businessman and philanthropist, Clinton and a few dozen friends were headed for Jeddah, the kingdom's second-largest city and its most important commercial center. Unlike many of his trips to the Mideast, Europe, and Asia, this midwinter tour would produce little in the way of speaking fees. But it would generate the seed of one of the most significant ventures of his post-presidential career.

Enjoying the crown prince's airborne hospitality was a truly Clintonian crew of companions that included former Brazilian president Fernando Henrique Cardoso; former Mexican president Ernesto Zedillo; comedian Chevy Chase; actor John Cusack; former undersecretary of state and Brookings Institution president Strobe Talbott; former ambassador to Portugal Elizabeth Bagley and her husband, Reynolds Tobacco heir and Democratic Party donor, Smith Bagley; former ambassador to the Bahamas, international lawyer, and Democratic donor Arthur Schechter; wealthy New York investors Alan Patricof and Stanley Shuman, both Democratic donors; New Jersey homemaker Sylvia Steiner, whose husband was another top Democratic donor; and the trio that built and rules Google, Sergey Brin, Larry Page, and CEO Eric Schmidt. Ron Burkle was also on board.

At the front of the plane with Clinton were Doug Band, Justin Cooper, Ira Magaziner, six Secret Service agents, and several additional foundation staffers. When the plane left Newark Airport, the full manifest included more than forty names.

The Saudi ruling family had been very generous to the Clinton Foundation, donating more than $10 million toward its library fund (or roughly the same amount that the resolutely bipartisan despots gave to George H. W. Bush's presidential library in College Station). While Clinton no doubt felt grateful for their largesse, the broader aim of the trip also appealed to him.

Hoping to mitigate the public relations damage done by the involvement of their citizens in the 9/11 attacks, top Saudi leaders wanted more Americans to visit their country and meet their people. The Clinton visit had been approved by Abdullah, next in line to succeed his half-brother King Fahd; Abdullah had been acting as regent ever since a stroke incapacitated Fahd almost ten years earlier.

Ambitious, sophisticated, and reform-minded, Amr al-Dabbagh had asked Band to bring a group of guests with him and Clinton to the annual Jeddah Economic Conference, a Red Sea version of the World Economic Forum held in the Swiss Alpine resort of Davos every January. Among the prominent figures participating in the Jeddah event would be the prime ministers of Turkey, Malaysia, and Lebanon, as well as Jordan's Queen Rania. When the forum concluded, the crown prince's jet would carry Clinton and his party onward to Davos, where he was scheduled to deliver the keynote speech at the conference's opening day luncheon.

Aboard Abdullah's plane, Clinton circulated among the travelers—most of whom had never visited the Saudi kingdom—offering greetings and reminiscing about his own previous visits. Unlike a commercial jet, the interior of the royal wide-bodied aircraft featured a large open space, styled like a living room, with couches and tables where passengers could sit, talk, and relax. The former president was supposed to spend time on this trip working with Cooper on his book, which was already overdue but still slated for publication in June, if he could finish in time.

Carrying a printout of the draft chapters he had completed so far, Clinton seized the chance to get some advice from readers he respected. He walked back to the seats occupied by Strobe Talbott and his wife, Brooke Shearer, an experienced journalist who had overseen the White House Fellows Program in the early years of Clinton's first term.

"My book," he said, smiling down at them as he hefted the massive typescript. "Would you mind reading this?" As someone who had known Clinton since both were in their early twenties, Talbott's perspective was valuable—and he couldn't help suspecting this might have been the real reason that he and his wife had been invited along. A formidable writer and editor, he spent most of the next several hours plowing into the text, and later went over his notes with Clinton on the plane.

The accommodations in Jeddah were luxurious and the Saudi guides friendly, but Clinton's party was ushered carefully to palaces and other venues where they were unlikely to observe much of daily life in the kingdom. Sylvia Steiner later told a reporter that they had felt "isolated." What the Saudis clearly wanted them to see, however, was the presence of many of their country's female entrepreneurs at the economic conference. Improving the role of women in the Saudi economy—and by implication, in Saudi society—seemed to be the event's overarching theme.

A leading Saudi businesswoman, financier Lubna Olayan, delivered the opening address for the first time in the conference's history. "Without real change, there can be no real progress," she said. "If we in Saudi Arabia want to progress, we have no choice but to embrace change," adding, "those changes can be embraced in a way that preserves our core Islamic values."

Inside the conference hall, a glass wall separated men from women in the audience. As she addressed them, Olayan's veil slipped off. But she simply continued, not bothering to adjust it, which provoked gasps and applause. The next day, Saudi newspapers published photographs of Olayan without her veil as well as pictures of unveiled women at the conference, evidently enjoying a few moments of comparative freedom.

In Clinton's keynote speech—for which he was not paid—the former president scolded the Saudis for "blaming other people for your problems," which he called self-defeating, and asked them not to dismiss American Mideast policy simply because of its commitment to Israel's security. Predicting the kingdom could not forever resist change sweeping across the world, he urged political and social reforms, including steps toward democracy, as well as broader science, technology, and civic education in the nation's schools.

With a touch of humor, Clinton reiterated the day's feminist themes. "How can you build a modern economy," he asked, "when you won't even let women drive?" The former president pointed out that Khadija, the first wife of the Prophet Muhammad, was a prosperous and independent merchant. "If they'd had cars 1400 years ago," he said, grinning, "she would have been driving one!"

As the female half of the audience applauded, the male section remained utterly silent, according to one of Clinton's guests, who sat watching in astonishment.

In a country where the veil is mandatory, and where women are neither allowed to drive cars nor to venture outside the home without a male relative, this was a shocking incident. If the visiting Americans regarded the presence of women as a minor gesture to modernity, the local religious authorities saw it as a revolutionary offense. The nation's chief religious authority, Grand Mufti Sheikh Abdul Aziz al-Sheikh, swiftly issued a condemnation:

"We followed what happened at the Jeddah Economic Forum, which should be denounced . . . namely, the mixing of men and women and the latter's appearance without wearing the Islamic hijab ordered by God. This is prohibited."

Warning of "dire consequences," the Mufti continued, "what is even more painful is that such outrageous behavior should have happened in Saudi Arabia, the land of the two holy shrines, whose rulers consistently abided by Islamic law without fear of criticism." He was also deeply disturbed by the publication of photographs of women, which he said was prohibited by Sharia law. Still worse was the implication in Arabic media that the conference represented "the beginning of the liberation of Saudi women—as if they were being constrained by Islamic law," he lamented.

The crown prince may have gotten a heavier dose of progress than he expected. When he received the American entourage at his palace in Riyadh, Clinton deliberately mentioned that his guests included Christians and Jews as well as Muslims, which the Saudi leader took in stride. But when Brooke Shearer started to ask him some pointed questions about the oppression of women in Saudi society, Abdullah answered sharply, reminding her how long American women had waited for the right to vote. Band then jumped up to curtail the exchange and a few moments later, the prince bid his visitors a gracious farewell and left, saying it was time for his evening devotions.

———

As the Boeing 767 roared into the sky toward Switzerland the next day, Doug Band lounged on a couch in the cabin, talking with the Google trio—Eric Schmidt, Sergey Brin, and Larry Page. He wasn't looking forward to Davos, which he had attended as a presidential aide to Clinton in the 1990s. While public exchanges of ideas could be important, such elite gatherings were too often, in his view, a waste of time. It was an opinion the young aide had communicated to his boss more than once.

Yet they were on their way again to the world's most exclusive confab, and Band couldn't help wondering aloud why. And why weren't all the important people who would be at Davos—and for that matter, all the people on this aircraft—doing more to address the world's most pressing problems, instead of just jabbering and networking and drinking little cups of espresso?

If there was anyone in the world who could convene a powerful group like the Davos crowd—and perhaps inspire them to *do something*—that person was Bill Clinton, mused Band. "We could do this differently, with a substantive agenda and a real purpose," he said as the Google guys listened.

"Do it!" blurted Page, the stubborn, idiosyncratic, and extraordinarily creative engineer, who often talked about his hope that Google would help solve the world's woes. "Do it," he said again, as the others nodded. "And we'll give you money to get started."

It was late morning when the Clinton entourage finally made its way up winding mountain roads and into the chilly, snow-covered town. Visible atop many of the taller buildings and discreetly stationed along major streets were armed commandos in gray-green camouflage gear, automatic weapons slung over their shoulders.

No fewer than two thousand Swiss Army troops were present to bolster the town's regular complement of several hundred police officers. With dozens of heads of states arriving, followed by hundreds of other prominent government, corporate, and nonprofit leaders, security was a deep concern, even in this isolated and inaccessible place. On the Davos schedule along with Clinton were such conspicuous targets as Iranian president Mohammad Khatami and Dick Cheney, vice president of the United States.

As was often his habit, Clinton had remained awake during the six-hour night flight. He was slated to speak at the opening luncheon in the town's Congress Centre, a sprawling modernistic pile that could accommodate well over 1,500 in its largest room. As *Newsweek* later reported, his appearance drew the largest crowd of the week to hear a sweeping, hour-long overview of the current state of affairs on planet earth, with a focus on "globalization," the buzzword agitating the few protesters who had found their way into Davos.

"Globalization works for half of us," he noted pointedly as he began. "The other half lives on less than $2 a day."

He went on in his usual diplomatic style: "I respect the anti-globalization people and I think a lot of their criticisms are valid. But they want to take us back to a time that never was. . . . Human history is the journey of going from isolation to interdependence to integration. A divided world is unsustainable and dangerous. Anti-globalists want to go from interdependence to isolation, and it's not possible. We are caught in the middle, and must systematize the process to make real economic difference for all."

To "smooth the rough edges of globalization," he said, would require much more from his powerful audience than emergency solutions and gestures toward social responsibility.

"The world is not organized systematically to deal with the fact that we are globally interdependent, whether it's AIDS or [violent] conflicts or economics," Clinton lamented. "You change the reality of human history by systematic action."

He asked his influential listeners to think about how they could help to develop more rational, orderly, effective ways to address the difficulties of a globalizing world. "When you hear about a good thing," he suggested, "think about how we can systematize it to scale."

Except to the most wonkish listener, "systematize it to scale" hardly sounded like a plausible solution to climate change, mass unemployment, or a raging pandemic. Yet that clunky phrase had real meaning for Clinton, reflecting his hope that the breakthrough his foundation had achieved in reducing the price of AIDS medications might indicate fresh approaches to other major problems. His call to action also reflected the frustration expressed by Band and others about the surfeit of chatter at conclaves like Davos.

But Band already was exploring the ways and means to do something very different. While Clinton took questions from the audience, the young aide stepped out of the hall to speak to an older, elegantly attired man with olive skin and graying hair. His name was Richard Attias, and aside from founder Klaus Schwab there was nobody who knew more about the inner mechanics of the World Economic Forum.

A Moroccan-born Jew whose family had immigrated to France, Attias earned a degree in civil engineering and worked for IBM before he founded an event-planning company. In 1995 he met Schwab, who hired him to help "reinvent" the Davos gathering while overseeing its planning and logistics—a job he would handle behind the scenes for well over a decade, keeping track of literally every aspect of the annual meeting, even the distribution of hotel rooms and the selection of menu items.

"How does this work?" Band asked, with a wave of his hand. "And how much does it cost?" He would remain in touch with Attias. And weeks later in New York, Band would start to develop an idea that he eventually called the Clinton Global Initiative.

———

When Clinton urged his Davos audience to encourage strategies that might benefit humanity, he was speaking from a renewed position of authority. Shortly before the former president boarded the plane that brought his entourage to Saudi Arabia and then Switzerland, he and Ira Magaziner had notched another critical advance in their effort to reduce the cost of HIV/AIDS treatment. It was a step that brought the world a little closer to the prospect of universal care—and "systematic" change.

On January 14, Clinton's aides summoned the press to the Harlem office, where the former president announced a new agreement between the Clinton HIV/AIDS Initiative and five of the world's largest medical equipment manufacturers to drastically reduce the price of laboratory testing for the disease in poor countries. Standing beside him as he spoke were executives of the five companies, notably including Edward J. Ludwig, chairman, president, and CEO of Becton Dickinson, along with executives from Bayer Diagnostics, Beckman Coulter, Inc., Roche Diagnostics, and the French diagnostics giant bioMérieux.

As the first step toward a course of treatment, and then to monitor blood levels of the AIDS virus, routine blood tests are essential to providing effective treatment. For new patients, the CD4 test measures the number of CD4 lymphocytes in the bloodstream, indicating the condition of the immune system and helping doctors determine when to start treatment with antiretroviral drugs.

For patients in treatment, the viral load test measures the amount of viral particles in a milliliter of blood, determining whether a particular drug regimen is effective. To administer them regularly was a prohibitive expense in poorer countries, and an obstacle to treatment almost as daunting as the cost of medicines.

Under the agreement negotiated with the medical companies, the cost of the CD4 test would be cut by more than half, Ludwig told the assembled journalists. The other executives present declined to be specific, but the foundation's press release stated that the reductions would cut costs by "up to 80 percent" below prices currently charged in developing countries.

Combined with the reductions achieved by the generic drug manufacturers, this meant that the cost of treating a single AIDS patient for a year in those countries would drop from around $800 a year to less than $250, a reduction of 70 percent. Initially, the lower-cost tests would be available in the sixteen nations where CHAI already was working to provide low-cost generic medicines and improved management of care—and eventually the new price regime would be expanded to other countries in Africa, Asia, the Caribbean, and Latin America.

Listening quietly in the fourteenth-floor office as the cameras whirred were Magaziner and the blue-ribbon team that had advised him, without compensation, during months of shuttle negotiations with the manufacturers—attorneys Steve Petras of Baker & Hostetler and Richard Zall of Mintz, Levin; and Harvard AIDS experts Trevor Peter and Dr. William Rodriguez.

"These companies are world leaders in their fields, and they deserve credit for their willingness and desire to make AIDS tests more affordable and more available to millions of people in the developing world," intoned Clinton. "They have stepped up to the plate and demonstrated tremendous compassion and corporate citizenship."

While the medical companies had earned Clinton's praise, the truth about the diagnostics deal was slightly more complicated than his remarks suggested. For months, in parallel with the negotiations Magaziner and his team were conducting with the generic drugmakers, they had simultaneously engaged in talks with the test manufacturers. And for months, those talks had moved very slowly, or not at all. When Clinton had announced the generic drug deal in November 2003, the pace quickened overnight.

Neither Ludwig nor his competitors relished the possibility of competition with companies in India—a threat that no longer seemed idle—and their attitude suddenly changed. The agreement was completed in a matter of weeks, despite the December holidays.

Around the same time, the pharmaceutical firms Boehringer Ingelheim and GlaxoSmithKline announced that they would license production of their AIDS drugs by four generic firms in India and South Africa for sale throughout sub-Saharan Africa—in return for a mere 5 percent royalty. A combination of threatened fines and the deal Clinton announced two months earlier seemed to have concentrated the minds of Jean-Pierre Garnier, the once dismissive GSK boss, and his counterparts at Boehringer Ingelheim.

The ramifications of CHAI's intervention appeared to be spreading well beyond the countries that initially joined with Clinton and into the broader market.

"We are systematically changing the economics of AIDS treatment in places where, before now, very few people have been able to receive life-saving care," said Clinton at the Harlem press conference. "By pushing down the price of HIV/AIDS medicine and laboratory tests, we are ramping up the ability of developing countries to treat millions of people, and to do so with the kind of quality of care that people with AIDS in the developed world usually receive."

———

Even as Clinton hailed the diagnostics and generic drug deals, he had no illusions about the reaction that attempts to bring systemic change provoke from powerful interests—in this instance, the branded pharmaceutical industry, which was fighting the adoption of generic drug formulations for AIDS treatment. He and Magaziner knew that Bush administration officials had warned CHAI's partners in Africa that PEPFAR's billions in aid and research funding would be withheld from any agency or country participating in the generic drug purchasing scheme.

On a visit to Paris early in 2004 at the behest of former treasury secretary and Citicorp executive Robert Rubin, who had invited him to address an event sponsored by the bank, Clinton encountered the opposition in person.

Over dinner at an opulent Parisian restaurant with Rubin's other guests, he sat near Hank McKinnell, president of the New York–based pharmaceutical giant Pfizer, Inc. Clinton knew that Pfizer was heavily involved in research, development, and production of HIV/AIDS medications, and was donating as many as sixty thousand doses a year. He also knew McKinnell's reputation as an aggressive advocate of legal and political action to protect his industry's intellectual property rights against foreign governments and generic manufacturers.

"Somebody at our table asked me about what we were doing," Clinton recalled later. He began to talk about CHAI's progress in bringing AIDS treatment to countries hit hardest by the pandemic, through the bulk purchase of generic drugs.

Almost immediately, McKinnell voiced his objections. "You know," said the Pfizer executive, "the generics are just not any good. They're only 60 percent as effective as my drugs." But Clinton had heard dozens of firsthand reports from communities across the Caribbean and Africa where people who had been dying were surviving, thanks to a generic drug regimen. And he had read several early studies of the impact of generics in AIDS-stricken communities.

"Well, Hank," Clinton said, smiling, "if I were you, I wouldn't make that argument."

"Why?" asked McKinnell, momentarily flustered.

"Just do the math. Now, I know you guys are making limited amounts of these drugs available in poor countries for $1,500 a year or so, which is a lot less than the $10,000 you used to charge over there, but that's still about ten times more than our drugs cost. And if you're charging ten times as much, and mine are 60 percent as effective, it means for any given amount of money, I'm still saving six times as many lives as you are.

"So I don't believe I'd make that argument, but you're free to do it, if you want. And actually, I dispute the premise. I think ours *are* effective."

Indeed, Clinton could rely on more than his personal opinion to support his foundation's decision to rely on generic drugs. In 2001, the World Health Organization had set up a "prequalification" protocol to help governments and aid organizations determine which generic formulations could be deemed safe and effective as well as affordable, not just for AIDS but for tuberculosis and malaria, too. Under prequalification, WHO scientists analyzed the purity and potency of every formulation, while teams of inspectors visited the factories where they were produced to ensure that they complied with international standards. With assistance from European, Canadian, and Australian regulators, the WHO prequalification process had achieved a reputation for probity.

The new generic formulations were central to the strategy created by public health experts to ensure that AIDS patients in developing countries reliably took their medicines on time and at the proper dosage. Instead of requiring patients to take six pills or capsules a day, as was necessary in using branded antiretroviral drugs, the generic medicine was packaged in pills that each combined three drugs and only needed to be taken twice daily.

Known in public health jargon as a "fixed-dose combination" or FDC, this innovation ensured easier storage, distribution, and patient compliance—all problems that medical organizations had faced for many years in the developing world when seeking to combat not only AIDS but tuberculosis. With approval by WHO, the use of FDCs had been adopted by CHAI, the Global Fund, and every other agency seeking to bring millions of victims into treatment as quickly as possible to stem the pandemic.

If Clinton won that dinner table argument in Paris, the Pfizer chief was prevailing in the White House, along with his comrades in PhRMA, the industry's supremely powerful Washington lobbying group. Like most pharmaceutical executives, McKinnell was a Republican whose company donated heavily to the party and to George W. Bush's campaign.

So much influence did the pharmaceutical interests enjoy in the Bush White House that the president had selected Randall Tobias—the former president and CEO of the giant Indiana-based drug maker Eli Lilly, Inc.—to serve as the administration's global AIDS coordinator, with the rank of ambassador. Although Tobias lacked any experience in public health, and his company didn't even manufacture any HIV/AIDS medications, Bush appointed him to oversee all the U.S. government's international AIDS programs, and PEPFAR in particular.

Within months of his appointment in July 2003, as Clinton and Magaziner knew all too well, Tobias and Bill Steiger, who oversaw international AIDS programs at the Department of Health and Human Services, had started pushing back against the campaign for generic drugs in the developing world. Magaziner believed that their reaction had included blunt threats against organizations and individuals cooperating with CHAI in its creation of a generic drug "buying club" in Africa and the Caribbean.

In Washington, PhRMA and its allies in conservative think tanks and media mounted a furious campaign against generics, with the American Enterprise Institute and the Hudson Institute producing a flurry of articles condemning generic AIDS medications as untested and potentially dangerous. These papers were rarely signed by doctors, or anyone else with field experience battling the pandemic, but penned instead by hired intellectuals.

Funded generously by tax-exempt donations from pharmaceutical companies like Pfizer and Eli Lilly, the writers and academics associated with Hudson and AEI mounted an attack not only on the generic manufacturers but on every institution that supported the use of generics. Their targets ranged from Doctors Without Borders, the Paris-based medical nonprofit that had pioneered AIDS treatment in Africa, to the World Health Organization itself, which had established a "prequalification" protocol to approve generic formulations.

The result of this concerted lobbying and propaganda campaign was a rule promulgated by PEPFAR, Bush's new international AIDS assistance program, prohibiting the use of its funds to buy generic drugs. Specifically, PEPFAR's rules required that drugs purchased with U.S. government funding had to be "approved by a stringent regulatory authority or otherwise demonstrate quality, safety and efficacy at the lowest possible cost"—a phrase that Tobias and Steiger interpreted to mean approval by the Food and Drug Administration. The foreign generic manufacturers could not even bring their drugs to the FDA, however, without risking patent actions in American courts by the branded pharmaceutical companies.

The campaign against generic drugs by PhRMA, the conservative think tanks, and their allies in the White House brought Clinton and his international allies into increasingly direct conflict with Bush. That conflict reached a crescendo in late March 2004, when the Bush administration sought to use an international conference in Botswana to enforce an international consensus around its position.

While vehemently denying any effort to curtail the use of generics, Tobias organized the conference in Botswana's capital city of Gaborone, inviting officials of WHO and the Southern Africa Development Council, along with European drug regulators, to discuss U.S. concerns about the prequalification program. But suspicions about American motives led the European Medical Evaluation Agency, roughly the European Union equivalent of the FDA, to cancel its participation. Days before the conference began, Representative Henry Waxman (D-CA), the ranking member of the House Committee on Government Reform, sent a long, angry letter to Bush protesting both the conference and PEPFAR policy rejecting generics.

"Your administration is circulating a proposal for consideration at an upcoming conference in Botswana that could impede access to the low-cost drugs needed to save the lives of millions of people living with HIV in developing countries," Waxman's March 26 letter began. "Adopting this proposal would be a tragic mistake."

The California liberal noted archly that U.S. agencies already purchased other generic medicines approved under WHO prequalification. He also mentioned that the Republican Party had received an estimated $40 million in contributions from pharmaceutical interests over the past several years.

A less pointed but equally passionate letter reached Bush's desk the same day from a bipartisan group of United States senators that included Massachusetts Democrat Ted Kennedy and Arizona Republican John McCain. "We question the purpose behind the Administration's duplicative process being developed to review the safety and efficacy of generic drugs used to treat persons with HIV/AIDS. A duplication of the existing and effective WHO review procedure will needlessly delay patients' access to these life-saving generic drugs. . . . Make no mistake, delay will cost lives."

Activists in Washington marked the opening of the Gaborone meeting with a spirited demonstration at PhRMA headquarters in Washington, not far from the White House. Denouncing Bush as a "puppet" of the industry, nine of the demonstrators chained themselves together and briefly blocked traffic in front of the building's lobby before local police arrested them. "The U.S. initiated the Botswana conference at the behest of the pharmaceutical companies, and its agenda is to protect their profits by blocking the procurement of generic AIDS drugs," said a spokesman for Africa Action, one of the groups sponsoring the protest.

Whatever Tobias intended to achieve in Gaborone, he succeeded only in galvanizing world opinion against the Bush administration, already stung by nearly universal condemnation of its ongoing misadventure in Iraq. Praise lavished on Bush when he announced PEPFAR was fading rapidly into skepticism, as the *New York Times* revealed in a front-page article on March 28, the day before the Botswana conference opened.

Headlined "Plan to Battle AIDS Worldwide Is Falling Short," the *Times* reported, "shortages of money and battles over patents have kept antiretroviral drugs from reaching more than 90 percent of the poor people who need them." While Bush had promised a year earlier in announcing PEPFAR that he would spend $15 billion over five years fighting AIDS in Africa and the Caribbean, "his budget requests have fallen far short of that goal," the story noted. He had requested only $200 million for the U.S. contribution to the Global Fund, despite a congressional authorization of $550 million.

The evident reason behind that budgetary decision, which went unmentioned in the *Times,* was the Bush administration's dispute over generics with the Global Fund as well as Clinton, WHO, and several other Western governments. It was a seething bureaucratic conflict that broke into public view on April 6—exactly a week after the Gaborone conference—when the World Bank joined the Global Fund in announcing that both organizations planned to assist the United Nations

Children's Fund (UNICEF) and the Clinton Foundation in purchasing generic drugs and discounted AIDS testing, to be made available in more than one hundred countries. Even though the ambitious partnership had not been fully elaborated—and aroused doubt in some quarters—its sharp divergence from U.S. policy could not have been clearer.

Only a year earlier, Clinton had welcomed Bush's bold intervention against the pandemic, unveiled by the administration in the wake of his own initiative. Now the former president and his successor were locked in worsening conflict.

———

Yet if Clinton was angered by the administration's rejection of his "systematic" plan for universal AIDS treatment, he never appeared to blame George W. Bush. And if Bush had once treated Clinton as a pariah over the alleged "trashing" of the White House, he displayed a far warmer attitude toward the Clintons when the opportunity arose. The occasion was the unveiling of the official portraits of Bill and Hillary Clinton at the presidential residence on the morning of June 14—only weeks after the tense confrontation over the Gaborone conference.

"President Clinton and Senator Clinton, welcome home," said Bush, smiling broadly as he stood on a dais in the East Room before an audience that included the entire Clinton and Rodham families as well as scores of former Clinton administration officials and aides who were invited to the unveiling and the luncheon that followed. The moment was both historical and intimate, marking the first time since their tumultuous departure that the Clintons had returned to the house they had occupied for eight years.

The pictures were historically significant, too, as the first portraits made by an African American to hang in the White House. Simmie Knox, son of a sharecropping family in Aliceville, Alabama, already had painted baseball great and childhood friend Hank Aaron, author Alex Haley, Bill Cosby, Muhammad Ali, and many equally celebrated figures, including the late Justice Thurgood Marshall and Justice Ruth Bader Ginsburg, who had personally recommended him to Hillary Clinton. At sixty-eight, Knox was finally receiving the national recognition he had earned many years earlier.

He had painted Bill Clinton facing straight ahead in a navy suit and light blue tie, and Hillary in a dark pantsuit with a wide smile. He felt a special affinity for Clinton, he later told reporters, because they both rose from "poor Southern families." He had the pleasure of sitting in the East Room and listening, as not just one but two presidents acclaimed his work.

While Bush's remarks were larded with characteristic banter, their longtime adversary greeted the Clintons in a surprising tone of warmth and respect. Noting that he and his father now called each other by their numerical order as president—"He's 41, I'm 43"—Bush turned to Clinton and said, "It's a great pleasure to honor number 42. We're glad you're here, 42."

He went on to praise both Clintons lavishly, calling attention to Bill's "incredible energy . . . great personal appeal . . . deep and far-ranging knowledge of public policy, great compassion for people in need, and the forward-looking spirit that Americans like in a president."

The laudatory description went on at length: "He's remembered in Hope, Arkansas, and other places along the way as an eager, good-hearted boy who seemed destined for big things. . . . He won his first statewide office at age 30, sworn in as governor at 32. He's a five-time governor of Arkansas; the first man from that state to become the president. He's also the first man in his party since Franklin Roosevelt to win a second term in the White House."

Bush even plugged Clinton's memoir, to be published within a few days. "I mean, I can tell you more of the story," he quipped, "but it's coming out in fine bookstores all over America."

Expressing admiration for Hillary's electoral triumph amid the "rough business" of New York politics, he called her "a person of great ability and serious purpose . . . a woman greatly admired in our country. . . . She inspires respect and loyalty from those who know her." Moreover, he noted archly, she happened to be "the only sitting senator whose portrait hangs in the White House."

It was Bush at his best—charming, funny, gracious—and the Clintons did their best to respond in kind. Each of them spoke about the emotional impact of the paintings of earlier presidents and first ladies, which had provided solace during difficult times in the Clinton years. Both gratefully acknowledged the kindness and cordiality of the current occupants, and the former president struck a note of bipartisan fellowship.

"Politics is noble work. I've just been doing some interviews in connection with my book . . . and I said, 'You know, most of the people I've known in this business, Republicans and Democrats, conservatives and liberals, were good people, honest people, and they did what they thought was right. And I hope that I'll live long enough to see American politics return to vigorous debates where we argue who's right and wrong, not who's good and bad.' My experience is, most of the people I've known in this work are good people who love their country desperately. And I am profoundly grateful that for a brief period I had a chance to be one of them."

Laura Bush concluded the ceremony with gushing congratulations. Gesturing to the paintings, the first lady said, "All who see them will be reminded of your dedication and all that you've done to strengthen our nation." Then she invited everyone to lunch in the State Dining Room.

––––––

The media barrage surrounding publication of *My Life*—a formidable 1,000-page-plus, three-and-a-quarter-pound tome—launched on the evening of Sunday, June 20, with a special episode of CBS's *60 Minutes*, an elaborate interview-travelogue taped by Dan Rather on location with Clinton at his boyhood home in Hope, Arkansas, at the site of the still unfinished Clinton Presidential Center and Library in Little Rock, and at his post-presidential residence in Chappaqua.

It took up the show's entire hour.

Making the most of the exclusive pre-publication access awarded by Clinton and his advisers, Rather led with probing questions about his childhood, his marriage, the Whitewater investigation, the Lewinsky affair, the Mideast peace negotiations, the Iraq War, and the Bush administration.

Aired on the eve of the release of the report of the National Commission on Terrorist Attacks Upon the United States, usually called the 9/11 Commission, the *60 Minutes* interview explored Clinton's failure to apprehend or kill Osama bin Laden at length. Explaining how he had tried to respond to terror threats during his presidency, Clinton told

Rather there was "not a shred of evidence" that Sudan had offered to turn over the al Qaeda leader. He refused to speculate on whether he or Bush could have prevented the 9/11 attack, preferring to leave that judgment to the commission.

The *60 Minutes* broadcast also featured a snippet of archived footage of Virginia Kelley, talking about her son not long before her death from cancer in 1994. "We had alcoholism in our family," she said. "And I think that Bill, in his mind, thought that I hadn't been dealt the best hand in the world. And he was determined to make up for that. Determined. He's just been a wonderful son, just a wonderful son." Clinton told Rather he had never seen that clip of his mother, and was visibly moved.

While hardly a puff piece, the cool and equable Rather interview could scarcely have prepared Clinton for what appeared the next morning on the front page of the *New York Times*—a long, scornful indictment of his book by Michiko Kakutani, the paper's lead reviewer. *My Life* was "sloppy, self-indulgent, and often eye-crossingly dull," she charged, "a hodgepodge of jottings" and "a messy pastiche of everything Mr. Clinton ever remembered and wanted to set down in print." She mocked him, "prattling away not for the reader, but for himself and some distant recording angel of history."

The result was an endless, stupefying sound as dull as his infamous 1988 Democratic convention speech, according to Kakutani, which had won applause only when he uttered the phrase "In closing . . ." Finally, she accused him of "lying" not only about the Lewinsky dalliance but about "real estate," a blunt allusion to the sore subject of the Whitewater land deal investigated by the *Times*.

Predictably, Kakutani's appraisal enraged Clinton and—although he later persuaded himself that the majority of reviews were positive—her harshly negative assessment seemed to influence the tenor of important reviews that followed. The *Washington Post* found the book "disappointing, even bizarre." The *Los Angeles Times* complained about "numbing stretches of tedious self-absorption." *USA Today* derided it as "more exhausting than exhaustive." The Associated Press review compared the experience of reading Clinton's memoir to "being locked in a small room with a very gregarious man who insists on reading his entire appointment book, day by day, beginning in 1946."

That summer and for years after, Clinton would seize any chance to rebut and criticize Kakutani in turn. "She couldn't have read the whole book," he would say. "Her attack on it said practically phrase for phrase the same thing she said about Hillary's book"—*Living History*, a major bestseller published exactly a year earlier by Simon & Schuster. "It was obvious to me [Kakutani] didn't care about people or politics or policy."

He also believed that her review was only the latest episode in a long history of caustic coverage of him and his wife in the paper of record, whose enmity he simply took for granted. "The people at the *Times* just wanted to make sure [the book] couldn't win any prizes," he said. "That was the only horrible review, which was because I pointed out the level of dishonesty in their coverage of Whitewater. And I was still quite complimentary, I said the *Times* was the best newspaper in America."

It was true that Kakutani's reviews of the two Clinton memoirs were similar, and that both echoed the rancor so often voiced over the years on the paper's op-ed pages by the likes of Maureen Dowd and William Safire. It was also true that Kakutani had simply failed to mention Clinton's criticism of the paper itself.

A week later, on the front page of the *New York Times Book Review*, Larry McMurtry's byline appeared over the most favorable review that *My Life* was to receive anywhere. To the great Western novelist, Clinton's book was a "big puffy plumcake of an autobiography."

According to McMurtry, "I happen to like long, smart, dense narratives and read *My Life* straight through, happily. I may not know Bill Clinton any better than I did when I started, but I know recent history better, which surely can't hurt."

Seeking to understand why Knopf had paid upward of $10 million for a heavy, concentrated narrative by "the world's premier policy wonk," McMurtry made a penetrating observation about the impact of "Clinton's long coyote-and-roadrunner race with the press."

Ironically, his memoir had commanded that huge advance because "the very press that wanted to discredit him and perhaps even run him out of town instead made him a celebrity, a far more expensive thing than a mere president. Clinton's now up there with Madonna, in the highlands that are even above talent. . . . And somehow, vaguely, it all has to do with sex—not necessarily sex performed, just sex in the world's head."

Much to Clinton's satisfaction, McMurtry concluded with a few sentences lightly ridiculing his fellow Texan, former independent counsel Kenneth Starr, who is depicted as a charlatan and criminal in *My Life*.

Dueling reviews aside, Clinton knew that the book had suffered from rushed writing and editing, especially the latter half about his presidency. He knew, too, that page after page of names, moments, scenes, and analyses had left everything somehow undifferentiated, of equal weight and thus little weight, despite the book's engaging prose and often inspiring story. He regretted that sections of the text that he considered important and revealing—such as his inside account of the disastrous 1993 Somalia intervention portrayed in the movie *Black Hawk Down*—had gotten lost within the book's massive bulk.

But so far as commercial success was concerned, none of that mattered at all—not the rush to publish, not the length, not the verbosity, not the negative reviews, and certainly not the sniping of Clinton's old antagonists in the conservative media, who instantly commenced a steady bombardment of abuse. ("It should be called *My Lie!*" bellowed Rush Limbaugh.) Even before its official publication date, the book ranked number one on Amazon.com's bestseller list.

On June 22, its first day in bookstores, *My Life* sold more than 400,000 copies, triggering an instant second printing of another 725,000, although initial orders were well over 1.5 million. The first-day sales broke the previous nonfiction record set by Hillary Clinton the year before with *Living History*, and the publisher announced on July 2 that his book had already sold over a million copies, with a third printing ordered.

Ultimate domestic sales in hardcover and trade paperback would exceed two million, pushed along by a wave of media coverage that stretched from *Oprah*, *Today*, and *Good Morning America*, whose producers surrendered their usual insistence on exclusivity, to nearly every little newspaper and radio station in the country.

Riding that wave, Clinton would spend the next four weeks promoting the book on a tour that took him from New York City—where he signed more than two thousand books at the first stop, a Barnes &

Noble store in Rockefeller Center, and another two thousand at a small Harlem shop near his office called Hue-man Books—to Los Angeles, San Francisco, Berkeley, San Jose, and Seattle on the West Coast, as well as Denver, Chicago, Philadelphia, Washington, Atlanta, Miami, and several stops in Arkansas.

The first man in line at the first Barnes & Noble had camped out all night on the concrete sidewalk outside the store, along with dozens more fans, some in sleeping bags. That night, feeling sore in the shoulders, Clinton greeted more than a thousand invited guests at a lavish book party hosted by his publishers at the Metropolitan Museum of Art.

———

The only obvious stop left off the book tour was Boston, where Clinton was scheduled to appear July 26 to deliver the opening speech at the Democratic National Convention. Determined to avoid drawing attention from Senator John Kerry, he had instructed the Knopf publicists that he would do no signings or other events there to avoid any risk of upstaging his party's nominee.

Clinton had always liked Kerry, and he deeply appreciated the nominee's decision to feature him on opening night in prime time—a clear break from the Gore campaign's decision to shun him four years earlier.

Unlike Al Gore, the Massachusetts senator sought Clinton's advice regularly. The former president had declined to endorse any candidate in the primaries, as an old friend of both former Vermont governor Howard Dean ("quite a good governor and a really able guy") and retired General Wesley Clark ("enormous regard for his intelligence and ability"), another son of Arkansas whom he had known since the 1960s.

But by late spring Clinton had known that Kerry would win the nomination. He had given the senator an impassioned earful about the campaign's halting response to the "Swift Boat" smears of Kerry's record as a Navy captain in Vietnam by an "independent" right-wing group.

Launched just as Kerry clinched the nomination, those attacks had been traced to political operatives and major donors from Texas, including several close associates of Karl Rove, chief political adviser to George W. Bush. Clinton had no doubt that the disgusting aspersions on Kerry's service—based on false claims that he had not earned his numerous medals and decorations—were directed from the White House.

"I was so angry at those Swift Boat people, I may even have called him [before he called me]," recalled Clinton. "I said 'John, I don't like the way this is being handled. You waited three weeks to answer!'" Clinton felt that the campaign's response had "legitimized the attack by being too detailed."

Naturally Clinton had his own ideas about the proper way to answer the media onslaught, as he told Kerry. "You should invite the president and the vice president to join you at a national press conference to talk about what you all did in the Vietnam War—and then smile."

Like Clinton himself, the hawkish president and vice president had both avoided serving in Vietnam—Bush by using his father's political connections to get a safe berth in the Texas Air National Guard, Clinton and Cheney with student deferments.

"If you do that, John, this thing will die," Clinton urged. "These people are *not nice.* You've got to hit 'em a gut shot." When he hung up the phone, Clinton believed that Kerry just might take his advice.

But by late July, when the Boston convention opened, the Kerry campaign had failed to mount an effective response. The Swift Boat campaign had inflicted real damage, shaping perceptions of the Democratic nominee while distracting public attention from both Bush's dubious National Guard service and rising doubts about the disastrous American occupation of Iraq.

In his convention speech, Clinton delivered a stinging rebuttal of the assault on Kerry, and a tough assessment of Bush's presidency, wrapped in a testimonial to his candidate's courage and constancy.

With Hillary standing beside him onstage, he looked out at the darkened auditorium. Beginning with gracious remarks about Gore and former president Jimmy Carter, who had preceded him at the podium, he lauded the record of his own presidency and Democratic policy in general, lambasted Bush's foreign and domestic failures, and concluded succinctly: "We tried it their way for twelve years, then our way for eight years, then we tried it their way for four more." He grinned broadly. "By the only test that matters—whether people were better off when we were finished than when we started—our way worked better."

Then he turned to the question of character.

"Now, let me tell you know what I know about John Kerry. I've been seeing all of the Republican ads about him. Let me tell you what I know about him.

"During the Vietnam War, many young men, including the current president, the vice president, and me, could have gone to Vietnam and didn't. John Kerry came from a privileged background. He could have avoided going too, but instead, he said: Send me.

"When they sent those swift boats up the river in Vietnam, and they told them their job was to draw hostile fire, to wave the American flag and bait the enemy to come out and fight, John Kerry said: Send me."

And he went on as the thousands in Boston's Convention Center picked up his refrain, rising from their seats, waving signs, shouting: "Send me!"

Journalists covering the convention seemed less impressed by the speech's impact on his fellow Democrats than the mundane fact that he had actually ended on time. As the *New York Times* reported the following day, "Mr. Clinton's prime-time speech instantly dominated a convention that featured two ex-presidents and an almost-president. . . . For nearly 30 minutes, Mr. Clinton held command over an arena packed with Democratic delegates, prompting laughter, cheers and finally roars of approval."

He still had it.

———

By necessity if not choice, Bill and Hillary Clinton led largely separate daily lives ever since she began her service in the Senate. He spent little time in Washington, while she came up to Chappaqua roughly two weekends every month. They also spent vacations together and usually escaped for a week in August to Martha's Vineyard, the island off Cape Cod long favored by literary intellectuals, artists, Democratic political figures, and an assortment of celebrities like their friends Mary Steenburgen and Ted Danson. The actors had a beautiful oceanside home with plenty of private space for the Clintons to relax. It was a pleasant habit they had established during White House days, when the presidential couple had visited the Vineyard every summer but one.

Late that August, both Clintons went up to stay with Steenburgen and Danson at their home. One afternoon, following nine holes at the

Farm Neck Golf Club, he returned complaining of a terrible pain in his back. Their hosts sent him and Hillary to their personal chiropractor on the island.

When they arrived at her office in Vineyard Haven, both Clintons noticed that the place had a slightly hippie, New Age atmosphere, with statues of the Buddha decorating the room, which he considered a bit much. But he hoped that she might do something to relieve the pain.

"I haven't had a backache in so long," he told the chiropractor, "but this *really* hurts." She asked him to extend both arms, and then began to tap on his chest with her fingers, directly over his heart.

"I sense blockage," the chiropractor said as she tapped harder on his chest. "I think there's blockage."

Looking directly at his wife, Clinton rolled his eyes slightly. "You know, I was just at the Mayo Clinic in Arizona, they gave me a lot of tests, and they said I was fine."

It was quite true that Clinton had submitted to a complete physical at the Mayo Clinic's campus in Scottsdale, Arizona, at the end of July, mostly because Hillary had insisted that he go. He had chosen Mayo because that was where Dr. Connie Mariano, the Navy officer who had served as White House physician during both of his terms, had located her post-government practice.

And it was also true that the assessment of his overall health by the Mayo specialists had been encouraging—in fact, his blood lipid tests were good enough that the doctors had told him to stop taking Zocor, the cholesterol-lowering statin drug he had used since leaving the White House, when his numbers had been frighteningly bad.

Having pushed him to seek medical attention, Hillary had felt a sense of relief when he went out to Arizona. She had grown increasingly concerned about her husband's health during their long walks on hiking paths in the Westchester countryside near their home. His difficulty climbing hills, his frequent shortness of breath, even on terrain that wasn't very challenging, had disturbed her.

More than once she had urged him to get himself "checked out," but usually he had brushed her off, saying he was "just tired" from his taxing schedule of travel, meetings, and long days working on his book. Yet for months he had often felt what he would later describe as "tightness" in his chest after exercising.

Returning home from the Vineyard, he had taken a speaking trip to Iceland and Ireland, then signed books in Pittsburgh, St. Louis, and Cleveland before flying down to New Orleans on September 1 for an event at the city's Barnes & Noble that had attracted more than three thousand people. That evening he had dined well in the Crescent City, but in Chappaqua the next morning his breathing problem worsened.

Seated comfortably at home while reading, without exerting himself at all, Clinton suddenly felt that same painful constriction around his rib cage. He mentioned the discomfort to Oscar Flores, who immediately told him to call Dr. Lisa Bardack, a Westchester physician who was among the doctors providing care for him and Hillary. After Flores prodded him once or twice, he placed the call. When he reached Bardack, she instructed him to proceed without delay to the nearest medical facility, Northern Westchester Hospital in Mount Kisco, just three miles north.

Hillary was in Syracuse that morning, waiting for him to join her at the annual state fair. He called her cell phone as he climbed into the black Suburban with two Secret Service agents to head for the hospital. Dr. Bardack met him at the emergency room, where tests swiftly established that he hadn't suffered a heart attack. Walking on a treadmill, he passed a stress test, but still felt "something was wrong."

Listening to Clinton and consulting with other doctors at the hospital, Bardack made an appointment for him to undergo an angiogram the next morning at Westchester Medical Center, a larger facility several miles south in the town of Valhalla.

He returned to Chappaqua wearing a heart monitor around his neck, with instructions to get some rest. By then, Doug Band and Justin Cooper had showed up at the hospital, having rushed there after hearing the news from Flores. The doctors directed the two aides to spend the night with Clinton in Chappaqua, and to remain awake to monitor his condition. Exhausted, they eventually fell asleep on couches in the living room, only to be awakened by Clinton standing over them at around 4 a.m., waiting to head to the hospital.

In the operating room, Clinton lay prone and strapped down on a special X-ray table. His chest was blanketed with electrodes; an intravenous tube snaked from one arm, and a blood-pressure cuff tethered the other. Through an incision in his groin, the surgeon threaded a catheter tube upward through his arteries toward his heart, where an injection of dye would reveal any blockage instantly on the X-ray screen.

Through a glass window, Band and Cooper could easily observe the doctors standing around Clinton—and saw their faces turn pale with horror as the imaging appeared. With two of his main arteries almost totally blocked, the former president was teetering on the edge of a serious and perhaps deadly heart attack.

CHAPTER NINE

The almost complete occlusion of Bill Clinton's arteries required immediate surgical correction to avoid a heart attack, but the discovery of that potentially fatal problem on the Friday before Labor Day weekend was inconvenient, to say the least.

The former president's family and many of his staff were scattered. Hillary Clinton was in upstate Syracuse, almost 250 miles north of Chappaqua, waiting for her husband to join her in a senatorial visit to the annual state fair, where he liked to say he "played the token redneck." Chelsea Clinton, then working for McKinsey & Company, was away in Paris on business. Doug Band was headed to Paris as well. Yet the people closest to Clinton could be summoned quickly in an emergency and all would return at top speed. On a holiday weekend, finding the best surgeon was a much greater challenge.

Within an hour after the angiogram revealed his dangerous condition—including two major blood vessels that were more than 90 percent blocked—Clinton, his physician Dr. Bardack, and some of her colleagues at Westchester Medical Center began to seek a top surgeon. Not long after 6 a.m., one of the Westchester physicians reached out to Wayne Isom, a renowned cardiac surgeon at Manhattan's Cornell Medical Center, who had performed successful operations over the years on TV host Larry King, former CBS news anchor Walter Cronkite, violinist Isaac Stern, and former treasury secretary William Simon—and had become something of a celebrity himself after a highly publicized surgical rescue of late-night host David Letterman in January 2000.

Unsurprisingly, Dr. Isom was not on duty. He took the call at his summer home in East Hampton where—perhaps even less surprisingly—he was looking forward to an early tee time at the exclusive Maidstone Club. According to him, the caller said that he was needed to operate on "an important person."

"Well, they're *all* important," drawled Isom, a blunt-spoken Texan. "Who is it?"

"I can't tell you."

"If you can't tell me," he said, "then I'm going to play golf." Before he hung up, however, the other doctor quickly asked whom he might recommend instead.

"I'd select Craig Smith," he answered, naming the head of cardiothoracic surgery at New York Presbyterian, the hospital associated with Columbia University, which was affiliated with Cornell Medical Center.

The doctors reached Smith's secretary, who rang him on his cell phone. He was in a car with his wife, speeding up the New York State Thruway toward their summer place in the Adirondacks, where they had planned to celebrate their thirty-fourth wedding anniversary that weekend. She answered the call and urged him to find the next exit, turn around, and head back to the city. Told that he was wanted to operate on Clinton, the bluff fifty-five-year-old surgeon mused, "This will be interesting."

On Smith's instructions, Band—with the assistance of four Secret Service agents—moved Clinton in an ambulance to New York Presbyterian, an imposing complex of buildings in northern Manhattan, about half a mile from the George Washington Bridge. In the meantime Band had alerted Herbert Pardes, the distinguished physician who served as the hospital's president and CEO, to Clinton's impending arrival. Cooper had gone ahead to prepare the way with Pardes so that Clinton's arrival would occur as discreetly as possible. When they showed up, hospital staff escorted them to an entire floor of VIP rooms, with stunning views of the Hudson River—and highly restricted access. Word of the former president's illness had somehow leaked to the press already, and reporters were beginning to swarm around the hospital. To contain them and hundreds of curious hospital employees who might be tempted to peek, special passes were issued to those permitted access to Clinton's floor.

Directly overseeing his care were Dr. Allan Schwartz, the hospital's forthright, laconic chief of cardiology, who also chaired that department at Columbia's medical school, and Robert Kelly, a physician and administrator who served as the hospital's chief operating officer.

Even with several top-ranked doctors and a world-class hospital on highest alert, Clinton could do little but sit and wait for another two days. The Westchester doctors, understandably frightened by the angiogram images, had pumped blood thinners into his system to prevent the seemingly imminent medical catastrophe. But the Presbyterian team had to wait for those drugs to wear off before opening up his chest for a quadruple bypass operation.

By all accounts, Clinton remained calm, even as tension built around him in the hours before his surgery. When Smith came by to see him, the surgeon found his patient "engaging" and "easy to talk to." Having escaped the worst, Clinton said later, he felt a certain sense of relief, understanding that his chances of survival had in fact improved enormously over the previous forty-eight hours. Coronary artery bypass grafting—colloquially known as a "cabbage" from its acronym—is a procedure so ordinary and so reliable that doctors as skilled as Smith could do two or even three a day, with a fatality rate below one percent.

The odds of death from an unexpected heart attack were far higher, particularly if it occurred while Clinton happened to be on an airplane. And not long after Labor Day, he had been scheduled for a three-week trip to promote his book overseas—beginning with a long, transcontinental flight to Asia.

While he waited, Clinton played cards with Band and Cooper, read books, watched television, chatted with the surgeons, and spent time talking with Hillary and Chelsea, who arrived late in the evening. Both Band and Cooper had their own rooms on the hospital floor to stay near their boss. When Hillary walked in and saw that the two young aides had ordered burgers and fries from a nearby Wendy's for dinner, she practically exploded.

"What are you *eating*?" cried the senator. Then she turned to the young doctors standing around. "Please get check-ups for these boys, as soon as possible!" They did.

Not too long after she arrived at the hospital, a tense but smiling Hillary went outside to deliver a brief statement to the press corps on the hospital steps.

"I want to report to you that my husband is doing very well. He's in great humor. He's beating us all at cards and the rest of the games we're playing."

Praising the "excellent care" provided by the hospital's doctors, nurses, and staff, she said, "We're delighted that we have good health insurance. That makes a big difference. And I hope someday everybody will be able to say the same thing." The Clinton Foundation posted a similar but longer statement online, in response to tens of thousands of email messages received from around the world.

During those two long days, which felt like weeks, an outpouring of goodwill messages swamped not only the foundation's website but Clinton's personal staff and Hillary's Senate office. Hundreds of telephone calls poured in from friends and strangers expressing concern—including Vice President Dick Cheney, who had undergone quadruple bypass surgery in 1988—as well as a stream of carefully vetted visitors, notably U2's Bono and Al Gore.

Renowned cardiologist and author Dean Ornish, a Clinton friend who had admonished him for years to adopt a low-fat vegan diet, tried to call several times, and finally got through. Hours before his surgery, Ornish tried to persuade Clinton to heal himself with dietary changes and exercise instead. At some point, a hospital employee who went into the computer system foolishly trying to look up "Clinton" was traced and swiftly fired. He was registered under an assumed name.

Outside the hospital, a sizable press contingent camped out, waiting for occasional word from the doctors and family. An enterprising photographer with a powerful telephoto lens set up on the elevated West Side Highway, and captured Clinton in his hospital room. After the *New York Post* published the grainy image on its front page, he quipped, "At least I wasn't wearing one of those open-backed hospital gowns."

Indeed, Clinton was deeply touched by the level of public interest in his condition—and the outpouring of sympathy symbolized by the thousands of messages and prayers posted to the foundation's website and the truckloads of flowers sent to his Harlem office. Contrary to the expectations of his critics, dismal memories of the final hours of his presidency seemed to be fading, in an atmosphere of renewed affection.

———

While Clinton had confessed to being "a little scared" of the impending operation, he felt a sense of relief when he was finally prepped for surgery shortly before 8 a.m. on Monday, September 6. He later told ABC correspondent Diane Sawyer that as the anesthesia put him to sleep, he had "an amazing experience," with dark visions of "death masks being crushed," and then images of Hillary, Chelsea, and others appearing in circles of light before flying away.

As he was wheeled into the operating theater, Band and Cooper followed, with two Secret Service agents. The hospital staff taped paper over the windows of the room to block any attempt to photograph the surgery. As the operation proceeded, Hillary waited outside. Band went in and out of the operating room to brief her at each stage.

Once Dr. Smith had sawed Clinton's chest open, he removed arteries from either side of the breastbone to create three grafts or shunts around the blocked blood vessels leading to his heart; he made a fourth from an artery taken from the left thigh. At first, everything proceeded smoothly and without incident.

But suddenly, after a couple of hours, the mood in the operating room changed.

The original plan had been to operate on Clinton without actually stopping his heart and putting him on a heart-lung machine—to perform what is called "beating heart" or "off pump" surgery, in which a device is used to limit the motion of a portion of the heart while the surgeon sews on a grafted artery. When surgeons elect to use this method, their aim is to limit the likelihood of future strokes, memory loss, and other potential problems that are believed to arise from completely stopping and then restarting the heart.

Midway through, Dr. Smith shifted Clinton to the heart-lung machine already set up for emergency use in the operating room. This change required very rapid and efficient movement by the surgeon—and all the other hospital personnel in the room—to ensure that the blood supply to Clinton's brain and other organs wasn't interrupted too long.

At a post-operative press conference, Dr. Smith would acknowledge that there had been "a few anxious moments" during the procedure. While he didn't explain further, he probably meant the unexpected shift to the heart-lung machine. For well over an hour, Clinton's heart was stopped completely while a machine took over the work of pumping oxygenated blood through his body.

Just before 1:30 p.m., Dr. Smith finished stitching up Clinton's chest. Still unconscious, strapped to a gurney, and breathing through a tube, the former president was wheeled into an intensive-care recovery room. Within minutes, Jim Kennedy began to call and email reporters with the news: The operation had been successful. The former president was expected to recover fully. The doctors would appear on the hospital steps to speak with the press around 4 p.m.

————

Tall, thin, dry, and deliberate in manner, Dr. Allan Schwartz loomed over the bouquet of microphones as he recounted again the timeline of Clinton's illness. The cardiologist confirmed that the surgery had been successful, that the patient was "in good spirits," and that had the former president not gotten effective medical attention when he did, he would have been in very deep trouble.

With characteristic understatement, Schwartz explained, "There was a substantial likelihood that he would have had a substantial heart attack." He went on to explain that once Clinton left the hospital, the former president would commence a daily regimen that included low-dose aspirin, a statin drug to lower cholesterol, a beta-blocker to prevent irregular heartbeats, and another medication to maintain lower blood pressure. Just as important would be strict adherence to a diet low in saturated fats and sodium—and, when he was sufficiently recovered, a course of rehabilitative exercise. Dr. Smith reported that aside from those few fretful moments, the surgery had been completed without incident.

By late Monday evening, nurses removed the breathing tube that had left Clinton uncomfortable and unable to speak for several hours. He began to take some liquid nourishment the next morning. Over the following three days, he underwent the same painful ritual endured by countless other bypass patients: sitting up in bed, putting his legs over the side, standing up, walking around his room, and then circling the hospital ward, slowly and exhaustingly. But his progress was steady. On Friday, September 10, he returned to Chappaqua.

When Clinton awoke from his surgery, he felt happy and elated to be alive, he later recalled—and that feeling lasted. While most heart patients awake with similar joy, many soon confront a sense of mortality, often for the first time, and suffer from sadness or even depression following surgery. One of Hillary's Senate colleagues had warned her that after his bypass, he had sat and wept for four days straight.

Clinton suffered no such bouts of melancholy. Having learned of his father's death at an early age, and then seeing several friends die young, he had contemplated death for many years—not obsessively, but as a simple and inevitable fact of existence. "I've never been under any illusion that I would live forever. I knew that sooner or later, my time would be up."

Physically, he was very sore, especially across his chest, where the rib cage had been cut down the middle, pulled apart, and then stapled back together. He had to work every day at restoring his own mobility, taking long walks through local parks with Band and Cooper (and a couple of Secret Service agents), and that required no small effort. Emotionally, he felt "grateful for every day of life I had." He was "more conscious of people," wanting to see and talk with friends even more than before.

Awakening to every new day at home, with no pressing responsibilities, Clinton also felt a refreshing sense of relaxation.

For the first time in decades, he was left to do more or less whatever he wanted—to read, watch movies or television, talk with friends on the phone, take a walk or a nap. Aside from brief vacations, which had almost always involved some kind of work, his life had included very little downtime since he first ran for an Arkansas congressional seat in 1974.

"By 2004, I had been working like crazy for more than thirty years. I'd had vacations, but I'd had thirty years of sleep deprivation, thirty years of exhausting work. I enjoyed the time off. I enjoyed the recovery process. I enjoyed learning how to walk and how to climb a hill again." Although recuperating his strength made him want to accomplish more, he was also learning to enjoy more—to shrug off feelings of guilt if he chose to take time off rather than work constantly.

Not all the changes in his personality were positive, as he conceded readily. He was more impatient, no longer quite so able to hide his "intolerance for dreck," a skill he had developed as a politician. He was more irritable when he grew tired, which happened more, and less able "to control my emotional and psychological responses to fatigue than I was before it happened." And he wasn't thrilled to notice these aspects of his recovery. "I didn't like becoming more of a whiner." He tried to notice when he was getting tired, so he could rest before he started to become irritable.

And for all his talk of learning to unwind, the enforced relaxation and isolation ultimately left him bored and frustrated. Sitting on the couch, watching movies and reading, even taking longer and longer walks every day, inevitably left him restless. "Those weeks felt like forever," he said years later. "It felt like we weren't doing anything, for the longest time."

———

At first the doctors had thought Clinton was joking when he told them that he planned to go out on the road for the Democratic ticket of John Kerry and John Edwards. When they realized he wasn't kidding, their reaction was roughly the same as if he'd announced a new interest in skydiving. The rigors of campaign travel were not advised for a heart patient who had not even begun, let alone completed, the slow march toward rehabilitation.

A month after surgery, he was still "pretty frail," by his own estimation, suffering pain from the chest incision and feeling quite exhausted after walking a mile. But he assured the doctors and his equally skeptical staff that he would be going, sooner or later. He appreciated Kerry—"I thought he was underrated"—and felt profoundly angered by the Republican attacks on the Democratic war hero.

But there was another consideration, as he acknowledged later. "I didn't want there to be any doubt that I was using this as an excuse not to weigh in"—so that Kerry would lose and leave the Democratic nomination open for Hillary in 2008. Besides, he had made a personal promise to the candidate that he would campaign, when Kerry called him in the hospital over the Labor Day weekend before his surgery.

The question was not whether to appear with Kerry, but where and when. Communication with the Kerry campaign was eased by the presence of several former Clinton White House staffers there, including former press secretaries Mike McCurry and Joe Lockhart, who maintained a close relationship with his old boss. If Clinton couldn't travel yet, he could still send out fundraising letters and record "robocalls," the taped messages, tailored to particular states and constituencies, that reached voters on their home telephones.

But the robocalls weren't enough for a Democratic campaign still struggling by mid-October to overtake Bush even in reliably blue states like Pennsylvania. At his own campaign appearances, Kerry started quoting his phone conversations with the former president ("Bill Clinton and I were talking, and he said . . ."); then on October 19, he told reporters in Wilkes-Barre, "I think it's possible in the next days former President Clinton may be here, working." McCurry quickly added that Kerry was only "expressing a hope."

Mediating the negotiation between Clinton and his doctors, Doug Band broached an idea that proved helpful. His older brother Roger, an emergency-care doctor at the Hospital of the University of Pennsylvania in Philadelphia, could travel with the Clinton entourage to keep an eye on the former president and administer immediate care, if necessary. He would be an unobtrusive and trusted presence—looking almost enough like Doug to be mistaken for him—with the skill to handle any medical incident. With the doctors' assent, Roger Band, MD, became the former president's traveling physician. Intended as a stopgap measure for a few 2004 campaign stops, "Doc" Band would join Clinton on many trips for more than a decade, charging no fees and flying around the world with him several times over.

"If this isn't a good idea for my heart, I don't know what is," Clinton told a wildly cheering rally as colorful confetti fell around him in downtown Philadelphia on October 25, with only a week left until Election Day. Standing beside him onstage at Love Park, overlooking a huge lunchtime crowd estimated at 100,000 or more, was a beaming Kerry—who embraced him not once but twice, and held up their clasped hands repeatedly. "Isn't it great to have Bill Clinton back on the trail?" he exulted. He was determined not to repeat the errors of Al Gore, who had coldly distanced himself from the president he served.

Looking pinched and pale, Clinton spoke for less than ten minutes—possibly a personal record for brevity on the stump. But his appearance made national headlines and thrilled the Kerry campaign. Later that same day, he flew down to Florida, another battleground state where he remained highly popular. He appeared for Kerry in New Mexico a few days later and then, on the final Sunday before Election Day, went home to Arkansas to mobilize black voters behind the Democrat.

On November 2, Bush defeated Kerry by only three million votes,

with a margin of 35 votes in the Electoral College. It was a narrow victory that only looked impressive in contrast with the deadlocked contest against Al Gore. Of the states where Clinton campaigned, only
Pennsylvania went for Kerry. But nobody would ever be able to deny he
had risen from his sickbed to try.

———

"It was wet."

That is how Clinton would always remember November 18, a day
he had awaited for nearly six years, when he returned to Little Rock just
two weeks after the election for the official opening of his $200 million
library, the William J. Clinton Presidential Center and Park. Thousands
of friends and supporters were expected to attend the grand event, including three other presidents—George W. Bush, his father, George
Herbert Walker Bush, and Jimmy Carter, all of whom were to deliver
speeches to mark the occasion. And with President Bush coming, the
entire White House press corps and national media would cover the
event, starting with live broadcasts from Little Rock days before the actual ceremony.

All over town, officials and residents prepared for a week of worldwide attention. Republican governor Mike Huckabee ordered a swift
renovation of the state capitol grounds. The municipal airport commission, chaired by a Clinton friend, already had spent as much as a
million dollars refurbishing its facilities, with fresh landscaping and
even a new fountain to impress the influx of distinguished visitors from
both coasts and beyond.

The city was excited, but the weather forecasts leading up to November 18 did not look promising; in fact, the ominous predictions had
inspired Stephanie Streett, the center's executive director, to procure
tens of thousands of umbrellas and plastic ponchos in advance. On
the day before, only a slight drizzle had fallen on the city. Doug Band
had kept checking the forecast with the crew of Air Force One, old
friends whose access to the latest meteorological data was unrivaled in
government.

At about 2 a.m. the night before, following a lavish pre-opening
party at the library, Band had checked with them again to determine
whether he should order a special tent for the dais where Clinton and

his presidential guests were to sit during the ceremony. According to the Air Force One forecast, rainfall was expected to stop in Little Rock before dawn. He didn't order a tent for the dais. Even if the rain continued, he thought, providing shelter for the presidents and their spouses would look wrong while everyone else in the audience endured the weather. It was a choice he would question hours later.

With almost biblical intensity, the pitiless rainstorm drenched everyone, from presidents to ordinary citizens, as Marine guards struggled to hold umbrellas over the distinguished guests on the dais. For the most significant day since he had left the White House—indeed, one of the most important days in his life—to be drowned in that deluge was a devastating disappointment to Clinton.

Dozens of foreign ambassadors, many former prime ministers and presidents, including Canada's Chrétien, Norway's Brundtland, and Israel's Peres, made the difficult journey to Little Rock from locations as distant as Beirut and Beijing. A planeload of former staffers and supporters had arrived from Washington, while loyal Hollywood friends like Barbra Streisand, Robin Williams, and Kevin Spacey had flown in from the West Coast. John Kerry showed up in one of his first public appearances since the election, evoking spontaneous cheers when the crowd recognized him. So did Al and Tipper Gore.

Clinton tried resolutely to maintain a cheerful affect, but he couldn't quite conceal how much the weather saddened and frustrated him. He looked better than he had during the campaign but with a lingering pallor. The long hours of a week's celebration had fatigued him.

Still, the overflowing crowd that had come to celebrate this monument to his presidency buoyed him. So did the two-hour ceremony, which included African drummers, Latin American singers, a choir from the local black college, and his pals Bono and The Edge, rocking out under the falling sky. Ordinary Americans were brought onstage to talk about the changes wrought in their own lives by his administration—a woman who left welfare for work, a student who served as an AmeriCorps volunteer, an older man who got precious time with his dying daughter thanks to the Family and Medical Leave Act. On his book tour, Clinton had encountered dozens of people with similar personal stories—the character witnesses for him and his presidency.

Years later, he would remember those little testimonials, which left

as vivid an impression on him as the gracious and amusing remarks offered by his White House predecessors. Rarely seen together on one
stage, his fellow members of the presidential club delivered the kind of
tribute that the first president to be impeached in more than a century
could scarcely have imagined. (Only Gerald Ford, who had suffered
two strokes and almost never appeared in public, at age ninety-one,
was absent.)

Jimmy Carter's Sunday-school demeanor and dour reputation
tended to overshadow his dry humor. But he opened with a funny
anecdote about his first meeting with a very young Clinton, whom
he claimed to have mistaken at first for a messenger. Since then they
hadn't always gotten along well—the prim Georgian was volubly judg-
mental during the Lewinsky scandal, and again when the Rich pardon
emerged. But on this occasion, he seemed eager to make amends for a
fateful incident that had occurred when he was president and Clinton
was serving his first term as governor.

"I made some mistakes in 1980 during the Mariel boat lift, and the
presence of Cuban refugees in Arkansas may have cost him his reelection," Carter said. "For that, I apologize. But I and the people of this nation are grateful he overcame that temporary setback and went on to
become our president." Coming from a man he had never much liked
but nevertheless admired, those words clearly touched Clinton.

The sitting president he had just worked so hard to defeat was
equally cordial, alternating between sober observations and laugh lines.
George W. Bush declared how pleased he and First Lady Laura Bush
were to be present for "this happy and historic occasion," congratulated
Clinton as "Mr. President," and went on to praise him extravagantly:

"His home state elected him to governor in the 1970s, the 1980s
and the 1990s because he was an innovator, a serious student of policy
and a man of great compassion.

"In the White House, the whole nation witnessed his brilliance and
his mastery of detail, his persuasive power and his persistence.

"The president is not the kind to give up a fight. His staffers were
known to say, 'If Clinton were the *Titanic*, the iceberg would sink.'"

Next Bush's father took the podium, and he didn't stint on the
wisecracks either. Playing on the cliché of "the man from Hope,"
George H. W. Bush spoke of how Clinton "went on to touch the lives

of millions around the world as president of the United States, bringing them hope.

"Of course," he quickly added, "it always has to be said that Bill Clinton was one of the most gifted American political figures in modern
times. Trust me, I learned this the hard way.

"And seeing him out on the campaign trail, it was plain to see how
he fed off the energy and the hopes and the aspirations of the American
people. Simply put, he was a natural, and he made it look too easy"—a
pause—"and, oh, how I hated him for that."

The crowd roared and Clinton chortled as the elder Bush continued in that self-deprecating vein, recalling his ill-fated 1992 encounters
with Clinton and a certain third-party candidate.

"You know, to be very frank with you now, I hated debates.

"And when I checked my watch at the Richmond debate, it's true, I
was wondering when the heck Ross Perot would be finished and how I
could get out of there."

When Bush had finished the fraternity-style ribbing, however, the
man Clinton had evicted from the White House concluded in a tone
of intimacy. Among the "great blessings" of leaving behind the presidency, he confided, "is the way one-time political adversaries have the
tendency to become friends, and I feel such is certainly the case between President Clinton and me.

"There's an inescapable bond that binds together all who have lived
in the White House. Though we hail from different backgrounds and
ideologies, we are singularly unique, even eternally bound, by our common devotion and service to this wonderful country." While typically
imperfect in diction, the older man's speech was distinctly warm and,
as he and Clinton both would soon learn, prescient.

By the time Clinton rose, he was absorbing energy from the remaining crowd and the presidents who had come to honor him. Peering out
into the rows of multicolored umbrellas, his mood seemed to lift, his
cheeks flushed, and he smiled. "I can't see through all the umbrellas
and all the ponchos, or whatever you call those classy things that make
you all look so beautiful," he said to rueful laughter. Mindful of the
downpour, which had not let up, he spoke for only twenty minutes—for
him, a very brief address on a momentous day.

He thanked everyone from his late mother to his wife and daughter, the workers who had built the library, the architects James Stewart Polshek and Richard Olcott, the exhibit designer Ralph Appelbaum, and the builder Bill Clark, another old Arkansas friend. He returned the accolades of those who had spoken before him, with a special word for Carter.

"John Quincy Adams once said, 'There is nothing in life so pathetic as a former president.' Well, he turned out to be wrong because of his own service, and President Carter has proved that nothing could be further from the truth."

Describing the library and its purpose, he returned to the themes of his presidency, focusing on the "bridge to the 21st century" that the building's shape and location were meant to symbolize. He spoke of how he had tried to combine progressive and conservative impulses in American politics—of trying to reduce both the deficit and poverty, of economic investment and government reform—and of specific achievements like the Family Leave Act, welfare-to-work, the peace agreements in Northern Ireland and the Balkans.

"That whole story is here in 80 million documents, 21 million emails—two of them mine," his electronic ineptitude provoking laughter, "two million photographs and 80,000 artifacts"—including complete life-sized replicas of his Oval Office and Cabinet Room, re-created by the Clintons' favorite interior designer, Kaki Hockersmith; the bulletproof presidential limousine that drove him to his inauguration in January 1993; and hundreds of gifts from citizens, schoolchildren, and foreign dignitaries, all on view in the library's exhibit spaces. (Thousands more were stored below ground, kept safe in the climate-controlled, highly secure archives structure that Polshek hid behind the main building's southeast corner.)

"Quite apart from all the details," said Clinton, "the thing I want most is for people to come to this library, whether they're Republicans or Democrats, liberals or conservatives, to see that public service is noble and important; that the choices and decisions leaders make affect the lives of millions of Americans and people all across the world."

After more than two hours, the ceremony finally concluded and the damp presidential party went into the library building, where a mildly dazed Clinton led them all on a quick tour before lunch. Polshek, Olcott, and Appelbaum were stationed inside to answer questions about design and construction.

White House political boss Karl Rove, a history buff if not a Clinton admirer, had joined President Bush on the trip to Little Rock. Ambling in ahead of the presidents, Rove introduced himself to Polshek. Pointing to the double-layered glass skin that suffused the spacious interior with light, the White House political chief wanted to know whether a bullet or a bomb could pierce it. "And . . . how much did this place cost, anyway?" he demanded, with a belligerent cackle. A lifelong liberal Democrat, Polshek smiled and answered politely.

In a white tent next to the building, the presidents, their families, and some of the honored guests dined on barbecue. Clinton then brought many of them upstairs to show the private apartment constructed for him and Hillary atop the building, surrounded by an ecologically advanced "green roof" (a space from which he intended to shank golf balls into the Arkansas River).

———

"Yes, this library is the symbol of a bridge, a bridge to the 21st century," Clinton had confided during his speech. "It's been called one of the great achievements of the new age—and a British magazine said it looked like a glorified house trailer."

Clinton would only repeat that snooty insult to the library's design—echoing local taunts that the 420-foot, rectangular glass-and-metal box resembled a "giant double-wide"—because he felt so confident of its status as outstanding architecture and urban development. Intimately involved with both the internal and external design at every step, he and the architects he selected were fully vindicated by the public and professional response. While the tone ranged from respectful to rapturous, the Clinton Presidential Center was judged a success—and, purely as art, surpassed the other ten presidential libraries in the nation's portfolio.

A few of the critics who toured the center expressed reservations, even a tinge of letdown, as if they had somehow expected a more edgy, flashy, charismatic design to reflect Clinton's compelling personality—particularly because, as the reviews knowingly mentioned, the former president had played a central role in overseeing and guiding the project.

Among them was Nicolai Ouroussoff of the *New York Times*. He praised the way in which the main building's "sleek cantilevered form thrusts out aggressively toward the river," ranking it "at the top of a long list of presidential libraries," above the John F. Kennedy Library on the Boston waterfront designed by Polshek's mentor I. M. Pei. Yet he found its style to be disappointingly "predictable" even if "dignified" and "solid."

Other reviewers were far less restrained, even effusive. Blair Kamin of the *Chicago Tribune* too ranked the Clinton library above the JFK, but went further: "Critics who once carped that the museum resembled a trailer on stilts should now be in full retreat," he wrote, describing the building as "architecturally refined" and "imbued with the dynamism of contemporary life." The interior "dazzles with its fine proportions, warm materials, and animating natural light." It is, he concluded, "a major design success"—a place where "monumental modernism is liberating, not oppressive. The monument to the ruler also benefits the people."

The *Washington Post* critic Benjamin Forgey detected "a certain magic in the transformation" of the derelict warehouse site, "a model of environmental responsiveness," elevated by architecture that "greatly enlivens its surroundings. . . . This is the way it is supposed to be, but usually isn't, in complex, prestigious projects such as this. Bravo to all involved."

Unsurprisingly, journalists who toured the exhibits that depicted Clinton's presidency found them lacking in objectivity, marred by insufficient emphasis on Monica Lewinsky and impeachment as well as an oversupply of historically biased, gauzily hagiographic spin. Scrutinizing the multimedia presentation in the library's main hall, *New York Times* critic at large Edward Rothstein complained, "Every object, every piece of text, every sound is harnessed in service to an almost relentless message about Mr. Clinton's achievements. . . . Perspectives of serious critics are nonexistent . . . the exhibits paint with such a broad brush and use such a limited palette."

Yet however justified—and certainly the exhibits reflected Clinton's viewpoint above all—the objections of critics like Rothstein mattered little to the public. Over the following year, tourists swarmed into the Clinton Presidential Center, in numbers rivaled only by the Reagan library in Simi Valley, California. Nearly 300,000 visitors showed up in 2006—and the city of Little Rock estimated total local investment stimulated by the project had by then reached nearly $2 billion.

————

Just before dawn on the day after Christmas, one of the strongest and longest earthquakes in recorded history erupted undersea off the coast of the western Indonesian island of Sumatra. Measured by the U.S. Geological Survey's seismometers at 9.1 or higher on the Richter scale, the tectonic disturbance launched a series of tidal waves, or tsunami, toward the shores of islands and coastal regions in South Asia. There was no tsunami warning system in the Indian Ocean and the huge waves came ashore with smashing force.

Within minutes, a wave more than thirty feet high hit the northern coast of Indonesia, destroying shoreline villages and towns instantly. More than 130,000 lives were lost there, more than half a million people were left homeless, and nearly two thirds of all the buildings in the coastal region of Banda Aceh were left in rubble. Within the first hour, waves hit Myanmar and the Andaman Islands, leaving thousands more dead; then Thailand, where thousands more were killed, including tourists in Phuket who drowned in their hotel rooms, then Sri Lanka, and southern India, where another forty thousand or more died as fishing villages on the Bay of Bengal disappeared under the onrushing ocean.

When the waters withdrew, hundreds of corpses were left tangled in trees on the beaches, along with boats and vehicles. Nothing was left standing within hundreds of yards of the sea. In some villages nearly all of the victims were women and children, found later by fishermen who survived when their boats simply floated over the waves.

Later in the day, the rippling giant waves struck the Maldives islands and Somalia on the east coast of Africa, claiming hundreds more lives and ruining potable water supplies. On the west coast of Mexico, rose water levels by as much as eight feet. By early morning on December 26, Americans began to hear disturbing news of the casualties and damage inflicted by the tsunamis. But the initial reports greatly underestimated the numbers of dead and homeless and the scale of property destruction. Tens of thousands more would soon be in danger of dying from disease and starvation.

George W. Bush, leader of the free world, was at his rural residence in Texas to celebrate the Christmas and New Year's holidays with his family. On the day after the tsunami, he issued a statement through Trent Duffy, his deputy spokesman at the White House, expressing "his sincere condolences for the terrible loss of life and suffering caused by the earthquake and subsequent tsunamis in the region of the Bay of Bengal." He promised "all appropriate assistance to those nations most affected." The Agency for International Development (USAID) announced that the United States would set aside $15 million for immediate relief—provoking the United Nations undersecretary-general for humanitarian affairs, a Norwegian named Jan Egeland, to describe Western aid allocations as "stingy." For comparison, as the *New York Times* noted, that $15 million was less than half the expected cost of Bush's upcoming inaugural festivities.

In the days that followed, as the estimates of death and destruction in South Asia mounted, Bush's decision to remain on vacation in Texas, with no public appearances or schedule, came under heavy criticism— as did the grossly inadequate commitment of American money for an unprecedented disaster, which would require billions of dollars for food, medicine, water supplies, shelter, and eventual reconstruction. With so many victims spread across such a vast geographic area, the entire world would need to mount the largest such effort in human history. The Bush White House did not seem nearly up to the task.

Into the vacuum of competence and compassion stepped Bill Clinton, whose voice could be heard warning on December 28 that without coordination of relief efforts, too little would happen too late—and that coordination would be impossible without strong leadership. "It is really important that somebody take the lead in this," the former president told BBC Radio. "I think one of the problems is when everybody takes responsibility, it's almost like no one's responsibility."

That same day, Bush decided to call together his national security team to plan American diplomatic and military responses to the tragedy, and to raise the initial U.S. relief commitment to $35 million. Yet he still remained in Texas, a decision questioned on the front page of the *Washington Post*, which reported "complaints that the vacationing President Bush has been insensitive to a humanitarian catastrophe of epic proportions," and noted that Clinton was, by default, "the predominant US voice speaking about the disaster."

Three days after the disaster, Bush finally stopped clearing brush long enough to deliver a formal statement to the assembled press corps. Wearing a navy suit and red tie, standing next to a flag at a podium adorned with the presidential seal, the president explained, "I felt like it was important to talk about what is going to be one of the major natural disasters in world history. . . . It's important for the world to know that our government is focused and will continue to respond to help those who suffer."

Meanwhile, Clinton's innocuous remarks had sparked an angry backlash from the White House. Bush aides told journalists and pundits that the president had purposely avoided mimicking Clinton's famous public displays of empathy. Appearing on MSNBC with host Joe Scarborough, *Post* reporter Jim VandeHei said, "A lot of White House aides do point to Bill Clinton. They say, we don't want to showboat. We don't want to take these disasters and try to use them for our political or foreign policy advantage." The conservative editorialists at *Investor's Business Daily* urged Clinton to remember that he was no longer president and didn't speak for the United States.

However gratified Bush aides may have felt in mocking Clinton's "I feel your pain" style, someone in the White House abruptly realized that such derision was worse than pointless. Appearances mattered, especially for a president disliked and distrusted across much of the world. On this tragic occasion, it would be better for Bush to repair his image—and the image of his country—rather than inflict further damage.

When they considered who might be able to help, among the first names that came up, ironically, was Bill Clinton.

———

On New Year's Eve, Doug Band called Andy Card to say that Clinton planned to raise money for the tsunami victims, much the way that he and Bob Dole had done after 9/11. The Bush chief of staff asked him to hold off for a day. When Card called Band again, he wanted to know whether Clinton would consider a request from the president to join his father, George Herbert Walker Bush, in a fundraising campaign for aid to the tsunami victims. While the plans were still sketchy, and the White House welcomed Clinton's ideas, the two former presidents would probably have to travel to the stricken region sometime soon.

Band knew the answer immediately, but waited until the next day, after a brief conversation with Clinton, to call Card back. Of course, he said, Clinton would be honored to assist in any way possible, especially in the company of Bush 41.

Card wasted no time, scheduling a White House appearance on the morning of January 3—the first workday after the holiday—where Bush, his father, and Clinton would announce the joint fundraising effort. Already the president had dispatched Secretary of State Colin Powell and his brother, Florida governor Jeb Bush, to assess the effectiveness of U.S. action and future needs in the region, as part of a frantic effort to regain control of the narrative. Over a few days, the early mention of an absurdly small $15 million in U.S. disaster aid had grown to $35 million, and then tenfold to $350 million, which would require a supplemental budget appropriation in Congress. (Within a few weeks, the White House would announce yet another increase, almost tripling the amount of aid to $950 million.)

But Bush aides believed their boss still needed to be seen doing more.

Flanked by the two former presidents behind a podium in the Roosevelt Room, Bush told the assembled White House press corps, "We've come together to express our country's sympathy for the victims of a great tragedy. We're here to ask our fellow citizens to join in a broad humanitarian relief effort."

He had ordered flags across the country to fly at half-staff all week, in memory of those victims, he said, noting that the dead were estimated at 150,000—with thousands more missing, and up to five million or more homeless, without sufficient food, water, or medical care, and in danger of illness. He talked about the $350 million that he expected to spend and noted that this amount didn't reflect the rapid, costly mobilization of American aircraft and ships in the region.

"But the greatest source of America's generosity is not our government; it's the good heart of the American people," Bush continued.

"I have asked two of America's most distinguished private citizens to head a nationwide charitable fundraising effort." His father and Clinton would spearhead a campaign to spur donations "large and small" to "reliable charities" such as the Red Cross and the Red Crescent, UNICEF, Catholic Relief Services, the Salvation Army, and Save the Children, among others. The president had a point: By midweek, those charities and others would tell reporters that they had already surpassed the pace and magnitude of earlier disaster appeals, raising about $337 million in the days since December 26.

Following the announcement President Bush, his wife, Laura, and the two former presidents set off in limousines to call on the embassies of the four nations most affected by the tsunami—Indonesia, India, Sri Lanka, and Thailand. Signing condolence books and visiting with embassy officials during the brief stops, Clinton embraced expatriate citizens of those countries drawn to him by his openness and sympathy. At one embassy, he met a sobbing woman who had lost both her parents and a brother in the disaster. It was a small glimpse of the tableau of horror that he and the elder Bush would soon encounter together.

On that day, however, they returned to the White House for a series of press interviews to kick off their campaign—and to bolster the international image of the president and the United States. Asked on CNN whether the younger Bush had fumbled the American response to the catastrophe, Clinton replied, "I don't see how he could have done more."

Enlisting the two former presidents was a stroke of public relations genius, not only for the sake of the current president's image but because their effort seemed to energize powerful players in the media, advertising, and entertainment industries. When Steven Spielberg announced that his family would donate a million dollars to tsunami relief, dozens of Hollywood figures, athletes, and other celebrities quickly followed, with several giving much more, in a movement that would culminate in a celebrity telethon.

And within two days, Clinton and Bush were back in the White House again to tape a public service announcement backed by the Advertising Council, which had never acted so swiftly before.

With consummate professionalism, the ex-presidents knocked off ten-second, thirty-second, and sixty-second versions of their scripted

pleas in under forty-five minutes, overseen by a director from the Mc-
Cann Erickson Worldwide advertising agency. Taking turns speaking,
they urged viewers to donate through USA Freedom Corps, a website
set up after 9/11 to encourage volunteer efforts. Clinton voiced the
kicker: "No one can change what happened. But we can all change what
happens next." The Ad Council anticipated that television and radio
networks would donate in excess of $100 million worth of airtime for
the Bush-Clinton ads.

In early February, Clinton agreed to a request from U.N. Secretary-
General Kofi Annan that he serve as a "special envoy" for tsunami relief, in the hope that his star power would continue to focus world
attention over the longer term. "The secretary-general wants to make
sure that once the television cameras leave, the world will not forget
the victims," said U.N. spokesman Fred Eckhard. The envoy position
would also engage Clinton's diplomatic skills, and not just in dunning
developed countries to fulfill their donor commitments. Annan hoped
that with his encouragement, the disaster's aftermath might compel
warring factions in Sri Lanka and Indonesia to engage in peace talks.
He would also assume leadership of a $45 million appeal by UNICEF to
ensure clean water supplies in the tsunami region.

As events propelled him forward—and into the global spotlight—
the most daunting problem that Clinton faced was his own failure to
recover fully from his heart surgery after five months. In a complica-
tion that occurs in only a very small number of bypass patients, bloody
fluid and then scar tissue had collected around the lower lobe of his left
lung. The excess tissue, which doctors described as a thick "rind" of
scarring around the lung, caused difficulty breathing and reduced his
lung capacity by more than 25 percent. He would need another operation, and soon, in order to avoid the threat of infection.

The symptoms had begun to occur before Thanksgiving, and surgery had been scheduled for early in the New Year. But he had post-
poned the operation, with his doctors' consent, when he agreed to
assist with tsunami relief. He felt well enough to work and travel, and
the risk seemed small compared with the responsibility he had been
asked to undertake.

On February 20, a blue-and-white Boeing 757 emblazoned with the
words "United States of America" landed briefly at Houston's Hobby

Airport to pick up George Herbert Walker Bush and his aides Jean Becker and Tom Frechette. From Houston it flew on to Los Angeles, where Bill Clinton, his chief of staff Laura Graham, Doug Band, and Justin Cooper boarded. Before 10 p.m. Pacific Time, the plane had refueled and departed on the first leg of a long flight that would land the presidential party in Thailand, to begin a four-day tour of the worst devastation seen anywhere on earth since the destruction of Hiroshima and Nagasaki in 1945. The former presidents and their aides had assumed the wrenching scenes they all watched on television would prepare them for this ordeal.

They were wrong.

CHAPTER TEN

On the morning of February 19, 2005, Bill Clinton, George Herbert Walker Bush, their aides, and several Secret Service agents finally deplaned in Phuket, Thailand, exhausted from nearly two days' travel with only refueling stops. Before descending the long flight of stairs onto the sweltering tarmac, Clinton waited politely for his older, slower companion. Over a few days in close quarters this new "odd couple," as Barbara Bush dubbed them, would establish not only a modus vivendi but a warm friendship. While they had gotten along just fine in recent years, the level of intimacy they both felt now was something new.

Even before their aircraft left Burbank Airport in California, Clinton had won Bush over by making sure that the older man occupied the plane's comfortable VIP stateroom, which featured the only proper bed and private bath on board. Bush later told reporters and friends how Clinton's concern about the sleeping arrangements had touched him.

"He was very considerate of the old guy, meaning me. . . . I mean, like the room on the plane. There was every reason in the world he should have had equal time if not priority, but he insisted. That's a tiny little thing . . . that meant a lot to me."

At the time Clinton was still recovering from heart surgery. He felt twinges of discomfort and shortened breath due to the scar tissue that still covered part of his left lung. But surrendering the stateroom for a few days was a tolerable hardship. He took the air mattress that Bush had brought along, placed it on the floor, and then spent most of the trip talking and playing cards in his habitual, endless way, sleeping only a few hours a night.

Waiting to greet them at the airport, where the temperature hovered near 100 degrees under a merciless sun, was an official party led by Khunying Potjaman Shinawatra, Thailand's first lady. From there, the Americans traveled by motorcade to a tiny fishing village where most of the boats had been wrecked by the waves. As in many places that they visited, people seemed more familiar with the younger of the ex-presidents.

To greet them the villagers had put up a big banner: "Welcome President Clinton." Such evidence of Clinton's international popularity popped up repeatedly, but if being in the younger man's shadow irritated Bush, he never showed it.

Under a scorching tropical sun, the heat grew steadily as the day wore on. Clinton and Bush dressed casually, wearing khaki pants and short-sleeves—the Democrat in a blue polo shirt and the Republican in a red one. Traveling by motorcade they toured the island resort, a legendary beach destination for many Westerners that had suffered severe damage from the surging wave, with residential and commercial buildings toppled, fishing boats overturned and reduced to splinters, cars and trucks rammed through narrow streets and storefronts, killing hundreds. In the Thai coastal resorts, half of the dead had been foreign tourists from more than thirty countries.

By late February, six weeks after the tsunami, the relief effort had removed many bodies and much of the debris. But more than 1,500 corpses, still unidentified, lay in a refrigerated facility there called the International Repatriation Center, next to a Wall of Remembrance where Bush and Clinton participated in a brief ceremony to honor the dozen Americans known to have died there.

From the Marine helicopters that took the presidential party on a sweeping aerial tour, they could see acre upon acre of flattened buildings. A few still stood, their lower floors gutted, amid the concrete rubble. Later in the day the choppers took them about ninety miles north to Ban Nam Khem, another coastal fishing village where nearly a third of the residents, including many children, had died when the towering wave smashed their homes. It was a wasteland of ruined buildings, dried mud, and toppled trees, surrounded by cement and stone fragments. But however awful, the physical destruction was far less affecting than the human distress.

Intense emotion visibly gripped both Clinton and Bush—along with their companions—as they encountered the existential reality of loss, again and again, in the eyes and voices of the village's survivors. Amid the noise of bulldozers and work crews engaged in rebuilding the little town, the former presidents met local residents and officials who told how they had watched their homes and families pulled away by the surging water. One little girl gave Bush a crayon drawing of a head out in the sea, depicting her own lost mother.

On that first afternoon they met with Prime Minister Thaksin Shinawatra and members of his cabinet back in Phuket to discuss how the donor nations and organizations could best assist the Thai government. When they emerged to talk with the press, Clinton tried to sound encouraging: "From what I saw today, the most urgent thing is to have people back in their homes and their businesses as quickly as possible. It seems to me that you are well on your way here."

Then newly reelected (and not yet ousted by the Thai military), Shinawatra expressed his nation's gratitude for the effort of the former presidents, men of differing parties and political views, and for the generous assistance of the United States, particularly including the Marines and the USAID personnel, at a time of grave need. That night, the prime minister hosted an informal dinner for the two presidents at the resort hotel where they were staying.

Early the next morning, they boarded the 727 and jumped across the Malacca Strait to Medan, the teeming, multiethnic capital of North Sumatra, where they landed amid pouring rain to meet with Indonesian president Susilo Bambang Yudhoyono. Their ultimate destination was to the north in the province of Aceh along the shore of the Andaman Sea, where the tsunami had struck with devastating force. Yudhoyono, a former general educated in the United States, had ventured north from the presidential palace in Jakarta to offer his personal guarantee that American money and goods sent to help the Indonesian victims would reach them without skimming or corruption of any kind—a concern increasingly voiced in U.S. media as the aid dollars, both government and private, mounted into the hundreds of millions.

Hours later the presidential party landed at the airport in Banda Aceh, the island's northwestern tip, where Indonesian security forces maintained a heavily armed presence due to a decades-old separatist insurgency that mostly kept Westerners away from the region. Then they quickly boarded a Marine helicopter that provided a vista of devastation along the entire coast, where nearly 130,000 people were estimated to have been killed.

They touched down again in one of hundreds of coastal villages, where nothing now remained of the little shacks where the fishermen and their families had once lived except scraps of wood, sheet metal, and cement along the beaches. Much of the debris had been cleared away, along with recovered corpses—yet even two months later, bodies of the victims continued to wash up onshore nearly every day. Many of the villagers refused to eat any fish, translators told the former presidents, fearing that the fish had consumed the flesh of family members lost to the sea.

As Clinton and Bush stepped away from their helicopter, they passed through long lines of people who had emerged from tents in the midday sun to see them. Tens of thousands of survivors were living in temporary shelter along the coastline hit hardest by the tidal wave. Few of the Acehnese spoke a word of English, but the former presidents listened as translators recounted their wrenching personal stories. A father stood staring, his arm around one surviving son, as he described losing his wife and four other children. Boys and girls, wearing the soiled T-shirts that were their only clothing, spoke softly, haltingly, of watching their parents swept away. Others stood by mutely, only their faces revealing a state of shock, sorrow, and hopelessness.

Moving through the hot and humid landscapes, confronted by dramatic vistas of ruin and throngs of destitute people, the rapid pace drained Clinton and Bush. Even in the middle of the day they slumped in their car seats, physically and emotionally exhausted. Clinton's words would catch in his throat as he tried to speak. As governor and president he had visited so many scenes of tragedy, from tornado-razed towns in Arkansas to the terrorist wreckage in Oklahoma City. But this was horror on a scale bigger than anything he had ever seen.

Whenever Clinton got cell phone service he called Hillary to tell her what he was seeing and feeling. It was so much worse, he said, than anything television could show. Publicly, he and Bush mustered the strength to express hope, empathy, and the determination to provide as much help as the tsunami victims needed to rebuild. The wire photographs showed them smiling, thumbs up, standing with heads of state and local officials. But away from the cameras, both men had wept.

In the late afternoon, the former presidents flew across the Bay of Bengal from Aceh to Colombo, the capital of Sri Lanka, where they dined at the home of President Chandrika Bandaranaike Kumaratunga.

Like many of the politicians they encountered in Asia, where ideological and communal enmities too often erupted in violence, she expressed wonder at the alliance of two men of opposite parties, who had once fought a bitter election.

"It means so much to me that the two of you who were political rivals in the U.S. . . . can rise above that to come and help us in this our hour of greatest need," she said, standing to toast them. In tribute to their example, the Sri Lankan president noted, she had invited the country's opposition leader and former prime minister to join her and her distinguished visitors at dinner.

For Clinton, the Sri Lankan leader's gesture to her own rivals meant more than a nice formality. In the months that followed, he would engage in quiet backstage diplomacy, covered by his role as the U.N. special envoy for the tsunami, in Sri Lanka, where the Tamil rebellion and its suppression had claimed many lives, as well as in Aceh. The memory of his successful intervention in Northern Ireland encouraged hope that he could achieve at least a cease-fire in these religious and ethnic conflicts on the other side of the world.

From Colombo they flew to the southern coastal city of Matara. There they stopped outside a temporary school, where they sat down on the bare ground with some of the island's orphaned children, looking over an exhibit of their artwork, and talking with them about the future. Hurt and frightened as these children were, they showed signs of beginning to recover from their trauma. They were more animated, and less withdrawn; they sang and danced for the former presidents. And although many of their pictures displayed tragic moments from the tsunami, some had more recently drawn sunnier scenes of rebuilt homes and gardens. Thomas Ward, a USAID official who accompanied Bush and Clinton on the trip, later told author Carol Felsenthal they could see "that we were making progress with these kids."

On the trip's final day they flew hours over the Indian Ocean to the remote Maldives, a cluster of coral atolls, whose population of 350,000 depended entirely on tourism and tuna fishing. While the islands hadn't suffered any damage comparable to the havoc wreaked in Indonesia or Sri Lanka, nearly one hundred people had died there. The point of the presidential visit was to show that the Maldives resort industry was up and running and ready to receive visitors.

Following a presidential greeting at the airport and a hotel lunch that Bush later described as "without a doubt the best tuna I have ever eaten," the former presidents sat for live interviews on the morning shows of the three major television networks, framed against the blue sky and sunlit sea.

On ABC News, *Good Morning America* anchor Charles Gibson asked what they had seen that "really surprised you or brought you up short." As usual Clinton deferred to his elder, who replied first.

"Well, I think it is far greater, far worse than what I had thought, particularly over in Aceh, in Indonesia," Bush said. "You can't tell from this background, this placid, beautiful background here, but there's a lot of suffering here. And every place we've gone, we have seen it. And what's affected me the most is the children, the heartbroken children whose families were literally ripped away by this tsunami. And so what we are trying to do is encourage more private giving in the United States. The people in our country have been generous, [are] continuing to be generous. But this work is far from over. The reconstruction is just beginning in many of these countries."

"We saw orphans in Thailand," Clinton confirmed. "We saw orphans in all these countries. We visited a village in Aceh where there had been 6,500 people living, all of the homes were destroyed, and only 1,000 people survived. You know, you can report on that, you can show it. But unless you physically see it and you look into these people's eyes, it is very difficult to communicate. . . . I was surprised by how much work has already been done, by how much people are working together. . . . I think people's money has been well spent so far. They are working hard and they are incredibly brave."

Then Clinton displayed the drawing that the little girl in Thailand had given to Bush, which showed her mother drowning. He held up another drawing that a child had given him, with helicopters dropping food and medicine.

"Every place we went," he said, "there's heartbreak and courage, and hope." These countries needed more aid, and a plan, and a coordinated effort to avoid waste and corruption. "But so far I have been impressed by what we have seen." Nodding toward his companion, Clinton added, "And I think he has, too."

Parting company in the Maldives—with Bush headed home to

Houston and Clinton scheduled for book tour and foundation events in Hong Kong, Beijing, Seoul, Tokyo, Taipei, Singapore, and Brunei—both felt that they had established a lasting bond. As he relaxed on the 727 that evening, Bush composed a three-thousand-word letter about the trip to his old friend Hugh Sidey, a retired *Time* correspondent. Pouring out his impressions, he described the personality of his old competitor as well as their compelling experiences together.

"I thought I knew him, but until this trip I did not really know him," Bush mused. "First of all, he has been very considerate of me. I think my old age had something to do with it." He explained how Clinton had surrendered the Air Force Two bedroom, and always waited courteously whenever they made an entrance together. But he also noted, in some detail, how often he had been required to wait patiently on "Clinton Standard Time," a perpetual and notorious tardiness that dated back to White House days.

Indeed, Bush catalogued his new pal's foibles with tart candor: "In grade school they had a place on our report cards, 'Claims no more than his fair share of time and attention in the class room.' Bill would have gotten a bad mark there." Everywhere they went, Clinton kept Bush waiting while he talked with waiters, cooks, shopkeepers, everyone he encountered.

And when Clinton finally showed up, he would usually ramble on at great length about his own experiences and opinions, of which there was an inexhaustible supply. "Does this purification system use reverse osmosis? This is diesel driven isn't it? I remember the hurricane damage I saw in X-land, or this reminds me of my trip to the Sudan, or I used to love to watch the kids singing in Ulan Bator. Boy, you haven't seen a wedding 'til you've seen one in Swaziland," Bush wrote, inventing a stream of Clintonesque patter. "I do think people were fascinated," he allowed. "Once or twice I got a clandestine high sign from the people we were talking to that we had to move on, that I had to get him going."

Yet as Bush generously acknowledged, neither lateness nor loquaciousness diminished the man's radiant charm. Moreover, Clinton actually knew a lot about many things, contemporary and historical; he could be relied upon to fill any awkward silence with engaging observations, usually relevant, and his confiding manner drew people to him in a way that Bush admired.

"He was far more easily recognized and to be frank got a warmer reception than I did, and mine was pretty darn good," he wrote to Sidey. "Rationalization: Not to detract from Clinton's star power with the crowds, but I have been out of office for a long, long time."

On the night of their dinner in Colombo with the Sri Lankan president, Bush recalled, they had planned to leave early and get some sleep in decent hotel beds. Keeping their remarks "short and sweet," they anticipated a swift departure—but then Clinton had lingered with President Kumaratunga and her ministers. He leaned up against a wall, talking and ignoring every signal that it was time to go. At long last, climbing into the limousine where Bush awaited him with diminishing patience, he blurted, "George, you owe me big time for getting us out of there a lot earlier than we expected."

At that point, wrote Bush, "I thanked him profusely. And I said nothing more. You cannot get mad at the guy. I admit to wondering why he can't stay on time, but when I see him interacting with folks my wonder turns to understanding."

At least once, however, Bush glimpsed a less endearing Clinton trait that was well known to his staff. Sometimes, when he felt things were going wrong, especially if he was fatigued or frustrated, Clinton blew up at Band, Cooper, and other staffers. Very rarely did this rage erupt in the presence of others—but just before their joint television interview on the Maldives, Bush had been startled by a loud burst of bad temper: "I heard him turn on his aide and take a huge bite out of his ass. It had to do with whether the mike for TV should go down through his shirt and out the bottom of the shirt or whether it could be hooked on the back. But at that juncture he was very tired."

––––––

To anyone puzzled by the comradeship of Bush and Clinton, stock explanations about the unique bonding force of the presidency may not be persuasive. Few ex-presidents ever spent much time together, in fact, except on ceremonial occasions. Their bond was real, and unusual. Jon Meacham, the journalist and author who wrote an acclaimed Bush biography, came to believe that his subject "was dazzled by Clinton's gifts of gregariousness and charisma; [while] Clinton sought Bush's fatherly approval and, given his historical imagination, enjoyed the company of this embodiment of the fading order of Cold War statesmanship."

In early March, the pair of them returned to the White House to brief President Bush about their efforts. Praising them before a gaggle of reporters in the Oval Office, the president described their mission as carrying "our message of compassion" so the world might have "a different impression of America"—an allusion, perhaps, to global revulsion against the continuing carnage in Iraq. When he asked the former presidents to offer any comments, his father said, "My comment is President Clinton was a joy to work with."

Clinton thanked the president for asking them to work together. The people they had seen, he added, "are very grateful for what the American military did, for what USAID did, for what the hundreds of non-governmental organizations have done. But there's a lot of work left to be done, and we want to see it through to the end."

The next day, Clinton and Bush flew down to a golf club in Hobe Sound, Florida, for a charity tournament hosted by former world champion Greg Norman. Returning to New York the next day, he headed straight to New York Presbyterian Hospital, where two surgeons finally performed the long-delayed decortication procedure to free his left lung from a band of rubbery scar tissue. Due to minor complications, the surgery took four hours to complete and was slightly more invasive than the doctors had originally planned. After twenty-four hours at the hospital he went home to Chappaqua for a month of recovery.

Clinton felt a distinct sense of satisfaction with the tsunami mission, though his work in the region was far from finished. Having agreed to represent the U.N., he would return to Indonesia, India, and Sri Lanka in May and again in November for meetings with Indian prime minister Manmohan Singh, among others, to monitor their progress, assess their needs, and try to prod peace talks forward. On that latter objective, he would find greater success in Aceh—where tsunami aid encouraged the separatist movement to sign a peace agreement with the Indonesian government in August 2005, under U.N. auspices—than in Sri Lanka, where the ongoing Tamil insurgency hindered reconstruction.

Whatever difficulties he confronted as U.N. envoy, the tsunami media blitz featuring Bush and Clinton achieved stunning results. In dollars raised, it proved to be the most successful private relief effort in history. While they would never seek any credit for that record, which obviously had required the efforts of millions, their leadership was important—and unprecedented in American politics.

A 2006 report by the Center on Philanthropy at Indiana University found that American individuals and families gave $2.78 billion for tsunami relief, with about a quarter of all households in the United States making at least one donation, often through churches, synagogues, mosques, or other religious institutions. Foundations and corporations donated another $380 million—and the former presidents had also bolstered public support for U.S. government spending of $950 million for relief and reconstruction. The world threw a large sum of money at the problems left by the tsunami, lending weight to the reconstruction slogan popularized by Clinton: "Build Back Better."

———

Campaigning for tsunami relief with George H. W. Bush—at the behest of the Republican White House—endowed Clinton with the nonpartisan aura that his aides viewed as essential to a successful post-presidency. Much as he disagreed with the Bush administration on political issues, and articulated those disagreements, the president and his father had elevated Clinton to a position of respected statesmanship. Forgotten were the dark times when the Bush apparatus leaked slurs about purloined furnishings and encouraged prosecutors and politicians to investigate Clinton's pardons. There was no more talk about restoring "honor and integrity" to the presidency, now that this old enemy of the first family had been transformed into an intimate friend.

So intense was the friendship between Clinton and the Bushes that it verged on the familial, with public references to Bill as "the fifth brother," and speculation by the elder George and Barbara that he saw in his presidential predecessor the father he'd never had. "I love George Bush, I really do," Clinton declared. Dubya called him "Bubba" or "the brother from another mother." And the flinty matriarch, who had once declared her distaste for the Arkansan upstart in no uncertain terms, allowed that she had come to "really like" and even "love" Bill Clinton.

Partisan Democrats and Republicans alike found these expressions of affection more unsettling than uplifting. Newt Gingrich, who had proved susceptible to Clinton's charm himself in years past, denounced the Bush family for "rehabilitating" the former president, and Gingrich wasn't alone. On the other side, liberal Democrats believed that Clinton was providing political cover to a president whose policies they—and he—had consistently opposed.

Such caviling irritated Clinton, who insisted on his own political course, especially in dealing with the president. "I'm not the leader of the opposition anymore," he retorted. "I will always be loyal to my party, but if I spent time being a leader of the opposition I wouldn't be able to save lives doing what I'm doing. . . . That's something we have to have Congressional leaders for, we have to have people like Hillary for, we have to have people like [then-Senator] Joe Biden and all these people who want to run for president—and I can be supportive, where it's appropriate. But I have a different life now and I've got to lead it."

The bipartisan Bush-Clinton rapprochement did not extend fully to Hillary. The Bushes said little about her publicly, and when her husband began to visit them occasionally in Kennebunkport, as he did that summer, she never joined him there. As a liberal Democratic senator who often criticized the Bush Republicans—and harbored presidential ambitions of her own—she may wisely have wished to avoid any photo opportunities at the exclusive Maine compound.

And that may have been why the elder Bush later told Meacham, "I don't feel close to Hillary at all, but I do to Bill—and I can't read their relationship even today."

Bush, whose own marriage had suffered painful examination during his political career, was hardly alone in that observation. After years mostly apart, the Clintons' marriage remained inscrutable even to longtime friends—an endless source of speculation in the media and among ordinary Americans. To cynics, it seemed to persist as some kind of political compact—but that didn't explain why he constantly called her from abroad, or why she seemed breathless and even "coquettish" to staffers whenever he visited her Senate office.

For Bill Clinton, an invitation to spend more time with the Bushes arrived soon after he returned to New York—and he made the most of the opportunity.

On the morning of April 2, 2005, the Vatican announced the death of Pope John Paul II. When the White House invited him to join a small delegation to the pope's funeral six days later, Clinton accepted—and departed for Rome from Washington on Air Force One with President Bush, his father, First Lady Laura Bush, and Secretary of State Condoleezza Rice.

Enjoying his first flight on the presidential aircraft since his departure from the White House, Clinton was suddenly summoned forward to Bush's office in the front of the cabin. As soon as Clinton sat down, Bush snapped, "Tell me what you're doing on AIDS. I want you to explain it to me. How do you relate to our program?"

The former president proceeded to describe the Clinton HIV/AIDS Initiative in some detail, focusing on its agreements with various countries—by then numbering in the dozens—and the generic manufacturers to provide low-cost medicine. And he was candid with Bush about the conflicts that had erupted early on between PEPFAR and CHAI.

"Well, in the first place it was terrible," said Clinton, "because your people thought we were the enemies of the [branded] drug companies and they didn't want to work with us at all in some of these countries." He went on carefully. "I know what you've been told about these generic drugs, but just look at our results."

Keenly aware of the pharmaceutical lobby's access to the White House, he knew that the American manufacturers had persuaded the president and his appointees at PEPFAR that the generic formulations were so inferior that, rather than relieving illness, they would probably worsen the pandemic. Now he had a chance to persuade Bush to reconsider the administration's hostility to his program.

"It's going to make a big difference if you participate in this," he pressed. "You could save a lot more lives for the money you've got." Even with price reductions by the branded manufacturers, the generic program would provide at least four times as many doses for the same cost.

"Well, what am I supposed to do about this?" Bush asked plaintively. "I can't ignore what these people are saying," referring to the manufacturers' warnings about the poor quality of the generic products.

Clinton tried a different tack. "How about this? What if we submit every single drug we buy from any of the other donors' money to the

FDA for approval? If the FDA concludes—not for approval for sale in America, but if the FDA concludes they're safe and effective, then you could say that in the countries where PEPFAR and CHAI operate together, if governments wanted to buy those drugs, then they could."

Bush looked across his desk at Clinton for a moment. "That sounds fair," he said. "I'll do it."

Outside pressures on the Bush administration to accept generic drugs for PEPFAR funding had been increasing steadily ever since the earlier clashes between Clinton's program and the Republicans in Washington. In January 2005, a few months before Clinton and Bush conferred on the way to the pope's funeral, the Government Accountability Office (GAO) had issued a harsh report on the issue.

Compiled during the course of a year's research at the request of Senators Ted Kennedy and John McCain and Rep. Henry Waxman, the GAO report scathingly criticized PEPFAR's refusal to approve funding for the kinds of generic formulations and two-drug and three-drug "cocktails" approved by the World Health Organization and purchased by the Global Fund and other major anti-AIDS initiatives in the developing world.

The yearlong study's most important finding was that the United States government was paying far more than necessary by purchasing branded drugs from U.S. manufacturers, paying a big premium above the cost of generics. The excessive payments ranged as high as $368 per patient per year—which suggested that in total, PEPFAR was wasting huge sums of money by insisting on branded medicines. "Such differences in price per person per year could translate into hundreds of millions of dollars of additional expense, when considered on the scale of the plan's goal of treating 2 million people by the end of 2008," the report warned.

Slowly and reluctantly, the coordinators of PEPFAR had begun to accede to those pressures as early as the summer of 2004, when they agreed in principle to an expedited process for FDA approval of generic AIDS drugs. By early 2005 they had allowed one generics manufacturer, South Africa's Aspen Pharmaceuticals, to apply for FDA approval of two-drug formulations, which won approval more quickly than normal under the usual extended process. But it would be months and years before the U.S. government began to purchase substantial quantities of generic drugs for distribution in PEPFAR target countries in Africa and the Caribbean—even though Bush aides argued that it had always been the president's intention. After Clinton's discussion with Bush, the approvals started to come more rapidly.

Meanwhile the Clinton HIV/AIDS Initiative was moving forward. Just over a week after Clinton's conversation with Bush, he held a press conference in Harlem to announce a new $10 million pediatric treatment program, focused on providing care for children and especially infants, and preventing mother-to-child transmission of the virus during pregnancy.

To start, ten thousand children in ten countries—including China, India, Rwanda, Tanzania, Lesotho, and the Dominican Republic—would receive low-cost medications under an agreement negotiated between Ira Magaziner and Cipla, the Indian generics manufacturer, which had agreed to reduce the prices of a special medicated syrup and child-sized pills by half. CHAI would spend $2 million on the drugs and another $3 million to support clinics where the program would train local medical personnel to oversee treatment.

At the same press conference, Clinton and Magaziner also announced a new $5 million program in Rwanda, where CHAI would support the takeover and renovation of an abandoned rural hospital by Paul Farmer, who had proved at his clinic in the mountains of Haiti that treatment could be effective among the poor in less developed countries (contrary to the assumptions of leading health authorities). Farmer's relationship with Magaziner—and the former president—had come a long way since he had mocked the Clinton administration's priorities in a 1999 book on AIDS.

Still a trenchant critic of the wealthy nations' failure to address the health care needs of the world's poor, Farmer couldn't help but point out to reporters that for anyone who had seen a child die of AIDS, $10 million was "too little, too late—but to let that paralyze us as a nation is a huge mistake." Also present was Stephen Lewis, the U.N. special envoy for AIDS, who described the CHAI plan as "a breakthrough. It always enrages me that children are on the bottom rung of the ladder in international priorities. Now it's clear that we will have these pediatric formulations."

It was the kind of advance that kept Clinton going even when he felt discouraged by the scale of the pandemic. He often spoke of the continuing AIDS death toll as depressing, and sometimes sounded like Farmer when he scourged the response of Western governments as "pathetic" and "unacceptable." When audiences applauded CHAI's efforts at a speech or public appearance, he would always hush them, because so few were still being treated.

Yet he drew encouragement from the progress that CHAI had enabled so far, along with its governmental and nonprofit partners. According to Magaziner, nearly 400,000 people were receiving treatment less than two years after the program began. He expected that number to rise to one million by the end of 2006 and two million by 2008. "Let's assume we need six million people getting their medicine," Clinton would say, when asked about the daunting numbers. "If our foundation can account for two million of that, if we can do a third of that by 2008, then we've done a heck of a lot there."

Fluent as he sounded when reciting the statistical data, those numbers alone revealed little about the realities on the ground, where CHAI's roughly two hundred young staff and volunteers had to surmount cultural stigmas and backward systems every day, without alienating their government partners. In July he planned to visit Africa again, a summer trip that would become an annual pilgrimage to the continent, where he and his entourage would cover seven countries—Lesotho, South Africa, Tanzania, Kenya, Rwanda, and Mozambique—in ten days.

To anyone who went along on Clinton's Africa trips, the march through clinics, hospital wards, community centers, and presidential palaces could feel dizzying and repetitive. But the annual tour served several important purposes. His appearance on site always provided an enormous lift to foundation staffers, toiling in difficult and distant places with very low budgets. His private meetings with heads of state and cabinet ministers rewarded them and fostered the critical relationship with government in country. His invitations to donors who accompanied him encouraged fresh funding and new networks of support. And his celebrity status attracted media coverage of the foundation's work, at least sometimes. Among the journalists on the plane in July 2005 were writers for *New York* and *Esquire* magazines and a TV crew from CNN led by Dr. Sanjay Gupta, the cable network's health correspondent.

Aside from those institutional considerations was the spiritual up-lift for Clinton himself, a man motivated above all by human contact. Barnstorming through Africa, from big cities like Nairobi to remote farm villages in Malawi, brought him close to the work he had set in motion, and offered him a vital opportunity to meet the people whose lives he was seeking to improve—or save. In grim hospital wards and tiny rural clinics, he got to see what his foundation had actually done with the millions of dollars given by his friends in Ireland, Canada, Norway, and the United Kingdom.

And Clinton always paid a call on Nelson Mandela in Johannes-burg, on or around the great statesman's birthday, just like a good son.

———

On the morning of July 18, when Mandela turned eighty-seven, a small motorcade passed through the gates of his walled home in a leafy Jo'burg suburb called Sandton, where the two former presidents were to enjoy a private luncheon. From within the yellow stucco of Mande-la's home his booming, cheerful voice could be heard quite clearly as he walked out to the stone portico to greet the Clinton entourage, which included four aides, six Secret Service agents, a few current and poten-tial foundation donors, and a couple of journalists. The graying Man-dela now used a cane and a hearing aid, but his eyes were clear and his mind focused as he greeted each awestruck guest. He made no attempt to hide his own boisterous joy at seeing Clinton again.

That evening, Clinton and his party attended a gala celebration of Mandela's birthday to raise money for his own foundation. Thousands of South Africans of all races showed up at a huge, wood-paneled civic auditorium to pay homage to the former guerrilla warrior who had led them peacefully out of apartheid. The event featured remarks by Clin-ton and various African dignitaries, including a speech by Wangari Maathai, the Kenyan environmental leader who had become the first African woman to win the Nobel Peace Prize in 2004.

When Mandela was seated onstage, he beckoned Clinton over to sit next to him. While the speeches and music continued, they could be seen whispering to each other and laughing, like the most intimate friends. Top aides to Madiba would say there were three sides of his relationship with Clinton—as father and son, as longtime friends, and as peers in statesmanship. Estranged from his own four surviving children after his lengthy imprisonment, the lonely Mandela found empathy and understanding in his American friend. They were so close that in later years, as he grew weaker and his appetite waned, he would eat at Clinton's urging.

And for Clinton, Mandela had become a spiritual mentor who provided counsel during impeachment, teaching him to liberate his own mind by refusing to reciprocate the hatred of his enemies. The public embrace of this secular saint continued to cloak Clinton in an impervious mantle of legitimacy—especially across Africa.

Later that night, the Clinton party would return to the Saxon Hotel, a luxurious retreat surrounded by woods where Mandela had lived after the Pretoria regime released him from prison. There the former president would linger quite late in the bar, talking and trading stories with anyone who had the stamina to stay up with him.

From Johannesburg, the Clinton party flew to Nairobi, Kenya, where the day's stops included a health clinic operated by the French charity Doctors Without Borders, whose volunteer doctors used AIDS tests and medicines provided through CHAI; a public elementary school whose fees had been abolished under a program urged by Clinton when he was still president; and a private "bilateral" meeting with Kenyan president Mwai Kibaki at the State House.

Dapper in a tan suit and striped tie, Clinton emerged from that meeting to praise Kibaki, a competent, low-key technocrat who had helped return Kenya to multiparty democracy, implemented the education reform, and welcomed CHAI into his country. The feisty local reporters who awaited him were bursting with questions about the upcoming national election and the perennial complaints of opposition leaders.

"I would tell the opposition to keep on trying," he said, grinning into a cluster of microphones. "It took my party 12 years to defeat the other side, but eventually we did it, and they can, too."

Clinton's evening hours in Nairobi were spent dining on room service with his aides in the Serena Hotel. After dinner he played cards and made telephone calls to the United States while chewing an unlit Cuban cigar and sipping occasionally from a glass of red wine. He talked with Hillary, as he did at least once a day, and with Rep. Donald

Payne, who then chaired the House Subcommittee on African Affairs, to update the New Jersey Democrat on the progress of his AIDS work.

From Nairobi, Clinton flew to Dar-es-Salaam, seaside capital of Tanzania, one of the most rapidly developing nations in East Africa. As his motorcade entered the city, thousands of people lined up along the roadside, cheering, waving, and simply staring—as they did in almost every big African city he visited. He was still immensely popular on the continent, where many remembered him as the first president who had seemed to truly respect and care about Africa.

His first appointment in Dar was at the U.S. embassy to participate in a ceremony marking the upcoming anniversary of the terrorist attack that killed eleven and wounded eighty-five there in August 1998, which had been timed to coincide with a similar truck-bomb attack on the embassy in Nairobi. As a former president, Clinton felt an obligation to provide support whenever possible to the Foreign Service corps, whose members were plainly delighted to see him. He offered brief remarks to the assembled diplomats and workers outside the embassy building, then went upstairs to the ambassador's office for coffee.

Central to Clinton's visit to Dar, as the capital is known, was the cultivation of Tanzanian president Benjamin Mkapa, a technocratic politician who was among the first African leaders to embrace CHAI. On this trip, Clinton not only held an hour-plus "bilat" with Mkapa and several of his ministers, but appeared with him at a lengthy outdoor ceremony, attended by many of Mkapa's supporters and government employees, to announce a new partnership between the Clinton Foundation and the government of Tanzania to provide advanced training in HIV/AIDS clinical care and treatment to "at least 30 medical professionals" in country every year. Prepared for deployment to rural areas and other medically underserved regions, they would be known as "Mkapa Fellows"—a legacy that would continue after the president was replaced by an election in six months.

The meetings were also a chance for Clinton, Magaziner, and local CHAI staff to establish a stronger relationship with Jakaya Kikwete, the Tanzanian vice president and former health minister expected to succeed to the presidency when Mkapa retired. Their aim—with the meetings, the fellowship program, and Clinton's visit—was to enable the swift scale-up of antiretroviral therapy under the National Care and Treatment Program that the foundation and the government had developed together in 2003, during CHAI's earliest days. Clinton nurtured the same kind of relationship in many countries, just as he had so often exercised his charm upon American governors, mayors, and legislators.

African leaders like Kibaki and Mkapa treated Clinton as if he was still the world's most powerful head of state. Standing proudly beside him, they seemed to feel that his presence reinforced their authority and integrity (sometimes to the dismay of human rights organizations). More importantly, from his perspective, they listened when he urged them to help remove the stigma from their HIV-infected citizens, to expand health services in rural areas, and to cooperate with the United Nations, Western governments, and nongovernmental organizations such as CHAI.

———

The most affecting moments for Clinton, however, occurred in the communities that were at last beginning to feel the direct impact of his foundation's efforts. From Dar-es-Salaam, he and his party flew across a small strait of the Indian Ocean to the Zanzibar archipelago, a semi-autonomous province off the Tanzanian coast. Until three months earlier, Zanzibar had provided no AIDS treatment at all—a situation that CHAI staff in country attributed to its overwhelmingly Muslim population and conservative culture.

He landed in Stone Town, an ancient Moorish city that had been a center of the spice trade for hundreds of years. The morning destination was an old hospital on the edge of the sea, where dingy, peeling walls and dark, muddy floors contrasted with the bright, clean blue of water and sky. Green scrubs hung on an outdoor clothesline, and pungent odors hinted at inadequate sanitation. Without hesitation, Clinton climbed the stairs to a second-floor ward, followed closely by his aides and security. He shook hands with patients in their beds, talked quietly with their doctors, and inspected the new HIV/AIDS clinic. With fifty-six HIV-positive clients, receiving mostly outpatient treatment, the hospital expected to scale up to serve two thousand before the end of 2005.

He stopped for several minutes to talk with a tall, young, bespectacled doctor in lab whites, operating a large, boxlike machine that resembled an old-fashioned computer printer. It was an essential piece of technology obtained for the hospital by the Swedish government through the Clinton Foundation, under a negotiated agreement with the manufacturer, which measured CD4 white blood cell counts—the only way to determine whether the ARV medications are working in each patient.

Not only did Clinton recognize the electronic box; he clearly knew how to read the paper tape that emerged from it, surprising the doctor and everyone else observing them. "I was really impressed," murmured a young woman from the U.S. Agency for International Development. "He was getting a lot of detailed information."

In the hotel parking lot, he held an impromptu press conference for the local media and Gupta's CNN crew. He was splendidly attired in a custom navy blue suit, red striped tie, and black Gucci loafers for a meeting with the island authorities. "I am thrilled to be in Zanzibar for the first time in my life," he exclaimed with a broad smile. "Just now, I shook hands with an 11-year-old orphan child who knows that he is HIV-positive. His circumstances have changed. He doesn't have to be stigmatized. And he doesn't have to resign himself to an early death."

In places like Zanzibar, where testing positive for HIV carried a disfiguring social stain, Clinton elevated the community's suffering men, women, and children. With his embrace came the endorsement of local government, as local officials began to follow his lead in promoting science and compassion instead of superstition and stigma.

For months before his visit, CHAI staff had been working in Zanzibar, led by Tanzania country officer Sandra Cress, an American who had seen the job in a business school listing, and Edwin Macharia, a young, American-educated Kenyan who had worked at McKinsey. They had found bureaucratic entanglements at PEPFAR delaying the hospital's purchase of lab testing equipment. Without tests there could be no treatment. Because CHAI could act swiftly, they arranged training for the hospital staff, and arranged a simple system to gather blood samples for transport via ferry to a private hospital laboratory in Dar-es-Salaam. Rather than wait until testing equipment arrived in Zanzibar, said Cress, who had accompanied Clinton from the capital, "we were able to get people on treatment very quickly, for a minimal investment." Now the Zanzibar hospital had its own testing facility and expanded treatment.

Later that afternoon, following a meeting in the State House with Zanzibar's president Amani Abeid Karume, Clinton walked across Stone Town to a tiny stone building near the city's center. Inside were several Zanzibari women, dressed modestly but colorfully, with young children and an American expatriate named Kathryn Sutton—the core of a local advocacy organization, the Zanzibar Association of People Living with HIV/AIDS, known as ZAPHA+. Fewer than a hundred of the thousands of men and women affected by the pandemic on Zanzibar had joined the group, whose leaders had worked with CHAI ever since its Tanzanian staff visited the island several months earlier.

Following introductions by a local interpreter named Faroque, Clinton shook hands with everyone and sat down in the small room. Taking a little girl and a young boy on his lap, he listened as each of the women, and one man, told their stories. With the interpreter, this took some time. They told him that before CHAI arrived on Zanzibar the previous spring, they had been waiting for medicines to arrive while watching their friends and relatives die. They thanked him for making the medicine available.

But they went on to say how worried they were that the medicine might suddenly disappear—or that the government would start demanding payments that they could not afford. Many of them were so poor already that they were always hungry. To stop taking the medicine would mean certain death. They had seen development agencies come and go over the years, many times, and that made them afraid.

Clinton waited to speak until everyone who wished to address him had finished. He praised their courage and urged them to spread the word that everyone could now emerge from the shadows for testing and treatment. He explained that he had just met with President Karume, and told him that the drugs must remain free. The president, he said, had assured him that was understood. And then Clinton made his own promise: He would work as hard as he could to ensure treatment for all the members of ZAPHA+ and every other HIV patient on Zanzibar, for as long as they needed it. He was not going to abandon them.

In every place he visited on that trip—and on similar trips that he would take nearly every summer thereafter, from Johannesburg to Nairobi to Kigali to Abuja to Addis Ababa—Clinton dropped in on clinics, hospitals, and community centers where hundreds and eventually thousands and hundreds of thousands of patients received treatment, thanks to his foundation's work, in concert with a global array of governments, organizations, and individuals he had helped to bring together. It was an achievement that the world's public health authorities had deemed impossible only a few years earlier. Millions of lives had been lost needlessly, as he continued to remind himself and everyone else. But millions of lives would be saved.

CHAPTER ELEVEN

Whenever Bill Clinton considered the shape of his sprawling post-presidential life, with all its thematic and geographical complexity, he tended to sort what he did into two broad categories. "There are things that I plan to do," he would say. "And then there are things that just . . . come up."

Not long after he returned to New York from Africa, something very big came up. During the early morning hours of August 29, the most destructive hurricane in American history landed on the Gulf Coast, destroying entire towns in Mississippi and Louisiana as well as much of the historic city of New Orleans. The storm and subsequent flooding killed almost 1,250 people, left many thousands injured and homeless, and cost well over $100 billion in property damage. In its awful aftermath, the callous and incompetent federal response inflicted political damage from which the Bush administration never fully recovered.

Watching the catastrophe unfold on television in Chappaqua, Clinton felt deep distress over the botched maneuvers of the Federal Emergency Management Agency and its director, Michael Brown—a Bush patronage appointee with no known qualifications who soon became notorious as "Brownie," his presidential nickname. Clinton hated to see the relief agency in the hands of such a dim nonentity.

With him in charge, the Bush approach to emergency relief, smacking of antigovernment ideology, had thoroughly undone the rebuilding and improvement of FEMA by Clinton's appointee and childhood friend, James Lee Witt, widely esteemed as the best chief executive ever to serve there. Combining the federal fiasco with the human suffering in the Superdome and the destruction of a city he loved, the former president found the entire spectacle nearly unbearable.

Within hours after the hurricane's landfall, the White House called Chappaqua to ask whether Clinton would rejoin George H. W. Bush to raise charitable donations for Katrina reconstruction, in a reprise of their "odd couple" routine, only nine months after the Asian tsunami. Although his fall schedule was already jammed with events—headlined by the debut of the Clinton Global Initiative in Manhattan in just over two weeks—there was no way he would or could refuse.

On September 1 President Bush announced the reunion, operating under the banner of the Bush-Clinton Katrina Fund. That same day, the two former presidents taped a series of three public service commercials in the White House library, urging Americans to give generously to help the hurricane's victims. But Clinton also wanted to see the victims up close—despite the fact that he was leaving a few days later for a grueling trip across Asia to deliver speeches, raise foundation money, and promote CHAI projects. So his advance team slotted a very brief trip to Houston into his packed calendar and hastily arranged air transport with assistance from John Catsimatidis, a New York billionaire, supermarket magnate, and political donor who owned a small fleet of jets.

Hours before dawn on September 5, Bill and Hillary Clinton left the gated compound on Old House Lane with Band, Cooper, and several Secret Service agents, heading to Westchester County Airport. There they boarded a Gulfstream IV, which delivered them to Hobby Airport before 8 a.m. In Houston, they joined the elder Bush and wife, Barbara, Oprah Winfrey, Rev. Jesse Jackson, several members of Congress, and a group of local ministers to visit the Gulf Coast evacuees at the Reliant Center, a smaller arena next to the Astrodome filled with cots and ice-chests, temporary home to nearly four thousand evacuees.

Outside the arena, Clinton and Bush held an early morning press conference to again announce the Bush-Clinton Katrina Fund. "I guess I could say on behalf of all of us that nothing we can do can be an adequate response to the agony we've seen," said Clinton. "The reason we decided to do this, not that we think the governments won't do their part, is we need to have a fund where we can fill in the blanks and help people who otherwise will be totally overlooked. A lot of people, they have no cars, no homes, nothing."

Unsurprisingly, reporters asked the two former presidents about the national eruption of fury at the Bush administration, which showed no sign of abating. The elder Bush shrugged off the controversy, admitting that while he didn't relish the harsh criticism of his son, "it comes with the territory" as president.

Ever the diplomat, Clinton brushed off any question of blame until days later, when he told a CNN reporter: "Our government failed those people in the beginning, and I take it now there is no dispute about it. One hundred percent of the people I've talked to here recognize that it was a failure, and I personally believe that there should be a serious analysis of it."

Among the elected officials in their party was a freshman senator from Illinois and budding political celebrity named Barack Obama. When Obama had called Clinton a few days earlier about raising money for the hurricane victims in his home state, the former president had invited him to join them in Houston. Sensing an opportunity to speak to a national audience about the poverty and neglect that the disaster had exposed, the young politician had immediately accepted Clinton's offer.

Shadowed by security, the Clintons and the Bushes walked through the Astrodome with Obama, stopping to greet families, embrace small children, and listen. At one point, Obama picked up a little girl who showed him a paper heart she had made in the shelter's daycare center.

"What's your name, sweetie?" Obama asked her. "You look so pretty. You made this heart and decided to give it to Bill Clinton, didn't you?" The girl, who said her name was Kearra, nodded shyly.

"Well, I give you my heart," said a beaming Clinton as he hugged the child. "You're beautiful. Thank you for the heart."

There were many less uplifting moments, as the evacuees poured out the stories of the losses they had suffered and the terror they had just barely escaped. Several days later, in an emotional speech on the Senate floor, Obama recalled their experience. "We heard, in very intimate terms, the heart-wrenching stories that all of us have witnessed from a distance over the past several days: mothers separated from babies, adults mourning the loss of elderly parents, descriptions of the heat and filth and fear of the Superdome and the Convention Center." Obama campaign consultant David Axelrod would mark that speech as a turning point, when the Illinois senator told his staff to start thinking about a possible bid for the presidency in 2008.

The political implications were even clearer for the Clintons, as speculation about Hillary's future presidential aspirations began to rise again. "Isn't it interesting that Bush realizes he's in trouble and has to phone President Clinton for cover?" crowed Bob Mulholland, a California Democratic leader, in the *New York Times*. "You've got all these photos of President Clinton with both Bushes. It's hard for a Republican in the national arena to be attacking the Clintons with these kinds of images out there."

———

By noon, both Clintons were again in the air, heading home to Chappaqua. A Secret Service detail took Hillary back to Old House Lane. But idling at the Westchester airport was another private jet, which would take Bill Clinton on the first leg of a world-girdling trip. It was owned by their old friend Ronald Burkle.

Like John Catsimatidis—indeed, like nearly all of the billionaires cultivated by Clinton—Burkle was a truly self-made tycoon. Starting out as a box boy in a grocery store managed by his father, he eventually built a leveraged-buyout empire of supermarket chains and, when his exit strategies produced big profits, created a diversified investment group called the Yucaipa Companies. As a generous Democratic donor and fundraiser, with strong ties to labor unions whose pension funds he invested, he had grown close to the Clintons during the White House years. They had become so close that in 2002, the former president chose to join Yucaipa as a paid adviser to two of its domestic funds, after rejecting many other offers to join corporate boards.

Burkle would explain that he had urged Clinton to work with Yucaipa because he didn't want to see his friend's dignity sacrificed to earning money as a cable TV host. "I thought, let's do something that is worker-friendly and community-friendly," he said. "If you need to make money, let's do something good." Clinton did need to make money, especially during the early and very difficult period on his own—and Yucaipa paid him millions. He had flown everywhere on the company's airliner, often with the owner aboard.

Upon returning from Houston, Clinton soon boarded Burkle's aircraft with Band, Cooper, and his Secret Service detail to cross the Atlantic Ocean overnight, on the first leg of a long journey that would take him through Central Asia, India, and China. In the early morning hours they touched down in Glasgow for refueling—and for breakfast with Sir Tom Hunter, then the wealthiest man in Scotland and that nation's first homegrown billionaire. He, too, had risen from nowhere, having started a business selling sneakers from the back of a van that became Europe's largest independent retail chain.

Hunter owned Learjets that he sometimes loaned to Clinton, and he had accompanied the former president several weeks earlier, during the first part of the Africa tour, to Mozambique and Lesotho—the latter, although tiny, being the most intense AIDS hotspot on the continent. Impressed with what he found at CHAI's clinics in those countries, the Scotsman had tentatively pledged to donate $100 million to health and education projects in Africa over ten years. At breakfast he confirmed that commitment to Clinton—and agreed to announce it at the inaugural meeting of the Clinton Global Initiative in mid-September in New York.

Much later that day, following an eight-hour flight direct from Glasgow across central Europe and Russia, the Clinton party landed in the mountainside city of Almaty, capital of Kazakhstan. Despite the late hour they proceeded directly from the airport to a meeting with the Kazakh president, the notorious autocrat Nursultan Nazarbayev; much as if Clinton were on an official diplomatic mission, they discussed political and economic conditions in the former Soviet republic and its relations with the United States and the international community.

At a joint press conference, Clinton praised Nazarbayev for destroying the nuclear arsenal left by the Russians, who had tested weapons in the remote territory. Before sitting down to a midnight banquet, Clinton signed an agreement with the Kazakh health ministry, permitting the government to purchase HIV/AIDS drugs through CHAI. And still later, around 2:30 a.m., Clinton met with Kazakh opposition leaders to hear their complaints against Nazarbayev's regime, which the State Department and international organizations routinely charged with serious human rights and civil liberties abuses.

Within an hour, Clinton and his party were again airborne, on a southeasterly course toward the city of Lucknow, India. But they had switched planes to a well-appointed private McDonnell Douglas MD-87, owned by a man named Frank Giustra—a wealthy mining investor from Vancouver who was also the founder and former chairman of Lion's Gate Entertainment in Hollywood.

The second-generation son of an Italian immigrant, Giustra's consuming interest in philanthropy had led him in middle age to seek out Clinton. His charitable endeavors had been low-key and anonymous, mostly centered on the poor and homeless in his own city—until the Asian tsunami struck and he decided to host a big fundraising event in January 2005 at his palatial waterfront home in an exclusive West Vancouver neighborhood. Through his entertainment industry connections, Giustra arranged for an evening in his living room featuring comic actor Robin Williams and the Barenaked Ladies band, which brought in nearly $2 million for tsunami relief.

Through a mutual acquaintance, Giustra had also arranged for Clinton to send a "thank-you" message to his event via pretaped video, a process that put him in touch briefly with Doug Band. Then a few months later, Giustra heard through another friend that the Clinton Foundation was soliciting the loan of an airplane (as the advance staff was almost always doing at any given moment) for a trip to Central America.

After Giustra offered his plane to the foundation, he received a call from Tim Phillips, an international consultant and fundraiser who sometimes worked for Clinton. On the telephone, Giustra quickly realized that Phillips was checking him out, trying to determine what he wanted. "Can I come along?" Giustra finally asked, only to be told that Clinton "doesn't know you." He felt brushed off, but soon Giustra called Phillips back with a slightly different proposal: Since he needed to visit Colombia on business himself, he would depart the plane there and let Clinton fly on without him. Band approved it.

Within an hour after Clinton shook hands with the short, graying Giustra, the initial ice was broken. Aboard his plane, they somehow alighted on the topic of *Rubicon*, popular historian Tom Holland's account of the end of the Roman Republic, a book they had both enjoyed. When Clinton started to quote verbatim from its text, Giustra was astonished.

On the way southward they had stopped in Little Rock, where Clinton dragged his new friend along to a meeting with three dozen Baptist ministers. They had flown on to Mexico City, where they dined with Carlos Slim, the magnate and philanthropist then on his way to becoming one of the very richest men in the world. And at some point on that trip, as Giustra tried to get to sleep late one night, someone knocked on his door: "The president wants to know whether you'd like to play cards"—his true initiation into Clinton's crew.

While playing cards, Giustra and Clinton talked about the foundation's work, with particular focus on CHAI, which the Canadian businessman judged "a brilliant idea." He offered to help any way he could. His initial pledge to CHAI amounted to $30 million, and he provided his plane whenever possible. On this occasion, his own visit to finalize a major uranium-mining deal in Kazakhstan had coincided with Clinton's stop there—and Giustra seized the chance to travel on with him through Asia. Years later, journalists would suggest that Giustra's presence with Clinton in the Kazakh capital had been no coincidence, but an attempt to promote the mining executive's prospects there. In fact, Clinton originally had been encouraged to visit Kazakhstan by the Indian steel magnate Lakshmi Mittal, another foundation donor who did business there.

Arriving in Lucknow, they crashed in hotel rooms until late morning. Thanks to his connections in the Indian American community, Clinton had tapped into the power networks of Uttar Pradesh, India's most populous state, where he met with several state ministers and business leaders.

Clinton hosted a fundraising dinner for his foundation in Lucknow that evening before departing on Giustra's plane for Zhengzhou, China—the beginning of another five days of frenetic plane-hopping to Kunming to Urumqi to Hangzhou to Beijing, where he marked the September 11th anniversary with the American ambassador and staff at the U.S. embassy. Along the way, as he visited CHAI-assisted clinics in Zhengzhou and Beijing, Clinton delivered paid speeches—including an address to a meeting in Hangzhou hosted by Alibaba, a then-obscure Chinese company that would become the largest online retailer in the world, with estimated annual sales of nearly $13 billion.

The last stop on this frenetic odyssey was Hong Kong, where he spoke at not one but two dinners on the evening of September 12, including a fundraiser for his library, which had not yet fully discharged its debts. He flew back to New York that same night. The Clinton Global Initiative was scheduled to open at the Sheraton in Midtown Manhattan in two days.

The first time Bill Clinton mentioned CGI in a public forum had been almost nine months earlier, when he took the World Economic Forum stage in Davos on January 27, 2005. Sitting for an interview with the American television journalist Charlie Rose before an audience of hundreds of corporate executives, heads of state, artists, scientists, academics, journalists, and nonprofit leaders gathered in the big auditorium, he waited for the question that the American TV anchor had been quietly directed to ask by Doug Band.

"You're creating something called the Clinton Global Initiative—September, New York," drawled Rose, "because you believe there is a necessity to do . . . what?"

"Give homework assignments!" retorted Clinton, to a ripple of laughter from the audience. "I'm a big supporter of Davos, but the world leaders of the rich and the poor countries and everybody in between come to the U.N. every year in September. . . .

"So what I thought we would do this year is to have a somewhat smaller version of what we do at the World Economic Forum, but that it would be focused very much on specific things all the participants could do. . . . Everybody who comes needs to know on the front end that you're going to be asked your opinion about what we should do on AIDS, TB, malaria; what the private sector can do about global warming . . . and then you're going to be asked to participate in very specific decisions about that and to make very specific commitments." He emphasized that final word, then paused and smiled. "We may only have ten people show up!"

Not wishing to denigrate the Forum, where he drew large and enthusiastic crowds every year, or its ingratiating impresario Klaus Schwab, Clinton said that CGI would be "very complementary to Davos"—although its stated aims implied a critique.

"I just see all these people leave here every year full of energy," said Clinton, "wanting to *do something* and wanting to know there is a place where they can actually go and say, OK, what is my assignment?" He would not only give out the assignments, he concluded, but grade the homework, too. It was vitally important to "keep score" of every effort to make change in the world, he admonished: "We need to know, we did *this thing* and it got *that result*," smacking his hand on the coffee table.

Clinton was inclined to grade his own humanitarian efforts quite harshly. "The AIDS thing drives me nuts," he told the Davos audience. "At the end of this quarter"—in March 2005—"we will be treating 100,000 people with our contracts with the Indian and South African [generic drug] companies. That's, I think, more than what any other country is doing except Brazil—and it's appalling."

But, he continued, "We have 30 other countries about to go onto our [generic drug purchasing] contracts through the World Health Organization, so we could have two million of the six million [AIDS victims] who need it by the first quarter of next year. . . . I feel better than I did three years ago. And I still don't feel that we're doing a very good job."

By the time Clinton announced CGI at Davos, a year after it was conceived there, Doug Band had brought together a small team of former White House aides with Richard Attias, the event planner and impresario who had long managed the staging of Davos.

The first person Band had called was Mary Morrison, an energetic, multilingual, and highly effective young woman who had started in 1995 as a White House intern, graduated to the scheduling office, and ended as deputy chief of operations in the Oval Office. All that they knew for certain at that point was that they wanted to put on a Davos-style event—but one that would require participants to "do things, not just talk about doing things."

Early on, the CGI team had chosen a conference date: three days in mid-September that coincided with the opening of the United Nations General Assembly, when many heads of state would be present in New York. (Clinton had met personally with U.N. Secretary-General Kofi Annan to ensure that he found the plan agreeable—and invite him to participate.)

The foundation's financing was still too insecure to justify a significant risk on a project that would clearly cost millions of dollars to produce. Within its first four years, Clinton and his associates had raised $168 million for the foundation, including CHAI and the library (which had consumed the great bulk of funding), plus another $74 million in pledges, but were still carrying a substantial debt. They had achieved that level of success without a dedicated development structure and—as Band, Bruce Lindsey, and others in the leadership well knew—without the kind of systems that raise money efficiently for other public charities.

At the same time that the foundation was attempting to launch its "global initiative," Clinton agreed to a formidable new domestic project—a national effort to reduce childhood obesity, in cooperation with the American Heart Association. A charitable powerhouse with thousands of employees and an annual budget in the hundreds of millions, the AHA had reached out to Clinton in the wake of his heart surgery, after he had expressed a strong urge to raise public consciousness about heart disease, diet, and exercise—and asked him to serve as a spokesman for its existing campaign. Having acknowledged his own difficulties as an overweight boy, and his lifelong history of poor eating habits, he could become a sympathetic role model for kids struggling to become fit. He could tape a public service announcement and appear occasionally at events.

But that role wasn't enough for Clinton, who believed he could do more to *solve* the problem than merely speak on behalf of AHA. On May 3, he appeared at a public school in Manhattan to announce that his foundation would join the AHA in creating and sponsoring a series of programs to turn back the growing wave of obesity among American children and adolescents. By his side, as he talked about how heavy he was at age fifteen (five feet nine inches, 210 pounds), stood Arkansas governor Mike Huckabee, an old political antagonist who had lost more than one hundred pounds after developing type 2 diabetes.

Glancing at Huckabee, Clinton quipped: "He is about half the size as when I first met him. While I am always trying to shrink the ranks of Republicans, I never really thought this was the way to do it."

But the potential cost of this fresh initiative was no joke—especially because in the months since Clinton first agreed to work with AHA, Ira Magaziner had developed an ambitious plan that involved engagement across the country with local schools, food and beverage companies, and health care providers, under the banner of a new organization to be called the Alliance for a Healthier Generation. It would cost millions of dollars that had yet to be raised.

By then, the foundation had raised at least some of the money required to launch CGI. The first "investor" was Jeffrey Epstein, the wealthy financial consultant who had traveled to Africa with Clinton on his plane in 2002, and their mutual friend Ghislaine Maxwell, socialite daughter of the late British publisher Robert Maxwell. Together Epstein and Maxwell provided a loan of $750,000 in CGI seed funding. The first-year cost would ultimately hit $7 million, with much of the additional financing provided by grants from Google (as promised), the Gates and Rockefeller foundations, and Thomas Golisano, an iconoclastic billionaire from Rochester who had once run as an independent for governor of New York.

Mary Morrison had started work on the still nameless conference during the spring of 2004, from a cubicle in Attias's offices at the Manhattan outpost of Publicis Groupe, the big French advertising and public relations agency. Joining her at Publicis over the summer was Ed Hughes, another former intern whose history with Clinton dated back to his volunteer work in the 1992 New Hampshire presidential primary as a college undergraduate.

Along with Eric Nonacs, the former president's foreign policy adviser, who worked from the Harlem office, the diligent Hughes oversaw program development—while Morrison handled every aspect of the event's logistics, from security arrangements for participating heads of state down to lunch boxes and the color of tablecloths, not to mention the process of designing and selecting a logo. (After much consideration, Clinton picked a starry blue swoosh that resembled the European Union flag.) From lighting and sound systems to communications, food service, press accommodations, and gift bags filled with donated items, the problems multiplied. Morrison and Hughes worked late into every night for weeks on end. Some days, Morrison felt so exhausted and overwhelmed that she put her head down on her desk and wept.

Still, the work moved forward.

Over the course of many meetings and memos, Clinton articulated four broad areas of focus for CGI—governance in the developing world, poverty alleviation, environmental protection, and conflict resolution. Those vague guidelines formed an early framework to which Nonacs gradually added ideas for specific topics, panels, and speakers, drawing heavily upon the advice of Clinton's former White House chief of staff John Podesta, former national security adviser Sandy Berger, former Mideast policy adviser Robert Malley, and former economic adviser Gene Sperling, as well as David Sandalow, a former assistant secretary of state for environmental affairs, and Gayle Smith, a former special assistant to Clinton and chief of staff at the U.S. Agency for International Development.

As he commented on the content memos from Nonacs, Clinton constantly emphasized the need for "doers as well as talkers" to participate, and his desire to bring together as diverse a group as possible, from geography to gender. The event's content would reflect not only Clinton's will, but his worldview. Every participant would have to agree in advance to undertake real action after the conference ended, each of which would be announced publicly as a "commitment."

And they had set the price of annual "membership" at $15,000, a very pricey ticket but well below the cost of admission at Davos, high enough to cover costs while allowing a significant percentage of complimentary admissions for those unable to pay. They had determined to limit attendance to eight hundred or so paid guests, plus two to three hundred who would be admitted free, in order to ensure a "substantive and interactive" experience for all.

As the days dwindled before CGI's debut, the new event began to draw excited media coverage—an hourlong CNN special with footage shot in Africa, interviews with Clinton on ABC's *This Week,* CNN's *Larry King Live,* NBC's *Today* show and *Meet the Press,* BBC TV, and National Public Radio—more attention than he had received since the publication of his memoir.

They had no idea what was going to happen when they opened the doors for the first time at the Sheraton Midtown on the afternoon of September 15.

———

The first couple of hours of the inaugural Clinton Global Initiative were inauspicious, if not quite disastrous. Long lines of grumbling "members" who had paid thousands of dollars to attend stretched further and further into the huge lobby of the Sheraton. Volunteers organized by Mary Morrison were trying to register them, photograph them for security badges, hand them gift bags, and see them through a rigorous security screening. But the unpaid staffers were inexperienced, the process slow and cumbersome. Just getting people into the building took much too long, cutting into the schedule and stoking frustration.

When the registration logjam finally cleared, the program began to move more smoothly.

With lights dimmed, the hotel's enormous grand ballroom had been set up to resemble an oversized television studio with a seated audience. Buzzing with conversation, hundreds of men and women, mostly wearing dark-hued business attire, milled about and then seated themselves in rows facing a blindingly white stage accented with sky blue. Looming behind them were several raised banks of TV cameras pointed at the stage, where a pair of mammoth video screens flanked a row of blocky, overstuffed white leather chairs.

Over the loudspeakers came the smooth baritone voice of a professional announcer, politely urging everyone to sit down. A few moments later, the announcer said simply, "Bill Clinton." To the cool techno hum of Moby's "Porcelain"—an instrumental tune often played as background sound in car and liquor commercials—he ambled out from behind the set as the audience rose to applaud.

Lean and at ease in a tailored blue suit coordinated with the décor, Clinton brandished a wireless microphone. Joining him moments later were Tony Blair, Condoleezza Rice, and King Abdullah II of Jordan, all prepared to engage in a rambling and agreeable chat, prompted by questions from Clinton about Mideast peace, terrorism, nuclear proliferation, clean energy, and international trade, sounding much like guests on a high-minded talk show. Lurking in the audience were current and former heads of state, such as Israeli president Shimon Peres, Ireland's Gerry Adams, and the presidents of South Africa, Ukraine, Nigeria, Turkey, and the Dominican Republic; pop stars including Mick Jagger, Barbra Streisand, Angelina Jolie, Brad Pitt, Leonardo DiCaprio, Tony Bennett, and Bono; and chief executives of several of the world's largest companies, notably Coca-Cola and Dow Chemical, seated with nonprofit leaders and social activists from around the world.

The theme music, the elaborate stage set, the mood lighting, the production values, and the surfeit of political, business, and entertainment celebrities—the "optics" of the entire event—were anything but modest. To Clinton's implacable critics, this could have looked like nothing more than a chance to shine the spotlight on himself. It looked slick—a term often applied unflatteringly to its impresario himself.

For much of the two days that followed, Clinton held court in a hotel suite forty-five floors above the panels and plenary sessions, conferring with the great and the good to commit themselves and their resources to global improvement. He discovered that many of the world leaders in town for the U.N.'s opening session wished to see him, and he seized the chance to advance his foundation's objectives in those meetings. CGI had created a completely new platform that enhanced his status and his causes. He would venture down to the stage from time to time to announce a major new "commitment," whether from basketball star Michael Jordan's mother, promising to build a new hospital in Kenya, or a Swiss Re insurance executive vowing to invest $250 million in clean energy; after making each announcement, Clinton stood still and smiled for a photo with each commitment maker.

The most heavily attended panel, unsurprisingly, featured a discussion of climate change with Hillary Clinton and former NATO commander Wesley Clark, the retired four-star Army general from Arkansas. Clark had run for president briefly in 2004 as a Democrat, while Hillary was expected to run in 2008. And in contrast to her husband's cordial exchanges with Condoleezza Rice, the New York senator lambasted the Bush White House.

Noting that she had recently returned from her second visit to the melting Arctic polar ice cap, she said, "We were a leader in the Kyoto process," referring to her husband's administration, "and since then we have abdicated leadership on this crucial issue." She called for a market-based cap-and-trade regime to reduce atmospheric carbon, a "crash program" to advance renewable energy technologies by the Pentagon's Defense Advanced Research Projects Agency, and intensified negotiations with the governments of China and India over emissions reduction.

But perhaps more surprising was the appearance of a special guest at the Saturday luncheon plenary session in the grand ballroom. Bill Clinton strode to the podium, accompanied by piano music, where he announced several CGI commitments—including a plan by Swiss Re to invest $250 million in European renewable energy projects. The insurance giant's chief executive, John Cooper, showed up for the photo and handshake with Clinton.

Then Clinton introduced his former vice president, noting that he had read Gore's prescient 1992 book, *Earth in the Balance*, "before I knew we would be running together" on their party's presidential ticket that year. "He is one of the most important thinkers our public life has ever produced," said Clinton. In his own remarks, Gore warned that Hurricane Katrina was the first harbinger of "a global emergency, a deepening climate crisis that requires us to act."

Not all of the panels were so high-minded, and one of the sessions moderated by Clinton himself proved rather comical, as News Corp chair Rupert Murdoch jousted with Time Warner's Richard Parsons and Sir Howard Stringer of CBS and Sony in a discussion of global media. When Parsons praised CNN—a division of Time Warner—as "the best and best-positioned global media company in the world," he provoked Murdoch to growl: "I don't think he watches CNN International. It's so unwatchable and so anti-American!" The audience roared.

When the first Clinton Global Initiative concluded, after two very full days of panels—and nights that saw the former president hopping from one restaurant to another, beginning with a dinner party on opening night at Nobu, the super-swank sushi restaurant—he would announce that the participants had signed agreements to sponsor, finance, and oversee more than two hundred separate projects valued at $2.5 billion. They had pledged to invest hundreds of millions of dollars in renewable energy, small business credit for women entrepreneurs, clean water for Ghana and terrorism insurance in Gaza, environmental protection for Tierra del Fuego and youth employment in the Balkans.

For his part, Clinton pledged publicly at the final plenary session that his foundation would monitor the fulfillment of all the bold promises made at CGI—an undertaking that would prove to be a perennial challenge. He also promised that he and the foundation would continue to host CGI annually for at least ten years.

The question that lingered beneath the surface was whether any of the hundreds of commitments would generate substantial improvement in the lives of the world's downtrodden, so distant and disconnected from all the very important people Clinton had summoned. Two and a half billion dollars was undoubtedly a decent down payment on progress, and a substantial marker of success for CGI, but that sum wouldn't go very far on a sweltering planet where more than a billion people existed in conditions of extreme poverty and untreated disease.

Clinton was well aware of the issues of scale—a word he used often—but nevertheless felt excited by the debut of CGI and grateful to those who had created the conference from what had once seemed like a fleeting notion. On a formal thank-you letter that went out on his personal stationery to everyone who had assisted with CGI, he scrawled a handwritten note to Doug Band: "This is yours [underlined twice]. I hope you're proud of it," signed "Bill."

While the outcome of the commitments was yet to be measured, CGI had inspired the usual suspects among the global elite—and a lot of other well-intended people—to *do something.* Interviewed a week later, Clinton said, "I don't know what I expected, but I didn't think it would do this well. Maybe not half as well! And I've had probably dozens of people come up to me and say it was the best meeting of this kind they'd ever been to." He smiled. "Because there weren't speeches, everybody was serious, everybody was working on very specific things, and they really did feel like they had the power to make a difference. It worked out even better than I thought it would."

He dismissed critics who complained that he had just put on the show to gain publicity, or to promote his wife's political ambitions. "This thing got a lot of media coverage because it was a big thing, and it was in New York so it was easy to cover, and it did a lot of good." He grinned and mimicked the critics. "Yeah, it's a good thing, yeah, it's gonna help a lot, yeah, it's going to do a lot of good for a lot of people, it's going to save a lot of lives—but he probably still shouldn't have done it because he just wanted publicity." He paused. "That's pretty lame, I think. I could think of all kinds of ways to get publicity. I could get lots of publicity if I just sat right out on the street."

Clinton had come to believe that the CHAI model—pointing toward a new system that would bring together governments, companies, nonprofit groups, international organizations, and private donors—had implications beyond its own mission of delivering medical treatment to AIDS victims. He thought great things could be achieved by leveraging the money and power of states and corporations with the flexibility and skills of the nonprofit sector. The enthusiastic response to the launch of CGI was a signal that the world in which he operated was ready for higher levels of cooperation and perhaps even global leadership.

"This movement has grown so rapidly, and there's so many people doing it, and it's so entrepreneurial, that I think it would profit from better coordination, more information sharing, and combining efforts. . . . I think that since so much money is going out there, and since on the whole it's fairly cost-efficient, it would be beneficial if we all worked together more." Even he had no idea then just how broadly and deeply CGI would reshape global philanthropy in the years to come.

———

Whatever Clinton's wonkish hopes, the first meeting of the Clinton Global Initiative had proved enormously beneficial to his image as a respected world leader. Media coverage of the event was overwhelmingly positive, although not every report could resist a touch of snark. Skeptical outlets suddenly found reason to praise him. Even his implacably Republican hometown daily, the *Arkansas Democrat-Gazette*, restrained its editorial mockery of CGI's do-gooding liberal internationalism and concluded with a stunning paean to its longtime target:

> Bill Clinton isn't just another politician. Say what you will about the old boy (and we do) but you can't just call him another pol. He can work not only the room but the world. If he can put all his mind and energy into fighting poverty, conflict, climate change and government repression, then . . . watch out poverty, conflict, climate change, and government repression. There are worse things an ex-president could do with his political capital.

In the *Washington Post*, another newspaper where he had few friends, Tina Brown suggested that "Clinton seems to have found his role as facilitator-in-chief, urging us to give up our deadly national passivity and start thinking things through for ourselves. Commandeering the role of government through civic action suddenly feels like a very empowering notion—the alternative being to find oneself stranded in a flood waving a shirt from a rooftop. . . .

"No one would have believed that Clinton—the king of spin, who went out under a cloud of indecency five years ago—could climb back to such credibility. Monica is fading and he's backlit now by his disciplined handling of the economy, the unsought comparisons of how well FEMA used to perform under his watch, and the enlightened nature of his global activism."

In that sense of astonishment, she was not alone.

CHAPTER TWELVE

If the true nature of the bond between Bill and Hillary Clinton continued to fascinate a curious public, the importance of their relationship endured for both—even during a long period when they mostly lived apart. With the onset of the midterm political cycle in 2006, as New York's junior senator looked toward her first bid for reelection and perhaps beyond, the stakes in their marriage again began to rise.

Leaving aside the Clintons' emotional connection—which few people who knew them well doubted, despite the humiliation inflicted upon her by his misconduct—their continuing impact on each other's lives and aspirations was complex. Bill had always admired Hillary, depended upon her, and promoted her. Having spent decades promoting Bill, Hillary had fully emerged from his shadow to become one of the most admired women in the world, a testament to her talents and her determination to vault every obstacle, including the misogyny that perpetually confronted female politicians. Despite their marital crises, they had been effective political partners while building a closely knit family around their daughter.

But the unfolding of his post-presidency and her Senate tenure exposed inherent tensions, as their paths diverged. Although Bill would never say so, Hillary's political prominence sometimes created difficulties for him as a former president and global philanthropic leader. From the perspective of the aides helping to shape his post-presidency, particularly Doug Band, partisan conflict continually risked damage to Bill Clinton as a statesman, by limiting his outreach and diminishing his broad appeal. But as a lifelong political pro, Clinton still loved the game that her career encouraged him to keep playing.

And although Hillary would never say so, Bill's fluency, skill, and even his renewed popularity sometimes created difficulties for her as a fledgling pol on her own. The invidious comparison between her and her husband—a man widely regarded as the most talented politician of their generation—had become a favored cliché among journalists sometime during her first Senate race. Like many banal observations it was more than a little true, as Hillary never tried to deny.

Early in February 2006, that contrast was highlighted at the funeral of Coretta Scott King, widow of the slain civil rights leader, who had died of ovarian cancer. King's televised memorial service, held in a suburban megachurch that easily accommodated a spirited throng of more than ten thousand mourners, included remarks by President George W. Bush, former President Carter—and both Clintons, who went up to the altar together.

The standing ovation they received went on for more than a minute, until Bill Clinton repeatedly gestured for quiet, biting his lip and smiling. He had the mourners laughing and applauding from the moment he started speaking. "I thank you for that wonderful reception. You might not feel like repeating it after you hear what I've got to say." He joked about his relationship with Bush 41, whom he gently mocked as an Episcopalian, "one of the frozen chosen."

Then his tone abruptly changed as he pointed to the casket.

"I don't want us to forget that there's a woman in there, not a symbol—not a symbol! A real woman who lived and breathed and got angry and got hurt and had dreams and disappointments." He spoke of the burdens she had borne every day as the great civil rights leader's wife, and of how her children must be feeling at that moment, as they prepared to bury their mother. He imagined Coretta King's conflicting emotions on the day after the assassination in 1968 when, instead of secluding herself, she went directly to Memphis to march with the impoverished sanitation workers in her dead husband's place.

"Now, that's the most important thing for us," said Clinton. "Because what really matters, if you believe all this stuff we've been saying, is what are we going to do with the rest of our lives? So her children, they know they've got to carry the legacy of their father and their mother now. We all clap for that; they've got to go home and live with it. That's a terrible burden. That is a terrible burden. You should pray for them and support them and help them."

In rising voice, bolstered by bursts of applause, Clinton built on this theme—the responsibility of all to carry on the work of Martin and Coretta—until he reached an electrifying conclusion: "We can follow in her steps. We can honor Dr. King's sacrifice. We can help his children fulfill their legacy. Everybody who believes that the promise of America is for every American, everybody who believes that all people in the world are caught up in what he so eloquently called the inescapable web of mutuality, every one of us in a way, we are all the children of Martin Luther and Coretta Scott King. And I for one am grateful for her life and her friendship."

Following him, Hillary delivered prepared remarks that, on paper, were touching and uplifting. But her reception didn't approach the wild clapping, laughter, cheers, tears, and roars of "Amen!" in response to his extemporaneous sermon. The reviews were unsparing: "As Bill riffed, Hillary stood by his side, looking like the gawky sidekick in a teen movie. . . . He stole the show and made his wife look like an ordinary politician."

Such nagging comparisons could be minimized, if not eliminated, by making sure that husband and wife didn't appear together in public too often. There were few occasions when a direct contrast would be unavoidable.

The clashes between her political ambitions and his global presence could not be so easily anticipated and deflected. The first came within weeks after the King funeral, in the midst of a furious national debate over the proposed takeover of American shipping facilities by Dubai Ports World, a company controlled by the ruling families of the United Arab Emirates.

The controversy erupted after the Bush administration approved the Dubai firm's $7 billion purchase of Peninsular & Oriental Steam Navigation, an old British company that operated ports in New York, New Jersey, Philadelphia, Baltimore, Miami, and New Orleans. To many in Congress, that approval appeared to have been rushed through, without sufficient attention to dubious connections between the Emirates and al Qaeda as well as the Taliban. In 1999, the presence of Emirati royals at Osama bin Laden's Afghan hunting camp had thwarted an American air strike against the terrorist sheikh; moreover, two of the 9/11 hijackers had carried Emirati passports, and the conspirators had used safe houses and bank accounts in Dubai. The Islamist nuclear weapons conspiracy overseen by Pakistani physicist A. Q. Khan had also operated behind a fake computer firm in the glittering Gulf city.

Although the UAE government had fully supported American efforts against terrorism following the September 2001 attack—maintaining that support in the years that followed—congressional opponents of the ports deal cited lingering security concerns. Some of those critics also pointed with suspicion to the deep personal and financial connections between members of the Bush family and the Emirates rulers, embarrassing the White House at a moment when President Bush's approval ratings were already in free fall. Both the president's father and his brother Neil had benefited from Emirati largesse.

In the midst of this bitter dispute—which pitted a presidential veto threat against a bipartisan legislative majority seeking to kill the deal—the *Financial Times* reported that executives of Dubai Ports World had consulted Bill Clinton about their troubles. On the evening of February 17, the Emirati businessmen had reached Clinton in Goa, India, where he had spent the day visiting the headquarters of Cipla, the big generic drug manufacturer that supplied antiretroviral formulations to CHAI partners in more than thirty countries. (The stop in Goa was part of a longer trip that included the Delhi society wedding of Vikram Chatwal, playboy son of the very wealthy Indian American hotelier Sant Singh Chatwal, a donor and friend.)

Clinton listened as the Dubai Ports executives recounted their troubles in Washington. His response was crisp: Their company should submit to a more thorough federal investigation, and must guarantee that should they eventually prevail politically, they would substantially improve security at all their American ports.

Whatever Hillary Clinton might have felt about her husband's advice to Dubai Ports, she had already come to a decision about the Emirati firm. While he was in Asia, she announced her plan to introduce a bill that would prohibit any company owned by a foreign government from acquiring American port facilities—on the same day that he spoke with the Emiratis. But that didn't discourage certain Republicans from fabricating a Clinton conspiracy as a distraction from Bush's veto threat.

Bill Clinton had received generous speaking fees and million-dollar library donations from the Maktoum family that rules Dubai, and the Nahyan family that rules the capital of Abu Dhabi and controls the national government there. And, one of Ron Burkle's Yucaipa investment funds, then partly owned by Clinton, had entered into partnership with a Dubai sovereign wealth fund, although not the same fund that owned Dubai Ports World.

The Persian Gulf monarchs had been generous not to Clinton alone, but to all his recent predecessors. Their millions of petrodollars had underwritten every presidential library, including that of George H. W. Bush. The investment funds and other businesses in the Gulf States had provided lucrative opportunities for various Bush family members, including two of the president's brothers.

Clinton's own relationship with the Emirati leaders dated back to his presidency. True to long-standing American policy, he had cultivated the Gulf Arab leaders, whom he viewed as moderate and modernizing forces in the region, despite their autocratic regimes, exploitive labor policies, and adherence to conservative Islam. Since leaving the White House he had maintained ties with all the Gulf States and especially the Emirates, whose comparatively progressive leaders were seeking to develop new projects with Western governments, cultural institutions, and universities.

Yet there was no evidence to support the charge—leveled by a few Republicans on Capitol Hill and the usual right-wing commentators—that the Clintons had covertly advanced the Dubai Ports takeover. "President Clinton now is on record as advising the emir [of Dubai] on how to make this deal go through," complained right-wing Representative Duncan Hunter of California on ABC News.

Senator Clinton had acted against the interest of the Emirates' rulers, in fact, despite her husband's connections with them. And Bill Clinton spoke out publicly in support of her restrictive legislation. "Whether [her bill] passes or not," said a statement released by his office, "he believes this purchase should not be approved unless the security of our ports can be dramatically improved."

Still, the Dubai Ports controversy provided an early warning about the problem posed by Clinton's worldwide network of partnerships with wealthy individuals, major corporations, foreign governments, and their leaders. If his affiliations appeared to compromise Hillary's role in government, the damage to both of their reputations could be severe. However innocuous the underlying realities might be, appearances mattered more, especially under the scorching spotlight of national politics. And perhaps because they felt so sure of their own probity and benign purposes, neither Bill nor Hillary Clinton would always be sufficiently sensitive to how things might appear—or might be made to appear.

———

Much more troubling to Hillary and her closest associates was the constant chatter concerning her husband's alleged extramarital romances, which buzzed in the background—and was always amplified by speculation about her presidential aspirations. If he appeared anywhere with an attractive and unattached woman, even in a group photo leaving a restaurant, her name would be "linked" to him in tabloid columns, as occurred regularly for a while with Belinda Stronach, a divorced Canadian heiress in her forties who held a seat in Parliament. He had likewise been "linked" to another wealthy, younger Canadian woman living in New York, to a divorced blond neighbor in Chappaqua, even to actress Gina Gershon—not much of a real connection was required to stimulate gossip.

Both Clintons resented this whispering as a damnable intrusion on their privacy, but the condition of their marriage wasn't a topic that could be brushed aside, at least not politically. The scars sustained in the Lewinsky affair had permanently sensitized not just their friends or their enemies, but the entire Democratic Party apparatus to the threat posed by any reprise of that kind of scandal. It was a subject that engaged the prurient, anxious gaze of everyone, from ordinary voters to congressional leaders.

It was also a matter that drew the attention of the editors of the *New York Times*, who assigned reporter Patrick Healy to conduct an exhaustive inquisition into the Clintons' marriage and its potential impact on her political career during the spring of 2006. After much internal debate among aides to both husband and wife over whether to cooperate with Healy, they sent forth press secretaries Jay Carson, representing Bill, and Philippe Reines, representing Hillary, to deal with his questions. In the meantime, Healy had reached out to fifty Clinton friends, acquaintances, and former aides.

On May 23, the story appeared above the fold on the paper's front page, under the headline "For Clintons, Delicate Dance of Married and

Public Lives." Aside from a suggestive mention of Stronach—who had been glimpsed emerging from a Manhattan steak restaurant with Bill Clinton and about ten other people—the article chronicled, somewhat poignantly, the difficulties of maintaining contact when both partners are exceptionally busy and often traveling.

"Mr. Clinton is rarely without company in public, yet the company he keeps rarely includes his wife. Nights out find him zipping around Los Angeles with his bachelor buddy, Ronald W. Burkle, or hitting parties and fund-raisers in Manhattan; she is yoked to work in Washington or New York—her Senate career and political ambitions consuming her time," Healy wrote.

While his article carped about a lack of cooperation from Reines and Carson, they had provided him with complete data from their schedules, showing exactly when they had been together since the beginning of 2005. On average, they had spent fourteen days per month in each other's company—a figure that, as Healy would later acknowledge, was "about average" for political spouses. They had constructed largely separate lives, as Healy noted, partly out of necessity and partly to keep Bill from overshadowing Hillary.

Refusing Healy's request to interview his subjects, Carson and Reines instead had given the *Times* a brief statement about their marital relationship:

> She is an active senator who, like most members of Congress, has to be in Washington for part of most weeks. He is a former president running a multimillion-dollar global foundation. But their home is in New York, and they do everything they can to be together there or at their house in D.C. as often as possible—often going to great lengths to do so. When their work schedules require that they be apart they talk all the time.

The remainder of the *Times* account read like boilerplate, featuring remarks from friends and political observers about how Bill tried to support Hillary politically, how their domestic relationship seemed to have healed, and how misgivings about Bill still made Hillary's allies wary. But what might have proved disastrous, from a public relations perspective, had turned out to be no worse than annoying.

For a man long acknowledged to be a master of American politics, Bill Clinton's role in his wife's Senate career had been humble and unobtrusive. "She knows a lot more than I do about the politics of New York and the decisions she has to make," he would explain. "Tons more! I am literally ignorant. . . . I'm almost totally worthless to her about either New York politics or the politics of the Senate. I just don't know enough. And besides, she's gotten better at this than I am because she's in it all the time." He smiled. "You get a little rusty. Except I do go to the State Fair with her every year, 'cause I'm real good up there."

He brushed aside discussion of Hillary's presidential prospects as premature until after November 2006. "I haven't permitted myself to think much about it, or to talk to her about it, for the simple reason that I believe that you have to be in the election you're in—and if you start thinking about the next campaign, you may not get to the next campaign," he said. "I think she will be overwhelmingly reelected, because she deserves to be, if and only if she maintains the present level of focus on this election."

Then he added, "But after she is reelected, if she wants to talk to me about it, I'll be honored to talk about it." And he admitted doubting that Americans were ready to elect "any woman" to the presidency, no matter what they might say to pollsters.

———

In May 2006, nearly a year after Clinton first presented the Alliance for a Healthier Generation with Mike Huckabee and the American Heart Association, the new group called the press to Harlem for an unexpected announcement. Following lengthy negotiations with the nation's largest beverage companies, led by Ira Magaziner, those firms and the industry's trade group had signed an unprecedented agreement with AHG to help curb obesity by ending the sale of sugary soft drinks in American public schools.

The ban on high-calorie sodas and "sports drinks" would be complete within four years, removing any drink with more than 100 calories per 12-ounce serving from school vending machines and cafeterias by 2010. According to the president of the American Beverage Association, Ralph Crowley, who ran a regional soda company in New England, the agreement would cost beverage companies an estimated

$100 million over four years to replace vending machines and other equipment.

Acknowledging how difficult it is to change an entire culture of consumption, Clinton told reporters, "We're turning a huge ship around in the middle of the ocean before it hits an iceberg."

The deal would entirely eliminate soda and other sugar-heavy drinks such as apple and grape juice from the nation's elementary schools, in the hope of inculcating healthy habits at the earliest age, while in high schools drinks such as diet soda, diet lemonade, and diet iced tea would be permitted along with bottled water.

By coming in to negotiate this agreement, Clinton and his allies may have saved Coca-Cola, Pepsico, Cadbury-Schweppes, and other soda manufacturers from lawsuits planned by the same public health advocates and law firms that had successfully pursued Big Tobacco a decade earlier. Such organizations, including the Center for Science in the Public Interest and the Public Health Advocacy Institute, had been threatening to sue the soft drink companies for endangering children by marketing their products in schools. Leaders of those groups immediately welcomed the deal, while casting doubt on the motives of the industry.

"The childhood obesity crisis isn't a partisan issue," said Eric Schlosser, author of the bestselling exposé *Fast Food Nation,* who lauded Clinton and Huckabee. "Republican and Democratic kids are becoming unhealthy. The sugars in soda make up a large part of the extra caloric intake in the diets of young people, and soda consumption has played a role in the rise of childhood obesity." Schlosser said he was "happy . . . the companies have agreed to do the right thing."

Richard Daynard, president of the Public Health Advocacy Institute and a law professor at Northeastern University, told the *Boston Globe* that he had sought a similar agreement with the beverage companies for several months—under a continuing threat of litigation. "I think this agreement is about as voluntary as a shotgun wedding," said Margo Wootan, director of nutrition studies at the Center for Science in the Public Interest. "Coke and Pepsi are doing this to address the wave of legislation and litigation they were facing."

Yet if Clinton was riding a wave of public concern, his intervention nevertheless had moved the beverage companies to adopt a more responsible approach, without wasting years in courthouses and legislative chambers. If the deal achieved its objectives, then millions of children across the country would consume billions fewer empty calories every year—which, as Magaziner quietly informed reporters, could mean that those same kids would weigh up to twenty pounds less by the time they graduated high school.

With the soft drink deal in place, Clinton told reporters that he looked forward to negotiating similar agreements to change the quality and quantity of the "snack foods" that were making American children fat and sick. "We are eating more fast food and got into this super-size culture. I used to be a part of it," he said, alluding to his own past poor eating habits. "I don't think there are any villains here. I don't think anybody realized this confluence of forces could produce such results."

Villainous as the corporate giants might indeed be, Clinton understood that demonizing them would delay their arrival at the negotiating table. His preferred way of doing business was to make friends, not enemies, and to seek consensus, not conflict. That style didn't always serve him or his causes well, but it was certainly a way of achieving deals in a combative atmosphere.

By then, the AHG had already hired an ambitious new executive director named Ginny Ehrlich, former director of school nutrition for the progressive Oregon Education Department—and they were already talking with industry behemoths like Kraft Foods about how to improve what kids ate as well as what they drank.

Within five months, Clinton would again summon reporters to Harlem to announce another agreement, this time in a high school gymnasium. Kraft, candy maker Mars, yogurt manufacturer Dannon, chip maker Pepsico, and Campbell Soup entered into a deal limiting saturated fat, sugar, and sodium and eliminating trans fats in the snacks sold in school vending machines—while promoting alternative choices such as baked chips that met nutrition guidelines set by the American Heart Association. This entirely voluntary arrangement met with more skepticism from health advocates than the soft drink deal, but Clinton defended it as a "first step."

In announcing the beverage deal, he had pointed out that state and municipal governments could still pass even more restrictive regulations. He didn't attempt to discourage them. "I think that the states are and always have been laboratories of democracy. Nothing in this agreement prohibits them from doing something else or something different."

———

If Clinton's post-presidential concerns sometimes appeared diffuse and unrelated, that didn't discourage him from pursuing problems that seemed urgent to him—sometimes arising from his own experience, other times arising from the frustrations of his presidency. Among the issues that had troubled him most as president was climate change, both because he had proved unable to draw attention to the problem, even among his fellow Democrats, and because he felt the consequences for civilization were likely to be so grave.

"During my second term, I spent a lot of time on it," he recalled. "I gave a couple of very serious speeches on it that elicited a giant yawn. And then even the Democrats voted against the Kyoto Treaty, Democrats from energy-producing states. I just could not get anybody to take it seriously."

Although as president Clinton had signed the Kyoto protocol in November 1998, he never submitted the treaty for ratification to the U.S. Senate, which had already passed a resolution condemning it. By 2006, however, many more elected officials in the United States and around the world were taking climate seriously—notably, an alliance of eighteen big city mayors led by the British Labour leftist Ken Livingstone, then mayor of London, who were seeking ways to move forward despite the repeated failures of national governments and the U.N. With cities accounting for an estimated 75 percent of energy use and greenhouse gas emissions, changing policies and habits in major urban areas could make a significant difference.

Magaziner had taken notice of the mayors' group and brought them to Clinton's attention in January 2006. Both were intrigued by the idea that the Clinton Foundation could somehow augment or even join their effort. He assigned some young researchers to explore how the foundation might address global warming. "I really wanted to do something in clean energy because I thought it was consistent with what we had done in the AIDS space, trying to figure out how to do more with less money, prove it's economically beneficial," Clinton later said.

And as with the AIDS crisis, he felt there was "no need for me just giving a lot of speeches about it. I thought Al Gore had done everything humanly possible in terms of making the arguments, trying to prove the science. . . . I didn't think there needed to be anybody else doing that. But somebody needed to be out there, proving we could do this"—that is, demonstrating the case for an economically viable shift from fossil fuels to conservation and renewable energy sources. For him the real proof of any concept—in retrofitting large commercial buildings to save energy or revamping bus fleets to run on renewable fuel—came when it could be brought "to scale." Big-city mayors had the political power to drive such plans.

In April, Magaziner went to London to meet with Nicky Gavron, the deputy mayor who ran the international cities group for Livingstone. As she later told a reporter for *The Atlantic*, Magaziner made a compelling pitch: "We've got this track record [on AIDS], and we can assemble talent very quickly." Her first thought was to ask Magaziner for money, but "he said, on the spot, 'We don't want to back you; we want to be your partner.'" Clinton and Magaziner also believed that they could indeed raise money for a climate initiative, from potential donors, eventually including Kathryn Murdoch, daughter-in-law of the notorious media mogul.

Over the next few months Magaziner and Gavron, along with representatives of other cities, began to negotiate an agreement, under which a new division of the Clinton Foundation, known as the Clinton Climate Initiative, would serve as the "operational arm" of the joint project as it grew to encompass more than forty major cities and became known as "the C-40." They drew in local leaders who were already friendly to Clinton, including the dynamic young Los Angeles mayor Antonio Villaraigosa and his San Francisco counterpart, Gavin Newsom.

On August 1, they announced this broad new international partnership in Los Angeles at UCLA's Anderson School of Business, with Clinton flanked onstage by Villaraigosa, Newsom, Livingstone—and the London mayor's political antagonist Tony Blair, whose centrist leadership of the Labour Party often irked the man known as "Red Ken." (Blair was in California to sign a climate-cooperation agreement with Arnold Schwarzenegger, the Golden State's maverick Republican governor, who dissented emphatically from his party's troglodyte approach to global warming.)

While Livingstone and Villaraigosa expounded on methods they had used to curb automobile traffic and plant millions of trees, Clinton explained how the Clinton Climate Initiative planned to help large cities work together to achieve an ambitious 80 percent decrease in carbon emissions over the coming decades. "It sounds like a daunting task," he said. "I don't believe it is."

Clinton believed that the climate initiative could succeed if it followed the methodology pioneered by the AIDS initiative, which was why he had encouraged Magaziner to take the lead. Like CHAI, which drew together national governments to achieve purchasing power, CCI would do the same for cities seeking to buy clean energy goods such as photovoltaic cells, lithium-diode street lights, or electric buses. Like CHAI, which advised government health ministries on best practices, training personnel, and implementing effective systems, CCI would provide similar expertise to cities needing technical assistance to reduce emissions. And like CHAI, which spent much effort on measuring outcomes—what Clinton always called "keeping score"—CCI would also create more precise tools to track the cities' progress.

But beyond all the wonkish projections and promises, Clinton didn't try to avoid the partisan aspect of climate change. He had never upbraided Bush publicly over his administration's fealty to the pharmaceutical manufacturers; now, however, he pointed out forcefully that the White House had failed to address global warming—and warned of a planetary catastrophe unless people and policymakers took concerted action. "The entrenched thought patterns and economic interests of yesterday are our common enemy," he said. To demonstrate its seriousness, CCI immediately dispatched several staffers on sales calls to introduce the cities project to mayors around the world.

————

For Clinton, his summer trip to Africa was becoming an important annual milestone, rendered more significant in 2006 by the presence of a *New York Times* reporter, who happened to be capable of examining the gritty philanthropic work beneath the glittering political surface. Celia Dugger, daughter of the radical Texas journalist and activist Ronnie Dugger, knew the territory well. She had traveled throughout Africa and Asia for years, covering issues of poverty and development for the paper.

During the previous winter and spring, Dugger and Donald Mc-Neil, Jr., had produced a compelling seven-part series for the *Times* on diseases such as guinea worm, measles, and river blindness that were "on the brink" of complete elimination, if only adequate support were made available from world health authorities. She had already won major awards for international reporting, and the series on eradicable diseases would earn a few more.

The difference in her approach was not a lack of skepticism about Clinton's motives and record. Dugger was more than willing to question the former president sharply about what he had (and had not) done to stop the AIDS pandemic during his presidency, and didn't hesitate to remind him of assorted other shortcomings. Yet she was deeply interested in seeing what he had accomplished out of office—and had the knowledge and experience to understand what she saw.

Following Clinton through Malawi, Rwanda, South Africa, and Lesotho, Dugger filed a 2,700-word dispatch that appeared on the paper's August 29 front page, which opened on a scene of the former president at a rural hospital, holding the hands of children who were "alive because of the AIDS medicines his foundation donated."

It was a hospital that the foundation had renovated, where he listened to "people once skeletal from AIDS tell of their resurrections to robust health." And as Dugger explained, it was a hospital that had lacked even a single doctor before Clinton persuaded Paul Farmer to come to Rwinkwavu, Rwanda, with the pioneering methods he had used to combat AIDS in the mountains of Haiti.

To balance those uplifting images, her story recounted the Clinton administration's failure to adequately address the international AIDS crisis and to intervene against the Rwandan genocide. To her it seemed ironic that the Bush administration had provided much more funding for AIDS relief, yet Clinton remained far more popular in Africa. And having asked whether his global AIDS work was "a form of redemption" for him, she noted his "scornful" dismissal of such questions.

"I'm 60 years old now, and I'm not running for anything, so I don't have to be polite anymore," he said.

But she also reported the unanimously positive assessments of the Clinton Foundation's work by international AIDS experts—from Harvard's Howard Hiatt and Richard Marlink to Bill Gates, who had joined Clinton's entourage in Africa—several of whom recalled wondering whether the former president was serious about fighting the pandemic, or merely seeking a form of cheap grace. She traced the history of CHAI, the role played by Magaziner and the generic manufacturers, and the foundation's profound impact on the delivery of treatment in more than two dozen countries, particularly in South Africa, where his pressure on President Thabo Mbeki had proved critical.

Clinton believed he had been "wrong" as president to protect the patents of the American pharmaceutical manufacturers as president, she wrote, but then quoted Dr. Bernard Pécoul of Doctors Without Borders, praising Clinton's "courageous" advocacy of generic medicines in his post-presidency.

Over the prior two years, Dugger wrote, Clinton and CHAI had been raising the issue of children with AIDS—and were beginning to succeed in drawing resources to those inexplicably neglected millions. According to Peter McDermott, chief of AIDS programs for UNICEF, "Children are alive in numbers we couldn't have imagined a couple of years ago because of what [Clinton has] done."

Dugger's article was more than just another confirmation of Clinton's status as a leader in the struggle against AIDS. It offered an unusual portrait of him as a joyful, energetic, ambitious, and compassionate figure, freed of guilt and anger but possessed by his work—a man of the world, embraced by throngs of appreciative people who cared only that he had come to help.

And to Clinton's surprise, not once did Dugger mention his wife the senator, her reelection campaign, or her presidential prospects.

———

With the autumn of 2006 came a virtual cyclone of events, meetings, controversies, and campaigns for Clinton. On August 19 he had celebrated his sixtieth birthday with Hillary, his brother, Roger, and about a hundred guests on Martha's Vineyard; the official celebration, scheduled for the end of October would feature a fundraising concert for the foundation at New York City's Beacon Theatre by the Rolling

Stones, whose lead singer Mick Jagger had become a faithful Clinton friend.

That fall, Clinton was expected at more than 120 events across the country to support Democratic candidates in the midterm election. On a single September Saturday, to mention just one of many frantic tours, he flew from a memorial service for Governor Ann Richards in Texas to a Governor Ted Strickland lunch in Ohio to a Senator Amy Klobuchar dinner in Minnesota, ending with a late-night dessert affair for that state's Democratic Farmer-Labor Party. Over a single week in October, he appeared at Democratic Congressional Campaign Committee events in Los Angeles, Atlanta, West Palm Beach, Chicago, Columbus, and Louisville, sprinkled between parties for Ohio senator Sherrod Brown, Massachusetts governor Deval Patrick, and Pennsylvania senator Bob Casey. As the current president's ratings fell, the Democrats were again ascendant, and their crowd-pleasing former president was in heavy demand.

Clinton's popularity couldn't deflect a wave of criticism on the fifth anniversary of the September 11 attack, which hit him from an unexpected direction. Familiar themes of blame and distraction, first enunciated with such vitriol in the wake of the 2001 catastrophe, were scheduled for histrionic repetition—this time in the shape of a big-budget "docudrama" titled *The Path to 9/11*, which ABC planned to air as a miniseries over two nights on September 11 and 12. The script had not been shared with Clinton or anyone from his administration, but the advance word was ominous. So was the pedigree of the production team, headed by a pair of avowed conservatives who were promoting the broadcast in advance to right-wing radio hosts and bloggers.

A friend inside ABC Television confirmed the worst that Clinton, Band, and others in their orbit had heard about the project. Although ostensibly based on the *Report of the National Commission on Terrorist Attacks upon the United States*, the script targeted Clinton, former secretary of state Madeleine Albright, and especially Sandy Berger as culpable for the 9/11 attack, while mostly letting the Bush administration escape responsibility.

As they learned more about the project and Cyrus Nowrasteh, the Hollywood screenwriter at its center, Clinton and his former aides became increasingly concerned. Nowrasteh's version apparently omitted important facts and literally invented scenes and events that had never happened. His most egregious fictionalizing depicted a strike on Osama bin Laden's Afghan redoubt, allegedly aborted at the last second by the feckless Berger.

Like several other scenes in Nowrasteh's script, in which he readily acknowledged using dramatic license, that incident simply never occurred. The 9/11 Commission's report certainly provided no evidence to support that exciting imaginary assault on bin Laden's compound, and further demonstrated that, dramatic or not, the underlying assumptions were completely wrong. Published in July 2004, the report stated explicitly that Clinton and Berger ordered the CIA and the military to use any force necessary to kill bin Laden.

In scenes sure to delight the far right, the script depicted the impeachment crisis as the engine driving Clinton as he confronted terrorism, acting or failing to act as he tried to shield himself politically. Here, too, the 9/11 Report provided no evidence to support that claim—a slur on the reputations of all the military officers who had supported the president's counterterror strikes during that period.

The script also fabricated scenes favorable to Bush and his aides, in particular Condoleezza Rice, then his national security adviser, who was shown ordering subordinates to implement "real action" against al Qaeda following the infamous August 6 presidential daily briefing. The 9/11 report stated clearly that neither she nor anyone else ever delivered such orders.

On a personal level, Clinton was distressed by the role of an old friend, former New Jersey governor Tom Kean, who had chaired the 9/11 Commission as a Bush appointee—and acted as consultant to the ABC production team with an "executive producer" credit. Was the nice but clueless Kean promoting the Bush White House line on 9/11 because his son, Tom Kean, Jr., was the Republican Senate nominee in his home state?

For several days Clinton, Berger, Band, Cooper, press aide Jay Carson, and Bruce Lindsey, among others, quietly debated how to proceed. Certainly, Clinton would draw much more attention by protesting. A prolonged battle would stimulate public curiosity and could backfire by provoking cries of censorship. They might end up looking more like bullies than victims. But Clinton soon concluded that he had no choice. He had to try to protect Berger, Albright, and himself from a partisan falsification of history. With only two weeks before the scheduled air date, as the network began to roll out publicity for the movie, the Clinton aides began their own counter-campaign.

Band called Robert Iger, the president and chief executive of Disney, ABC's parent company, to explain Clinton's concerns and ask that Iger, a longtime friend and supporter of the former president, look into the 9/11 project to ensure its fairness. Iger responded that the movie still was undergoing final editing and he was unaware of any problems with its content. But he agreed to look into it. Band also contacted former Maine senator George Mitchell, another close Clinton friend who had served as his special envoy for Northern Ireland. The highly respected Mitchell now sat on Disney's board.

On September 1, with no guarantee that Iger or Mitchell would be able to help, Clinton's team decided to go public. After consulting with Berger and Clinton defense attorney David Kendall, Band and Lindsey sent a bluntly worded letter to Iger, with copies to Mitchell, ABC News president David Westin, ABC Entertainment president Stephen McPherson, as well as Berger, Albright, and the members of the 9/11 Commission.

Opening with "Dear Bob," the letter's first paragraph quoted McPherson, who had said, "When you take on the responsibility of telling the story behind such an important event, it is absolutely critical that you get it right."

But, the letter continued, "By ABC's own standard, ABC has gotten it terribly wrong. The content of this drama is factually and incontrovertibly inaccurate and ABC has a duty to fully correct all errors or pull the drama entirely. It is unconscionable to mislead the American public about one of the most horrendous tragedies our country has ever known." Complaining that the producers had refused to let them see the film, despite several requests, Band and Lindsey alluded to Nowrasteh's alleged reputation for inaccuracy, and quoted him explaining, with respect to an earlier project on the shooting of Ronald Reagan that had also been criticized for its errors: "I made a conscious effort not to contact any members of the Administration because I didn't want them to stymie my efforts."

As a result, they warned, Nowrasteh's film included at least three significant mistakes: the Berger scene, which was "complete fiction";

a scene that showed Albright halting a missile strike against al Qaeda until she can inform Pakistan's military, which also never occurred; and a newsreel clip of Clinton denying his affair with Lewinsky, used to suggest that he had been too preoccupied with impeachment to focus on al Qaeda, an allegation directly refuted by his former counterterrorism adviser Richard Clarke.

With copious citations from 9/11 Commission testimony and its report, the letter dismantled Nowrasteh's version of events. "While ABC is promoting *The Path to 9/11* as a dramatization of historical fact, in truth it is a fictitious rewriting of history that will be misinterpreted by millions of Americans. Given your stated obligation to 'get it right,' we urge you to do so by not airing this drama until the egregious factual errors are corrected, an endeavor we could easily assist you with given the opportunity to view the film."

Within a few days the letter leaked to the media, prompting a three-sided media battle that embroiled Clinton's office, Nowrasteh and his supporters in the right-wing media, and the corporate public relations apparatus at ABC, which sought to create an appearance of fairness and balance. But ABC's position was contradictory: The network chided the Clinton team for attacking a movie they hadn't seen, while refusing to let them view it before airtime.

Kean came under intense pressure from other members of the 9/11 Commission, who didn't appreciate the misuse of their work. And actor Harvey Keitel, who played John O'Neill, the heroic FBI counterterror agent killed in the World Trade Center collapse on September 11, openly expressed doubts about the movie's veracity. "I had questions about certain events and material I was given in *The Path to 9/11*," said Keitel. "Yes, I had some conflicts there. You can't put these [events] together, compress them, and then distort the reality."

In at least one important way, this episode of political warfare differed from previous Clinton skirmishes. Unlike so many times in the past when the Clintons had faced a barrage of criticism alone, a new corps of liberal web bloggers opened a loud, aggressive second front against Fox News, talk radio, and the conservative media.

Ultimately, the Clinton forces won on substantive and symbolic points. Conceding that the invented material about Berger and Albright was indefensible, ABC edited those scenes before the film aired, cutting the offensive dialogue. (The Lewinsky newsreel footage remained.) The educational publisher Scholastic deleted from its website a series of *Path to 9/11* pages that were to be used by 25,000 high school teachers in conjunction with the movie, a decision explained in a press statement by its chairman: "We determined that the materials did not meet our high standards for dealing with controversial issues."

ABC broadcast the film over two nights but despite the furor stirred up by Clinton, its Nielsen ratings were disappointing, with only 13 million viewers, or less than half what the network had expected. Disney never issued a DVD of the film, taking a financial loss on the project.

So angry was Nowrasteh over his film's fate that he spent the next two years making a documentary about its political suppression by Clinton, titled *Blocking The Path To 9/11* and produced with the assistance of Citizens United president David Bossie. The documentary received little attention outside right-wing circles.

Grateful for the support of the bloggers, Clinton invited about a dozen of them to his Harlem office for a celebratory two-hour lunch and discussion. Serving up fried chicken, cornbread, and cherry cake, ordered in from Sylvia's, the neighborhood's legendary soul-food restaurant and political haunt, he engaged them in a wide-ranging discussion of current issues—including the role of the Internet in countering disinformation from the right. As *TalkLeft* blogger Jeralyn Merritt later wrote, their meeting with Clinton was "a heady experience" for them. In attendance was Peter Daou, a former blogger who had signed on as Hillary Clinton's online communications director.

———

Looming beyond the controversy over 9/11 and the intensity of midterm elections, the second annual conference of the Clinton Global Initiative was set to commence on September 20, with the opening address to be delivered by Laura Bush. Her game attempt to persuade the liberal-leaning audience in the Sheraton ballroom that her husband's administration was engaging the world with compassion—by emphasizing his multibillion-dollar PEPFAR program—earned a standing ovation.

The first lady concluded her remarks by announcing a $16 million commitment to provide thousands of African villages with "play pumps"—clever merry-go-round devices that used the energy of children to pump clean water. (Years later, the play pumps proved to be a development fiasco, but that wasn't her fault.) Standing next to her with AOL chairman Steve Case, who had agreed to help underwrite the pumps, Clinton beamed with bipartisan pride.

With climate change as a principal theme, however, the second iteration of CGI represented a profound rebuke to the priorities of the Bush administration, which scarcely acknowledged global warming. The morning after Laura Bush's speech, Clinton introduced billionaire Virgin Group magnate Richard Branson to announce an extraordinary commitment. Over the coming decade, Branson promised that Virgin Airlines and Virgin Rail would devote all corporate profits, estimated at $3 billion, to research and investment in clean energy technologies, with an emphasis on environmentally benign automobile and airline fuels.

In a burst of enthusiasm he would later have cause to regret, Clinton said, "No matter how cynical you are, that's serious money."

On the same day, Al Gore delivered a passionate address calling climate change the challenge of a generation. And in a moment stage-managed by Clinton, political adversaries Rupert Murdoch and Barbra Streisand rose to that challenge by publicly pledging donations of $500,000 and $1 million, respectively, to the Clinton Climate Initiative. By the second day, thanks to Branson and dozens of others, CGI had more than doubled the first year's commitments of $2.5 billion; by the final day, the tally had reached nearly $7.5 billion, "or so my staff swears," said Clinton.

Branson's commitment alone had spurred dozens of headlines around the world. The wave of favorable CGI coverage included a story on page A5 of the *New York Times*, under Celia Dugger's byline.

For the first time, CGI's plenaries and panels had been made available via webcast, and more than fifty thousand people around the world had watched. And at the conference's gala dinner, the food was "sustainable" and organic, eaten from dishes made from biodegradable bamboo.

The only sour note was sounded a day or two later, when Clinton appeared on *Fox News Sunday* to talk about CGI—or so he believed. Sitting in a studio at the Sheraton, host Chris Wallace instantly departed from the agreed topic. "Why didn't you do more to put bin Laden and al Qaeda out of business when you were president?" he asked.

Speaking calmly, with a slight smile, Clinton never raised his voice—nor did his face redden, as critics later claimed—but he didn't attempt to conceal his anger at this ambush.

"OK, let's talk about it," he replied.

Now, I will answer all those things on the merits, but first I want to talk about the context in which this arises. I'm being asked this on the Fox network. ABC just had a right-wing conservative run their little *Pathway to 9/11* [sic], falsely claiming it was based on the 9/11 Commission report, with three things asserted against me directly contradicted by the 9/11 Commission report.

And I think it's very interesting that all the conservative Republicans, who now say I didn't do enough, claimed that I was too obsessed with bin Laden. All of President Bush's neo-cons thought I was too obsessed with bin Laden. They had no meetings on bin Laden for nine months after I left office. All the right-wingers who now say I didn't do enough said I did too much—same people.

I tried. So I tried and failed. When I failed, I left a comprehensive anti-terror strategy and the best guy in the country [counterterror director Richard] Clarke, who got demoted. So you did Fox's bidding on this show. You did your nice little conservative hit job on me.

Wallace tried to protest his own innocence, but Clinton leaned forward and cut him off.

"And you've got that little smirk on your face and you think you're so clever," he went on. "But I had responsibility for trying to protect this country. I tried and I failed to get bin Laden. I regret it. But I did try. And I did everything I thought I responsibly could. . . . And so, I left office. And yet, I get asked about this all the time."

In closing he noted that the Bush administration had "three times as long" as his government to retaliate against al Qaeda for the terrorist bombing of the USS *Cole* in October 2000, but "nobody ever asks them about it. I think that's strange."

Later, Wallace suggested that Clinton had tried to intimidate him, saying, "former President Clinton is a very big man. As he leaned forward—wagging his finger in my face, and then poking the notes I was holding, I felt as if a mountain was coming down in front of me. The President said I had a smirk. Actually, it was sheer wonder at what I was witnessing." But the liberal blogs erupted in glee at Clinton's combative response to Fox, where Democrats rarely get the final word.

———

The event that almost entirely escaped notice, amid much tabloid commotion over *The Path to 9/11*, Richard Branson, the Clinton Global Initiative, and Fox News, was a rather quiet announcement on September 19 at the United Nations. On that day, representatives of four countries, led by France, told reporters that they had agreed to impose a surcharge on international airline tickets—an "international solidarity levy"—to fund treatment for children with HIV/AIDS, malaria, and tuberculosis. Its main partner in that endeavor, seeking to shape the worldwide market for pediatric medicines and diagnostics, would be CHAI.

Hosted by the World Health Organization at the U.N., this new multinational entity, which promised to raise $300 million annually, would be called UNITAID.

The man responsible for the creation of UNITAID was French foreign minister Philippe Douste-Blazy, under the direction of Prime Minister Jacques Chirac. But the inspiration for its mission, according to the French minister, was Clinton. During the summer of 2005, Chirac had decided that he wished to create an international legacy as he neared retirement, and deputized Douste-Blazy, his newly appointed foreign minister, to set to work on a suitably significant project. When Douste-Blazy prepared to visit the United States for the first time a few months later, he told the French ambassador, "I want to meet with the world's greatest living politician." He meant Clinton.

Their meeting in Chappaqua was casual, with Clinton in jeans and a yellow Lacoste polo shirt. In a meandering discussion that touched on the Mideast peace process and the next Olympic Games, Douste-Blazy finally got down to business. He wanted to talk about "innovative financing" to advance humanitarian projects in the developing world, specifically about an airline passenger tax, which he believed could eventually generate up to $600 million annually, perhaps more.

"What do you think I should do with the money?" asked the French minister.

"I know what you have to do," Clinton said. "You have to do on a big scale what I do with my foundation. You have to work on drugs to fight HIV/AIDS, malaria, and tuberculosis." He paused. "You have to say to the drug companies, 'I'm giving you money, not for one year but for several years—for example, $300 million per year for five years. How much do you agree to reduce the price?'"

According to Douste-Blazy, that conversation was the beginning of the process that brought UNITAID to fruition. "Thank you very much, Mr. President," he said. "I knew I could find an idea here." In his memoir, Douste-Blazy wrote, "The meeting with Bill Clinton left me energized and eager to move forward."

Many months later, by the time that UNITAID was ready for its unveiling in New York by Chirac and U.N. Secretary-General Kofi Annan, the French foreign ministry had recruited several other countries to join the airline tax regime (although the resolutely antitax Bush administration had rejected it for ideological reasons). With a charge of $51 on every first-class ticket and about $5 on every economy seat, the officials in the Quai d'Orsay estimated that the first year would bring in an estimated $250 million—to be topped up with $25 million from the United Kingdom, Brazil, Chile, and Norway, and as many as nineteen other countries were expected to join.

At the same press conference, UNITAID announced that it would engage the experts at CHAI to negotiate prices of diagnostics and drugs, in exactly the way Clinton had suggested. Buying in bulk at reduced prices would permit the organization to finance treatment of 100,000 children with AIDS immediately, as well as 100,000 adults and children who needed so-called second-line AIDS drugs, whose cost CHAI was also working to reduce—plus as many as 150,000 children suffering from tuberculosis, and 28 million infected with malaria.

Magaziner, who spoke with reporters at the U.N. press conference, was elated. "We'll have a sustainable way to assure a supply of drugs and tests for the long term." Jean Dussourd, the French official who had implemented Douste-Blazy's vision and negotiated the deals from which UNITAID emerged, was blunt. "We would not permit thousands of children to die in the United States and France," he said. "Why should we allow that in Asia and Africa?"

––––––

Throughout that autumn, Clinton fulfilled an intense schedule of political appearances for Democrats, although he would later say that Hillary's possible presidential candidacy had "surprisingly little to do" with how he allocated his time, "because I didn't know whether she was going to run."

Her own race for reelection to the Senate was more of a leisurely stroll. She trounced an energetic but unknown opponent from the left with 87 percent of the vote in the Democratic primary. Early polls made her look invincible, and the New York state Republican Party—chaired by Nixon son-in-law Edward Cox—was unable to find a viable November challenger.

After a prolonged comedy of errors, culminating in a GOP primary that attracted the lowest turnout in thirty years, Clinton defeated John Spencer, a former upstate mayor, winning 67 percent of the vote in the general election. With her victory, Hillary had fulfilled a promise to serve a full term, and could resume the fitful discussions with her staff, friends, supporters, and husband about whether to run for president in 2008.

"She adored being a Senator from New York," Clinton later said of his wife. "She remained ambivalent about whether to run for president for a long time."

Over the New Year's holiday, the Clintons went to Anguilla, where they stayed at the vacation home of Robert Johnson, the billionaire founder of Black Entertainment Television. On the beach, she asked him what he thought she should do.

"I told her I thought she should run, because I thought she would be the best president. But I told her she should only run if she believed that too." In his mind, neither the campaign nor the presidency would be easy. "I knew we had huge structural problems with the economy, [and] we had to unwind what we had done in Iraq. America was already in trouble and people were already hurting."

He also recalled making a prediction: "If you run, either you or Obama will be the nominee."

CHAPTER THIRTEEN

In the brief video that launched her as a candidate for president, after months and years of public anticipation, Hillary Rodham Clinton perched on a sofa in the sunroom of her Washington home, gazing directly at the camera.

Smartly attired in a maroon jacket over a simple black top, she said: "I announced today that I'm forming a presidential exploratory committee. I'm not just starting a campaign, though. I'm beginning a conversation with you, with America." For just under two minutes, she talked about the war in Iraq, Social Security and Medicare, universal health care, energy policy, women's rights, her middle-class background, and the ill effects of "six years of George Bush."

Sitting alone, she did not mention her husband, the former president. From the outset, her campaign—presenting its candidate without surname as "Hillary!"—kept Bill Clinton mostly in the background as a matter of policy. During the year to come, his schedule would devote well over a third of his waking hours to political trips, appearances, and fundraisers for her, according to records later tallied by his aides. But the persistent concern that he would overshadow her meant directing the spotlight away from him, with few exceptions. Bill and his top aides were rarely asked to participate in meetings of her campaign staff, although he maintained a back channel into their deliberations via Mark Penn, the pollster and strategist who had helped to guide his 1996 reelection campaign. And Band, who feared the likely damage a political campaign would inflict on his boss, stayed in constant contact with Hillary's closest aide, Huma Abedin.

The same records show that Bill Clinton spent somewhat less time on foundation business than politics in 2007, but the first few months of the year saw him increasingly preoccupied with the foundation's growing pains. After more than five years, Clinton had overcome most of the early problems of his post-presidency, from paying off personal and library debt to largely restoring his reputation and popularity. He had found a compelling mission—indeed, more than one—that excited him. But perhaps inevitably, the foundation's rapid growth brought complications and conflicts.

Not only was the progress undeniable but, in many respects, it was accelerating. The Clinton Presidential Center was no longer in debt and would welcome its millionth visitor before year's end. The Clinton Global Initiative had logged almost six hundred commitments, with an estimated value above $10 billion, assisting people in more than one hundred countries—such as the thirty thousand schoolchildren in Nicaragua vaccinated against the deadly rotavirus by Merck & Co., and the scores of nonprofit groups awarded "Google Grants" of free advertising by Sergey Brin and Larry Page, the company founders who had supported CGI in the concept stage. The Alliance for a Healthier Generation had established new guidelines for better drinks and snacks in schools across the country, and reached out to nearly a million students directly to engage them in improving their eating and exercise habits.

The foundation's long-standing effort to assist small businesses in Harlem, since renamed the Clinton Economic Opportunity Initiative, had provided pro bono assistance valued at $14 million to entrepreneurs across New York City—and meanwhile had launched an Earned Income Tax Credit Awareness program that helped survivors of Hurricane Katrina in New Orleans and nine other cities obtain $10 million worth of assistance. Promising new projects were getting under way, such as the Clinton Climate Initiative and the Clinton Hunter Development Initiative, seeking to improve the lives of small farmers in Rwanda and Malawi.

Looming over all the initiatives was CHAI—still an inspiration for many of the foundation's projects—which employed more than five hundred staff and volunteers around the world in late February 2007. Over the course of four years, CHAI operations had expanded urgently, spurred by a sense of crisis; by 2007, nearly seventy countries were purchasing medicine through its consortium, which had negotiated sharply reduced prices on forty treatment regimens and sixteen diagnostic tests. With Clinton's personal intervention, CHAI had succeeded in penetrating China and India, persuading those governments to act against AIDS before the epidemic overwhelmed them.

During 2006, Magaziner had focused CHAI on children with AIDS, a subset of victims that was inexplicably neglected. Negotiating a drastic cut in the annual price of antiretroviral medicine per child from $567 to only $54, CHAI's pediatric program had doubled the number of children receiving treatment in thirty-three countries. With fresh financial assistance from UNITAID, CHAI's drugs were reaching 135,000 children, or two thirds of all the children getting treatment in the world. Over time, said Stephen Lewis, U.N. Special Envoy for AIDS, this program would "keep hundreds of thousands, indeed millions, of children alive who would otherwise die."

CHAI had embarked on a new program to rebuild the health system in Rwanda, under the direction of Paul Farmer, and a pilot program in Tanzania to reduce the cost of malaria treatments, which would reduce the price of effective drugs from $10 per dose—far beyond the reach of most people there—to less than 50 cents. Thousands of Tanzanians had already obtained medications for themselves and their children. With CHAI's technical assistance, the central government had appropriated a new subsidy for every Tanzanian child under five to receive malaria treatment if needed.

More than 1.5 million people were receiving AIDS treatment supported by CHAI in early 2007—and with the efforts of the Global Fund, PEPFAR, and UNITAID, all strengthened by CHAI's impact on the pharmaceutical marketplace, the world was finally combating the pandemic in a systematic and serious way.

Behind the foundation's record of achievement, however, was an escalating bureaucratic battle between Ira Magaziner and Clinton's senior staff, particularly Doug Band. At a meeting in Chappaqua during the fall of 2006, Band and others had gone so far as to urge the former president to "curtail" or even dismiss his old friend, whom they suspected of attempting to take over the foundation. Clinton, who considered Magaziner one of the smartest, most creative, and hardest-working people he had ever met, summarily rejected that recommendation. But his demand that they all find a way to get along had not ended the conflict.

The likelihood of Band and Magaziner working smoothly together was never great; their differences were too obvious and grating. For instance, Magaziner's irreverent habit of addressing Clinton as "Bill" rather than "Mr. President" irked Band, who considered protecting the former president's dignity among his chief responsibilities. To him, Magaziner's uninvited informality reeked of presumption if not disrespect. Band tended to be short with anyone who violated this sense of propriety, and his flashes of temper had earned him a tough reputation.

Determined as he was to maintain an aura of statesmanship around Clinton, Band expected proper attire and demeanor in the office. Magaziner, with his unruly gray hair and rumpled suits, no necktie, usually looked as if he had just completed a long sojourn on an airplane—which very often he had. He was unwilling to take direction, let alone criticism, from someone so much younger and less experienced.

Their contrasting styles reflected more substantial disagreements over how to run the foundation. After years of ad hoc administration, Band wanted to impose organizational rigor, strategic planning, and uniform procedures that would encourage growth while avoiding fiscal and programmatic pitfalls. Magaziner continued to operate CHAI from suburban Boston, in a space that was formerly a dentist's office, beyond the reach of the foundation's main offices in Harlem and Little Rock. He bridled at such controls. To him, CHAI's success depended on his ability to function nimbly, without burdensome managerial restrictions.

Barrages of emails and memos flew between the two sides, filled with complaints about Magaziner's failure to consult or even inform foundation colleagues when he contacted donors on behalf of CHAI, when he made commitments that implicated foundation resources in other countries, when he hired or fired personnel, and when he spent money.

One such critique of Magaziner, written in early 2007, ran to eleven angry single-spaced pages. Another letter, addressed to Clinton from Lindsey, upbraided the CHAI chairman for alienating major donors and claiming credit for big donations that others had actually arranged. Dueling memos to Clinton from Band and Magaziner argued, to cite only one example, over who had fostered the foundation's close relationship with Bill and Melinda Gates; the Microsoft billionaire had become one of the foundation's most generous supporters.

Even worse, in Band's view, was Magaziner's repeated pattern of making promises that were impossible for Clinton to fulfill. He regarded Magaziner as a poor manager, operating without transparency or communication, hiring inexperienced young people, micromanaging them, and then driving out anyone who challenged him. While he inspired great loyalty among some CHAI employees, others found him "terrifying." One who had worked closely with him before being pushed out said he ran the organization "by the seat of his pants."

What troubled Band the most, however, was the feeling that unlike him, Bruce Lindsey, and nearly everyone else in Clinton's orbit, Magaziner didn't seem to put the former president's interests and image first. By Band's most important standard, personal loyalty, he felt that Magaziner didn't measure up. And Magaziner's approach to management left the organization exposed to potential trouble.

Painfully aware of the turmoil swirling around him, Magaziner felt increasingly resentful. His own efforts to raise money received too little credit—much of the foundation's fundraising capacity was based on CHAI's success anyway. He sometimes threatened to quit and take CHAI with him—tantamount to staging a coup—because he found working with Band so difficult and unpleasant.

Behind all the anger and distrust, Band and Magaziner couldn't completely suppress a certain respect for each other's work. In a mutually indignant email chain, Band praised Magaziner's "great strategic vision" without a trace of sarcasm; in his reply, Magaziner acknowledged the creation of CGI as "a great accomplishment and your vision and drive made it happen. . . . You are a smart and talented guy. You work very hard. You are capable of being very gracious, friendly and charming when you want to be. . . . But those are not the parts of your personality that we see most often now."

Every few months, these ongoing disputes would become so rancorous that Clinton would have to step in to establish a truce. By early 2007, however, Magaziner had accumulated a budget deficit of at least $9 million, a number that would ultimately rise to almost $24 million—all of which had to be covered by the foundation's general revenues. CHAI had raised programmatic funds, but not enough operating money. Clinton couldn't ignore the financial misdemeanor, especially because he was trying to establish a significant rainy-day reserve fund and, eventually, an endowment of $250 million. Without stricter cost controls, he would never meet those objectives.

The wrangling between Magaziner and Band was symptomatic of a larger problem: how to maintain the entrepreneurial spirit of the foundation's early years with the fiscal rigor, forward strategy, and organizational structure essential to achieving its global ambitions. Within the foundation, Band's opinion that Clinton should rein in Magaziner was widely shared.

Toward that end, Bruce Lindsey sent a memo to Clinton in March 2007, setting forth ideas to better integrate Magaziner into the overall structure despite his resistance. His two projects, CHAI and the Clinton Climate Initiative, would be required to report monthly data on staffing, management, finances, development, and communications to Lindsey and other senior staff. The memo even hinted at closing down Magaziner's operation in the Boston suburbs and moving its functions to the offices in Harlem and Little Rock.

What followed was a tense telephone conversation between Clinton and Magaziner, during which the former president demanded change and his old friend pushed back, hard. They hung up without reaching any agreement.

———

Having predicted that Barack Obama might become the most competitive challenger to Hillary didn't make the Illinois senator's sudden rise any less irritating to Bill Clinton. He considered Obama, a freshman with little experience in government and almost none in foreign affairs, both poorly prepared and arrogant. While Hillary was constantly criticized for ambition, Obama was seen as charming and cool. Nobody in the press, complained Clinton, showed any interest in the way that Obama played both sides—touting his opposition to the war in Iraq for progressive audiences, while telling the "serious people" in Washington that he might have voted for Bush's war resolution in October 2002—a time when, luckily for him, he was still a state legislator. Instead, the media stoked liberal anger over Hillary's Iraq vote.

As his wife's campaign unfolded, those who observed Clinton closely saw his unconcealed frustration. But by wading into the Democratic primary, his aides worried he would stain his status as an international statesman. If engaging in primary politics was unavoidable, it was also un-presidential. The question was whether the damage could be limited.

His wife's campaign staff viewed him as an asset—a formidable strategist, spellbinding orator, prodigious fundraiser, political shepherd—and an irritant. His loquacious charm could spill over into excessive chatter about himself and his presidency. When they were scheduled together on a trip to Iowa over the Fourth of July, the staff fretted over how to manage them, where to send them—and whether he would keep his introductions of her short, sweet, and to the point.

"Yeah, okay guys, *I got it*," Clinton sighed after five separate lectures from Penn and her other top staffers, according to Mark Halperin and John Heilemann's *Game Change*. "I'll try not to screw it up for her too bad while I'm out there." He didn't screw up, sticking to the script at the brunch and rally in Des Moines, the barbecues in Davenport, Waterloo, and Cedar Rapids, and the big parade in Clear Lake.

Except for the days he was overseas, his 2007 monthly schedules were strewn with his wife's initials: "HRC Wkly Donor Calls," "HRC Event/Miami," "HRC Event/Aspen," "HRC Event in Destin, FLA," "Hold for HRC in New Hampshire." One exception was July 23, when Hillary debated Obama and John Edwards in Charleston, South Carolina. He was away on his annual Africa trip, meeting with the president of Tanzania in Dar-es-Salaam.

In contrast to 2006, when he had spent 80 days abroad—visiting 53 foreign cities in 32 countries—and 84 days in U.S. cities, his 2007 schedule showed 44 days abroad, and 121 days spent visiting 150 U.S. cities (not including several trips to Washington and Little Rock). Rarely did Clinton's 2007 calendar reflect any involvement in campaign strategy sessions or conference calls, however. One of his aides later recalled, "Basically, we just went wherever they told us to go."

———

Dispatched to locations across the country by his wife's handlers, Clinton tried to make the best use of his travel time. When he wasn't reading, he spent many airborne hours scribbling his thick longhand into notebooks—not just tweaking speeches, but working on a new book. After the massive sales and worldwide barnstorming tour for *My Life*, the former president and his publishers at Knopf had been eager to formulate a fresh idea.

Inspired by the remarkable success of the Clinton Global Initiative, they eventually came up with a concept to be titled *Giving: How Each of Us Can Change the World*. Justin Cooper remained Clinton's literary collaborator, a role he was well trained to fulfill while overseeing trip logistics and advance, whether they were working together during a long flight or in the Chappaqua barn. The book's purpose was to "democratize CGI" by creating a new, inspirational platform for citizen philanthropy, from the lemonade stand to the sustainable corporation.

Published in September, just before CGI's third annual conclave, *Giving* struck many reviewers as an exercise in cheerleading rather than analysis, with praise lavished on any altruistic act—the plucky child picking up litter as well as the kindly billionaire financing scholarships and microloans. By highlighting organizations and activities addressing every conceivable problem, from hairpieces for kids with cancer to peace in the Mideast, the book gently argued that there is a charitable niche for everyone and that happiness depends more on giving than taking. The dozens of examples blurred into a fuzzy panorama of good feeling, proving Clinton's homily: If only everybody gave money or time, this would be a different world.

The most compelling sections detailed his own efforts, including a concise explanation of the theory and practice that made CHAI successful and a moving recollection of his work with former President Bush to raise money for the communities wrecked by the Asian tsunami and Hurricane Katrina. (For the frontispiece, he chose a photograph of a beautiful baby named Basil, born with HIV in Thailand, whose life was saved by a Clinton Foundation clinic with pediatric medicine provided by UNITAID.)

The book mentioned nearly everybody connected with his post-presidential endeavors, from Ron Burkle and Carlos Slim to Frank Giustra and Tom Hunter, and included a long and quite moving paean to Paul Farmer, writing, "I hope I live to see him win the Nobel [Peace] Prize."

Giving was launched on September 5 in a Harlem gymnasium, under the auspices of a local nonprofit—not with the usual round of cocktails and canapés, but a panel discussion on philanthropy led by PBS host Tavis Smiley, with a roster of celebrity guests that included Princeton professor Cornel West, home cooking guru Rachael Ray, and sportscaster Pat O'Brien. (The day before, Oprah Winfrey hosted Clinton on her television show.) The initial print run was 750,000 copies.

Planning the book tour, Clinton had hoped that *Giving* would afford him a chance to go to places he didn't usually visit and take the country's political temperature, as a sort of advance mission for Hillary. Once her campaign got under way, however, that plan no longer made sense. It was impossible to mesh promotion of the book—and its warm, nonpartisan, we're-all-in-this-together message—with the cooler, hard-edged dynamic of Democratic primary politics. He did book events in only ten major cities, and sales never reached the spectacular level anticipated by the publisher.

Still, the slender, two-hundred-page volume made its September 23 debut on the *New York Times* nonfiction bestseller list at #1 and Clinton pocketed a $6 million advance—of which he donated $1 million to charity.

At the Clinton Global Initiative meeting in New York that month, the publication of *Giving* was amplified by three new components. The gala dinner featured the advent of the Clinton Global Citizen Awards, a prize to be given to leading philanthropists, activists, or public officials, nominated by CGI members, whose work had demonstrated "innovative and effective approaches to making positive global change" and "potential for scalable growth and sustainability." The award's inaugural recipients included tennis star Andre Agassi, who ran an education-oriented foundation; Cisco Systems chairman John Chambers, a Republican who had made significant donations to CGI and CHAI; Vicky Colbert, a renowned Colombian educator; and Sir Fazle Hasan Abed, founder of the Bangladesh Rural Advancement Committee, a major South Asian antipoverty organization.

Clinton also announced the Clinton Global Initiative University, a new program based on CGI that would challenge college students to create fresh solutions to global problems. Students wishing to attend CGIU, which would be held at a different campus each spring, would submit a "Commitment to Action" in advance—and thus become eligible for a scholarship covering the costs of travel and attending the conference.

And in keeping with the egalitarian thrust of *Giving*, Clinton established a new CGI website, MyCommitment.org, which he hoped to develop into an "online community" for like-minded citizens to connect with each other and foster positive change.

———

As Clinton's publishers anticipated, *Giving* drew the attention of all the major broadcast, cable, print, and online outlets. What they didn't expect was a highly favorable feature in *Newsmax*—the largest-circulation conservative news magazine in the country, which was owned by two men who had fanatically pursued the destruction of Clinton's presidency.

Yet there on the cover of its November issue was a smiling photo of Clinton, hyping a friendly interview conducted by editor-in-chief Christopher Ruddy.

A lifelong conservative, Ruddy had earned a measure of journalistic fame on the right for his bloody-minded investigation of the tragic suicide of Vincent Foster, the deputy White House counsel who shot himself in suburban Virginia's Fort Marcy Park in July 1993. Although he never accused the Clintons of murdering Foster—who had been Hillary's law partner in Little Rock and Clinton's friend since early childhood—Ruddy disputed the official finding of suicide by six separate investigations, and insisted that lawyers in the Clinton White House had covered up the real circumstances of his death.

Ruddy published his theories about the Foster case in the *Pittsburgh Tribune-Review*, a right-wing daily owned by Richard Mellon Scaife, heir to the Mellon oil and steel fortune and one of the chief financial backers of the American right. So powerful was Scaife's disdain for the Clintons during those years that he spent more than $4 million on the "Arkansas Project," a secret effort to defame Bill and Hillary Clinton by any and every method available.

Several months after the Arkansas Project was exposed in 1998, Ruddy started Newsmax Media, a new conservative website, and eventually added a printed monthly magazine edition and a variety of health and financial newsletters. His main financial backer was Scaife—and Newsmax continued to bash the Clintons, their fellow Democrats, liberals, and progressives with predictable regularity for several years, while establishing itself with a large audience and big profits.

Ruddy was a Long Island native who had worked at the *New York*

Post in the 1980s, and had become friendly with Ed Koch, then the city's Democratic mayor. That friendship endured—and one day in 2005, Koch had suddenly told Ruddy over lunch how much he had come to like Hillary Clinton, then New York's junior U.S. senator. Ruddy said he wasn't interested in meeting her. But two weeks later, he received a note from Clinton, saying she was "pleased to know we have a mutual friend in Hizzoner."

To Ruddy, that note was a sign of "tremendous guts" on her part, and he wondered whether he should invite her to lunch. Scaife told him not to do it, and he sent back a friendly note without an invitation. Almost two years later, when Ruddy saw Koch again, the retired mayor mentioned that he intended to support Hillary for president.

At that point, Ruddy recalls, "I started looking at [Bill] Clinton and his foundation." He discovered that Clinton wasn't calling for "socialization of industry," but promoted development and entrepreneurship. He was deeply impressed by CHAI's work on health care and AIDS treatment.

After Koch offered to set up a lunch with Bill Clinton, Ruddy raised the issue with Scaife again—and discovered that the eccentric billionaire had been reevaluating their old enemy, too. But after Koch sent a message to Clinton's office raising the possibility of lunch with Scaife and Ruddy, he received no reply.

Finally in July 2007, Ruddy found a message on his cell phone: "This is Douglas Band. I'm counselor to President Clinton. I'm in Iowa and I'd like to talk with you." When Ruddy called, Band said, "Sorry we didn't get back to you sooner. Do you want to set up a meeting?"

"Yes, let's get together," said Ruddy.

"Are you taking back what you said in the Nineties?" Band asked.

"No," Ruddy replied, "but let's get together and talk about things we agree on."

After a few more calls, they scheduled a meeting on July 30. When he told Scaife, Ruddy recalls that the older man was "thrilled." They flew down to New York together from Scaife's summer home on Nantucket in his personal DC-9, then took a limousine to Harlem. They waited in a Starbucks on 125th Street for a Clinton aide to take them up to the foundation offices. Merely sitting at a coffee shop in the nation's legendary African American neighborhood was an adventure for

Scaife, a tall blond man with bright blue eyes, whose privileged life had rarely led him to meet any black people who weren't servants.

Only minutes after Band settled them in a conference room, the door opened and they heard that familiar voice. "Hi Dick. Welcome! Hey, Chris! Thanks for coming," said Clinton, smiling broadly as he brought them into his private office, where he showed off the magnificent view and some of the books, paintings, and artifacts he had collected from around the world.

Although Ruddy felt "pretty nervous," he said Clinton "soon put us at ease." Over a catered lunch of Mediterranean chicken, they listened as Clinton explained the inner workings of CHAI and the foundation's other projects for forty-five minutes, and then spent almost two hours more talking about presidential politics. Before they left, he gave each of them an inscribed copy of *My Life*.

When a reporter for *Newsweek* learned about the remarkable Harlem meeting months later, he asked Ruddy to comment—and Ruddy called Doug Band. "Doug said, say whatever you want. And President Clinton wants you to know, he doesn't care whatever they might say about you and all that old stuff." Eventually Ruddy told a writer for *Vanity Fair* that, looking back, he could have been "more level-headed" in his reporting on the Clintons: "I was overzealous." And around that same time, one of Scaife's foundations sent the Clinton Foundation a check for $100,000.

While Ruddy and Scaife were hardly alone in reconsidering Clinton, their reversal was a symbol of how far the former president had come from the dark time after his departure from the White House. For his part, Clinton had lived up to Mandela's lesson, liberating himself with generosity toward those who had grievously wronged him.

Now even his most ardent former enemies had come to acknowledge and support his humanitarian work. The press that once vilified Clinton now sought him out and even celebrated him. Prominent journalists— *New York Times* columnists Thomas Friedman and Nicholas Kristof, *Financial Times* editor Lionel Barber, NBC News' Tom Brokaw, among others—participated in CGI sessions. Many Republicans in the corporate world supported the Clinton Foundation, and Republican officials had appeared at CGI in the wake of his entente with the Bush family.

Bill Clinton's poll ratings both at home and abroad were strongly favorable. By some measures he was the most popular man in the world. As the election year loomed, there was nowhere to go but down.

———

Until late autumn, Hillary seemed poised to walk away with the Democratic nomination. Polls over the summer had showed her with substantial leads over every other contender, including Obama. With her strong performance in the first debates, the attitude of "inevitability" cultivated by Penn from the beginning seemed less imperious and more assured.

Then she stumbled in a debate at Drexel University—over the obscure issue of driver's licenses for undocumented immigrants—and her opponents pounced. So did her old adversaries in the political media, many of whom had never quite reconciled themselves to her unscathed emergence from the conflagrations of Whitewater, the independent counsel investigation, and impeachment.

A few weeks later, at the Jefferson-Jackson Day dinner in Des Moines, the combination of weak planning by her staff and a boilerplate speech, delivered poorly, left Hillary suddenly looking like a loser. The hall was filled with Obama loyalists, who responded with wild enthusiasm to his inspirational address, in which he rejected cynical Clintonite "triangulation" to build toward a soaring promise: "A nation healed. A world repaired. An America that believes again." From that evening forward, Hillary remained at a disadvantage in the kickoff Iowa caucuses. And she soon turned to her husband for help.

Clinton had long believed that his wife's campaign should go after Obama more aggressively. He knew that the Obama campaign had been quietly leaking negative material on him and Hillary for months. Media hostility toward Hillary had been amplified by favorable coverage of Obama, a phenomenal politician who was quickly becoming popular with the press.

But the Clinton campaign's experiments with potential negative advertising themes about the Illinois senator—his financial relationship with a shady real estate developer in Chicago, his shifting statements about the Iraq War, his equivocal record as a state legislator—were all flops when tested on Iowa voters. Clinton spent much of December in

Iowa, without effect. Hillary came in third, behind Edwards, in the caucus on January 3.

When the polls there showed that she might lose again in New Hampshire, Hillary unexpectedly displayed the emotions roiling inside, as she talked earnestly with a roundtable of undecided voters at a diner in Portsmouth. "It's not easy. . . . You know, this is very personal for me. It's not just political, it's not just public. I *see* what's happening." Cameras caught the pain on her face, her eyes welling with tears.

The next day, during a town hall meeting at Dartmouth College in Hanover, Clinton finally ripped into Obama. Wagging his finger, in hoarse, angry tones, he complained bitterly about the media's failure to vet the young senator.

"It is wrong that Senator Obama got to go through 15 debates trumpeting his superior judgment and how he had been against the war . . . and never got asked one time, 'Well, how could you say that, when you said in 2004 you didn't know how you would have voted on the [war] resolution? You said in 2004 there was no difference between you and George Bush . . . and there's no difference in your voting record and Hillary's ever since.' Give me a break! This whole thing is the biggest fairy tale I've ever seen!"

Then Clinton turned to another rankling story—a leaked document from inside the Obama campaign, urging an assault on both Clintons over campaign contributions and speaking fees from Indian American business leaders, referring archly to her as "Hillary Clinton (D-Punjab)."

Although Obama had rejected that idea, Clinton spoke as if he had been personally attacked. "What did you think about the Obama thing, calling Hillary the Senator from Punjab? . . . Or what about the Obama handout that the press never reported on, implying that I was a crook, scourging me, scathing criticism over my financial reports. . . . The idea that one of these campaigns is positive and the other is negative, when I know the reverse is true and I have seen it and I have been blistered by it for months, is a little tough to take."

When the primary returns came in with a narrow but crucial victory for Hillary, Clinton took special notice of the vote in Hanover. He felt certain that his double-barreled blast had held down Obama's margin in the college town, and perhaps beyond.

Following New Hampshire, the management at Hillary 2008 headquarters underwent a rapid change. Worried about the upcoming contests in Nevada and South Carolina, where she felt at a disadvantage, Hillary recruited Maggie Williams, who had served as chief of staff in Clinton's Harlem office, to join Patti Solis Doyle as campaign "comanager"—and Williams quickly drew Bill Clinton into the campaign's brain trust. In a meeting at Whitehaven, political director Guy Cecil briefed him and his top aides on the campaign's outlook. Cecil's candid observations worried Clinton—the campaign had spent a lot of money and time without achieving anything like the inevitable path to the nomination that Penn had predicted.

What bothered him still more, as the South Carolina primary drew closer, was the sense that this political contest was turning into some kind of vaguely racial dispute—with the press and some politicians holding him responsible. Rep. James Clyburn, a black member of the Democratic House leadership from South Carolina who had made no primary endorsement, criticized Clinton's Hanover speech as if the former president had mocked the idea of a black man running for the nation's highest office.

"To call that dream a fairy tale, which Bill Clinton seemed to be doing, could very well be insulting to some of us," he said. While Clinton had meant no such insult, Clyburn was reacting to an emerging racial theme. More than one Clinton surrogate, including Penn, had referred publicly to Obama's admission that in his youth he had not only smoked plenty of marijuana but had sampled cocaine ("a little blow") a few times.

In another incident, Hillary and Obama tweaked each other on the theme of "hope" versus practical politics. "Dr. King's dream began to be realized when President Johnson passed the Civil Rights Act," she responded to one of his jabs. "It took a president to get it done." A *New York Times* editorial twisted that remark into a criticism of King.

To suggest that he or Hillary might be subtly trying to inflame racism made Clinton furious. Nobody who knew them believed that either was racially prejudiced. Mandela's adopted son had been fighting racism his entire adult life, standing up against Klan-backed political adversaries in Arkansas, erasing the last vestiges of Jim Crow from the state constitution, appointing the first African Americans to top positions in state government and his presidential cabinet, and, more recently, insisting that Africans were just as deserving of AIDS treatment as Americans and Europeans. He understood the evil of racism better than most white politicians, and certainly had done far more than most to extinguish it.

When Hillary won a narrow victory in the Nevada caucuses, her campaign had to decide quickly whether to put time and resources into South Carolina, a state where she lagged Obama in polls—and where African Americans dominated the Democratic primary. Although her campaign's consensus was to spend little effort there and move on to the Super Tuesday states that would vote on February 5, Bill Clinton disagreed vehemently, arguing that he could win South Carolina for his wife. Rather than head off elsewhere to stump and raise money, he would spend the week before the primary crusading in the Palmetto State.

To say that week went poorly would be a profound understatement. Within the space of a few days, Clinton fulfilled the baleful predictions of Band and Cooper, who worried that his intense campaigning and acid comments about Obama were "un-statesmanlike," to say the least.

The first warning came from Tom Daschle, the former Senate majority leader, who had eagerly sided with Obama against Hillary. Daschle said Clinton's verbal attacks on his wife's principal opponent were "not in keeping with the image of a former president." Former Democratic state chairman Dick Harpootlian, another former ally, started to follow Clinton around, spouting sound bites that accused him of using racial tactics and the "politics of personal destruction."

On January 23, outside a Charleston auditorium, Clinton finally took the bait when a reporter asked him about Harpootlian's remarks. With video recording every word, he vented about Nevada, Obama's negative campaigning, and the "Senator from Punjab" memo. Jabbing his forefinger, he accused the Obama camp of using race against him, with the connivance of the media. "This is almost like once you accuse somebody of racism or bigotry or something, the facts become irrelevant. . . . They are feeding you this because they know this is what you want to cover. This is what you live for." He walked away, then turned once more to the gaggle of reporters: "Shame on you!"

This astonishing display of raw fury was a turning point in the primary, confirming what Daschle had said and causing some close to Clinton to wonder whether he truly wanted Hillary to win. He had eclipsed his wife—exactly as he had vowed not to do—and harmed his own reputation.

On Primary Day, Clinton made an offhand remark as he was about to exit the state. Flanked by a pair of African American members of Congress who had endorsed Hillary, he tried to explain what was happening in historical context. "Jesse Jackson won South Carolina in '84 and '88," he said. "Jackson ran a good campaign. And Obama ran a good campaign here." He didn't know yet that her principal opponent would crush her by almost 30 points.

With that loaded observation, Clinton had confirmed the racial indictment—or so his critics insisted, although black politicians, including Jackson himself, said they took no offense. Badly timed and clumsy, but surely not racist, Clinton's remark fell well within the bounds of acceptable commentary in American politics, where analysis of ethnic voting preferences is unavoidable and utterly mundane. Yet the press and Clinton's political foes swiftly imposed the worst interpretation: The former president was attempting to "blacken" Obama.

The next blow came within a few days, when Caroline Kennedy and her uncle Ted, the dean of the Senate Democrats, stepped forward to endorse Obama at American University in Washington. Senator Kennedy's move followed a long series of telephone calls from Bill Clinton, asking him to support Hillary. Clinton believed that Hillary not only deserved Kennedy's endorsement but was owed it, for many reasons— including his appointment of the senator's sister Jean Kennedy Smith as ambassador to Ireland. They had spent time with the Kennedys in Hyannis Port and felt a connection with them.

None of that made any difference to Ted Kennedy, immensely attracted by Obama's charisma and, he told friends, troubled that the Clintons were playing racial politics. On the day of the endorsement, he called Bill Clinton to inform him of his decision, in a very brief conversation. Minutes later Clinton called back, asking him to spell out his reasons. Kennedy replied that Obama's capacity to inspire the young had impressed him, and that he felt Obama might be able to heal the nation's divisions. In a way, Clinton appreciated the call—other old friends who endorsed Obama, including John Kerry for whom Clinton had risen from his sickbed, never bothered with that courtesy—but Kennedy's defection hit him hard.

————

Following the Kennedy endorsement by only three days, the *New York Times* struck an even harder blow at the former president—and his foundation. The front-page headline, "After Mining Deal, Financier Donated to Clinton," sat atop a suggestive lead:

> Late on Sept. 6, 2005, a private plane carrying the Canadian mining financier Frank Giustra touched down in Almaty, a ruggedly picturesque city in southeast Kazakhstan. Several hundred miles to the west a fortune awaited: highly coveted deposits of uranium that could fuel nuclear reactors around the world. And Mr. Giustra was in hot pursuit of an exclusive deal to tap them.
>
> Unlike more established competitors, Mr. Giustra was a newcomer to uranium mining in Kazakhstan, a former Soviet republic. But what his fledgling company lacked in experience, it made up for in connections. Accompanying Mr. Giustra on his luxuriously appointed MD-87 jet that day was a former president of the United States, Bill Clinton.

Clinton was not, in fact, aboard Giustra's aircraft when it landed in Almaty that evening. He would not arrive until four days later on Ron Burkle's plane with an agreement for the Kazakh government to purchase HIV/AIDS medicine for its citizens through CHAI.

However he got there, the article by Jo Becker and Don van Natta hinted strongly that Clinton's influence with Kazakh president Nursultan Nazarbayev had greased the way for Giustra to obtain a lucrative uranium mining deal there, in exchange for a later $31 million donation to the foundation. Recounting a "sumptuous midnight banquet" hosted by Nazarbayev, the *Times* reporters noted that Clinton's toast to him for "opening up the social and political life of your country" whitewashed his authoritarian record and ignored severe criticism of his regime by none other than Senator Hillary Clinton. Two days later, according to the *Times*, Giustra won the Kazakh deal, despite his "newcomer" status.

The *Times* account was not only misleading on the minor question of how Clinton arrived in Almaty. Far from being a novice in Kazakhstan, Giustra had completed successful mining deals there for more than a decade. He had been working on the uranium deal, which was done well before Clinton left New York, for months. The deal he made was with two private firms that owned uranium interests there, not the Kazakh government (although officials there would later say government approval was important). By then Giustra had already donated $5 million to CHAI. Although the *Times* reporters had no way to know it, Giustra would continue to work closely with Clinton, pledging more than $100 million toward antipoverty and development projects in the decade that followed the Kazakh trip. And the generous foundation donor who had urged Clinton to visit Kazakhstan was not Giustra but Lakshmi Mittal, the Indian industrialist who had major mining and steel production facilities there.

Yet neither Giustra nor the foundation complained to the paper's editors about the mistakes or the story's thrust at that time. (The errors would remain uncorrected until January 2009, when *Forbes* magazine published an article by Robert Lenzner titled "Clinton Commits No Foul in Kazakhstan Uranium Deal.") They ignored it in the hope that it would fade away.

Preventing such negative coverage was the reason that Clinton had decided, in the weeks before the publication of the *Times* story on Giustra, to withdraw from his personal business relationship with Ron Burkle and the Yucaipa Companies. Three of Burkle's companies were registered in the Cayman Islands, as Bloomberg News and other outlets had discovered. And the *Wall Street Journal* had opened up the matter of a Burkle investment that was about to draw still more unfavorable press, thanks to a twenty-nine-year-old Italian playboy and con man named Raffaello Follieri.

More than two years earlier, Band and Burkle had met Follieri simultaneously through Aldo Civico, a Columbia University anthropology professor who was assisting the Clinton Foundation. Follieri said he was helping the Vatican and local Catholic bishops to sell church property. His connections in Rome meant he could get valuable properties at low prices, and he was looking for investors. Burkle signed a deal with Follieri, but ended up suing him for misspending the proceeds on fancy hotels and chartered aircraft to woo his girlfriend, actress Anne Hathaway.

Meanwhile, Band had helped to introduce Follieri to another friend of the foundation, Canadian investor Michael Cooper, who put up a few million dollars toward the real estate deals—and had paid Band a finder's fee of $400,000. The *Journal* headline—"How Bill Clinton's Aide Facilitated a Messy Deal"—caused embarrassment, although Band gave half the money to another friend who had made the introduction, and returned half to Cooper.

The amounts earned by Clinton from the Yucaipa Cayman accounts were minimal, although he stood to make much more if the investments prospered. He had not avoided taxation on those earnings, which were listed in Hillary's personal financial disclosures as a senator and presidential candidate. But all the Democrats had criticized the misuse of offshore shell companies to avoid taxation—and Mitt Romney, a Republican candidate for president, was reported to have used such entities while working at Bain & Co., his Boston hedge fund. Competing with Obama, who had sponsored legislation to curtail offshore tax shelters, Hillary could not afford any hint of financial taint.

In early April, after verbal jousting between campaigns over "transparency" and "vetting," Hillary Clinton released her joint tax returns with Bill for all the years since they had left the White House. Combined with the returns they had already released, dating back to his tenure as governor, they had put almost thirty years of personal tax data in the public record—far more than any other political candidates in American history.

The impact of the release was stunning, as reporters learned for the first time how rich the Clintons had become. Their earnings over seven years totaled $109 million, described in the *New York Times* as "an ascent into the uppermost tier of American taxpayers that seemed unimaginable in 2001." Based strictly on annual income, they had flown to the top of the one percent. The returns showed $12 million or more from Burkle, which didn't include possible future payouts of up to $20 million; another $3 million or so from Vin Gupta, the controversial chairman of telemarketing firm infoUSA; about $29 million in book advances and royalties; and $52 million from Clinton's speeches, even though, as the *Times* noted, his paid speeches represented far less than half of all those he had delivered.

While urging greater transparency from the Clintons—although Obama had failed to disclose nearly as many years of tax returns as they had—the Obama campaign had insisted they should disclose all of the donors to the Clinton Foundation as well. For the moment, they could ignore that demand.

———

Over the next few months, as Obama steadily accumulated victories and delegates, Clinton spent almost every day on the road for Hillary and continued to provide his strategic wisdom to the campaign. His public appearances, however, were largely confined to places like Billings, Montana, Blowing Rock, North Carolina, and Yankton, South Dakota. "We were going to Indian reservations in the middle of nowhere," recalled one of his traveling aides.

Keeping her husband away from the limelight didn't brighten her prospects. Even when she won big primaries in March and April, the Democratic Party's superdelegates—party officials whose convention votes either she or Obama would need to secure the nomination—seemed allergic to her. The task of calling them had fallen largely to Bill Clinton, but his appeal and persistence were failing. The supers were gravitating steadily to Obama. On April 30, Penn emailed Hillary a memo outlining his concerns.

"I am worried generally that we are doing what we need to do in the races but that the super-delegate operation is not picking up despite the wins. . . . Overall, about 45 announced for Obama, 20 for HRC, and 3 switched from HRC to uncommitted," noting that Obama had won more women, more liberals, more moderates, and every region except the Northeast. "He even has more Senators," the consultant wrote. "So I am just taking a look at a primary operation that has been winning primaries but it would appear that the super-delegate operation is unsuccessful and there is no evidence we can get the numbers we need."

Forwarding his analysis, Hillary attached a note. "I feel the way Mark feels. I'm working as hard as I can, winning where I must, and bleeding superdelegates every day. . . . The hill is getting steeper as [Obama] gets weaker."

In fact, he was only a month away from winning. Numerically, Obama clinched the nomination on June 3 with a victory in Montana and a final rush of superdelegate endorsements.

With the primaries over, the Clintons confronted a massive debt, owing almost $13 million to Penn and other contractors, and the loss of another $12 million they had borrowed from themselves. Bill's reputation was badly bruised; so were some of Hillary's relationships in the Senate. Those problems would only deepen unless they did their utmost to elect as president a man they had come to dislike deeply—and who seemed to have no great regard for them.

––––––

Bill Clinton knew very well that he had no choice in coming to terms with Obama, despite the dismissive chill he felt emanating from the Obama camp in the wake of his wife's concession. Although Hillary knew her Illinois colleague well, Bill had only spoken with him very briefly on a few occasions. He faced the prospect of campaigning for someone he felt that he didn't know at all.

He believed they had to discuss the charges of racism that had wounded him so badly; a joint appearance would bury those accusations. He wanted Obama to personally ask for his help in the campaign, before public pressure forced him to make the endorsement. A former president should be treated with at least that much respect.

After weeks of waiting, however, the message from Obama headquarters in Chicago was more insulting than encouraging. Evidently the prospective nominee was too busy to meet with the only Democratic president who had served two terms since FDR. Or perhaps, as Clinton suspected, Obama and his advisers wanted to avoid appearing to pay homage to him, which might blur their rejection of "old politics." But Obama's staff promised to make time for a telephone call.

The call came on a Monday morning, a few days after a highly choreographed "unity rally" in Unity, New Hampshire, where Hillary had sworn "our hearts are set" on electing Obama. He and Bill talked for twenty minutes, a brief chat that the nominee's aides later described as "terrific."

"He has always believed that Bill Clinton is one of this nation's great leaders and most brilliant minds," said Obama spokesman Bill Burton, "and looks forward to seeing him on the campaign trail and receiving his counsel." But Clinton thought their chat had been perfunctory and superficial. He was not impressed and not mollified.

The cost to his image could be measured by "The Comeback Id"—a vitriolic, ten-thousand-word profile in the June issue of *Vanity Fair* by Todd Purdum, the magazine's national affairs editor and husband of former Clinton White House press secretary Dee Dee Myers. Replete with unattributed quotes and assertions, allegedly from concerned friends of the former president, Purdum depicted Clinton as an angry narcissist and aging satyr, jetting around with loose women on Burkle's plane, which was supposedly known to the cognoscenti as "Air Fuck One." The writer attributed Clinton's "questionable" choices to the bad company he kept, naming his friends Steve Bing and Ron Burkle, and possibly to the emotional impact of his heart surgeries—while conceding there was no "proof of post-presidential sexual indiscretions on Clinton's part, despite a steady stream of tabloid speculation and Internet intimations" on that score.

> Among the not-so-small cadre of Clinton friends and former aides, concern about the company the boss keeps is persistent, palpable and pained. No former president of the United States has ever traveled with such a fast crowd, and most 61-year-old American men of Clinton's generation don't, either.

To Clinton and his staff, the article was nothing but low-down gossip in the guise of high-minded anxiety. "Air Fuck One" was strictly a myth, as Band and others who had traveled with Clinton on Burkle's plane would attest. Jay Carson issued a statement denouncing the piece as "the journalism of personal destruction at its worst. . . . President Clinton has helped save the lives of more than 1,300,000 people in his post-presidency, and *Vanity Fair* couldn't find the time to talk to even one of them for comment." Purdum acknowledged Clinton's post-presidential achievements—he had included at least one or two laudatory sentences about the foundation—but insisted that good works weren't relevant to his profile.

———

By the time Clinton left for Africa on his annual summer trip in late July, his indignation about Obama had swollen to volcanic proportions. Not only had the Democratic victor treated his overtures with complete indifference but, far worse, he had bluntly rejected Hillary as a possible running mate. "Barack Obama would rather have every one of his teeth pulled out without Novocaine than accept Hillary on the ticket!" Clinton roared. The campaign to promote her for vice president had hardly been subtle; Bill had played his part, trying to send messages through various intermediaries to the Obama camp. As one friend later said, "He really seemed to want them to choose her." He left the country knowing that it wouldn't happen, partly because of him.

On Clinton's summer tours of Africa, the long hot days began around dawn, when his entourage would depart from their hotel, usually the best available, and end very late in the evening—often at a different hotel in another city, where the former president could be found playing cards with weary aides and friends, chewing an unlit cigar, nursing a glass of red wine, and talking on the telephone with someone back home.

The summer trip of 2008, spanning the last few days of July and the first few days of August, provided respite for him from the pressures and disappointments of presidential politics. The conflict with Obama had marred his image and frayed his unique bond with the African American community. In Africa, where public admiration had not been diminished by campaign controversies, he could again immerse himself in the duties and rewards of his post-presidential life. There he could begin to redirect the narrative.

But given the inclinations of the political press corps, that was a forlorn hope. And the trip did not begin auspiciously.

Although the itinerary was shorter than normal, covering only four countries in six days, the traveling contingent was bigger and included Chelsea Clinton, still on campaign hiatus from her job at a New York hedge fund; traveling physician Roger Band; Roger Clinton's son Tyler; former Democratic National Committee chair Terry McAuliffe; former ambassador Joe Wilson; former transportation secretary Rodney

Slater; and actors Ted Danson and Mary Steenburgen, longtime friends of the Clintons from Arkansas days.

The media contingent, which tended to range from very small to nonexistent on the annual trip, was larger than usual, too, with correspondents from ABC News, the *Washington Post*, and the *Guardian* of London, a young blogger from the *Huffington Post*, and a crew dispatched by Hollywood directors Steven Spielberg and Ron Howard to shoot video for a prospective documentary on the foundation.

Transporting this oversized retinue required not one but two passenger jets. Traveling aboard a luxuriously appointed Boeing 767 loaned to the foundation by a group of Google executives were the former president, his family members, several personal friends, and his Secret Service detail. The press corps, the documentary crew, some foundation staff, and assorted other passengers were assigned to an older, more modest 727 chartered for the trip, which turned out to be in dismal condition.

For more than two days after the former president and his entourage lifted off from Newark Airport, the aging 727 suffered one malfunction after another: a broken air conditioner, an aborted takeoff due to fuel tank problems, a cracked cockpit window, a minor fire, and a defective fuel valve. Several passengers, including Slater, abandoned ship in frustration, while frantic foundation staffers tried to locate another large aircraft available on short notice. Rocker Jon Bon Jovi intervened to make a last-minute rescue by providing an even older Boeing 707 used by his band for touring, which was quickly cleaned up and flown to Newark from a Bahamas hangar.

By the time the media contingent reached Addis Ababa on Air Bon Jovi, the staff had been forced to cut back the schedule. The aviation jinx continued when the 767 suffered an engine malfunction on takeoff and had to turn around immediately for an emergency landing at the Addis airport. The press plane turned around, too, and returned to Addis to retrieve the Clinton group, forcing everyone to find seats on the smaller plane.

Yet despite the endlessly irritating and occasionally frightening aviation difficulties, those few days in Africa lifted Clinton. The curtailed visit literally flew by as he and his companions moved through Ethiopia to Rwanda, then across the continent to Liberia and Senegal on the western coast, before he headed to the annual World AIDS conference in Mexico City and then homeward.

They visited Rwandan coffee and cassava farmers, whose production had grown substantially thanks to fertilizer grants, technical assistance, and marketing help from the Clinton Hunter Development Initiative. They spent a few hours in the Liberian capital, Monrovia, where Clinton delivered an address to President Ellen Johnson Sirleaf, her cabinet, and Liberia's parliament concerning the foundation's new agreement with pharmaceutical manufacturers to slash the price of malaria medicine, enabling the government to pay for the treatment of tens of thousands who might otherwise die. He joined representatives of the United Nations and the French government at a hospital in Dakar, the capital of Senegal, to announce a new protocol and funding for the treatment of infants born with HIV/AIDS, which would eventually save hundreds of thousands from death before their second birthday.

Nearly everywhere they went—even to remote places like the village of Debre Zeit in Ethiopia's northwestern highlands, where the traveling party made one of its first stops to inspect a new health clinic—throngs showed up to greet the ex-president with a joyous enthusiasm that never failed to astonish jaded Americans. People chanted and waved flags (including American flags) and sometimes danced to welcome Clinton, with a spirit that seemed almost anachronistic, as if the United States still enjoyed the lost prestige of an earlier time.

The Godino Health Clinic in Debre Zeit was a modest single-story structure with a white corrugated roof, one of fifty built by the Clinton Foundation to serve rural families in a partnership with the national government. Those sites represented the beginning of an effort to develop thousands of clinics across Ethiopia, a nation of nearly 80 million, and tens of thousands spanning the continent.

Fanning out from each of those clinics every morning were dozens of rural health workers, mostly young women without high school diplomas, trained by CHAI to deliver medicine and care to AIDS and malaria patients in even more remote places. That strategy was designed not only to eradicate those diseases within the next decade, a project requiring much more than simply dropping off truckloads of cheap medication, but to construct a functioning health care system across Africa.

Hundreds of people, led by schoolchildren in spotless dress clothes, lined the rutted road as the Clinton motorcade slowly pulled up outside the clinic. Greeted by the clinic director, a middle-aged gentleman in doctor's whites, Clinton and Chelsea quickly toured the facility before walking up the road to the town center, where a small stage had been erected behind a twine cordon.

A length of string wasn't much to hold back the surging wave of humanity, but then the Secret Service detail that traveled with Clinton had long since come to understand that he would no longer tolerate the security constraints of his White House years. People wanted to touch him, and he wanted to touch them, so the agents would simply stand as close as possible and hope that nobody wanted to do him harm.

More than once, intense emotions had driven spectators forward suddenly, shouting with excitement while stampeding over fences and cars and scaring everyone—except Clinton, who would turn, hold up his hands, and grin happily as the rushing crowd surrounded him. On that particular morning, however, there was no impassioned stampede. The people of Debre Zeit gathered to listen quietly as Clinton thanked the Ethiopian government for supporting his foundation's work, discussed the plans for the new clinic, and described what the health workers would be doing. They applauded and cheered loudly, then jostled to get near him for a touch or a handshake before allowing him to depart.

The roster of countries on Clinton's annual Africa tour varied from year to year, but he always visited Rwanda, the scene of what he has often described as the worst failure of his presidency—the tribal massacres in 1994 that killed hundreds of thousands, unimpeded by U.S. or any other outside forces. One of the stops on the 2008 summer visit to Rwanda was the groundbreaking for a rural hospital in the last district that still lacked one—and that would become, when completed in 2009, the most modern health facility in Africa.

Surely Clinton felt a degree of personal redemption in Rwanda, prompting critics to complain that behind his foundation's good works was a mixture of narcissism and angst. He shrugged off these putdowns. "I have never met anybody who spent all their time talking about everybody's motives who, at the end of their life, could talk about very many lives *they* had saved," he once said.

By the summer of 2008, his foundation's programs had expanded well beyond the capital to reach the most distant, neglected rural villages—places such as Rwinkwavu, in the country's southeastern corner, where the foundation had paid to renovate a derelict hospital that reopened in late 2006. Accompanied by President Paul Kagame, Clinton flew down to Rwinkwavu to visit the hospital and meet the rural health workers who were fanning out into the countryside.

It was a health worker paid and trained by his foundation—a young woman named Beatrice—who brought Clinton to meet one of her very young patients. Fifteen-year-old Jean Pierre lived with his sister Eugenie, nineteen, who had looked after him ever since both of their parents died of an illness that was probably AIDS in 2002. Three years later, Jean Pierre was diagnosed with advanced AIDS symptoms and could no longer attend school. For many months he lay ill in their hut, waiting to die, until Beatrice showed up one day to deliver care, medication, and human kindness. Jean Pierre's health improved dramatically and he returned to school.

As they shook hands, the thin dark boy told the smiling white-haired man that he would like to become a doctor who helps sick children. Clinton spoke about that moment for many weeks after he returned from Africa. To him the recovery of that brave child, with real hope for a full life, symbolized his foundation's mission. Six years after the creation of CHAI, there were still far too many children and adults dying of AIDS in Africa and elsewhere. But there were also well over a million alive, like Jean Pierre, because they were at last receiving treatment—and there was now the prospect of bringing proper care to all.

Reporters on the trip seemed fixated on Clinton's reaction to the defeat of Hillary and the rise of Obama rather than his global vision or his foundation's achievements. Evidently unaware that he had visited Africa every summer since 2002, the *Washington Post's* reporter thought he had scheduled this particular trip to commence his political "rehabilitation." In a 1,600-word story, she confined her account of actual events on the ground to a few paragraphs. She didn't find space to mention Jean Pierre, the rural health workers, or the new hospital in Rwinkwavu.

———

When he arrived back in Chappaqua, Clinton was tired but happy to be home. Within a few days, he would need to start thinking about a speech for the Democratic convention, where he would endorse a man he had come to dislike intensely. Anita Dunn, the communications director of the Obama campaign, had sent Band an email advising that the former president was scheduled to speak on Wednesday evening at 9 p.m. They wanted him to talk about national security and foreign policy. They wouldn't mind if he outlined "contrasts" with Republican nominee John McCain. And separately, they let him know they wanted to see the text in advance.

Band had ignored that last demand, knowing Clinton wouldn't submit to any vetting of his words. He also knew that his boss would talk about whatever he wanted to discuss, unconstrained by any themes ordained by the Obama campaign. With Clinton's assent, he asked speechwriter Jeff Shesol to start working on a first draft.

In a certain way, Shesol was an ironic choice to draft the endorsement speech. Years earlier, before joining the White House staff, he had written a well-received history of the feud between Lyndon Johnson, a controversial Southern president of great ambitions and appetites, and Robert F. Kennedy, a gifted politician and eloquent reformer to whom Obama had been compared by his surviving brother, among others. Its title was *Mutual Contempt*.

As Band had anticipated, Clinton did not even glance at the Shesol speech until the Friday before the convention. He took the draft, whose motivating idea might be called "What a Democratic President Can Do," replete with direct and implied references to what he had done during eight years in power, and began to add and whittle. Sitting out in the Chappaqua barn, he went through one draft, and then another.

He continued to craft the speech as he boarded a private jet in New York on Monday, August 25, the convention's opening day, to fly out to Denver so he would be present for Hillary's speech the next evening. The aircraft belonged to Steve Bing, a rakish film and music producer and philanthropist who had inherited a shopping mall fortune estimated at $700 million. He was a dedicated Democrat and Clinton supporter who had spent huge sums promoting Hillary's candidacy in 2008.

The fortyish bachelor had been involved in not one but two colorful paternity cases. He was an exceptionally loyal and close friend, but his presence in the Clinton entourage always encouraged gossip.

Bing's other traveling companion was Jesse Dylan, the oldest of Bob Dylan's five children and a respected film and video producer in New York. Modest and low-key, Dylan was a fervent supporter of Barack Obama, for whom he had directed the emotionally powerful "Yes We Can" music video, featuring will.i.am of the Black Eyed Peas and a dazzling cast of singers and actors poetically affirming Obama's New Hampshire primary concession speech.

Dylan had pulled them all together and put up his own money to produce the video. He had expected nothing in return, and nothing was what he got: Not a telephone call from the candidate, not a thank-you note, not even an invitation to celebrate at the convention. More than 57 million viewers had watched "Yes We Can" on YouTube by the time Obama delivered his convention speech, resulting in many millions of donated dollars and many thousands of volunteer hours.

When Bing told Clinton how the Obama campaign had treated Dylan, the former president shook his head. To Clinton, who had prided himself all his life on remembering people and writing appreciative notes, such unfeeling behavior was worse than a sin; it was a mistake.

Arriving in Denver, Clinton and his small entourage settled into luxurious quarters on the same floor as Bing at the Brown Palace Hotel. For a few hours, he set aside his own draft to work on Hillary's speech. Over the following two days, Doug Band fended off a series of increasingly agitated calls from the Obama camp, requesting to see the draft. He blew them off repeatedly, trying hard not to be rude without always succeeding. Obama aide Anita Dunn didn't get a glimpse at the text until Band brought her up to a hotel conference room to read it, only hours before Clinton arrived at the convention center on Wednesday evening.

There was simply no way to read Clinton's speech—a litany of indictments and guarantees, well-crafted but lacking great inspiration on paper—and actually hear its uplifting spirit and the way it would resound in the hall as he delivered it. Many of the reporters listening to him rated it the best address he had delivered in years, perhaps the finest since he had left the White House. It gave Obama everything he needed, and more, with generosity:

My fellow Democrats, sixteen years ago, you gave me the profound honor to lead our party to victory and to lead our nation to
a new era of peace and broadly shared prosperity.

Together, we prevailed in a campaign in which the Republicans
said I was too young and too inexperienced to be Commander-
in-Chief. Sound familiar? It didn't work in 1992, because we were
on the right side of history. And it won't work in 2008, because
Barack Obama is on the right side of history.

His life is a 21st Century incarnation of the American Dream.
His achievements are proof of our continuing progress toward
the "more perfect union" of our founders' dreams. The values of
freedom and equal opportunity which have given him his historic
chance will drive him as president to give all Americans, regardless of race, religion, gender, sexual orientation or disability, their
chance to build a decent life, and to show our humanity, as well as
our strength, to the world.

We see that humanity, that strength, and our future in Barack
and Michelle Obama and their beautiful children. We see them
reinforced by the partnership with Joe Biden, his wife Jill, a dedicated teacher, and their family.

Barack Obama will lead us away from the division and fear of
the last eight years, back to unity and hope. If, like me, you still believe America must always be a place called Hope, then join Hillary, Chelsea, and me in making Senator Barack Obama the next
President of the United States.

Those final few paragraphs electrified the delegates, who rose up
shouting, waving signs frantically, and embracing across the differences that had divided them. The African American delegates looked
especially joyful in welcoming errant brother Bill back into the family.
They didn't question his sincerity. They wanted to believe that he believed.

———

Within days after the Democratic convention, the comfortable polling
lead that Obama and his running mate, Joe Biden, held over McCain
and his surprise choice, Alaska governor Sarah Palin, began to evapo-

rate. In several polls, McCain led by the first week of September. And suddenly, Obama was no longer too busy to meet with Bill Clinton, whose sustained popularity among white working-class voters seemed essential to Democratic hopes for carrying states like Ohio and Pennsylvania.

When Clinton learned that Obama was coming to Manhattan for the seventh anniversary of 9/11, he extended an invitation for lunch at his office—just the two of them—and this time, his courtesy was reciprocated. The Democratic nominee came up to Harlem after a morning memorial ceremony at Ground Zero. Before going into Clinton's private office, they spoke very briefly with reporters gathered in the foyer. "I've agreed to do a substantial number of things—whatever I'm asked to do." As for his view of the race, Clinton said, "I predict that Senator Obama will win, and win handily." Smiling broadly, Obama interjected: "There you go. You can take it from the president of the United States. He knows a little something about politics."

Over a catered lunch of grilled chicken and vegetables, they talked about the race and the best use of Clinton's available time to ensure victory. The mood was cordial. Clinton was delighted that Obama had finally showed up to repair their relationship. When it was time for his guest to leave, the former president accompanied him downstairs to 125th Street. Outside the glass doors, an enormous crowd had gathered, and when they saw Obama and Clinton, a chant of "Yes We Can!" went up. Surrounded by agents, Clinton put his arm behind Obama's back and they walked out together, waving.

The Clinton Global Initiative convened in Midtown two weeks later, with Obama and McCain appearing there on the opening day. The Obama campaign had sent sincere regrets that the nominee would be unable to attend in person, due to campaign commitments, and planned to appear via satellite instead—but much to Clinton's dismay, they also asked that he rescind the Republican's invitation.

That would not happen, replied Band. McCain was a longtime political adversary, but both Clintons regarded him as a friend; CGI was a nonpartisan event; and Clinton would never do something so rude, under any circumstances. They dropped the request.

———

Both Obama and McCain were scheduled to appear on September 25—
in the midst of delicate bipartisan negotiations in Washington over a
bank bailout in the wake of the Wall Street credit crash. But on the eve of
his appearance, McCain shocked the country by declaring that he would
suspend his campaign so he could return to Washington to shepherd the
bailout legislation through Congress. He urged Obama to do likewise.
And the Arizona senator said that he would not attend the first presidential debate of the general election, set for September 26 in Mississippi.

"I'm an old Navy pilot, and I know when a crisis calls for all hands
on deck," McCain told the CGI audience, standing behind a lectern on
the Sheraton ballroom stage. "As of this morning, I suspended my campaign. With so much on the line, for America and the world, the debate
that matters most right now is taking place in the United States Capitol—and I intend to join it."

But neither Obama nor the Democrats were willing to entertain
this obvious ploy, which they dismissed as a "rescue plan" for the fal-
tering Republican campaign. Gazing down from giant screens in the
Sheraton ballroom, Obama transfixed the CGI audience and the press
corps, his image beamed from a hotel in Florida. "It's great to speak to
you this morning. I'm sorry that I can't be there, but I did enjoy the opportunity to sit down with President Clinton recently in New York . . ."
The candidate knew what was on the minds of everyone in the country,
and he got quickly to the point.

"You are meeting at a time of great turmoil for the American economy. We are now confronted with a financial crisis as serious as any we
have faced since the Great Depression. Action must be taken to restore
confidence in our economy," he said.

"Let me be clear: it's outrageous that we find ourselves in a position
where taxpayers must bear the burden for the greed and irresponsibil-
ity of Wall Street and Washington. But we also know that a failure to
act would have grave consequences for the jobs, and savings, and retirement of the American people. . . .

"Our election is in 40 days," he went on. "The American people deserve to hear directly from myself and Senator McCain about how we
intend to lead our country. The times are too serious to put our campaign on hold, or to ignore the full range of issues that the next president will face."

Ultimately McCain folded, agreeing to Obama's terms for the bailout and appearing as originally planned at the Mississippi debate.

Clinton spent most of those final weeks in the purple states campaigning for Obama, with appearances in Florida, Ohio, Nevada, New Hampshire, Pennsylvania, and back to Florida again for a gigantic midnight rally with Obama on October 29 in Kissimmee, a small city just south of Orlando. Estimated at 35,000, the waiting throng looked as if everyone in the state had showed up—blacks, Latinos, whites, young and old, poor and middle-class—waiting for hours before the gates opened to see the two Democratic "rock stars."

For their first and last campaign appearance together, Clinton and Obama took the stage with their arms around each other's shoulders. Even more effusive than in his convention speech, Clinton held back nothing. Speaking for just under fifteen minutes, he made a cogent case for Obama, reviewing his philosophy, his platform, his intellectual strength, and his determination to create change.

"He's got the right policies—I've read them all. And I've read his opponent's," he told the diverse crowd. "People used to make fun of me for being a policy wonk, but after the last eight years, it really matters what people advocate."

Pointing to Obama's calm handling of the financial crisis, he said, "We know we need a president who wants to understand and who *can* understand. . . . I think it's clear the next president of the United States should be, and with your help will be, Barack Obama!"

The man who had been his bitter antagonist now embraced him warmly. Then Obama took the microphone, gestured toward Clinton, and said loudly: "In case all of you forgot, this is what it's like to have a great president." As he listened to those words, Clinton was touched, his face etched with emotion.

On November 4, Barack Obama was elected the forty-fourth president of the United States, carrying twenty-eight states plus the District of Columbia, with 365 electoral votes, and almost 53 percent of the popular vote. As Clinton predicted, he had won handily.

CHAPTER FOURTEEN

For all the pundits and politicians across the ideological landscape who had believed that Barack Obama would at last extirpate Bill and Hillary Clinton from American public life, the weeks following his election victory became repetitive episodes in cognitive dissonance. With astonishment and chagrin, they watched the president-elect name friends, allies, and former employees of his former rivals to run his transition—and then his government.

To oversee the wrenching shift from the Bush administration, Obama had chosen John Podesta, a veteran of both Clinton administrations, including a stint as White House chief of staff. To serve as his own new chief of staff, Obama chose Rahm Emanuel, who had also worked as a senior political adviser to Clinton. And he had followed those startling selections with a lengthy roster of Clintonites slated for top positions in the West Wing and cabinet agencies.

But anyone distressed by hearing so many of those familiar names—at the very dawn of what was supposed to be a merciless cleansing—might have simply passed out upon hearing that Obama would name Hillary herself as secretary of state. By the time that rumor appeared as an item inside the *Washington Post* on November 14, only ten days after the election, the process leading to her appointment was well under way.

It began when Bill Clinton's cell phone rang on the morning of November 9, as he and Hillary were taking a Sunday hike around the Mianus River Gorge, a nature preserve about ten miles from Chappaqua. The voice on the phone was Obama, who greeted him warmly and said he needed to talk with Clinton "and Hillary." Neither of the Clintons had spoken with him since election night, when she had called to offer congratulations, and he had thanked them both for the hundreds of campaign events, calls, and appearances they had logged on his behalf.

With weak cell reception on the trail, Clinton suggested resuming the conversation when they got home. He told Hillary that the president-elect probably wanted to discuss the transition, and perhaps ask their opinions about a few people. When they connected again later in the day, Clinton turned out to be right—Obama wanted to talk over the names of former Clinton administration figures he was considering for positions involving the economy, his top priority. At the end of their conversation, he mentioned that he looked forward to seeing Hillary "sometime soon."

If that sounded mysterious, there were already clues, as Hillary learned when she called her adviser and press secretary, Philippe Reines. He told her that George Stephanopoulos—another former Clinton hand—had said that same morning on ABC News' *This Week* that her name was being mentioned for secretary of state. Still, she didn't take the idea very seriously, or so she later wrote in her memoir *Hard Choices*.

A few days later, when she and aide Huma Abedin traveled to Chicago for a secret meeting with Obama, however, she learned that the rumor was accurate. Only minutes after they sat down in the transition office, he asked her to consider becoming secretary of state because, as he put it, she was "the only person" who could handle the job (although his short list also included John Kerry and New Mexico governor Bill Richardson). He needed someone who could run the nation's foreign affairs immediately and competently, Obama explained, while he revived the ruined economy.

Hillary's first impulse was to turn him down, and she did, saying she wanted to return to the Senate. She would do her utmost to support him there. But he prevailed on her to agree to consider the offer, insisting he needed her in the cabinet. She agreed to think it over and went home.

Sometime after she returned to New York, amid clamorous speculation in the press, a call came from Rahm Emanuel saying she had seventy-two hours to respond: yes or no. With a touch of sarcasm, Doug Band reminded Emanuel of a recent interview in which he had confessed to taking two weeks to decide whether he would join Obama's White House staff.

During the week that followed, Hillary leaned heavily on her husband and his staff, while reaching out to many friends and several of her Senate colleagues. She was truly and deeply conflicted. Bill Clinton's attitude was negative but equivocal—he would support whatever decision she made. Band and Mills both were outspokenly opposed to her accepting the nomination. Apart from whether she was inclined to shoulder the exhausting responsibilities of leading the State Department, there loomed the issue of how such a decision would affect her husband's work.

As soon as news of her possible appointment leaked, journalists and commentators began to revive dormant questions about the sources of Clinton's income, the donors to the foundation and the library, the sponsors of his speeches, and his relationship with Burkle, among others. How Bill Clinton earned, raised, and spent money had been media obsessions for a long time.

In this instance the questions were appropriate, even if many of the underlying assumptions were wrong. Unquestionably, conflicts could arise between the State Department and the private interests of the secretary's spouse—and the same might be true for anyone in the job. The new administration's procedures had to ensure probity in dealing with such issues, whether real or merely apparent. Having vowed to restore integrity to the government, and to rebuild American relationships around the world, Obama had to demand transparency from every appointee, especially Clinton.

So while the president-elect and a few of his aides attempted to persuade Hillary to join him, teams of lawyers discussed what the new administration would require from Bill Clinton and the foundation. Everything would have to come together, including Hillary's final decision, by December 2.

Leading the Clinton side in the negotiations was Cheryl Mills, the longtime trusted aide best known for her impassioned defense during the Senate impeachment trial, along with Band, Lindsey, and former communications aide Jim Kennedy. On the Obama side were Podesta, former Clinton White House deputy Todd Stern, and Thomas Perrelli, a transition team attorney who had worked in the Clinton Justice Department.

It was a sign of how much Obama trusted Podesta—and desired Hillary's assent—that he put someone so close to her in charge of the process. Podesta had worked with Mills and the rest of the Clinton team for years; he had even taught Band law at Georgetown University when the young White House aide was studying for his degree at night.

Yet the initial positions set forth by Obama's side seemed rigid: Bill Clinton must "step down" from his foundation and stop hosting CGI every year; the White House would vet and possibly veto every paid speech and business relationship. As more than one internal Clinton memo noted, the impulse to "walk away" in response to such imposing demands was strong.

Bill Clinton wasn't about to leave the foundation, but neither he nor Hillary felt any grave concern about the financial disclosures that might be imposed on them. They had revealed the sponsors of his paid speeches and his business partnerships every year on Hillary's Senate disclosure forms. They had disclosed their joint income tax returns for many years, too, dating back to his tenure as attorney general in Arkansas, and released still more during the 2008 campaign.

Nor would Clinton object to revealing the names of future donors to the foundation—a requirement that made perfect sense to him, at least going forward. CHAI in particular depended heavily on subsidies from foreign governments—almost all close U.S. allies such as Canada, Norway, and the United Kingdom—a situation that could raise questions for the secretary of state. The foundation had long publicized the major Clinton Global Initiative sponsors. Much more vexing was Obama's insistence that they reveal every *past* donor to the foundation and the library, people whose gifts had been made with a guarantee of privacy.

No such disclosures had ever been demanded from any of Clinton's predecessors, although every recent president had raised money from foreign sources for the construction of their presidential libraries and other post-presidential endeavors. When George W. Bush ran for president, nobody had insisted that his father reveal the millions of dollars in donations from foreign potentates that he had collected to build the George Bush Presidential Library in Texas. Clinton had come to expect such disparate application of the rules, however.

On November 18, while Joe Biden, Senate majority leader Harry Reid, and New York's senior senator Chuck Schumer sought to persuade Hillary to take the job, her team prepared a memo outlining "issues and proposals" regarding her possible nomination. Its theme was how to preserve Bill Clinton's "robust set of activities" without compromising her.

"There has, at various times, been considerable pressure to release the list of donors to the Clinton Foundation," the memo acknowledged. "The sensitivity about doing so is that donors understood that their donations were private." The memo sought to preserve that confidentiality by letting the Obama transition team "vet" any donors who declined to permit public release of their identities, with all donors disclosed in the future.

It also proposed to set up the Clinton Global Initiative as "an entity separate from the Foundation," with Clinton himself as emeritus chairman but continuing as "the principal host and master of ceremonies" for the annual conference. He would not solicit financial support for CGI, nor would CGI accept contributions from foreign governments. The first CGI conference outside the United States, scheduled to open in Hong Kong on December 2, would also be the last, at least for the duration of Hillary's government service.

As for CHAI, the Clinton team argued that to cut off financing from foreign governments would endanger millions of impoverished people who relied on the initiative for treatment. They proposed "no change with regard to existing donor countries," unless those donors increased their contributions substantially. In that case, and with new donor countries, the proposed donations would be reviewed by the State Department's ethics officers and perhaps by White House counsel as well. The Clinton Climate Initiative, whose only foreign nation donor was Australia, would follow the same protocol.

The memo foresaw no problem with Clinton continuing to write and publish books. Noting that all of his speeches were "a matter of public record," and that he delivered no paid speeches to foreign governments, the memo suggested a review procedure for his speeches to other overseas entities: His office would submit a list of planned speeches to the State Department ethics officer for review, with further possible review by the White House counsel. They would articulate any concerns, "with the expectation that appropriate action would be taken." (The ethics office only ever flagged one speech, in Shanghai, which Clinton canceled.)

Finally, the memo noted that Clinton had exited his consultancy with Vin Gupta's infoUSA firm in October 2007—and that he had begun the process of disentangling himself from Ron Burkle's ventures around the same time. "Going forward, President Clinton intends to continue to provide consulting advice, but not to enter into any further partnerships." Any proposed consultancy, including a "green construction venture" he was then discussing with Steve Bing, would be submitted for the same kind of review and potential action as his speeches.

After several loud, heated discussions, the negotiators found ways to accommodate Obama's concerns without eviscerating the foundation. The Clintons had no need to conceal anything and wouldn't let disclosure become the obstacle to her appointment. Band and Lindsey began to reach out to the foundation donors, mostly via letters, letting them know that their donations might be disclosed publicly. (Not one of the more than 200,000 individuals and entities that had donated to the foundation ever objected.)

The negotiators also reached agreement about two issues Hillary had raised. She wanted to be certain of regular access to the president, and she needed reassurance that his apparatus would help to retire her campaign debt.

By November 18, however, those points of agreement appeared moot, with Hillary leaning strongly toward returning to the Senate. That afternoon, Mills circulated a letter to Podesta that she had drafted, laying out the reasons why Hillary had decided to reject the president's offer. "We need the best rationale that we can share with others," she explained. "We also will need talking points."

The draft letter began, "I am glad we were successful in developing a plan to ensure that many of the activities of the Clinton Foundation can continue and not create conflicts, or the appearance of conflicts, if Senator Clinton were to serve as Secretary of State." But those protocols, said the letter, would likely hinder the growth of the foundation's HIV/AIDS programs—"programs that have saved millions of lives." Although "honored to consider service in his Cabinet," she had "concluded that it was best . . . to continue her lifetime commitment to public service as the Senator from New York."

When Hillary called Obama on November 19, she had a set of talking points, reviewing the process, expressing her gratitude, but explaining why she would remain in the Senate. The Clinton team had prepared a statement for release to the media. Much as she appreciated his offer, it said, "in the end, this was a decision for me about where I can best serve President-elect Obama, my constituents and our country. And as I told President-elect Obama this afternoon, my place is in the Senate."

But she didn't reach Obama until after midnight on November 20. She talked about the foundation, her campaign debt, and whether she could accomplish more in the Senate or the State Department. He listened sympathetically and promised to make sure her concerns were addressed. When she reiterated her reluctance, he refused to accept her refusal. They hung up without reaching a conclusion.

The next day Hillary changed her mind for the last time—above all because, as she later wrote, "When your president asks you to serve, you should say yes." Obama announced her appointment to the press in a Chicago hotel ballroom on December 1, with her standing beside him. He briskly dismissed questions about their campaign criticisms of each other, and they left the podium arm in arm.

Bill Clinton watched their press conference on a hotel television in Hong Kong, where he was hosting the first—and for several years to come, the last—CGI International gathering. Tentative plans for a 2009 CGI conference in Brazil would soon be canceled in accordance with Obama's strictures.

Over the following weeks, with a break for Thanksgiving, the Clinton and Obama teams worked on a final "memorandum of understanding," to be signed by Bruce Lindsey and Valerie Jarrett, Obama's top adviser and cochair of his transition team. This document codified the arrangements they had already negotiated concerning foreign donations, speeches, and business arrangements.

The foundation released the names of its donors on December 18, provoking a frenzy of coverage—"In Clinton List, a Veil Is Lifted on Foundation," announced the *New York Times* on page A1—that focused on contributions from celebrities like Barbra Streisand, big sums collected almost a decade earlier for the library from Saudi Arabia and the Gulf States, and donations from a small collection of figures whose pedigrees might raise an eyebrow—"a businessman who was close to the onetime military ruler of Nigeria, a Ukrainian tycoon who was son-in-law of that former Soviet republic's authoritarian president and a Canadian mining executive who took Mr. Clinton to Kazakhstan while trying to win lucrative uranium contracts."

The unprecedented revelation, which Clinton's office said "would insure against even the appearance of a conflict of interest," didn't mollify their critics. Neither did a statement from Obama's spokesperson insisting, "Past donations to the Clinton Foundation have no connection to Senator Clinton's prospective tenure as secretary of state." The *Times* story dismissed those reassurances with an editorial tone: "Such contributions could provoke suspicion at home and abroad among those wondering about any effect on administration policy." The editorial pages and cable commentators tended to agree, describing the disclosure protocols as inadequate and doomed to failure.

Her Senate confirmation nevertheless appeared certain—so certain that between Christmas and New Year's, she started serious discussions with potential recruits for top State Department positions. To keep that process quiet, she invited prospective aides and envoys to a location in New York rather than Washington. Anyone entering her home in the capital was likely to be spotted. But nobody noticed who went in and out of a busy tower overlooking Central Park, where Hillary had borrowed the residence of Doug and Lily Band as a "State Department annex" to conduct interviews and meetings.

———

When Hillary appeared before her colleagues on the Senate Foreign Relations Committee the week before Obama's inauguration, the mood was jovial, even celebratory. She offered smooth, smart answers to every question, displaying her impressive grasp of policy issues, from the international Law of the Sea treaty to tensions between Turkey and Armenia. Senator Richard Lugar of Indiana, the ranking Republican on the committee and a moderate who had befriended both Hillary and Obama when they arrived in the Senate, sounded the first discordant note.

He hinted at concerns that the former president, whose personal network encompassed most of the world's heads of state, might say or do something damaging to U.S. prestige—"freelancing," as other critics put it. After eight years of Bush, however, nobody could name a single instance when Clinton had embarrassed the president. On several occasions, he had helped, despite their many policy disagreements.

But that largely imaginary concern wasn't what troubled Lugar most.

"Foreign governments and entities may perceive the Clinton Foundation as a means to gain favor with the Secretary of State," said the Indiana senator, warning Hillary that "even well-intentioned foreign donations carry risk for United States foreign policy." She responded evenly that the memorandum of understanding negotiated as a condition of her appointment would ensure full transparency and ethics review. Senator David Vitter, a Louisiana Republican best known for his own ethical lapses, suggested that the Clinton Global Initiative might serve as a conduit for hidden donations; she replied that the CGI donors had always been public and would continue to be disclosed regularly.

But Lugar, veteran of a more bipartisan Senate, whose intentions were undoubtedly benign, was not fully persuaded. Neither was John Kerry, who had ascended to the committee chair. Before the committee voted, Lugar urged changes to the agreement governing the foundation, including the immediate disclosure of all actual or pledged donations over $50,000, with all foreign donations submitted for ethics review by the State Department.

"If there is a slightest doubt about the appearance that a donation might create," he said, "the foundation should not take that donation. If there are issues about how a donation should be disclosed, the issue should be resolved by disclosing the donation sooner and with as much specificity as possible."

Hillary said she took his point. "I respect you so much, Senator," she said directly to Lugar. "And I can, you know, certainly guarantee to you that I will remain very sensitive to this and I will work with you and [Kerry] as we go forward." The committee voted to affirm her nomination almost unanimously; Vitter voted no.

On January 20, the day of Obama's historic inauguration, the full Senate still had not yet confirmed her. At the inaugural luncheon, Senator John McCain ran into Doug Band and Huma Abedin, who asked him why no action had been taken on Hillary's nomination since the Foreign Relations Committee vote. "I'll take care of it," he assured them.

The next day, the Arizona Senator moved to cut off debate on her nomination to speed a full Senate vote. "We had an election and we also had a remarkable and historical time yesterday and this nation has come together as it has not for some time," said McCain. "The message the American people are sending us right now is they want us to work together and get to work right now." Later that afternoon the Senate confirmed her, with only two voting no—Vitter and South Carolina's ultraconservative Jim DeMint.

Not many months into Hillary's tenure, Madeleine Albright—the first female secretary of state, appointed by Bill Clinton, and a close friend—hosted a small, low-key, celebratory dinner at her home in Georgetown. All the others at Albright's table, too, once held the responsibilities Hillary had recently assumed: Henry Kissinger, who had served under Presidents Nixon and Ford; Warren Christopher, who had served under President Clinton before Albright; and Colin Powell and Condoleezza Rice, both of whom had served under President George W. Bush.

Toward the end of the evening, over dessert, Albright asked all the former secretaries to offer one salient bit of counsel to the nation's next top diplomat. Much of the advice was joking, like Warren Christopher urging her never to vacation in August, a month when crises always erupted. But Powell suggested that she use her own email, as he had done, except for classified communications, which he had sent and received via a State Department computer on his desk. Saying that his use of personal email had been transformative for the department, Powell thus confirmed a decision she had made months earlier—to keep her personal account and use it for most messages. She would also continue using the email server from her presidential campaign, which aides had installed in Chappaqua. Those were choices of convenience that would, years later, cause her untold trouble.

———

Scarcely a full week into the Obama administration, Bill Clinton and his small retinue—including Band, Cooper, hedge-fund manager Marc Lasry, and Los Angeles sports entrepreneur Casey Wasserman—arrived in snowy Davos, Switzerland. Exactly five years earlier, in this same setting, Doug Band had first envisioned an international conference that would not just inspire but require action on global problems.

That had been a more optimistic time. Amid a worldwide recession, with no economic revival in sight, the mood among the hobnobbing elites at the 2009 World Economic Forum was glum.

More accustomed to flattering themselves and each other as benevolent masters of the world, the corporate, media, and philanthropic titans had no choice but to confront a catastrophe that had badly diminished their financial assets and moral credibility. Nobody doubted where the blame belonged, namely on the criminality and stupidity of American bankers and the government that had failed to constrain them—an undeniable fact that the Russian and Chinese leaders present in Davos mentioned more than once.

Yet even on this uncertain terrain, the former U.S. president drew a full and attentive auditorium at a special plenary session interview with Klaus Schwab, the Davos impresario. There at least, the indignities and errors of the presidential campaign no longer clung to him. Clinton didn't attempt to evade or minimize his country's responsibility. Referring to an earlier speech by China's prime minister, Wen Jiabao, he said, "The Chinese premier was right: It all started in the United States." Even so, he quickly added, China had no choice but to continue underwriting U.S. budget and trade deficits for the sake of its own economy. "Global interdependence is more important than anything else in the world today," he said. "We cannot escape each other. Divorce is not an option." Speaking out forcefully in defense of the Obama administration's economic priorities, especially its $800 billion stimulus plan, he insisted that world leaders had to act resolutely, in the tradition of the West's wartime leaders.

He had little patience for the bathos he sensed in his audience. "This is not a time for denial or delay," he urged them. "Do something. Give people confidence by showing confidence." He scolded them at a panel discussion of a "philanthrocrisis," as donors grew stingier and charitable budgets tightened. The responsibilities of the fortunate had not shrunk with their declining portfolios.

"We're all still doing pretty well, or we wouldn't be here," he said with an edge of sarcasm. "So many private planes here, some are parked as far away as Milan!" The financial implosion had exposed a world that "is unequal, unstable, and unsustainable, and inequality is the cause of this crisis. . . . Too much of the wealth went to too few people."

According to Clinton, many at Davos were suddenly asking themselves, "What are we supposed to do about the fact that we have less money?" For him, the answer was that efforts to provide better health care and more robust development in poor countries should be redoubled, not reduced. His greatest current worry, he told Schwab, was that "because so much wealth has been lost, the impulse to help the poor will be lost too." Redressing the world's gross inequalities remained the moral imperative for humanity, regardless of cost. Like all nonprofits and charities, his foundation had suffered a steep decline in donations, he noted. "But we went into our endowment to sustain our AIDS work, because otherwise people would die."

Staying only one day in Davos, Clinton remained busy all afternoon, meeting privately with foreign dignitaries such as the prime minister of Qatar. That evening, the Clinton Global Initiative hosted cocktails and snacks at the Kirchner Museum, a glassy box across the road from the Congress Centre where the forum was held—a motley scene typical of Davos, with faces ranging from actor Jet Li , Prince Haakon of Norway, and San Francisco Mayor Gavin Newsom to Israeli president Shimon Peres and U.N. Secretary-General Ban Ki-moon.

But not long after greeting the assorted party guests, Clinton and his entourage bundled into a black Volkswagen van for a quick trip down the mountainside, stopping at the entrance to Hotel Waldhuus, the local Sheraton franchise.

Waiting to greet them inside the hotel lobby was Vladimir Putin himself, ready with a small glass of vodka to toast the arrival of "our good friend" Clinton. The Russian prime minister, whose early days in office had overlapped with the end of Clinton's presidency, was hosting his own celebration, attended by the likes of Oleg Deripaska, billionaire oligarch and principal shareholder of the world's largest aluminum company. For several minutes, Clinton and Putin stood with drinks while a pianist pounded out "In the Hall of the Mountain King" from Grieg's *Peer Gynt*, as waiters passed vast trays of smoked salmon and caviar canapés and poured more iced vodka.

When the musical entertainment ended, Putin swiftly escorted Clinton and Band to a table at the far end of a separate room, with an interpreter, guarded by a phalanx of Secret Service and Russian security agents. Visible on the other side of a glass wall, they talked intensely for nearly ninety minutes, before finally rising and walking out together for a few handshakes and photos with the other guests.

Later Clinton declined to comment publicly about the substance of their conversation, except to hint that the Russian leader seemed ready to resume discussions on missile defense issues. (It was a topic they had last discussed when Clinton, still president, had made a final trip to Moscow in 2000.) Putin wanted to learn more about Obama, but their conversation ranged widely, touching on Iraq and Afghanistan.

"Do you think we can prevail in Afghanistan?" Clinton asked. "No," replied Putin sardonically, "no more than we could. But that doesn't mean you are wrong to be there—at least until you get rid of al Qaeda."

In keeping with his practice when Bush was president, Clinton had diligently informed Jim Jones, the retired Marine general who served as Obama's national security adviser, about his trip to Davos and the likelihood that he would meet with foreign heads of state. Despite his incautious conduct in the campaign, Clinton was no loose diplomatic cannon. Obama would soon learn that he and his team were capable of handling the most sensitive and difficult mission without trouble.

———

Without seeking or gaining much notice in the North American press, Clinton and his friend Frank Giustra traveled to Colombia and points south in March on the Canadian mining magnate's MD-87 jet. It had been two years since Giustra, who had gained so much unwanted notoriety for his uranium venture in Kazakhstan, thanks to the *New York Times*, first committed $100 million of his personal fortune to what would become known as the Clinton Giustra Sustainable Growth Initiative—and later renamed the Clinton Giustra Enterprise Partnership. They had persuaded Carlos Slim, the Mexican billionaire whose fortune was thought to be the fourth largest in the world, to match Giustra's commitment with another $100 million.

As a business executive who had climbed from a very modest background, Giustra believed in Clinton's vision of alleviating and perhaps someday eliminating poverty through "social enterprise." To provide lasting jobs and significant income to the poor, the most effective programs would encourage investment based on market demand—preferably with environmental, social, educational, and health benefits that addressed the broadest needs of a community. Giustra had earned most of his money from mining industries that rarely left anything of value behind after depleting a region's valuable commodities.

The communities in greatest need often lacked the basic elements of enterprise: affordable financing, technical skills, a trained workforce, marketing networks, and even basic transport for farm and craft products. With a boost of capital and advice, for instance, small agricultural producers could obtain inputs like fertilizer at lower bulk prices, and sell value-added produce to supermarkets or hotels—in short, by connecting small cooperatives into the supply chains of much larger corporate businesses.

Giustra was eager to see whether this theoretical approach would work. Visiting Colombia, they were able to glimpse the beginnings of progress, stopping first in Cartagena, the beautiful coastal city whose old architecture and alluring beaches were drawing tourists—and hotel investment.

There Giustra and Clinton visited an "inverse trade fair," organized by CGEP, where executives from six local hotels displayed their purchasing needs—and 150 people, representing fifty-five local makers of everything from vegetables, fruits, and bread to candy, linens, dolls, and other souvenirs, showed up to present their wares and make connections. Many of the potential suppliers represented disadvantaged groups, including teen mothers and the disabled, who were brought to the fair by NGO sponsors. The hotels had agreed in advance to buy at least 20 percent of their needed goods and services from local sources. Next, CGEP planned to train young people from poor neighborhoods for hotel employment.

From Cartagena, they flew northward along the coast to Barranquilla, where they visited one of several successful schools funded by the singer Shakira, who had grown up there. Giustra and Clinton had agreed to provide $2 million to her charity, known as Pies Descalzos (Bare Feet) after the title of her first major-label album, to provide income and food support to the 1,500 poor students in her schools for two years.

Finally they traveled inland, deep into a mountainous jungle region, to visit an organic spice cooperative run by a group of local Afro-Caribbean women. For hundreds of years, women in this rural area had been growing abundant crops of cilantro, basil, ginger, turmeric, and paprika.

With sporadic NGO assistance, a few local women had created a small business they named Taná and established marketing ties with supermarkets in Colombia's larger cities. They had drawn together more than sixty of their neighbors. They had earned some extra money for their families, and had even obtained an organic certification, but were never able to amass enough capital—or qualify for a loan—to expand much. The low volumes and primitive packaging had left them unable to rise above a subsistence level. Now CGEP was proposing to help them redesign their packaging, improve their processes, recruit more growers, and expand their marketing, even to other countries— to grow and prosper.

Investing in this kind of project, Giustra understood, was only possible for "patient capital"—and the most patient capital would be the kind of money made available by him and Slim, which would be reinvested in employment rather than taken as profit. Years would pass before they knew whether CGEP's approach was working, whether they had the right staff and strategies. And if it did work, that uplifting knowledge surely would have to be its own reward. The chance of any American media outlet featuring this kind of story was nil. On that score, neither of them harbored any illusions.

————

Owing to his experience in dealing with the aftermath of the Asian tsunami and then Hurricane Katrina, Clinton had come to be seen as an international "master of disaster." His work as the U.N. special envoy overseeing tsunami aid had been successful, although little noticed in the media. Nobody who had been paying attention was surprised when, on May 18, the United Nations announced that Clinton would become the international body's "special envoy" for Haiti, at the secretary-general's request.

During 2008 the impoverished Caribbean island, one of the poorest and worst governed countries in the world, had been struck by four destructive hurricanes that killed eight hundred of its people, destroyed more than half of its agricultural production, and drowned its cities and villages in avalanches of mud. Damage to buildings and infrastructure was estimated at $1 billion. But again the worldwide recession had victimized the poorest of the poor, with pledges of international aid slow to materialize as the Haitians struggled to survive, let alone recover.

Having spent his 1975 honeymoon with Hillary there, Clinton had long been fascinated by Haiti—and, for an American politician, he was popular with the Haitians who remembered how his threat of armed force had dislodged a military junta and then restored the elected left-wing president, Father Jean-Bertrand Aristide, to office in 1994. Little had improved since then, and much had gotten worse. In addition to its chronic economic and governance problems, the country was an ecological ruin, as the harvesting of trees for fuel left mountainsides bare, letting fertile soil wash out to sea.

Clinton had responded to the crisis by devoting much of the September 2008 session of CGI to the creation of a "Haiti Action Network" that would focus commitments and investment on the island. In March he had visited some of the CGI commitment sites there, and in April he had helped to raise $324 million for relief and reconstruction at an international donors conference in New York. When the secretary-general asked him to take the job of special envoy—which meant, among other things, making sure those donors fulfilled their pledges—he agreed instantly. It was an undertaking he approached with characteristic if not justified optimism.

"It is an honor to accept the secretary-general's invitation," he told a reporter for the *Miami Herald*, which broke the story of his appointment. "Last year's natural disasters took a great toll, but Haiti's government and people have the determination and ability to 'build back better,' not just to repair the damage done but to lay the foundations for the long-term sustainable development that has eluded them for so long."

In Haiti, however, the response from political leaders and commentators was equivocal. While President René Préval welcomed Clinton's appointment, local politicians from left and right suggested that this was merely another ploy used by foreign authorities to control Haitian affairs and exploit the Haitian people. Clinton had broken promises to rebuild Haiti in the past, they said, so why should anyone believe him now?

Short of a massive emigration from the broken island, Haiti's troubles were intractable and likely to frustrate everyone who sought to solve them. Despite Clinton's insistent optimism, he had no illusions about what he would face as the special envoy. He also had no idea how much worse the island's misfortune would soon become.

CHAPTER FIFTEEN

Sometime early in the summer of 2009, Clinton first learned of a strange invitation. From various people, his staff had heard that Kim Jong-il, the "dear leader" of North Korea, desired his presence in Pyongyang, the capital of the outlaw communist regime. Specifically, the Hermit Kingdom's dictator had suggested that if Clinton came to visit, his government would release a pair of American journalists imprisoned there and allow them to return home with the former president.

Four months earlier the journalists—Laura Ling and Euna Lee, both employed by Al Gore's Current TV—had stepped across the border from China into North Korea, where soldiers immediately seized them. A colleague who escaped then reported their capture. Diplomatic efforts to secure their release had failed. Held in a Pyongyang guesthouse rather than in prison, the two women were nevertheless subjected to a trial for the crime of attempting to defame the Democratic People's Republic of Korea, and sentenced to twelve years hard labor.

As time went on there appeared to be a real risk that Ling and Lee would be sent to a prison camp. Laura's sister Lisa Ling, a well-known U.S. television correspondent and anchor, was terrified that unforeseen circumstances—such as the death of Kim, then sixty-eight and thought to have suffered a stroke—could lead to disaster for the prisoners.

The rumors about a potential Clinton rescue took on greater reality in early July. The North Koreans had permitted the women to make a few telephone calls directly to their families, and in the most recent conversation, obviously monitored by their captors, Laura and Euna had told their families the U.S. government would have to request "amnesty"—and send Bill Clinton—to secure their release.

Nobody else was acceptable, as their mother, Mary Ling, explained in a pleading letter to Hillary. The North Koreans, she wrote, "do not want former Vice President Al Gore as they consider him only as the girls' employer." They also rejected other potential rescuers, including

Bill Richardson and Jimmy Carter. The message was clear: If Clinton didn't come, the women would be sent to a labor camp.

On July 10, Hillary called publicly for a grant of amnesty, shifting from the tone of earlier statements urging the release of Ling and Lee on "humanitarian" grounds. The women and their families, she declared, "have expressed great remorse for this incident, and I think everyone is very sorry that it happened."

In the meantime, Clinton had heard directly from Gore as well, who reiterated the North Korean demand and asked him to go. Over the ensuing weeks, Clinton and Band talked several times with Thomas Donilon, Obama's national security adviser. The White House was nervous about any such "freelance" contact with the North Koreans, who had recently tested another nuclear weapon and come under heavier U.N. sanctions as a consequence. Tensions had risen to a new level on the Korean Peninsula, in Japan, and even in China, which had denounced its ally's reckless action.

Donilon, his deputy Denis McDonough, and others in the administration seemed especially wary of any mission that involved Clinton, due perhaps to lingering political animosity. But in the face of a continuing, heavily publicized campaign to free the women spearheaded by Lisa Ling, the administration had to act if there was any possibility of freeing them.

Backchannel sources in New York, at the North Korean embassy to the United Nations, and in Pyongyang had reiterated to State Department officials the regime's demand for Clinton to visit Kim. No one else would be acceptable.

In desperation, Lisa Ling had sent a letter in July directly to Obama via his half-sister, Maya Soetoro-Ng, whom she had met and befriended in Hawaii. "I took my journalist hat off last year to stump for you during the campaign," she reminded him. Indeed, she had been among the celebrity organizers of Asian Americans for Obama, speaking for him and raising money across the country. (Both Clintons and Band were well aware of Ling's activism for Obama, which was of "no concern" to them.)

"I know that President Clinton is a complicated request," she admitted, "but the signs that the [North Koreans] are ready to deal are more apparent than ever. Mr. President, our families beg you to send President Clinton as an envoy to secure the release of my sister Laura and Euna Lee. . . . With terror in her voice, my sister said, 'If something is not done very soon—this week—we will be sent to a labor camp.' Please help her avoid this, there's no one else who can."

From Clinton's perspective, the only question was whether the North Koreans were serious about letting him bring the women home. With assurances from the White House, he agreed to go without hesitation—as he had already told Lisa Ling he would, through a mutual friend.

Within the White House, a debate still raged over whether or not to send Clinton, but on July 30 Obama ordered a green light. The anticipated departure date was August 4—a tight schedule with even tighter operational security. A leak might ruin the chances of success. The list of those "read into" the mission at the White House and State Department was very limited. Clinton's staff cleared his schedule, without revealing the reason to anyone.

To arrange aviation, they approached Steve Bing. "I'm taking your plane," Clinton told him. "But I can't tell you right now where we're going." Bing's white Boeing 737 was in a hangar near Los Angeles, in Burbank. For transportation to Burbank, they asked Andrew Liveris, the chief executive of Dow Chemical, who readily agreed to lend them the company's plane without knowing why.

Indeed, the trip would be depicted as a "private humanitarian mission," with the State Department and the White House maintaining a largely fictional distance from it for diplomatic reasons. In reality, Denis McDonough, the deputy national security adviser, and Cheryl Mills, Hillary's chief of staff at State, oversaw the process in detail, including the preparation of talking points for Clinton, guidance for press contacts, and draft statements from Clinton and his office, to be released once the mission was complete.

Besides Clinton, the "head of delegation," those on the plane would include Band, Cooper, John Podesta, Dr. Roger Band, Korean interpreter Min-ji Kwon, and a Stanford University professor of Korean studies named David Straub—accompanied by a squad of seven Secret Service agents. They all received a fat "Mission Briefing Book," a binder filled with briefing papers on topics that would arise while Clinton was in Pyongyang.

Keeping the mission secret for as long as possible was vital, but that was only the first imperative.

In pre-departure briefings, State and NSC officials clarified what must not be done in Pyongyang: The members of the delegation should avoid smiling, clinking of glasses, or any displays of sociability. Such overly warm behavior toward the North Koreans would surely be captured on video and then replayed over and over again, to the embarrassment of Clinton and Obama. They should not appear at any public events with the North Koreans, nor tour around the capital with them. They should spend no money and accept no gifts. They should not get separated from each other and, whenever they spoke, had to be careful not to comment on any political or diplomatic issues, nor to criticize Kim or his country in any way.

But a few events could not be avoided, such as a meeting with Kim Jong-il and a state dinner.

On August 1, two days before he departed, Clinton spoke with Gore and members of Ling's and Lee's families on a conference call. They all thanked Clinton, as did Gore, who was genuinely grateful after working for months to secure his employees' release. "You know, Al, this means you have to go to Port-au-Prince with me," Clinton joked. "Yes, Mr. President!" replied Gore.

———

Late on Sunday, August 2, the Clinton group left Westchester Airport heading west. In Burbank, Straub and Kwon joined the Clinton group long after midnight. Steve Bing's white aircraft departed a few minutes before 3 a.m. on Monday, August 3, for a roughly four-hour flight to Elmendorf Air Force Base in Anchorage, Alaska, where they stopped to refuel.

At this point, the White House notified South Korean and Japanese authorities of the mission, letting them know that a plane carrying the former president would be passing through their airspace—and landing in Japan both inbound and outbound to ensure they had enough fuel to leave North Korea without refueling there.

One hour later, they were in the air again, landing at Misawa Air Force Base in Japan just before dawn, and then flew on to arrive in Pyongyang at around 10 a.m. (Band would later discover to his surprise that the U.S. government had declined to pay about $62,000 in aviation fuel costs, which the Clinton Foundation picked up.) Not long after their plane left Japan, news of the mission broke in the South Korean media: "President Bill Clinton Is on a Secret Mission to North Korea to Negotiate the Release of the Two American Journalists." The story was out.

During the entire flight, Band and Cooper had been in touch with the United States, including Lisa Ling, via email. She later wrote that when she lost contact with them, she knew they must have landed in North Korea. From that point forward, Band's only method of communication with Washington would be a satellite phone that he would only use with caution.

At Pyongyang's Sunan Airport, Kim Kye-gwan—the country's chief nuclear negotiator—greeted the Clinton party as they deplaned. Photographs of them shaking hands showed a stone-faced Clinton, suppressing his usual broad smile.

A convoy of limousines took the delegation to an immense guest palace, where the North Koreans presented a busy itinerary of tours to various sites and monuments. Band begged off, explaining that they needed rest after the long flight.

Instead, after lunch at the guesthouse, their hosts brought them to a meeting with the Speaker of the Supreme People's Assembly, who launched into a loud, long tirade about the crimes of the United States against his country. They listened politely to his monologue and said nothing. Podesta, Band, and Straub would later endure a similar ceremonial tongue-lashing at an "apology ceremony," where another official berated Lee and Ling as well as the United States.

As Clinton recalled, before he would meet with Kim, "we insisted on seeing [the two women], and they took us to a hotel in downtown Pyongyang to see them." There, guards brought the journalists to meet with Clinton—a moment that Laura Ling later described as surreal, the former president surrounded in what she saw as a celestial halo of light. Bursting into tears, they embraced him. Telling them he was sure they'd be leaving together the next day, he asked Roger Band to make sure they were well enough to fly home.

Finally, their escorts brought Clinton and his party back to meet with Kim himself, an encounter that he later described as "really good."

Greeting Clinton effusively, Kim cried, "I've always wanted to meet you!" He reminded Clinton that when his father, Kim Il-sung, died in 1994, "you were the first [world leader] to send a letter of condolence, even before my allies." That gesture made a powerful impression on Kim, who recalled that relations had improved under Clinton and then worsened under Bush "and the neoconservatives."

Clinton expressed gratitude for the amnesty and assured Kim that their apology was heartfelt. For the next hour or so, they talked about past and present relations between the two countries and the history of nuclear disarmament talks. Sticking closely to his talking points, Clinton urged Kim to permit Ambassador Stephen Bosworth, the U.S. special representative for North Korea policy, to again visit Pyongyang, and to revive the "six-party talks" on the nuclear issue. He also tried to persuade Kim to release several South Korean prisoners and resume his "investigation" of Japanese citizens abducted into North Korea.

The moment that Lee and Ling stepped off the plane in the United States, said Clinton, public opinion would surge in favor of dialogue with North Korea. If Kim followed his advice, the same would occur in South Korea and Japan.

"You see what happens when these girls go home and how the international community reacts," he said. "You'll get a similar reaction if you release the South Koreans." That was the way forward, he said. "You don't need nuclear weapons to be a great nation," he said. "You should return to the path we were on, toward a Korean peninsula that is free of nuclear weapons."

When the meeting concluded, the entire party posed with Kim for the official photo. Clinton sat next to the dear leader, holding the expressionless gaze they had all practiced at home and on the plane; behind them in a row stood Roger Band, Cooper, Podesta, Doug Band, Straub, and Kwon with the same blank stare. Released by the state news service, that photo appeared on the front pages of most major newspapers the next day, provoking much laughter.

Clinton was impressed by Kim's mental acumen, energy, and commanding presence, as were his aides. But Roger Band observed that while the dictator looked in decent health, one of his arms appeared to be immobile, presumably the result of a stroke.

That evening, Kim hosted them for what Clinton described as an embarrassingly lavish state dinner, with steak, lamb, chicken, various local delicacies, an entire fish for each guest, and a selection of French wines. Kim and his minions repeatedly importuned them to attend a celebration in their honor at a stadium, featuring ten thousand child gymnasts performing for a crowd of forty thousand North Koreans. Band and Podesta yawned and made excuses, as Clinton turned away, pretending not to know what was going on. Sometime during the dinner, Band left the table and went outside to call Cheryl Mills on the satellite phone, letting her know they were all fine, had spent time with the two journalists, and expected to bring them home the next day.

They went back to Clinton's suite in the guesthouse and played Oh Hell, his favorite card game, for hours.

———

Shortly after dawn on Wednesday morning, Podesta and Band went to observe a brief "court hearing" where a military general delivered the message that Kim had pardoned the women. They were returned to their rooms and instructed to write a thank-you note to Kim. Then they were free.

On the drive to the airport, the two Americans were in a limousine just ahead of the car carrying Ling and Lee, and a worried Band kept glancing back to make sure they were still behind him. Clinton, Cooper, and the rest of the party were already on the plane. When the wheels went up on takeoff, Band emailed Lisa Ling: "We have them. We're on our way to Japan. They're both doing well."

On the way home, Band received an irritating message from Denis McDonough in the White House. Before Bing's jet pulled into the hangar in Burbank, Clinton and his aides should deplane and depart the airport on their own plane. Then the hangar doors would open, and the jet would proceed to bring Ling and Lee in to meet their families and the press. He wanted no photos or video of Clinton on the ground with the women and their families. The reason for this guidance, as stated by McDonough, was to avoid any undue emphasis on the former president's role as a reward to the North Koreans—but Band could only suspect that the real motive was petty and political. That suspicion intensified when he learned that the White House had also planned to keep Gore away from the hangar arrival.

Lisa Ling would have none of that, as she recalled later. Intensely grateful for the strenuous efforts of Gore and both Clintons to ensure the return of her beloved sister, she insisted in frantic emails to the White House and State Department that the families wanted Gore and Clinton to be present.

Her final message to her government contacts, sent after midnight, warned them bluntly that "as someone who works in the media, I would be remiss if I didn't say one more time that keeping President Clinton [out of sight] may very well invite a whole shit-storm of speculation and chatter that you may not want." Under pressure from a professional journalist with easy access to television, they ultimately relented. Nobody would have to pretend that Clinton and Gore weren't there.

When the plane rolled into Bing's hangar at 5 a.m. Pacific Time, scores of reporters and television crews were waiting to transmit the emotional scene around the world. Descending from the plane, Lee and Ling embraced their families at the bottom of the stairs, followed discreetly a few minutes later by Clinton and his aides. Gore hugged Clinton fervently, and then did the same to Podesta.

Reading a statement she had written on the plane, sometimes holding back tears, Laura Ling said: "Thirty hours ago, Euna Lee and I were prisoners in North Korea. We feared that at any moment we could be prisoners in a hard labor camp. Then suddenly we were told that we were going to a meeting.

"We were taken to a location and when we walked through the doors, we saw standing before us President Bill Clinton." She looked over at him and put a hand to her chest, half-sobbing and half-laughing. "We were shocked, but we knew instantly in our hearts that the nightmare of our lives was finally coming to an end. And now we stand here home and free.

"Euna and I would just like to express our deepest gratitude to President Clinton and his wonderful, amazing, not to mention super-cool team," she continued, "including John Podesta, Doug Band, Justin Cooper, Dr. Roger Band, David Straub, Min-ji Kwon, and the United States Secret Service." She thanked Bing, Liveris, Gore, Hillary, Obama, and the government officials who had overseen the rescue mission. Gore stepped to the microphone to express gratitude to "my friend and partner, President Bill Clinton," who offered no comments. Then the women and their families went home. And the super-cool team flew back to New York.

On the White House lawn, President Obama delivered a short statement praising Clinton and Gore, noting that he had spoken with Clinton when the plane landed. Broad public reaction to the successful mission was strongly positive, marking a recovery from Clinton's decline during the Democratic primaries. As Obama said, "the reunion that we've all seen on television I think is a source of happiness not only for the families but for the entire country."

It was, as former secretary of state Lawrence Eagleburger observed, an effort that exemplified the best of America—a society that values the lives of its citizens enough to send a former head of state to the aid of two women in distress; a happy reunion, bringing wives home to their husbands and a mother back to her little girl; a moment of national pride and joy.

Not quite the entire country embraced the joy, however. On the Republican right, politicians and analysts inveighed against the "propaganda victory" supposedly gained by Kim. And the credit redounding to Clinton and his "super-cool team" predictably enraged certain commentators.

On AM radio, Rush Limbaugh and G. Gordon Liddy, the demented Watergate felon, cackled about the two women with Clinton "on that long flight home." A paranoid *New York Post* columnist insisted that "the whole shebang was nakedly scripted and staged as a device to help rehabilitate" Clinton's image. But even Maureen Dowd could not deny that he had emerged once more as "a dazzling statesman"—and put South Carolina behind him.

Within six months, Kim Jong-il implemented Clinton's advice by inviting Bosworth to return to Pyongyang and releasing the South Korean prisoners. He died two years later, to be succeeded by his son, Kim Jong-un.

———

In the weeks that followed Clinton's return from North Korea, he and his staff spent several hours briefing NSC, State Department, and intelligence officials about the trip's details. Whatever tensions may have lingered from the trip dissipated quickly, because on August 18, Obama invited Clinton to brief him personally at the White House. They spent twenty minutes talking in the Situation Room—attended by other officials, including Cheryl Mills—and then the president invited Clinton up to the Oval Office to continue their conversation for another half hour.

During the White House visit, they also made plans for a lunch in New York. On September 14, they met at Il Mulino, a legendary Italian restaurant in Greenwich Village—the owners, friends of Band, turned the place over to the Clinton-Obama party. The two presidents sat at a table alone, dining on salad, pasta, and fish, while their staff members ate at a separate table.

Eight days later, Obama was with Clinton again—as the main attraction at CGI's opening session. The president drolly described how Clinton, over lunch, had secured his "commitment" to show up that evening. "You know how it is," he said, gazing out into the audience from the Sheraton stage. "He looks you in the eye. He feels your pain. He makes you feel like you're the only person in the room. What can I say? I was vulnerable to his charms."

Then Obama took a moment to talk about his host. "After a lifetime of service, he would have been forgiven had he settled for a life of quiet, a life of ease, a life of improved golf scores. I understand they have not improved that much," he said, deadpan. "But he chose a different path. He asked, what can I do to keep making a difference. . . . Around the world, Bill Clinton has helped to improve and save the lives of millions. That is no exaggeration."

For several minutes the president talked about the meaning of service, recalling his mother's work against poverty in the slums of Indonesia and his own stint as a community organizer in Chicago. He said that he hoped "the spirit of this gathering" would infuse his own administration.

With Obama's enthusiastic embrace of CGI, the clouds over Clinton and his work clearly had dissipated, along with the sonorous warnings that he would somehow embarrass the United States. Typically, Clinton couched his boasting in data: "We're announcing over 250 commitments to action, sponsorship is up 20 percent, and—more than ever before—over 60 current and former heads of state will be discussing the major challenges of our time." So confident were Clinton and CGI director Bob Harrison—who was acknowledged personally by Obama from the podium—that they opened all the sessions to the media.

————

Even as Clinton's public image recovered dramatically during 2009, the internal disagreements that had long divided the foundation's leadership became an urgent problem. Ira Magaziner resisted ceding control of the two programs he had built—the Clinton HIV/AIDS Initiative, by far the largest, and the Clinton Climate Initiative, still comparatively small—and continued to argue with Lindsey, Band, and others over fundraising, governance, and procedures. As the discord intensified, major donors to CHAI such as the ELMA Foundation, the CIFF Foundation, and the Bill and Melinda Gates Foundation were drawn into the dispute.

Magaziner had persuaded the principals of those foundations, which had given millions to Clinton's projects over the years, not to oppose him in the ongoing bureaucratic battle. As a result, he and Lindsey began a lengthy negotiation over how to restructure CHAI and its relationship with the Clinton Foundation, with both sides contemplating a permanent rupture—not the outcome desired by the former president under any circumstances. After seven years, CHAI and its mission were too important to him and his post-presidency for him to walk away.

Before the year's end, Magaziner and Lindsey reached an agreement, with Clinton's assent, to reorganize CHAI as a separate 501(c)(3) charitable entity. It would remain under the foundation's umbrella, but with separate financial and operating systems. Clinton would chair its new board, with Magaziner as the vice chair, and the three major donors would also be represented. Imperfect as this arrangement seemed, especially to Band, who believed that Magaziner had attempted a coup, it prevented a public split that would have embarrassed Clinton and possibly diminished CHAI's capacity to serve as a lifeline and a source of hope for impoverished and ill people around the world.

On December 10, the foundation's press office issued an announcement of the changes, describing the new structure and noting how CHAI's mission had changed, from dealing solely with HIV/AIDS treatment to encompass malaria, tuberculosis, and the improvement of health systems in developing countries. In recognition of CHAI's expanded purpose, its new incarnation would be renamed the Clinton Health Access Initiative.

This agreement didn't resolve the fate of the Clinton Climate Initiative, a contentious issue that flared again within weeks of the CHAI announcement. Despite cordial conversations with Clinton that suggested a "new spirit of cooperation" to Magaziner, suspicions remained strong on both sides—thwarting the prospects for the strong climate program that Clinton yearned to build.

———

Shortly before sunset on January 12, 2010, a cataclysmic earthquake with 7.0 magnitude struck just west of the Haitian capital of Port-au-Prince, shaking the entire island and locations as distant as Puerto Rico and Venezuela. Thousands of buildings fell instantly, filling the streets with tons of rubble and killing as many as 200,000 people in the initial moments of the disaster while injuring even more.

Among the buildings destroyed or badly damaged in the capital's central district were the Port-au-Prince Cathedral, the Presidential Palace, and the National Assembly building; much of the city's main hospital collapsed, as did the hotel that served as headquarters of the United Nations Stabilization Mission in Haiti (MINUSTAH). The government estimated that the quake had destroyed as many as 250,000 houses, leaving a million Haitians homeless.

It was a crushing blow to the hopes of the Haitian people, then just beginning to see signs of real recovery from the ruinous hurricanes of 2008.

The next evening, Bill Clinton arrived at the United Nations building in Manhattan with Band, Cooper, Paul Farmer, and a Secret Service contingent, to address an emergency plenary session of the U.N. General Assembly at the request of Secretary-General Ban Ki-moon.

Standing next to Ban before the rows of seated ambassadors, Clinton exhorted the member countries to honor the memory of the lost U.N. workers and officials by saving the survivors. Nobody knew yet how many had died in the collapsed MINUSTAH headquarters and around Port-au-Prince, but among those missing was the mission's chief, Tunisian diplomat Hédi Annabi (whose body was found two days later).

Talking about how rescue efforts would proceed, with the assistance of the U.S. military and the immediate release of $10 million by U.N. agencies, Clinton said, "We have a thousand details to work out, but we'll do that. I ask for your support. . . . We owe it to our colleagues who perished in that earthquake yesterday. No one can ever doubt again what the relevance of the United Nations is in the 21st century, or what the devotion of its employees is to the common cause of humanity. We owe it to them to respond in the right way."

Soon after delivering his remarks, Clinton left the General Assembly Hall—while the special plenary was still in session—for a series of media appearances on NPR, CNN, and on *ABC World News Tonight* with George Stephanopoulos to appeal for relief funds. Between interviews, he was editing an op-ed "call to action" for the next morning's *Washington Post*, outlining Haiti's immediate and long-term needs.

Those who are still alive under the rubble must be found. The bodies of those who have died must be taken away. Power must be restored and roadways cleared. But what Haiti needs most is money for water, food, shelter and basic medical supplies to bring immediate relief to those who are homeless, hungry and hurt," he wrote. "The entire United Nations system is working hard to meet these needs and to regroup on the ground in Haiti after the collapse of our headquarters building and the loss of many of our colleagues. . . .

But after the emergency passes, the work of recovery and reconstruction will remain. . . . Already, the Haitian government and citizens, the Haitian Diaspora, neighboring countries and allies, NGOs and international groups were committed to a plan for long-term development. These efforts will need to be amended because of Tuesday's disaster, but they cannot be abandoned.

Within the first twelve hours or so of Clinton's fundraising appeal, his foundation's dedicated web page raised $2.6 million for Haitian relief—a total that didn't include money raised via the new technique of mobile texting at $10 per call, which immediately began to catch on, according to a foundation spokesperson, "like wildfire."

For almost two years, Clinton had been trying to raise hundreds of millions of dollars for Haiti from international donors, with intermittent success. Now in the face of unspeakable tragedy, he felt that the checkbooks of the wealthy governments as well as ordinary citizens might open.

That same evening, Ban quietly asked Clinton to assume still greater responsibility for Haiti. Raising money to clear the wreckage and rebuild was sure to be hindered by lack of faith in the notoriously corrupt and incompetent Haitian government. But if Clinton agreed to cochair an interim reconstruction commission, donors would feel more confident.

To his advisers, including Band, this was like asking Clinton to enter a minefield wearing a blindfold. The obstacles to getting anything done in Haiti, as they had already discovered, were numerous and daunting. Many of the Haitians, disillusioned by decades of promises left unful-filled by foreign agencies and nonprofits, were understandably suspi-cious, even hostile to outside forces. Nor was the U.N. mission popular there. Any realist could see that the likelihood of failure—and blame—was very high. The chance for success was almost nil.

For those reasons and others, Band urged Clinton not to take on Haiti's reconstruction. But he understood that he had lost the argument before he uttered a word. Clinton accepted the assignment and, four days later, agreed when President Obama asked him and George W. Bush to chair another ad hoc relief effort—the Clinton Bush Haiti Fund.

The former presidents appeared on five television talk shows the fol-lowing Sunday, and taped a public service announcement in the White House Map Room. Clinton flew home to Westchester, only to rise early the next morning to head out to Kennedy Airport, where a comfortably furnished Boeing 737 owned by Google waited to take him, a group of foundation staffers and friends, and several pallets of medical supplies to Port-au-Prince. Joining the trip were Chelsea Clinton and her fiancé, Marc Mezvinsky, as well as Google founder Sergey Brin, clad in T-shirt and jeans and toting a camera with a huge telephoto lens. On the flight down, Brin lounged on the plane's beige leather seating while he asked Clinton about China, where his company was encountering difficulties with the government.

By then, almost a week after the earthquake, most of the Port-au-Prince airport was under the command of the United States Army, with State Department and National Security Council officials present to oversee the relief effort. When the plane landed, soldiers unloaded the pallets of medical supplies into a cinder-block warehouse, while Clinton and his entourage climbed into jeeps that took them through the capital's rubble-strewn streets to the Central Hospital. The vista of destruction was extraordinary, even more shocking than what he had encountered in post-tsunami Indonesia and Thailand.

Driving past the ruins of the Presidential Palace in the center of town, Clinton shook his head and talked about what the city had looked like before the quake. It was hard to imagine the army that would be needed to clear the thousands upon thousands of chunks and blocks of concrete that filled every sightline. The hospital, too, was a ruin, with patients lined up in makeshift cots outdoors, for fear that more buildings would collapse, many surrounded by weeping family members. Doctors had flown down to volunteer, including Clinton's friend Mark Hyman, but there seemed to be few nurses or attendants to provide a service as simple as bringing water.

Clinton escaped at day's end and returned to New York. The contrast between the jet's luxurious interior and the squalid chaos of the broken city felt almost grotesque. He would return many more times to that frustrating, heartbreaking, and yet seductive place.

————

The Haitian earthquake slammed Clinton's usually hectic schedule of travel, speeches, and events into overdrive. When he flew down to Port-au-Prince with his cargo of medical supplies, he had been working for five days straight without rest, alternating between planning meetings in the daytime, nights of telephone calls with world leaders, and media bookings that often began around dawn. He could be excused for thinking that overwork was what caused him to wake up one day in mid-February, feeling exhausted and looking pale, with a disturbing ache in his chest. He was supposed to fly to Washington that morning.

He called Allan Schwartz, his cardiologist at New York Presbyterian Hospital, who listened to Clinton's complaint. "Oh, you've dropped a vein," he said.

"What do you mean?"

The doctor told him that roughly 25 percent of patients who undergo a quadruple bypass "drop a vein" within five years because the veins used in those procedures are thinner and weaker than the original arteries. "We can fix it," Schwartz assured him. "But you're not going anywhere." When he checked into the northern Manhattan hospital later that day, Hillary and Chelsea came up to join him. After a series of tests, surgeons placed two stents into a coronary artery.

"I was awake for the whole thing. I watched them do it on the screen," he later recalled. "It was fascinating. And then [the doctors] went out," to talk with reporters who had gathered at the hospital. "They were trying to reassure the public that I wasn't on the verge of death, and so they said, 'You know, this is actually fairly normal.'"

Clinton was up and walking around the ward within two hours of the operation, and went home the next day. According to Schwartz, who had become accustomed to answering media questions about his famous patient, Clinton's "very active lifestyle" had not caused the narrowing of the artery. There was no reason, his doctor said, for Clinton to slow down. And the prognosis for a full recovery was "excellent."

For Clinton, however, it was nevertheless troubling to learn that one of the bypass grafts to his heart had already become blocked, five years after the original operation. Soon after leaving the hospital he had heard from Dean Ornish, the cardiologist and author who advocated drastically reducing dietary fat to cure heart disease. Ornish had read Schwartz's comments in the press and sent his old friend a "blistering" email: "Yeah, it's normal, because fools like you don't eat like they should."

When Clinton got home, he reread Ornish's *Reversing Heart Disease* and two other studies that made the same point. He wanted to live to be a grandfather and not go under the knife again. With some prodding from Chelsea, he decided to drop at least twenty pounds before he walked her down the aisle at her July wedding. To reach that goal—and to protect his arteries from further blockage—he immediately stopped eating meat, poultry, fish, milk, cheese, and eggs.

Overnight, he became that rarest of Arkansans: a vegan.

Giving up meat didn't make Clinton feel deprived. His reputation for wolfing down McDonald's hamburgers in Little Rock was always a myth, although he did love French fries. But while Hillary had tried for years to encourage him toward healthier eating, now he went further than she had ever imagined. (And she continued on as a carnivore, with no signs of heart disease.)

On his new diet, Clinton reduced the total intake of fat in his diet

and consumed very little saturated fat. At first that meant too little protein, leaving him terribly fatigued. For a more nourishing breakfast he
added a smoothie prepared from almond milk, protein powder, and
fruit; for lunch, a salad of some kind; and for dinner he would have a
dish of legumes or grains, often quinoa, which he liked. Between meals
he ate nuts, "because those are good fats," or hummus, a favorite snack.
He easily met his goal and kept the weight off. He underwent regular
blood tests to monitor his levels of iron and other minerals; whenever
they dropped too low, and to maintain muscle tone, he ate eggs or wild
salmon occasionally. Otherwise, he kept to his regimen zealously.

———

When Clinton went to Africa for his annual trip in late June, he carried a new title that he had acquired a month earlier, when he was
named honorary chairman of the United States bid committee for soccer's World Cup. Along with an assortment of soccer enthusiasts that
included Henry Kissinger, film director Spike Lee, boxing champion
Oscar de la Hoya, and a number of business and media figures, Band
was already a member of the committee, and he had persuaded Clinton
to join the effort to bring the World Cup to the United States.

He arrived in South Africa as the 2010 World Cup competition was
under way there. It was the first time that FIFA, the international soccer federation, had ever held the championship in Africa, a source of
enormous pride and excitement for the entire continent.

Although he was a devoted—some said "crazy"—follower of football, basketball, and baseball, Clinton quickly picked up an enthusiasm
for soccer, the sport that best suited his global outlook. He even developed a multicultural pitch for the U.S. bid: "In our country, every team
from around the world will be able to attract a hometown crowd in at
least one of our cities."

While he would still make his regular visit to Mandela in Johannesburg and his stops at foundation projects in several countries, Clinton
and his party had box seats for what seemed likely to be the final World
Cup match for the U.S. team against Algeria, at a stadium in Pretoria.

That match turned into one of the most exciting and momentous
in U.S. soccer history, when at the very end, captain Landon Donovan scored a stunning overtime goal to win. As the stadium erupted,

Clinton and his party were escorted from their box to the team's locker room. The American players roared with pride as the former president walked in and was enveloped in a maelstrom of embraces, handshakes, chest bumps, and high fives.

With an arm around Donovan's shoulder, he congratulated them. "I'm so proud of you. . . . You are amazing!" He posed for photographs with the shirtless, whooping players. They invited Clinton to join them in their inner locker room, where he could be glimpsed toasting them with a can of beer, amid much additional hollering.

The surprise victory meant an abrupt change in schedule, since the Americans would play again a few days later, in the northwestern city of Rustenburg. They lost when Ghana scored in overtime to break a 1–1 tie. But Clinton enjoyed the game and welcomed an unexpected friend—mad soccer fan Mick Jagger—to his box.

His thrilling experience at those matches intensified Clinton's desire to bring the World Cup to his own country. The bid committee had turned in a heavy proposal, the size of two telephone books, to FIFA, the sport's governing body, in Switzerland a few weeks earlier. Decisions on both the 2018 and 2022 World Cup locations would come before the year ended. In a corrupt process, the U.S. lost both.

———

Between World Cup matches, Clinton spent time with Mandela and visited health clinics in the city and countryside that had partnered with CHAI. The new South African government of President Jacob Zuma had fully endorsed the partnership with Clinton and CHAI that his predecessor Mbeki had undertaken only hesitantly. More than 700,000 AIDS victims were on treatment there, but millions more needed it and as many as 365,000 were estimated to have died due to the Mbeki government's delay in responding seriously to the pandemic.

After several years, the foundation's work in Africa was starting to be felt beyond the clinics and health systems that CHAI strengthened. In Dar-es-Salaam, he met with Tanzanian president Jakaya Kikwete, who complained that under Western policy, it was possible to open forests to loggers for profit and then receive carbon-credit subsidies as a reward for replanting the raped land. Kikwete hadn't done that, but he had watched his neighbors in Kenya exploit the system.

Such stupidity astonished Clinton. The Tanzanian leader expressed frustration as well over the imperial style of Western environmental efforts, with foreign personnel parachuted in to certify projects for carbon credits—precisely the opposite of the Clinton Foundation style of guiding and assisting governments, letting them take responsibility and credit.

Later that day Clinton traveled hundreds of miles south to Kikere, a rural village where foundation staffers were assisting a local clinic—in essence a very basic hospital, serving thousands of destitute farm families—to improve its services with solar electricity. Using a photovoltaic system, the clinic produced enough clean energy to power lights (replacing dirty kerosene lamps), refrigerators for medicine, lab equipment, a laptop computer, all displayed proudly by the young technician trained to maintain the system. For a capital cost of $38,000 it provided enough wattage for five clinic staff houses, where, as a doctor said, "our children can now do schoolwork at night."

Although much of the clinic's operation still appeared rudimentary by U.S. standards, electrification had enabled doctors there to treat illness much more effectively and save many lives. Across Tanzania, more than fifty clinics had installed similar solar arrays, at very low cost. To Clinton, this pointed toward a simple climate bargain: Western capital and technology, free or deeply discounted, in exchange for preserving African forestlands.

Coping with climate change was a major aspect of the Clinton Development Initiative as well, whose outposts he visited in both Rwanda and Malawi. (Its name had changed after 2009, when recession losses forced Tom Hunter to reduce his financial commitment.) To reach one of the projects run by CDI in Malawi, one of the poorest countries in the world, his party flew into the capital's airport, Lilongwe International, which boasted a single asphalt runway next to a rusting Quonset hut.

Hours later, after a bumpy and extremely hot ride through flat, arid countryside, they reached the CDI "anchor farm" in Mchinji district. There Clinton met with farmers growing soy and maize whose incomes had risen by 150 percent since the program began to provide them with certified seed, cooperative buying of fertilizer and marketing of their crops, and training in advanced agronomic techniques—with a special emphasis on "climate smart" methods of conserving water and improving soil.

Wielding a shovel and a watering can, he planted a sapling, one of more than 1.9 million trees that the farmers in the program had planted for fruit and wood. As those trees grew, they had captured nearly a quarter of a million tons of carbon dioxide. With the right incentives of better nutrition and cash crops, the project's aim was to begin to reverse the deforestation still occurring across Africa.

The farmers and their families were excited to see Clinton, and to show him the low, dark grain warehouse where they stored the harvested maize, and the small health clinic that had been erected by CDI. A woman told him that with more money, more local children were in school. The government of Malawi wanted to expand the program to 56,000 farmers in three districts.

When the farmers and their families started dancing in celebration of the Americans' visit, McAuliffe suddenly joined in, jumping and spinning around, his arms waving in the air, as Clinton laughed.

———

For Clinton, the International Conference on AIDS had become a semi-annual marker, ever since he had attended the 2002 conference in Barcelona with Mandela as a private citizen for the first time. Since then he had spoken at every one, and on July 19 in Vienna, he delivered the keynote address to an audience of physicians, academics, health workers, and activists estimated at 25,000. While much had been achieved—five million were then receiving treatment—much still remained to be done before the pandemic could be ended.

"To paraphrase what Winston Churchill said when the British finally started winning a battle or two in World War II," he said, "this is not the end. It's not even the beginning of the end. It is only the end of the beginning. In other words, we ramped up. You've done a great job. But we have to transition now from what has essentially been a make-it-up-as-you-go-along emergency response to one that we can sustain."

Rather than debate whether to spend more on global health or on specific programs such as AIDS treatment or maternal health, Clinton said that as PEPFAR and the Global Fund had increased spending on health care around the world, fewer women and children were dying every year.

"The fight against AIDS has raised a lot of boats," he explained, "to fight tuberculosis and malaria, to improve health systems, to challenge and motivate governments and NGOs alike, to deliver more and better health care. Fighting AIDS in the right way clearly improves maternal and child health."

Clinton went out of his way to defend Obama, under harsh criticism at the conference and at home for failing to fulfill a promise to increase PEPFAR's funding. After saying he would increase the AIDS treatment program created under Bush to $50 billion a year, the federal appropriation had fallen far short and wouldn't reach that figure while he was president.

"I do not think it is either fair or accurate to say the president has gone back on his promises, as if this was a callous walking away," he said. "When he signed that petition saying he would support greater AIDS funding, it was before the American economy led the world into the worst financial crisis since the Depression. Since then, he has tried to keep his commitments." He urged them to lobby Congress instead, because he was certain Obama "would never veto an increase in AIDS funding."

They gave Clinton a standing ovation, less for what he said than for what they knew he had done.

———

To friends, Clinton jokingly complained about the cost of his daughter's wedding, sounding rather like a sitcom dad all year. But the projected expense of the lavish event, estimated at well over $2 million, wasn't a joke. As the location Chelsea had chosen Astor Courts, a 1904 Beaux-Arts mansion with a fifty-acre estate on the Hudson River in Rhinebeck. That rental alone was over $200,000 for the weekend. The catering for over four hundred guests was probably more than three times as much.

The July 31 wedding had become a source of friction not only due to the enormous bills but the problem of the guest list, which couldn't possibly encompass the vast number of people in America and around the world who regarded themselves as close friends of the Clintons.

People who had done major favors for Bill Clinton—loaning him a plane, or donating millions to the library or the foundation—were offended to learn that they had not been invited.

And then there was Donald Trump, who had hosted a somewhat reluctant Bill and Hillary at his third wedding in 2005. The real estate mogul was the sort of person who, though not an actual friend, still aspired to attend Chelsea's wedding, which he clearly considered a prestigious event. An avid reader of gossip columns, he had probably seen mentions of a guest list that was expected to include the likes of Oprah Winfrey, Barbra Streisand, Steven Spielberg, and Ted Turner (none of whom ultimately turned up). And having given Bill Clinton free access to his northern Westchester golf club, Trump National, where he proudly hung photos of the former president—and had even cleared the links once for the Clintons to play on Bill's birthday—Trump may well have felt that there was simply no way he was not on the guest list.

So when the wedding invitation didn't arrive, he called Doug Band with his characteristic self-assurance.

"I'm supposed to be at the wedding, Doug," said Trump briskly, "but I didn't receive the invitation, and I need to know where to go." Band knew Trump wasn't on the list, of course, and politely urged him to get in touch with Chelsea for directions. After a fruitless call to another Clinton staffer, Trump apparently gave up.

Conducted jointly by a rabbi and a Methodist minister, the celebration of Chelsea's marriage was described as "a storybook wedding" by *People* magazine, with media coverage resembling a royal event. The bride wore a beaded Vera Wang gown, while her mother wore a dress designed by her friend Oscar de la Renta.

Following the ceremony, the secretary of state and former president released a statement: "Today, we watched with great pride and overwhelming emotion as Chelsea and Marc wed in a beautiful ceremony at Astor Courts, surrounded by family and their close friends. We could not have asked for a more perfect day to celebrate the beginning of their life together, and we are so happy to welcome Marc into our family."

———

On the morning of the very last day of the midterm election campaign, Clinton awoke well before dawn to fly upstate from Westchester to

Saratoga Springs. It was a cold morning, but 1,500 upstate Democrats had risen early to see him.

He confided jokingly that he had originally expected only "to do a few events this year to honor the people who had supported us," noting that his wife, as secretary of state, was prohibited by law and custom from campaigning. "This is my 127th event," he recalled as they laughed appreciatively. "And I've kept going because I am so concerned that in the fact-free environment of this election, people are going to choose exactly what they don't want."

That concern spurred him on a grueling series of jet hops, from two stops in the northern reaches of his adopted state on to McKeesport, Pennsylvania, then Beckley, West Virginia, Louisville, Kentucky, and finally Orlando, Florida, for a midnight rally.

The former president drew enthusiastic crowds everywhere, and they listened raptly to his latest political pitch, which included point-by-point explanations of the student loan reform, the health care reform, and the banking bill, as well as his argument that he and his fellow Democrats—not the Republicans—deserved the affections of the Tea Party.

Despite the big crowds, Clinton had a bad feeling about the election, and not just from reading polls. He had gone out on the road so often that fall, he said, because the American people "are starving for explanations. They want someone to tell them what the hell is going on. And in the present media environment it is imperative to repeat the same message again and again for anyone to hear it."

What made him angry was that his party's elected leaders had endured a crescendo of attacks from Republican politicians and right-wing media without even trying to answer them. As his small plane flew south, he expressed bewilderment that Democratic leaders had done so little to promote their legislative achievements, which he touted at every stop.

He was deeply frustrated with the White House, too. For the past year, Clinton had tried to persuade the president and his economic advisers to back an innovative green jobs program devised by his foundation staff. That proposal, which he had first brought to Vice President Joe Biden in an October 2009 memorandum, suggested that the Obama administration could stimulate $100 billion in private lending for energy efficiency improvements in all kinds of buildings—with as little as $9 billion in U.S. Treasury commitments to a Federal Energy Efficiency Loan Guarantee Program.

Every billion dollars invested in building conservation would create as many as nine thousand new jobs in construction, design, and manufacturing, swiftly adding up to a million or more Americans rescued from unemployment. And a million new jobs would have lifted Obama's popularity and Democrats' midterm prospects.

But Obama had ignored this idea until, in July, he had finally invited Clinton to the White House for a conference with a group of business executives from companies such as GE and Johnson Controls that might benefit from the program. That meeting had amounted to little more than a photo op. It was portrayed in the media as Obama's attempt to use Clinton to stroke corporate leaders alienated from his administration—and accomplished nothing.

Still, he defended the administration vigorously as he flew from rally to rally down the East Coast on that last day. In populist tones, he framed the election as a clear choice between destructive Republican policies that favor "people like me, who make more than a million dollars a year" and the great majority of Americans who don't.

"Last weekend, I read a touching article about two ladies who started the Tea Party movement," he said, referring to a profile in the *Wall Street Journal*. "They were outraged by the bailout. And who wasn't? President Bush told me that signing the bailout made him sick."

Yet the Dodd-Frank banking reform enacted by Democrats in 2009 against Republican opposition would "outlaw" future bailouts and make financial executives and shareholders pay if they recklessly squander assets. "So why would the Tea Party support the Republicans, who have promised to repeal that bill because their friends on Wall Street don't like it?"

And, he noted, it was President Obama and the Democrats in Congress who have actually cut taxes for most Americans in the stimulus bill—not the Republicans. If the Tea Party movement wants more jobs, balanced budgets, lower taxes, and smaller government, he insisted, they should be supporting Democrats.

"Where is the love?" he cried. "I ought to be the Tea Party's poster child."

The crowds roared appreciatively every time. But when the plane landed in Westchester around 4 a.m., Clinton's tired face broke into a wry smile and he muttered that the exhausting day of electioneering had been "a fool's errand." He had a point. Republicans won big majorities in both the House and Senate the next day—defeating every candidate for whom he campaigned in that final trip except Joe Manchin.

————

The strangest incident in Clinton's vexed relationship with Obama occurred toward the middle of December, when the president invited him to the White House to discuss a controversial tax agreement drawn up by White House negotiators with the Republican congressional leaders who would assume control of Congress in three weeks. The deal preserved the Bush tax cuts benefiting the wealthy, while providing cuts in payroll taxes for working Americans, tax credits for manufacturing jobs, and an extension of benefits for the unemployed.

Having talked in the Oval Office for nearly ninety minutes, Obama and Clinton walked over to the press briefing room, which was dark and deserted. They found someone to open it up, and Obama instructed press secretary Robert Gibbs to summon reporters from a holiday party in the East Wing.

"It's a slow news day, so I thought I'd bring the other guy in," quipped Obama when they returned. Standing beside him was Clinton, with whom he had just been discussing the tax deal. Clinton had "presided over as good an economy as we've seen in our lifetimes, so I thought it would be useful for him to share some of his thoughts."

He had been studying the country's economic woes for an hour a day, Clinton said, "trying to figure out what to do." And he had studied the deal that the president struck with the Republicans.

"The agreement taken as a whole is, I believe, the best bipartisan agreement we can reach to help the most Americans," he said, then paused to digress. "I want to make full disclosure. You know, I make quite a bit of money now, so the position that the Republicans have urged"—to preserve the expiring Bush tax cuts—"would personally benefit me. And on its own, I wouldn't support that. . . . However, the agreement taken as a whole is," he repeated, "the best bipartisan agreement we can reach to help the most Americans."

As soon as Clinton started taking questions, on Haiti, the START nuclear treaty, and the mortgage crisis, the president smoothly excused himself to join the first lady at a holiday party—but the conversation between the former president and the press continued for nearly another half hour.

Understandably, some accounts described Clinton's sudden reappearance at the White House lectern after nine years as "surreal" and "bizarre," but it was a moment for Clinton to savor. After so many spats and slights, his relationship with Obama had turned in a very different direction. They might never become close friends, but they understood each other. With that understanding had come respect.

CHAPTER SIXTEEN

According to Bill Clinton's calendar, the year 2011 was dotted with a series of significant dates: On January 21, he would complete a full ten years since his departure from the White House, to begin another life as private citizen and philanthropic leader—the period that his foundation would brand "A Decade of Difference." On August 19, he would turn sixty-five, an age he once doubted that he would ever reach. And on October 3, he would commemorate the twentieth anniversary of his 1991 announcement of his presidential candidacy.

But before Clinton could mark any of those occasions, he would have to acknowledge on January 12 that a year had passed since the calamitous earthquake in Haiti. That destitute and deforested island nation was a place where he exercised considerable authority: as the U.N. special envoy; as the cochair, with Haitian prime minister Jean-Max Bellerive, of the Interim Haiti Recovery Commission (IHRC); as the cofounder, with George W. Bush, of the Clinton Bush Haiti Fund; and, not least, as the spouse of the secretary of state, who oversaw the American assistance mission there, through agencies run by State Department staff, such as the U.S. Agency for International Development.

The initial rush to help Haiti had resulted in pledges of nearly $10 billion from donor nations, plus hundreds of millions of dollars raised by private charities; as many as ten thousand nonprofit organizations had mounted projects to help rebuild the island's wrecked physical and social services—to "build back better," as Clinton often said. In the aftermath of the cataclysm, a time of mourning and deprivation, he had tried to encourage optimism about the future.

But a year later, that optimism was becoming more difficult to sustain. Anyone who visited the cities and towns on Haiti's western coast, where the earthquake struck hardest, would still see the jagged dunes of smashed concrete, stretching into the distance, while over a million people in and around Port-au-Prince lived in hundreds of temporary camps or, if they were less fortunate, in the streets.

Only 5 percent of the debris left by the quake had been cleared, according to the best estimates, mostly on the major avenues in the capital. The international airport had been repaired, but major infrastructure projects to construct new roads, ports, and housing had not yet been started.

To make matters much worse, a cholera epidemic had broken out the previous October, eventually traced to poor sanitation practices by a division of U.N. peacekeepers from Nepal. The bacterial disease had killed at least 3,000 Haitians so far, and threatened to infect as many as 250,000. Dealing with the outbreak had distracted the government and aid organizations, and again, the level of international assistance proved woefully insufficient. The U.N. had appealed for about $150 million to pay for medicine and sanitation, and had raised only $44 million so far.

By early January, only 10 percent of the money pledged by foreign donors had been collected, and not even all of the first billion had been spent on projects yet. Politically, the Haitian government had been frozen since an inconclusive national election two months earlier, which had excluded the most popular political party, Father Aristide's Lavalas, along with many eligible voters. The political stasis discouraged donor nations from fulfilling the multibillion-dollar donations they had pledged in 2010. They didn't know what would happen to the money.

The chaotic electoral process appeared likely to conclude with a former pop singer—Michel "Sweet Micky" Martelly—as the country's new president, although for the moment President René Préval remained in power despite rioting by Martelly's supporters in the slums. But Préval's role was more symbolic than real. He and his ministers could block progress, but they could accomplish nothing on their own.

The journalist Amy Wilentz, author of two books on Haiti, described him as simply "an old-fashioned Haitian politician" who in the aftermath of the quake had found "the horror on the ground was too much for him to handle, both emotionally and practically." Préval had failed to appear or make any public statement for three days after the earthquake, later explaining that he had been "in shock."

Nobody had really expected the Haitian government to function in the wake of disaster, since it had scarcely functioned before. That was why the country's politicians and ruling elite had reluctantly ceded authority to the IHRC, which to them represented an unwanted infringement of sovereignty. With Clinton as cochair, that body was supposed to ensure a measure of effectiveness and transparency in a place known for neither.

Before he accepted that position—or any responsibility for Haiti—Clinton had known very well that no degree of progress would ever be sufficient and that there would be far more blame than credit, no matter what he achieved. Still, he, too, was frustrated by the slow crawl of relief and reconstruction.

Blame was already coming his way, although any knowledgeable observer understood that reconstruction on such an unprecedented scale, in such a miserably underdeveloped country, would inevitably require years and perhaps a decade. Removing the remains of the World Trade Center from Ground Zero in Manhattan, a much smaller job in an efficient modern environment, had required two full years. A relatively developed country like Indonesia, where Clinton had worked closely with government officials after the tsunami, had likewise required years to clean up its devastated coastline and begin to rebuild.

On the eve of the earthquake's anniversary, the global charity Oxfam—one of the most active nongovernmental organizations in Haiti—released a report that criticized the overall reconstruction effort and the IHRC specifically in what news reports called "blistering" language. Oxfam analysts blamed the slow pace "on a crippling combination of Haitian government indecision and rich donor countries' too frequent pursuit of their own aid priorities." While praising the emergency relief campaign that had saved "countless lives," Oxfam declared that the IHRC "has failed to live up to its mandate."

Clinton realized there was little point in arguing with such criticism, but when reporters asked, he would answer. "It's easy to see what hasn't been done," he said, "with so many still living in camps, so many homes still collapsed, and so much debris that hasn't been cleared." He pointed to the recovery effort's advances, with three million cubic feet of rubble carted away, 50,000 families gaining access to potable water, 350,000 Haitians put to work, and hundreds of thousands of children returning to school—although many of their teachers had lost their lives in the disaster.

While the IHRC had approved construction of nine large housing projects, those units would not be nearly sufficient, as Clinton was painfully aware. "In every natural disaster in which I have been involved for over 30 years now, the one thing that is always too slow is moving people from temporary to permanent housing . . . [but] we are on track to move hundreds of thousands of people within the year into permanent housing."

As the effective substitute for an actual government, the IHRC had been heavily preoccupied with meeting the immediate needs of millions of Haitians for food, water, clothing, medical care, and temporary shelter. With donations stalled, Clinton and Bellerive had been forced to transfer a billion dollars in funding from construction and cleanup to meet those needs.

The criticism of Clinton and the IHRC tended to be somewhat self-contradictory. Critics worried that the commission was infringing on Haitian sovereignty and weakening the government, despite Bellerive's role; yet those same critics complained that the commission was not making decisions quickly enough, which would have required it to ignore the dithering government.

Beyond Préval's personal inadequacy and rampant corruption in many ministries was the inherent ineffectiveness of the Haitian state, which lacked basic tools of twenty-first-century governance. Many of its offices had no cars and no computers. But according to the agreement that created the IHRC, those ministries had to give the final authorization on every project.

Behind the "Build Back Better" slogan that Clinton had popularized was a fifty-six-page document titled "Action Plan for National Recovery and Development," written by his IHRC cochair Bellerive, with guidance from U.N. and World Bank experts. That paper's vision for a new Haiti reflected the outlook of the Clinton Foundation as well—emphasizing value-added agricultural production and processing, clean energy, tourism, and industrial investment that would mobilize Haiti's inexpensive labor force. To Clinton, "sustainable development" implied private sector financing and the creation of profitable businesses at every level, from tiny craft cooperatives to luxury hotels.

Engaged as Clinton himself was with Haitian affairs, he delegated the daily business of the IHRC, the Clinton Bush Haiti Fund, the Haiti Action Network, and the coordination of those entities to Laura Graham—a former deputy on his White House scheduling team who had served as the foundation's chief of staff since 2005. Graham had been deeply involved in the relief efforts for the Asian tsunami and had co-chaired the Bush-Clinton Katrina Fund, and had overseen Clinton's work in Haiti since he signed on as the U.N. special envoy in 2009.

Smart and dedicated, Graham had risen from a struggling, working-class family on Staten Island, and she empathized deeply with the Haitian poor. She drew both praise and criticism as Clinton's eyes and ears on the island, working twelve-hour days and traveling back and forth from New York at least three times a month. Despite her other responsibilities at the foundation, she estimated in a 2011 interview that she devoted almost 70 percent of her time to Haiti.

Nobody questioned Graham's energy or good intentions, but she had little experience in government or development at the level where she found herself after the earthquake. She got along well with her Haitian counterpart on the IHRC, executive director Gabriel Verret, but there were officials in the U.N. bureaucracy who resented so much clout in the hands of a thirty-eight-year-old woman without an appropriate résumé. And among ordinary Haitians, her presence did not compensate for the absence of Clinton, whom they had expected, perhaps unrealistically, to see more frequently in their country.

As Haitians marked that first anniversary with tears and prayers in the ruins of the Port-au-Prince Cathedral, there was at least one notable sign of recovery: the city's historic Marché en Fer, or Iron Market, a remarkable nineteenth-century structure that had partially burned down in 2009 and then almost completely toppled in the earthquake, was open again—rebuilt and fully restored by an Irish billionaire named Denis O'Brien. Derelict for years, in its glory days the market had sheltered nearly a thousand sellers of everything from live poultry, turtles, fresh produce, and flowers to perfumes, herbal potions, toys, crafts, and housewares.

It had been, and would be again, the commercial and cultural heart of the capital.

The founder of Digicel, Haiti's largest cell phone company and one of the biggest in the Caribbean, O'Brien had seized a leading role in the country's recovery well before the earthquake struck. He and Clinton had become fast friends. When Clinton went down to Port-au-Prince with medical supplies a few days after the quake, O'Brien met him at the airport to assist with logistics. The largest foreign investor by far in the local economy, he had worked tirelessly in the relief effort, giving away tens of millions of dollars in direct aid and free phone credits as well as the use of his corporate aircraft.

Sharing Clinton's affection for Haiti, O'Brien had joined CGI and become chair of its Haiti Action Network, one of the organization's most active groups, which meant that he oversaw more than a hundred commitment projects on the island valued at over $200 million. In fact the Iron Market restoration, funded through his Digicel Foundation, was itself a CGI commitment.

With his team of architects and builders, O'Brien had restored the old market—consisting of two huge covered sheds, connected by an archway under a gorgeous red clock tower with four ornate, turreted minarets—in a matter of months rather than years. Aside from his personal drive and willingness to spend roughly $12 million of his own money, rather than wait for international donors to write a check, O'Brien had enjoyed the assistance of one of the few competent political leaders in Haiti, the capital's mayor, Jean-Yves Jason.

It was nevertheless an amazing feat, not least because the builders had so diligently taken care to salvage and reuse materials from the old building, and to accurately re-create its original louvers and tiles. Yet the new market was modern, too, with mobile money transactions available, and all of the vendors registered, each with his (or more often her) own stall number. It was built to withstand hurricanes and earthquakes, its lighting and electricity powered by the sun.

More than nine hundred jubilant merchants reclaimed their stalls amid a massive grand opening celebration on January 11 that featured speeches by O'Brien and Clinton.

Something in Haiti truly had been built back better.

————

The difficulty of rebuilding Haiti was proving as intractable as Clinton's aides had predicted—and fairly or not, a degree of blame for the lack of progress had stuck to the former president. But as with so many stories about the troubles of other countries, public attention to the Haitian tragedy had waned in the United States, even though millions of Americans had donated to relief funds. In his own country, Clinton's reputation sustained little if any damage from the disorder and confusion in the island republic.

Instead, he seemed to be climbing new peaks of popular esteem.

Back when he was president, Clinton's pettier critics had often accused him of cheating at golf, an accusation that became a staple of late-night comedy routines. By early 2011, however, the Professional Golfers Association had determined that Clinton would be the ideal partner to resuscitate the Bob Hope Classic, a long-standing PGA tour event on the edge of extinction after losing its namesake, the entertainment legend, who died in 2003, and its corporate sponsor, Chrysler Motors, which withdrew several years later.

As keen golfers and fans, Clinton and Band were eager to work with the golf tour if they could find a way to fit the Bob Hope event's traditional charitable purpose with the work of the Clinton Foundation. In late January, the PGA issued a press release announcing that talks with Clinton had begun. Within a few months, they negotiated a three-way agreement that brought together Humana Health Care, the Clinton Foundation, and the PGA to rename the tournament after its corporate sponsor, with Clinton as its host and spokesman. "I think everyone knew there had to be some sort of reorganization in order to save [the tournament]," said Clinton. "We thought this would be an opportunity to focus on the health and wellness of children, and that's a big part of what my foundation does now."

———

Still more surprising, given the animosity he had routinely expressed on air toward both Bill and Hillary Clinton, was the sustained courtship by Chris Matthews, host of *Hardball*, MSNBC's nightly political show. Except for the hardline conservatives on Fox News, few television personalities were more consistently hostile, during Clinton's presidency and impeachment, and later during Hillary's presidential run. But Matthews's opinion of Bill Clinton had changed—or so he had sought to persuade Band, inviting the Clinton aide to a very public lunch at Michael's restaurant, preferred watering hole for the city's literati and media elite, just blocks from NBC headquarters in Rockefeller Center.

What Matthews wanted was more ambitious than a *Hardball* appearance by Clinton. He proposed a one-hour documentary special—billed as *President of the World: The Bill Clinton Phenomenon*—on the post-presidential works and influence of the man who had once been merely president of the United States.

Eventually Clinton assented to this project, which featured interviews with him and friends such as Terry McAuliffe and Tony Blair, video of him on trips to Africa and domestic political campaigns, and "exclusive behind the scenes access" of Matthews following him around, even to a conference in Northern Ireland. At one point, the MSNBC host observes, "You're like a one-man Peace Corps."

The special aired on February 21, Presidents Day, provoking the *Chicago Tribune* reviewer to ask why Matthews had produced "a fawning special on Bill Clinton, complete with worshipful comments from celebrities such as Ben Stiller, Kevin Spacey, and Mary Steenburgen." The *Washington Post* reviewer wasn't impressed either, disdaining the documentary as "a promotional film for someone who isn't running for anything."

But the *Post* review conceded that Clinton "has busied himself in a number of worthy ways, especially when he heads toward human and natural disasters (wars, tsunamis, earthquakes, hostage crises) to raise relief funds or broker a solution. He loves the world and, as we see on many a tarmac and in convention halls and hotel lobbies hither and yon, the world still loves him back."

———

The world's apparent appreciation of Clinton encouraged hopes that he could rescue other Americans in trouble abroad, as he had done for Euna Lee and Laura Ling. Ever since his return from North Korea, his office had received entreaties on behalf of Americans held captive by unfriendly regimes, such as the three young hikers taken prisoner by Iranian border guards in July 2009. His answer was that he would go anywhere to save an American if there was a reasonable expectation of success—and the U.S. government authorized the trip.

In March 2011, Band and Cooper secretly visited Cuba for a day, to see whether Clinton might be able to bring back Alan Gross, a USAID contractor who had been arrested in Havana on December 3, 2009, convicted of "crimes against state security," and sentenced to ten years in prison. After two years, his mental and physical health were deteriorating, and the Cubans had sent signals that they might release him in exchange for concessions by Washington—possibly including an exchange for the "Cuban Five," a group of Cuban spies serving prison sentences for serious crimes committed in the United States.

Fidel Castro was known to like Clinton, dating back to an occasion at the U.N. in 2000 when the Cuban president had lingered to speak with the American president, who was about to leave office and bidding farewell to the heads of state gathered there.

"Of the six American presidents I've had to deal with, you're my favorite," said Castro in Spanish, as an interpreter translated. "I wish you and your family well." Their handshake made national news and on two or three occasions since then, Castro had sent Clinton a signed box of cigars through a third party. Clinton and Band had also gotten to know Bruno Rodríguez, Castro's foreign minister, when he had served for several years as U.N. ambassador. It was Rodríguez who suggested that Band visit Havana.

When Band asked whether the Obama administration wanted him to go, the answer was positive. White House officials arranged briefings at the State Department and the special Treasury Department license necessary to allow Band and Cooper to travel to Havana legally. They flew down and stayed at the legendary Hotel Nacional—only to learn that neither the Cubans nor the Americans were then prepared to reach a deal. But it was a gesture that showed, late in Obama's first term, that his administration might explore a thaw in the Cold War freeze between the two nations. That controversial process wouldn't begin in earnest until after his reelection.

———

After ten years in Harlem, where his post-presidency had commenced with about a dozen employees, Bill Clinton's operations had outgrown their quarters on 125th Street. The foundation had more than one thousand employees worldwide and hundreds in New York who needed more space—and cheaper space. Ironically, Clinton's presence had helped to spur a rise in the value of uptown real estate that made renting downtown much cheaper per square foot—which had forced America's "first black president" to leave the neighborhood, like too many other African American residents forced out by its growing gentrification.

So that summer the foundation would move to 77 Water Street, a financial district building where the rent would cost less for a considerably bigger headquarters. The configuration of the Water Street building made it possible to house the entire foundation on a single floor, rather than on several floors. Clinton would still continue to use a smaller portion of the Harlem space for his personal office.

But deeper, more consequential changes were occurring beneath the surface in Clinton's world. In May, a former journalist named Declan Kelly resigned his position as the State Department's special economic envoy for Northern Ireland, an unusual (and unpaid) position created by Hillary to employ his special connections and talents. After making a fortune as a business consultant in his native Ireland, Kelly had come to New York. He had gotten involved in Hillary's 2000 Senate race and brought millions of dollars into her 2008 campaign, but she hadn't hired Kelly for his prowess as a fundraiser. He was exceptionally well connected with business leaders around the world, including the leadership of Coca-Cola and Dow Chemical, and his tenure in the State Department had been widely praised for its success.

But Kelly was moving on, with a longtime associate named Paul Keary, to create a new corporate consulting firm called Teneo, Latin for "to guide"—and their new partner Doug Band would be going with them. Early on, Clinton himself had urged Band to work with Kelly, whose acumen impressed him, and the two younger men had indeed become friends. The opportunity to make money was attractive to Band, but he also felt the pull of family life. Life with Clinton was a great adventure, exciting and exhausting—and not the life for a man nearing forty with a wife and children.

For well over a decade, Band had spent more time with Clinton than anyone else, including the former president's family, and inevitably, such intimate knowledge had tempered his admiration. He felt that he understood what was good about Clinton, and what was less good. Yet he also felt an intense gratitude for the remarkable experiences and opportunities that their relationship had afforded him. He and his new partners intended to offer Clinton a share of their new company, without expecting that his involvement would be more than peripheral.

Band and Kelly explained their plans for Teneo and their invitation to Clinton at a meeting in his Harlem office before they launched the firm in June. Present at that meeting was Chelsea Clinton, along with her husband, Marc Mezvinsky. In the months before Band began to withdraw from full-time engagement with the foundation and the former president, she had arrived—and began rapidly expanding her role.

Emulating her parents, Chelsea was tough, smart, and driven, with an enduring interest in public health issues. (As she would later put it, she was "obsessed with diarrhea," a reference to diseases that still killed hundreds of thousands of infants and children every year in developing countries.)

Before turning her attention to her father's institution, she had worked for several years in the private sector, logging three years at McKinsey & Company, the management consultants, and two years at Avenue Capital, a financial firm owned by her parents' friend and supporter Marc Lasry. She had taken time off from Avenue to campaign for her mother between 2007 and 2008.

Then for a year or so, she had taken on a job as an assistant vice provost working on international programs at New York University, whose president John Sexton had known her since childhood. And meanwhile, she had completed a master's degree in public health at Columbia University in 2010, studying nights and weekends. Not long after receiving her master's, she had renewed her Oxford connection to seek a PhD in international relations with a remote study course. She had also worked as a "special correspondent" at NBC News.

Although she had shown scant interest in the foundation during most of those years, her attitude changed sharply in the months after her July 2010 wedding. She would later suggest that the publicity whirlwind had revealed that she, too, was an American celebrity—and that the foundation could serve as a platform to direct the energy surrounding her toward humane and useful purposes.

Both Band and Magaziner, who had known Chelsea since White House days, welcomed her involvement in the foundation. But both had also hinted that she might want to spend more time out in the field, learning its operations from the bottom up—a suggestion she ignored. With her father's support, she joined the foundation board as vice chair, armed with her credentials in management consulting and public health.

In the jargon of Silicon Valley, where she had gone to college and imbibed the new tech culture, she believed the time had come to "disrupt" the foundation with data-driven metrics and to "break down silos" between its sprawling programs.

At the meeting with Band and Kelly, Clinton seemed eager to participate in Teneo, with an honorary title and annual compensation of $3.5 million, an amount similar to what he had been paid by Burkle and Bing. The Teneo founders would have been glad to award him an equity share, but Hillary's job at State precluded Clinton from accepting that form of compensation. For the same reason, he couldn't take an executive or board position with the firm.

Chelsea would later insist that her father understood Teneo to be "something different from what it became," although what she meant by that distinction was unclear. As for Band, he still expected at that point to continue as a senior adviser to his longtime boss—and believed, correctly, that his new venture would position him to raise additional money for the foundation. But in what was later described as a move to isolate Band—who had relinquished his foundation salary in 2010—Chelsea Clinton urged her father to bring in the law firm of Simpson Thacher & Bartlett for a study of the foundation's operations.

———

For his part, Clinton was preoccupied that summer with another book project, reflecting his continuing concern over the domestic and global economy and the malign influence of the antigovernment "Tea Party" movement within the Republican Party. He had spoken out forcefully against the Tea Party and its extreme ideology during the 2010 midterm campaign, only to see its influence increase as the Democrats lost control of both the House and Senate.

Furious over his party's paralysis and the president's passivity, he decided that the time had come to write another book. Rather than a benign ode to generosity and civic involvement, this would be a defense of Obama's effort to revitalize the economy, a review of how his own economic policies had succeeded, an agenda for action—and a straight-talking takedown of the Tea Party. Its blunt title was *Back to Work: Why We Need Smart Government for a Strong Economy.*

Clinton believed that a Tea Party Republican takeover of the federal government in the 2012 elections, including the White House, would be nothing less than tragic for America and the world. Wholly aside from their retrograde domestic policies, they had adopted a troglodyte attitude toward climate change, which he, like many others, suspected was a reflection of the fossil fuel investments of the billionaires, Charles and David Koch, whose money financed the movement. Clinton and his publishers at Knopf agreed that the book should be published no later than November 2011, which would allow a year for its arguments to percolate through political and media networks.

He finally began to write in June, working closely with Justin Cooper in the same style they had honed on his previous books: While Clinton typed pages, Cooper would provide additional research and read the pages, then return them marked up with notes about clarity and accuracy. Facing a deadline just after Labor Day, they continued through the summer, concluding with two weeks of labor in late August.

By then, Clinton and Hillary were vacationing, more or less, at a beachside estate they had rented on East Hampton's Lily Pond Lane, where the neighbors included Jon Bon Jovi, Martha Stewart, and Steven Spielberg. Clinton sat in the sunny dining room, writing and faxing back and forth with Cooper, until the 196-page manuscript was finished.

———

Between the moment that he turned in the draft of *Back to Work* and its publication in November, Clinton enjoyed a peripatetic festival of events to celebrate his sixty-fifth birthday and to commemorate his entry into national politics.

Over the weekend of October 1, Clinton and his family returned to Little Rock, where the foundation's popular executive director Stephanie Streett had overseen the planning of parties, luncheons, speeches, and panel discussions.

The kickoff event on September 30 was the dedication, after seven years, of the Clinton Presidential Center's final elements—a stunning

$10 million pedestrian bridge across the Arkansas River, connecting the library and surrounding park to the city of North Little Rock, and thirteen acres of restored wetlands named for the late Bill Clark, an old Clinton friend, outdoorsman, and city civic leader whose construction firm built the library. Clark had died in 2007. In his brief remarks, Clinton couldn't help repeating favorite jokes about the critics who had initially disparaged the library for resembling an oversized house trailer—which somehow kept winning architectural plaudits for its handsome appearance and environmental design.

That night, James Carville hosted a lavish party at Doe's Eat Place, the ramshackle steakhouse that had served as a Clinton campaign hangout, with big platters of superb porterhouse, beef tamales, and broiled shrimp circulating while he and his old comrades-in-arms held forth over beer and wine. Vegan though he was, Clinton turned up at a long table with Carville, pollster Stan Greenberg, and several other campaign cronies, nursing a glass of red wine while expounding on the latest research into red meat and heart disease.

The next morning, hundreds of veterans of the 1992 campaign, from former cabinet secretaries to the many rank-and-file "Arkansas Travelers" who fanned out across the country, showed up in front of the Old State House, yelling and applauding in the place where Clinton had announced his candidacy so long ago.

When Carville took the stage, he thundered, "Let me tell you something that this day is not about. It is not about *nostalgia*! This is a day about *pride*! Pride in the kind of presidency that President Clinton had, pride about his humanity, as evidenced by the unbelievable work that goes on in the Clinton Foundation and Clinton Global Initiative all over this world."

The former president then took the lectern. Wiping a tear from his eye, and then another, he confessed that the Little Rock weekend—and all the anniversary events—were at least a little about nostalgia. "I want this anniversary weekend more than anything else to be about thanks from me to you."

But after he had thanked them all, his forty-minute speech reflected political themes from *Back to Work*, emphasizing the grossly unequal distribution of income in the nation's fitful recovery, and the raging debate about "whether government is the problem, or whether we need smart government in a changing world to create the opportunities of tomorrow."

No politics intruded on the Hollywood Bowl birthday concert that honored his foundation's tenth anniversary (on October 15, almost two months after his real birthday), where Lady Gaga made gossip headlines with a crooning, flirting reprise of Marilyn Monroe's 1962 "Happy Birthday, Mr. President" serenading of JFK. As Clinton sat in the front row next to Hillary and Chelsea, the singer gazed directly at him.

"Bill," she sighed, "I'm having my first real Marilyn Monroe moment. I always wanted to have one. And I was hoping that it didn't involve an accident with some pills and a strand of pearls, so here we are." As she sang and swiveled, Gaga stripped away her costume until she was wearing nothing but a pale bodysuit and high heels. "It's a good thing I used to dance on bars, right?"

Live-streamed on Yahoo.com as a fundraiser for the foundation, the "Decade of Difference" concert featured a stellar cast, including Stevie Wonder, Usher, Kenny Chesney, the Colombian singer Juanes, and, not surprisingly, Clinton friends Bono and The Edge of U2, who closed their set with "Sunday Bloody Sunday."

Smiling gamely, his wife and daughter had clapped along with Lady Gaga's risqué routine, but her boldness had clearly discomfited the love object himself. When he took the stage to speak later, Clinton joked: "I got nervous when Gaga said she was planning to have a Marilyn moment. I thought, my God, I get Lady Gaga and I'll have a heart attack celebrating my 65th birthday."

In an amusing contrast that defined the cultural poles of Clinton's life, that month's final event was very wonkish and almost sedate: a morning conference at Georgetown University, Clinton's alma mater in Washington, D.C., on "Clinton-Gore Economics: Understanding the Lessons of the 1990s," which featured several former Clinton administration officials.

Former treasury secretary Robert Rubin described his old boss in opening remarks as "a visionary. . . . He recognized what all of us know today, that the global economy was in the early stages of transformation that would create enormous opportunities but also great pressures, and that information technology and communication were on the threshold of revolutionary changes that would have enormous impact on our economy."

The discussion highlighted the deficit reduction and public investment strategies that Clinton liked best to recall, with considerably less attention to the financial deregulatory legislation—the repeal of the Glass-Steagall Act and passage of the Commodity Futures Modernization Act—that many critics had blamed for the financial chaos that led to the 2008 crash and the Great Recession. Now that he was promoting the role of "smart government," Clinton didn't dwell on those bills, although he had admitted that he had listened to the wrong advisers on derivatives regulation, if not Glass-Steagall. (Among those providing the mistaken counsel had been Rubin, of course.)

Introducing Clinton to deliver the morning's closing address was Scott Murphy—a former Democratic congressman from upstate New York, whose reelection campaign had drawn Clinton northward on that cold morning before Election Day in 2010. Like all the others whose races Clinton had flown around to support on that very long day, save one, Murphy had lost his seat. Clinton thanked Murphy, praised him as a smart fellow who should be returned to Congress—and then launched into a speech drawn heavily from his new book, which had been born out of Clinton's anger and concern over the Tea Party midterm.

> Today, there is not a single solitary example on the planet of a truly successful economy that is pursuing this militant anti-government theory," he said, wagging a finger. "You can be a little to the right or a little to the left, but all the successful countries have both a vibrant private sector and an effective government. . . .
>
> I ask you again to ask yourself, is it better to have a partnership or an anti-government strategy? Is it better to believe in 'invest and grow' or 'trickle down'? Is it better to believe in shared prosperity, or you're on your own? I don't think it's a close call. Everybody needs to calm down and do what we know is best for the future.

Nearly a week before Knopf officially released *Back to Work* on November 8, the Associated Press previewed its contents in a story that led with the book's criticism, implied or stated, of Barack Obama. It noted Clinton's complaint that a summer-long struggle between the president and the Republican Congress over the nation's debt ceiling had made America look "weak and confused," and questions he raised over White House strategy in that fight.

"While he generally praises Obama for taking steps to mitigate the financial crisis and deep recession," the AP reported, "he also gently dings the president for poor communication and strategic misfires." Specifically, Clinton expressed the dissatisfaction he had felt for well over a year with the president and other Democratic leaders for failing to fight back against the Tea Party—and make a strong positive case for Obama, as Clinton's book finally did.

Reviews of *Back to Work* were more balanced and largely positive, focusing on the dozens of ideas that Clinton had gleaned from many hours studying economic issues, whether in the business press, journal articles, or obscure government reports. He offered concrete ideas for reducing government waste, for creating millions of jobs, for conserving vast amounts of energy and moving toward clean power, and for rebuilding the country's decrepit infrastructure.

While many of these ideas weren't new, as Clinton forthrightly acknowledged, they were almost certainly new to most Americans.

Even Michiko Kakutani, the antagonistic *New York Times* daily book critic, found much to like, although she didn't entirely resist the urge to snark in her review. Within the slender volume, she wrote, readers would find "a lucid one-man rebuttal of the Tea Party's anti-government agenda. A series of shrewd talking points for Democrats trying to hold on to the White House . . . . . . A self-serving reminder of the prosperity the country enjoyed during Mr. Clinton's tenure in the White House, meant to burnish his legacy. And a practical set of proposals—some borrowed and some new, some innovative and some highly sketchy—for restoring economic growth and creating jobs."

Within two weeks, the book made its bestseller debut at #4 on the *Times* nonfiction list.

While the initial reports of Clinton's mild censure irritated the president and his staff, they quickly adjusted to make the best of it. The popular ex-president had weighed in heavily on behalf of Obama. Besides, they could scarcely have been surprised by his comments on the debt ceiling, since Clinton had openly disagreed with Obama's strategy in a July interview that had made headlines on nearly every news outlet. He had told *The National Memo* that as president, unlike Obama, he would have invoked "the constitutional option" by raising the debt unilaterally—and challenged congressional Republicans to try to stop him in court.

After the book was published, Clinton corrected himself on one important issue. Having written that Obama and the Democrats should have raised the debt ceiling when their party controlled Congress, he subsequently discovered that had not been possible. "Everybody was talking about why didn't we do it, why didn't we do it, including members of Congress," he recalled. "I assumed, wrongly, that it wasn't subject to the filibuster, but it was. They did try to raise it, but [Kentucky senator Mitch] McConnell"—then the minority leader—"told them he was going to filibuster it."

None of that mattered to Obama and his advisers anymore. Indeed, the president would admit eventually that Clinton was right about his failure to consistently and persuasively "tell the story" of his policies to the American people (as he said in an interview on CBS with Charlie Rose). By November, a year before facing reelection against what looked like long odds, they were working with the former president on a much broader agenda.

The process of enfolding Clinton into Obama-Biden 2012 had begun while he was finishing his book in August. Patrick Gaspard, an Obama political aide from New York, called Band to ask whether the former president might do the White House a favor. Would he go down to Florida to visit a few senior citizen homes, as a "preemptive" campaign swing?

Flabbergasted, Band told Gaspard bluntly that the relationship needed additional attention before anything could be asked of his boss. He thought golf would be the best way to bring the two presidents together in a private setting. The following day, Obama called Clinton personally to invite him for a round at Andrews Air Force Base, where they played on September 24. Their foursome included Band and White House chief of staff Bill Daley. The golf outing was awkward, with conversation lagging sometimes. After the show of presidential respect, however, the ice was again broken.

Six weeks later, on the day after Clinton's book came out, Obama's top political operatives traveled from Chicago and Washington to converge on Harlem, in a second phase of the charm offensive. The president's chief campaign adviser David Axelrod, campaign manager and former deputy White House chief of staff Jim Messina, pollster Joel Benenson, and Gaspard, working out of the Democratic National Committee headquarters, met for more than two hours with Clinton to review their outlook and strategy. Band and Cooper were also present.

Messina brought a PowerPoint display on his laptop to give a sense of how the Obama camp foresaw their campaign unfolding. Working on the assumption that the Republicans were likely to nominate Mitt Romney, he explained that they were considering two approaches. One was to portray the former Massachusetts governor, who had adopted sharply contrasting positions over the years on abortion, taxes, gun controls, gay rights, and health care, among other salient issues, as a "flip-flopper." The alternative was to paint him as a right-wing zealot who would attempt to repeal a century of progressive reforms, including Medicare and Social Security.

They went over polling numbers, looked at swing states, and told Clinton that they needed his advice.

Clinton urged them to take the more ideological approach, which would mobilize Democratic voters—and motivate liberal donors. "They tried to do the flip-flopper thing to me," he recalled. "It doesn't work." More important than Clinton's specific advice, however, was the meeting's symbolism. From that point forward, until Election Day 2012, he would be closely integrated into the campaign.

To bring Clinton inside was not a painless process for anyone, including Obama himself. The former president was no longer at the peak of his powers, as they had observed in 2008, and now he was four years older, remote from the daily scuffle and technological advances of national politics. But they couldn't risk leaving him outside, either—especially when they were already running slightly behind Romney in national polls, with the odds-makers betting against them.

CHAPTER SEVENTEEN

Less than five months after launching Teneo in June 2011, Doug Band and his new firm were sideswiped by the humiliating crash of a formerly venerable Wall Street trading house. On the morning of Halloween, MF Global filed for Chapter 11 bankruptcy protection when its management, led by former New Jersey governor Jon Corzine, could no longer avoid the crushing burden of its long position in Eurozone debt, which had gone very sour. It was the biggest bank failure since the fall of Lehman Brothers in September 2008.

The news of MF Global's demise swept through financial and political circles with smashing force, not only because Corzine was a former leading Democrat, who had served in the U.S. Senate as well as the statehouse, but because he was also a former managing partner of Goldman Sachs. The son of an Illinois farm family, Corzine was a completely self-made figure who had endured more than one defeat, first when he was forced out of Goldman by Hank Paulson in 1999, and then when he lost a bid for reelection ten years later to Republican Chris Christie.

Corzine's mismanagement of MF Global meant the end of his remarkable Horatio Alger career—and, as the story of his ruinous investment in Eurobonds unfolded, hints of something worse than a bad bet emerged. Ominous reports in the financial press warned that more than $1.5 billion in client funds had gone missing in the firm's final hours of frantic trading.

Unfortunately for Band and his partners, a senior Teneo executive—who formerly worked as Corzine's chief of staff in the Senate and the statehouse—had signed MF Global as one of the new firm's first clients, billing as much as $125,000 per month for public relations counseling. On December 6, the *New York Post* revealed the relationship in a brief but sensational story headlined "Jon-Bubba Twist: MF Global Hired Clinton's Group." The story was picked up by wire services.

The *Post* story suggested wrongly that Teneo somehow shared culpability for the ill-fated Euro-trades, while highlighting both Bill Clinton's role as chairman of Teneo's advisory board and Corzine's long-standing political connection with both Bill and Hillary Clinton. "MF is now bankrupt and is the subject of investigations by federal prosecutors and regulators," it noted gravely.

The *Post* exposé was strictly an example of guilt by association, with no evidence of actual wrongdoing by anyone at Teneo. Ultimately, investigators would find that MF Global or its management had committed no fraud or crime of any kind. Its dissolution would proceed in an orderly way, with customers getting almost all of their money back and creditors getting about 40 percent of their bills paid. (Ironically, the Eurobonds held by MF Global never defaulted.)

Under pressure from both Hillary and Chelsea, Clinton decided to resign his position with Teneo, and return almost all of the $2 million the firm had paid him on signing.

With Chelsea Clinton's ascendancy in the foundation, Band's tight relationship with her father began to unwind. Clinton was well aware of what Band had done for him and the foundation, expanding his global influence and prestige and, in the process, helping to raise tens of millions of dollars for his projects. Band had continued to raise money for the foundation even after moving to Teneo, encouraging the firm's clients to join CGI and donate.

Over the years that followed, many articles would implicate Band in "conflicts of interest," although the accusations were almost always vague. What the conflicts might be was never spelled out in any specific way. The same articles would claim that Band had acted as a gatekeeper who, in creating Teneo, had built a kind of corporate tollbooth, charging big fees to business leaders for access to the former president.

Certainly, Band had tried to manage Clinton's schedule while protecting his time and reputation. He had said no to many people and yes to others, and made some enemies as well as friends. But to anyone who understood how the world actually works, the tollbooth metaphor was plainly false. What Band had done, with considerable reluctance and distaste, was to shoulder much of the fundraising burden at times when nobody else around Clinton could or would do so.

The chairman of Coca-Cola or Dow Chemical or any of the major corporations that hired Teneo didn't need to pay Band or Kelly in order to meet with Bill Clinton. They could gain access to him through his speakers' bureau, through the foundation, or simply by calling his office. Some of them had his personal cell phone number. (This became still more obvious after Band severed his ties with the foundation, when all of the same business leaders nonetheless maintained their support of the Clinton Foundation and Clinton himself. They also continued to retain Teneo, despite the fact that Band spent little time with Clinton and played no part in his schedule or decisions.)

Meanwhile, Simpson Thacher & Bartlett had completed its "corporate review" of the foundation's operations, after an investigation that included thirty-eight interviews of senior staff and others, asking them questions about its efficiency, governance, budget, and employment practices, as well as "potential conflicts of interest." But the white-shoe law firm's brief report identified no actual conflicts.

Those who were interviewed "uniformly praised the effectiveness of the Foundation and its affiliates, noting the enormous amount they have accomplished over a ten-year period, including building the Presidential Library in Little Rock, the number of people receiving life-saving drugs through CHAI, the agreements negotiated by the Alliance [for a Healthier Generation] with the beverage companies, and the commitments made through CGI."

The report offered a series of recommendations to improve the effectiveness of the foundation's board of directors and, in general, to instill "best practices" appropriate to a large and complex organization—such as hiring a full-time foundation president. While the report clearly implied that more rigorous administration was needed in some areas, it was difficult to understand why this anodyne document was so closely held for nearly two years.

In news reports that winter, led by coverage in the *New York Post*, Clinton was depicted as seeking distance from Band and Teneo because of the imputed conflicts. Whatever others thought, however, Clinton didn't seem to view Band's role in a negative light. In a foundation-wide conference call, he had defended his longtime aide vigorously, telling the staff that they all owed their jobs largely to his efforts.

Finally in March 2012, Clinton issued a public statement that served as his response to negative media coverage of Band and the foundation:

In 2011, the Clinton Foundation marked ten years of rapid growth and significant achievements. From the start, the foundation has operated with a lean, flat management structure and a high level of operational independence for its ongoing projects. Two of our largest efforts, CGI and CHAI, our health access initiative, have independent boards. . . .

The foundation's rapid growth, the management strains caused by our work in Haiti—following similar efforts in the Gulf after Katrina and in Southeast Asia after the tsunami—and the fact that our Chairman Bruce Lindsey and I aren't getting any younger, convinced me to undertake a management review to clarify what we needed to do as an organization to assure another decade of success.

The review produced several positive suggestions, the most important of which was that we hire a full time New York-based foundation president, which we are currently in the process of doing. . . .

I am so proud of the work we have been able to do around the world; and the staff that has worked alongside me for these past ten years has played a key role in that success—Doug Band among them.

I couldn't have accomplished half of what I have in my post presidency without Doug Band. Doug is my counselor and a board member of the Clinton Global Initiative, which was created at his suggestion. He tirelessly works to support the expansion of CGI's activities and my other foundation work around the world. In our first 10 years, Doug's strategic vision and fundraising made it possible for the foundation to survive and thrive. I hope and believe he will continue to advise me and build CGI for another decade.

Finally, I did not sever my financial relationship with Teneo. I changed it. Because of the invaluable help I continue to receive with my business relationships and speaking engagements, as well as with CGI and other philanthropic activities. . . . I felt that I should be paying them, not the other way around.

Despite Clinton's kind words, their once close and almost paternal relationship never fully recovered from the MF Global incident. The distance between them would grow, in fact, as Band was turned into a media scapegoat for the real and, more often, perceived or even imagined shortcomings of the Clinton Foundation. But they still spoke from time to time, at events and on the telephone, especially when the former president felt he needed his former counselor's advice.

———

With the conclusion of a year of meaningful anniversaries, there was still one more to consider. As a legal entity, collecting donations and planning the library, the Clinton Foundation had existed well before 2001. But Clinton had needed many months after leaving the White House to recover himself and find a mission worthy of his skills, passion, and intellect—and on the calendar, 2012 would mark ten years since he had promised to bring HIV/AIDS treatment to all who needed it, regardless of their ability to pay.

Since that day at the Barcelona AIDS Conference in 2002, when Denzil Douglas and Nelson Mandela had asked Clinton to take on what seemed an impossible objective, he had achieved great progress toward fulfilling that commitment. When he and Ira Magaziner had launched CHAI, only seventy thousand people in the less developed countries, outside Brazil, were getting the antiretroviral medication that would keep them alive; at the beginning of 2012, more than six million patients in nearly seventy countries were receiving those vital treatments, more than half through agreements negotiated by CHAI.

Clinton would never claim to have accomplished any of that by himself, nor would Magaziner, for that matter. They had continued to work together, sometimes when they were barely on speaking terms, and they had each contributed their own passion and talents—along with hundreds of dedicated doctors, nurses, CHAI and Clinton Foundation staff, volunteers, individual and institutional donors, American politicians, World Health Organization and United Nations officials, government leaders, and bureaucrats in the aid agencies and health ministries of many countries.

Behind their success had been a powerful element of fortune, as well, in the emergence of the Global Fund to Fight AIDS, Tuberculosis and Malaria, in George W. Bush's decision to create PEPFAR, and in Bill and Melinda Gates's determination to apply their wealth to world health—all of which enabled treatment of millions more people, thanks to the CHAI formula for reducing generic drug costs.

Nor would Clinton ever suggest that their progress had been adequate, in its urgency or breadth. He knew too well that millions had died, and would still die, because the world response to the pandemic had been too slow, too narrow, and too parsimonious. It was still a constant struggle, every year, to obtain adequate funding from the developed world's governments.

That was why, on so many occasions during the "decade of difference," he had chastised those who applauded when he talked about CHAI's work. And yet, they had accomplished something great, and were still working toward something greater. In a five-country study by CHAI analysts that would be released in 2012, the decline of AIDS treatment cost per patient showed that providing care to all 15 million of those infected was indeed affordable. "We now have compelling evidence that universal access to high-quality HIV treatment is achievable, sustainable, and within our means," said Clinton. "Together, the costing study and price reductions open the door to scaling up and sustaining services for the 7 million people who currently lack access to HIV treatment. Providing treatment will save lives and help prevent the spread of HIV." Ten years on, he still hoped to fulfill his promise.

Along with the leaders of the other Clinton Foundation initiatives, Magaziner was asked to brief the foundation's "trustees"—really a group of major donors—on CHAI's latest endeavors when they arrived for an annual conference in Harlem on February 10, 2012. The series of briefings began at breakfast, after welcoming remarks by Dennis Cheng, a veteran political fundraiser for Hillary's campaigns.

Bob Harrison, the Clinton Global Initiative's longtime chief executive, explained how CGI had expanded internally rather than abroad, by sponsoring its first "CGI America" the previous summer in Chicago, which had attracted such luminaries as Treasury Secretary Timothy Geithner, Agriculture Secretary Tom Vilsack, Colorado governor John Hickenlooper, Mississippi governor Haley Barbour, as well as top corporate executives, city mayors, and nonprofit leaders.

Among the one hundred commitments that Harrison said would create 150,000 new jobs was a pledge by the AFL-CIO to allocate $1.4 billion in pension fund financing to retrofit buildings for green energy. He also reported on CGI University, whose fourth annual conference in San Diego had attracted more than one thousand students from 368 universities and colleges; one out of five had received "scholarship" aid to attend.

Each of the initiative leaders offered a similarly uplifting report. Among those who went deeper was Walker Morris, a former broadcasting executive who headed the Clinton Development Initiative, working with smallholder farmers and other agriculture projects in Rwanda and Malawi for several years.

"These are the people with an income of $1 a day that we hear so much about," Morris said. The Rwandan project had grown to 9,000 farmers, mostly growing soybeans and cassava; the 21,000 farmers in Malawi had set up two hundred community nurseries to begin a project that would eventually plant millions of trees, with carbon credits as well as wood and fruit to raise their incomes.

When the briefings concluded, Chelsea rose to engage the initiative leaders in a "dialogue" about their programs. "It's impossible, even for my father, to wrap his mind around all of it," she said. "How do you learn from and work with each other?" Later she invited the trustees to raise questions of their own. And at the end of the morning, just before lunch, her father took the floor, speaking with great familiarity about all the projects, with numbers and anecdotes from the fields of Africa to the streets of Haiti, as if he were working on every project personally.

That evening, the trustees sat at big round tables with Clinton and Chelsea at Del Posto downtown, where chef Mario Batali would greet them all like family. Dennis Cheng would be at dinner, too, working away at his daunting goal: to raise an endowment for the foundation of $250 million.

———

The conflict between Magaziner and the Clinton foundation management had not disappeared, but remained in abeyance as Band gradually withdrew. Placing CHAI under a separate board had submerged those disagreements, for the time being, but they would emerge and intensify with Chelsea's increasing influence.

———

When Obama's campaign aides approached him, Clinton had agreed to a series of 2012 events supporting the president's reelection, with an emphasis on raising money in the spring and, after the late-summer convention, rallies and speeches to inspire the Democratic base before Election Day.

On a Sunday afternoon in late April, he and Obama appeared together in the spacious yard of Terry McAuliffe's home in leafy McLean, Virginia, just across the Potomac River from Washington. The cocktail reception attracted five hundred guests, each paying $1,000 to hear Obama and Clinton, with a dinner afterward for eighty high rollers who had each paid $20,000, all proceeds split between the president's reelection committee, the Democratic National Committee (which McAuliffe had once chaired), and Democratic Party committees in the battleground states.

"You guys get two presidents for one out of this event, which is a pretty good deal," Obama told the guests. Although at least one news report later portrayed the president as uncomfortable on what was clearly Clinton turf, he eventually loosened up, perhaps while listening to Clinton's introduction.

Even that early in the campaign season, political observers had noticed that two favorite Republican themes revolved around Bill Clinton, who by then had been out of office for more than a decade. The first was a claim, emphasized by writers in right-wing media and on talk radio, that the Clintons and the Obamas continued to despise each other, even though Hillary served in Obama's cabinet without rancor, and both she and her husband had worked hard to elect him in 2008. The conservative publisher Regnery had just published a book on Obama by tabloid writer Ed Klein, titled *The Amateur*, which was replete with alleged quotes from Clinton—uniformly nasty and almost certainly fabricated—disparaging the president.

The second theme was less gossipy and more substantial, voiced by Romney himself and other Republican officials. They complained that Obama had betrayed the steady, centrist, fiscally responsible Clinton style of governance—which somehow they had never appreciated when Clinton was president—and embarked on a reckless left-wing spending spree.

Understandably reluctant to associate themselves with the unpopular George W. Bush, the Republicans instead were trying to claim Clinton—and turn his achievements against Obama. Romney attempted this rhetorical maneuver repeatedly, usually quoting the famous 1996 State of the Union address when Clinton had declared "the era of big government is over." According to the Republicans, "President Obama tucked away the Clinton doctrine in his large drawer of discarded ideas, along with transparency and bipartisanship."

To say that Clinton disliked hearing this line, especially from Romney, was a grave understatement. Such right-wing boilerplate irritated him and didn't reflect his views at all, no matter what trope he had once uttered. He had spoken out strongly against austerity policies both at home and in Europe, and written a book that demanded more and smarter public investment while sharply criticizing the antigovernment ideologues of the Tea Party. At McAuliffe's house party, he left no doubt of his opinions concerning Obama and the Republicans.

"When you become president, your job is to explain where we are, say where you think we should go, have a strategy to get there, and execute it," he began. "By that standard, Barack Obama deserves to be re-elected president of the United States. And I'm going to tell you the only reason we're even meeting here. I mean, this is crazy—he's got an opponent who basically wants to do what they did before, on steroids"—his audience laughed—"which will get you the same consequences you got before, on steroids." They kept laughing.

Clinton went on to endorse Obama's "forward-looking" plans for economic renewal, first outlined in the 2008 campaign, which were derailed by the financial crash "only seven weeks before the election." Such fundamental collapses, noted Clinton, historically render nations unable to achieve full recovery and job growth for as long as a decade, "so he's beating the clock, not behind it."

Obama responded with fervent praise for Clinton's "remarkable record" in the White House—and in particular, his capacity as "a master communicator" to persuade his fellow Democrats, "at a time when, let's face it, the Democratic Party was a little bit lost, to refocus not on ideology, not on abstractions . . . but on where people live, what they're going through day to day." He couldn't help ribbing Clinton a little, too, noting that the former president must miss Air Force One. "I'll miss it too," he mused. One of the guests shouted, "But not yet!" Obama smiled. "No, not yet," he replied, as Clinton clapped.

———

Late in August, Clinton took his summer trip to Africa, with Chelsea and the usual cohort of donors and associates, including Magaziner, hitting the usual stops in South Africa and Rwanda, with detours to Uganda and Mozambique, all in six days aboard a chartered Boeing 737. Owing to his scheduled speaking slot at the Democratic National Convention on the evening of September 5, when he would nominate Barack Obama for a second presidential term, the *New York Times* had sent political reporter Amy Chozick along with him.

Her story, datelined Rwanda, appeared the day before Clinton's address. It lightly tweaked his idiosyncrasies while respecting his philanthropic work, and noted Chelsea's gradual "evolution into a more public and less press-averse figure." It also mentioned Hillary's determination to step down from the State Department after Obama's reelection, when she would join the foundation and "go back to being a professional advocate for women and girls" in her daughter's words.

At Entebbe Airport in Uganda, Clinton had met and embraced "the other Bill Clinton"—a boy named after him, Bill Clinton Kaligani, whom he had held in his arms as a tiny baby during his first visit to Africa in 1998. A photograph of that scene hung on the wall in Chappaqua. Clinton had promised young Bill Clinton's mother that he would pay for the child's education, and the fourteen-year-old boy said he hoped to become a doctor, which delighted his namesake. "I feel good," Bill Clinton Kaligani told reporters. "He told me he also wanted me to be a doctor, that I should work hard and pass in my studies."

———

In late July, Obama had called Clinton to ask him to deliver the nominating speech, a prime-time rebuttal to the Republicans who questioned their alliance. The aura of cooperation could scarcely have differed more from the frozen atmosphere four years earlier, when the Clinton camp barely acknowledged requests from the Obama team to see his convention speech.

This time the line of communication with Cooper was open, with Axelrod and communications director Stephanie Cutter providing guidance, which was welcomed, during the weeks leading up to the convention. Obama himself had assured Clinton, "We will give you whatever you need." Gene Sperling, director of the National Economic Council, who had held the same job in Clinton's White House, soon started to send memos with fresh economic data.

According to the framework suggested by Axelrod and Cutter, Clinton was to make the case explaining why the economy had not grown faster, the reasons behind Obama's actions as president, and the argument for the country to stick with him, despite dissatisfaction with the lagging recovery—and all while drawing contrasts with the Republicans.

What they proposed made sense to Clinton and to Cooper, who assisted with the speech, and to his other advisers. But it was only the barest outline. Paul Begala began to work on a draft toward the end of August, with help from Bruce Reed, another domestic policy adviser in Obama's White House who had once worked for Clinton.

Finally, over Labor Day weekend, just two days before the convention, Clinton sat down in Chappaqua with a lined white pad and pen. "I'm working on it," he told anyone who asked, but not much was on paper by Tuesday morning. Around noon, Clinton got on a chartered Gulfstream IV jet at Westchester Airport to fly down to the convention in Charlotte, North Carolina.

Clinton was in a good mood, but pensive. About an hour into the flight, he started handing pages of cryptic handwriting to Cooper to type into his laptop. By the time they landed, the speech had just begun to take shape. On the twentieth floor of the Hilton Center City downtown, he sat at a dining room table, still writing longhand pages. Around 5 p.m., they took a break to attend a party thrown by Arkansas governor Mike Beebe, but he was preoccupied with the speech and passed on a second party that evening at the home of Erskine Bowles, one of his oldest friends.

He went back to the hotel room where he skipped dinner, snacking on a bowl of hummus and sipping coffee as he continued working until almost 2 a.m. Through the evening he had dispatched questions to Reed and Sperling via Cooper's email. While the text had gained structure during the night, it had also gained a lot of words—and would need to be cut nearly in half for his twenty-five-minute time slot.

On Wednesday morning he had breakfast in the hotel room, then got on the phone with Cutter and Axelrod at around 9 a.m. to discuss a television appearance later in the day. He gave them a preview of the speech and, while they liked what they heard, they frankly worried about the amount of factual data piled into the text. Begala, John Podesta, and former White House press secretary Joe Lockhart turned up in the suite. They were soon sitting around the dining table with printouts, adding lines. Around noon, Sperling showed up, then Reed, and later still, former presidential assistant and journalist Sidney Blumenthal and Mark Penn.

By then the text was complete, yet still too long, and everyone in the room began to discuss how best to state the essential facts. But the speech still had no ending—and while they had cut it down to twenty-eight minutes, Clinton kept adding back material that had come out. At 5 p.m., they sent excerpts of the speech out for distribution to the political reporters, then broke at 7:30 to shower and change. Cooper sent a draft to Sperling's staff for a swift fact-checking.

Obama's staff showed him the speech, and he approved, asking only that Clinton strengthen a certain sentence defending his record on welfare, which the Republicans had attacked.

A teleprompter and podium sat in a room down the hallway from Clinton so that he could practice. He hadn't used a teleprompter in years, but as his aides, old staffers, and Chelsea watched him rehearsing, it was, as one later put it, "a wow moment." And he had hit the mark in twenty minutes.

Cooper printed it out in a thirty-point font—as Clinton liked to say, quoting George Washington, he had gone blind in the service of his country—and handed off a thumb drive for the prompter in the convention hall at 9:50 p.m.

The convention schedule was running behind, so there was no way Clinton would finish his speech until after 11 p.m. But they were confident that the networks would continue to broadcast him, no matter how late the speech went. For an introduction, the Obama campaign had produced a video about him, the foundation, and his post-presidency. As the lights came up, he strode out into the spotlight and stood behind the big wooden lectern, wearing a dark suit, white shirt, and striped tie, to the strains of that old Fleetwood Mac tune.

When the delegates finally stopped cheering, it was 10:35. "Fellow Democrats," he began, "we are here to nominate a president. And, I've got one in mind. . . . I want to nominate a man who ran for president to change the course of an already weak economy and then just six weeks before his election, saw it suffer the biggest collapse since the Great Depression; a man who stopped the slide into depression and put us on the long road to recovery, knowing all the while that no matter how many jobs that he saved or created, there'd still be millions more waiting, worried about feeding their own kids, trying to keep their hopes alive.

"I want to nominate a man who's cool on the outside—but who burns for America on the inside. I want—I want a man who believes with no doubt that we can build a new American Dream economy, driven by innovation and creativity, through education and—yes—by cooperation.

"And by the way, after last night, I want a man who had the good sense to marry Michelle Obama."

In short, Bill killed it. He brought to bear the full weight of his political experience and forensic skill on behalf of the man who was once his sworn adversary. This was among Clinton's finest campaign speeches, presenting an exhaustive argument for Obama—and against the Republicans.

With professorial flair, he delivered a lesson in presidential economics, acknowledging complexity while keeping the lesson understandable and even simple. No political leader since FDR had developed Clinton's capacity to perform such rhetorical magic. He possessed a singular authority to discuss employment, spending, and debt, having proved his GOP opponents wrong so comprehensively in the past that they had started citing him as a model.

To call Clinton out that way—as both Romney and his running mate, Paul Ryan, had done—had been a woeful mistake. He merrily repaid the cynical compliment by "scoring" them and their party on budgetary arithmetic and job creation, an exercise from which they did not emerge unscathed.

Republicans have ruled the country for more presidential terms than Democrats over the past fifty-three years, Clinton recalled, but they have overseen the creation of only 24 million jobs, compared with 42 million credited to Democrats. He then praised Obama for enabling creation of 250,000 new jobs in the restored auto industry and castigated Romney for advising Bush to bankrupt the industry, which would have created "zero" jobs (and probably would have caused the loss of millions).

The "country boy from Arkansas" did the sums that exposed the Ryan budget as a hoax, doling out tax breaks to billionaires that would supposedly be offset by reforms—which they promised to detail "after the election."

On both welfare reform and the expansion of health care for poor children, he was passionate and highly articulate, explaining "what really happened" with the welfare work requirement that Republicans had accused Obama of gutting—and how Ryan and Romney planned to hit Medicare with the same level of cuts that he accused them of wrongly attributing to Obama.

Obama had added eight years to the Medicare system's solvency, he said. "Now, when Congressman Ryan looked into that TV camera and attacked President Obama's Medicare savings as, quote, the biggest, coldest power play, I didn't know whether to laugh or cry"—the audience laughed—"because that $716 billion is exactly, to the dollar, the same amount of Medicare savings that he has in his own budget!

"You got to give him one thing," he said to roaring cheers, "it takes some brass to attack a guy for doing what you did." As the cheers and applause went on, he wagged a finger. "Now, you're having a good time, but this is getting serious, and I want you to listen." He went on to explain, in detail, how the Republican plan "would end Medicare as we know it."

Finished with his dismantling of the GOP program, he vindicated the president's economic record in a way that neither Obama nor his campaign could do without sounding defensive. "President Obama started with a much weaker economy than I did. Listen to me, now. No president—no president, not me, not any of my predecessors, no one could have fully repaired all the damage that he found in just four years."

He mockingly summarized the other party's case: "In Tampa, the Republican argument against the president's re-election was pretty simple: We left him a total mess, he hasn't finished cleaning it up yet, so fire him and put us back in." Instead, he said with the authority vested in him by his enduring popularity, Obama had earned another term by saving the country from depression and laying the foundation for renewed prosperity.

Finally, he described America's moral foundation, as a nation where "we are all in this together," a society that had grown strong because the benefits of growth and innovation were shared broadly. What Democrats believe to be morally decent, he said, is also economically sound.

Even as he excoriated the Republicans, Clinton contrived to seize the high ground, saying he had never learned to hate them the way they seemed to hate Obama (and once hated him, too). Republican presidents had done too many good things, from Dwight D. Eisenhower's interstate highway system to Bush's PEPFAR spending, to pretend that they were all bad. He was very proud, he said, to have worked with Bush's father on Katrina and tsunami relief; in his foundation work, he didn't bother looking at who belonged to which party, because they were all too busy getting things done.

Cooperation, even with people whose views are disagreeable, was the way forward for the country, he said—and the president had persisted in trying to work with his opponents, even when all they wanted to do was defeat him.

It was a very long speech, almost fifty minutes, but spellbinding as Clinton put forward a defense in detail of everything significant the president had achieved, from the auto bailout and green energy to Obamacare. From memory, he had restored about two thousand words cut from the first draft. He could feel the audience with him at every word and went on.

"Are we better off today than four years ago?" he demanded, again and again. The answer was always yes.

For the ending, he cribbed directly from the conclusion of *Back to Work*.

"Look, I love our country so much. And I know we're coming back. For more than 200 years, through every crisis, we've always come back. People have predicted our demise ever since George Washington was criticized for being a mediocre surveyor with a bad set of wooden false teeth. And so far, every single person that's bet against America has lost money, because we always come back. We come through every fire a little stronger and a little better.

"And we do it because in the end we decide to champion the cause for which our founders pledged their lives, their fortunes, their sacred honor—the cause of forming a more perfect union. My fellow Americans, if that is what you want, if that is what you believe, you must vote and you must re-elect President Barack Obama. God bless you and God bless America."

Backstage, the Obamas greeted him warmly. Among the aides who had worked on the speech until the final moments, there was a palpable feeling of relief. But it was less a climactic moment than an opening salvo. Clinton would return to the campaign trail, aiming to make Romney and Ryan regret they had ever mentioned his name.

———

During the weeks leading up to Election Day, the race between Obama and Romney felt tighter than the results proved to be, partly because the Republicans and their media outlets insisted that polls showing the Democrat leading were "skewed," and partly because the economic fundamentals pointed toward a Republican victory. But those polls showed unmistakably that the Democratic convention—and in particular, Clinton's masterful speech—had lifted the party's ticket beyond reach of their opponents.

The campaign kept his face before the public in television and on-line advertising, such as an ad that kept running in some states for weeks after the convention. Touting Obama's investments in education, job training, and manufacturing innovation, he looked straight at the camera and said: "It only works if there is a strong middle class. That's what happened when I was president. We need to keep going with his plan."

The strategy for surrogate Clinton was simple: Persuade white working-class voters in battleground states like Ohio and Pennsylvania to stay with Obama. No other surrogate had the credibility to reach those voters, which meant that the former president spent day after day in October flying into Scranton, Pittsburgh, and Cleveland, sometimes driving at breakneck speed behind a police convoy from one platform to another.

Frenetic as the end of a campaign invariably is, Clinton was having fun. If anyone expressed surprise to see him campaigning so hard for Obama, he would laugh and say, "I might be the only person in this country who is happier to vote for Obama this year than in 2008," then explain that the president had proved himself during the past four years in ways that Clinton had not expected. It wasn't a line he used often on the stump, where he reprised the themes of the convention speech on the economy, student loans, health care, and, depending on where he happened to be, a strong emphasis on the auto bailout.

On a Thursday evening, five days before the election, the campaign sent Clinton to Cuyahoga County Community College, just outside Cleveland, for a special event. Waiting backstage as he spoke was Bruce Springsteen, so he wisely kept his remarks shorter than usual, just half an hour. "We love Ohio," he said, referring to himself and Hillary. "And now I'm here to tell you something important. When you were down, President Obama had your back. You've got to have his back now." He talked about student loan reform—"one of the most important things President Obama has done that nobody knows about"—and the benefits of Obamacare.

"This is the first time in my life I ever got to be the warm-up act for The Boss," he quipped. "I'm qualified for it, because I was 'born in the USA.'" He gazed out at the overflow crowd, nearly all white, knowing that he had to sell the African American president, at least a little. He shook hands along the ropeline, stepped backstage to greet the waiting rock star, and then returned to the stage in his shirtsleeves.

"It is my honor to introduce one of the most important voices in American music in the last 50 years, and a man who has always stood for true American values, the incomparable Bruce Springsteen." But he couldn't stay to listen as Springsteen broke into his anthem, "We Take Care of Our Own." Clinton was out the door and hustling to the next stop, in a remote corner of the state near the West Virginia border.

On election eve, with the Republicans claiming that Pennsylvania was still in play, the campaign had scheduled Clinton for a giant rally at the University of Pennsylvania campus gym in Philadelphia to push Democratic turnout. Everywhere he had gone, the crowds had been too big to be contained in the booked venue; sometimes, as at a suburban college rally, the event had simply been moved outdoors, with a makeshift stage. That wasn't possible at Penn, where the big gym was filled beyond capacity. The best guess was sixteen thousand inside, and a couple thousand more lined up around the superblock.

"I want you to vote your hopes, not your fears," shouted Clinton, trying to be heard above the echoing din of the crowd. "I want you to imagine what America can be like ten years from now. And I want you to go out tomorrow and make Barack Obama president for four more years." He saluted and left the stage, wild cheering in his ears.

The election wasn't close, despite all the Republican chatter. Obama carried Pennsylvania with 52 percent of the vote; he took Ohio, too, with 51 percent. And in Cuyahoga County, where whites outnumbered minority voters by two to one, the Democrats carried 70 percent of the vote.

CHAPTER EIGHTEEN

With the advent of the thirteenth year of the new millennium came a momentous change for the Clintons and their works, as Hillary made her long-promised departure from the State Department.

Rather than the fond and orderly farewell she had earned after four years of ceaseless toil at the State Department, Hillary's return to private life was just as tumultuous as her husband's exit from the White House had been a dozen years earlier. She had spent New Year's Eve in a room at New York Presbyterian Hospital, imbibing blood thinners to dissolve a clot in a blood vessel just behind her right ear and dangerously close to her brain. The clot had appeared after she contracted a stomach virus on a trip to Egypt, and then, fainting from dehydration, fell and injured her head in mid-December.

With her public approval rating close to 66 percent, most of the country sympathized with Madam Secretary in distress. But Republicans in Washington, stricken with fear that she might run for president again, couldn't decide how to spin her illness: Was she actually far sicker than the official story suggested, disabling any presidential ambitions she might still harbor? Or was she merely faking, so she wouldn't have to testify in Congress about the September 2012 consular attack in Benghazi, Libya, that had left Ambassador Chris Stevens and three other Americans dead?

Her usual antagonists, from Rush Limbaugh to John Bolton to Karl Rove, had skipped any expression of concern over her medical condition to promote theories contradicting the doctors' explanation. Bolton bluntly accused her of malingering with a "diplomatic illness," while Rove insisted that she was actually much sicker than advertised. The *National Enquirer* ran a screaming front-page "Breaking News" headline—"Brain Cancer Drama"—over an unflattering photo. To conservative columnist Kathleen Parker, the chorus of callous doubters revealed a "viciousness" that was "disheartening and disgusting."

Hillary effectively quelled the conspiracy mongers by showing up on the Hill to answer questions about Benghazi from Senate and House members on January 23, assuming responsibility for what had happened on her watch while sharply rebutting the worst insinuations about her supposed negligence. And although she had suffered a previous blood clot in her knee many years earlier, she wasn't deathly ill. After 401 days spent traveling to 112 countries, logging 956,733 air miles or the equivalent of three full months airborne, she was simply very, very tired.

"I just want to sleep and exercise and travel for fun and relax. . . . I'd like to see whether I can get untired," she had told the *New York Times*. On February 1, John Kerry took over as secretary of state.

Hillary's new civilian life had been the subject of careful planning for months. Fresh from maternity leave, Huma Abedin had resigned as her deputy chief of staff in June 2012 and settled down in New York City, where her status as a "special government employee" of the State Department allowed her to work simultaneously for the Clinton Foundation (and for Teneo, where Doug Band hired her temporarily to work on special events, mostly as an act of friendship). Abedin's multiple jobs were legal but complicated, and the Republicans dogging Hillary on Capitol Hill would later question her arrangements. But they were never able to show what she had done wrong or demonstrate any conflict of interest that had arisen between her public and private employments.

As she departed the government, Hillary had declined several lucrative opportunities to join corporate boards. Instead, when she felt sufficiently rested, she planned to deliver speeches booked by her husband's representatives at the Walker agency, for the same fees that she frankly considered "ridiculous." Reporting that the agency had signed her, the New York *Daily News* quoted prices no less than $200,000 in the U.S. and as high as $750,000 in "the high-priced Asian and Middle Eastern markets." The same article quoted the head of the National Speakers Association predicting she would earn somewhere on "the lower end of her husband's speeches, but she'll be incredibly desirable."

Independent experts said that at $250,000 or even more, Hillary's projected fees would not exceed those of comparable speakers. Kofi Annan, the former U.N. secretary-general, commanded $170,000 per appearance; Rudolph Giuliani, the former New York mayor, asked

$270,000; Ben Bernanke, the former Federal Reserve chair, got $200,000 at home and $400,000 abroad; and to book former treasury secretary Timothy Geithner required up to $200,000. She may have been the first woman expected to command speaking fees of that magnitude, but then she was also considered more likely than any other woman to become the first female president of the United States.

Unlike her husband and many of his fellow top-level lecturers, however, Hillary would not be available for appearances in the high-rolling overseas venues. Somewhat naively, she believed that by rejecting the dozens of foreign speaking offers, and accepting only stateside invitations, she could avoid any political backlash. It was a policy she had adopted just in case she should ever decide to seek public office again.

At that moment, Hillary wasn't obsessing over another run for the presidency—as the rest of the world already appeared to be doing on her behalf—but she surely didn't want to foreclose her candidacy. Within days of leaving the government, her aides had set up a new website, hillaryclintonoffice.com, and blasted out a mass email from Bill and Chelsea to the foundation's list.

"She inspires us every day—and we hope she inspires you, too. Please take a moment to send Hillary your personal note of thanks," it said, providing a convenient link. The site collected the names and email addresses of everyone who did.

Whatever her ultimate decision, she would be ready to run in 2016. And that looming possibility would inexorably affect elite and public opinion about the foundation. While Hillary served in office, her approval ratings hovered at high levels; the Gallup Organization had identified her in its surveys as America's "most admired woman" for seventeen years in a row, a status usually reserved for first ladies. But whenever she ran for office, her popularity would drop rapidly amid the partisan clash. No longer would the foundation remain insulated from that political turbulence.

Before settling into a corner office at the foundation's new Midtown headquarters that spring, Hillary had briefly considered starting her own nonprofit, focused on issues affecting women and girls. It soon became clear that would make little sense with her family already toiling together, and substantial funding in place, at the foundation. She preferred to be with her daughter, which offered a chance to inquire regularly, in person, as to when Chelsea and Marc Mezvinsky planned to produce a grand-child. (To the inexpressible delight of both Bill and Hillary, they would deliver the first, Charlotte Clinton Mezvinsky, on September 26, 2014. The second, her little brother Aidan Clinton Mezvinsky, would be born almost two years later, on June 18, 2016.)

By spring, Hillary had begun to construct her niche, hiring former aide Maura Pally away from the Bloomberg Foundation to serve as the executive director of her foundation office. Pally had started as an assistant in the White House counsel's office when Clinton was president, later working in Hillary's 2008 campaign, and then rising at State to become a deputy assistant secretary in the Bureau of Educational and Cultural Affairs.

Pally's job would be to build and operate Hillary's signature programs, most notably the No Ceilings initiative—a partnership with the Gates Foundation to measure female progress worldwide over the previous two decades, and encourage "full participation" by women in all spheres of economic, social, and political life. Its name echoed Hillary's Democratic convention speech in 2008, where she boasted of leaving "18 million cracks in the glass ceiling" that had kept women from winning the presidency. And although it was officially part of the Clinton Foundation, No Ceilings built its own website, noceilings.org.

Another signal of Hillary's renewed authority in her husband's world was the choice of a replacement for Doug Band, who had drastically wound down his involvement in 2012. Tina Flournoy, a former American Federation of Teachers official with long-standing ties to both Bill and Hillary—but especially the latter—became the chief of staff in his presidential office. Flournoy would be the new gatekeeper.

And there was still another change heralding Hillary's arrival. Once she decided to join her husband and daughter, a decision was reached to reflect her arrival—and Chelsea's increasingly high profile—by adopting a new corporate name. What had been the William J. Clinton Foundation would henceforth be known as the Bill, Hillary & Chelsea Clinton Foundation.

———

The renaming of the Clinton Foundation set off renewed chatter about Chelsea's instant rise to power in her family's philanthropic enterprise, both inside and outside. More than a few staff and friends of the foundation believed that she would be more welcome—and morale would be improved—if she had "paid some more dues," as one former high-ranking staffer said. But her parents manifested complete confidence in her, and encouraged her to pursue the objectives that she felt were important. Indeed, her indulgent father often mentioned in public that she "is a lot smarter than I am."

Certainly Chelsea's influence as a member of the Millennial generation was positive in modernizing her parents' attitudes on technology, culture, and social issues. When her mother announced in March 2013 that she had changed her views about homosexual marriage—in support of full equality for gays and lesbians—she credited Chelsea as a powerful influence. When her father accepted an award from the Gay and Lesbian Alliance Against Defamation, an important media sentinel, he spoke extensively about how his daughter's friendships with gay and lesbian couples had provided a "model" for him to change his own outlook. Neither he nor Hillary could fairly be described as bigoted, and as president he had fought hard to appoint the nation's first openly gay ambassador, James Hormel. Having signed the Defense of Marriage Act as president in 1996, however, he had come around to urging that states legislate full marriage rights—and that the Supreme Court should strike DOMA down.

Chelsea's impact on the operations of the foundation was also striking. A self-proclaimed nerd, she enjoyed working with pivot tables and other powerful data processing tools commonly used in business and finance, but that most people would consider impossibly arcane. While her father had always liked to talk about "keeping score," she had encountered some of the most sophisticated statistical methodology while working at McKinsey and Avenue Capital, and earning her academic degrees.

Very soon after arriving at the foundation, as she told reporters, she had sought to "harmonize the tracking of data" across all of its initiatives—and to make sure that all of the programs were operating on the same computer platform. Without any unified database, the managers couldn't compare the costs and efficiencies of the various initiatives or encourage "best practices."

It was not long before she sought to impose a different vision of how the foundation should operate.

———

As U.S. senator and then as secretary of state, Hillary had participated many times in the Clinton Global Initiative annual September conference in New York, where she had delivered plenary speeches and participated on panels devoted to international issues. In June 2013, she spoke for the first time at CGI America, the annual spinoff conference devoted to domestic issues and originally designed as the foundation's answer to the loss of jobs and fraying social cohesion caused by the Great Recession. Held in her hometown of Chicago, CGI America presented a prime opportunity for her to highlight the social and economic issues—childcare, education, family leave, and women's equality—on which she had made her reputation.

And not incidentally, as the *New York Times* and other publications noticed, addressing those concerns before an American audience meant drawing renewed attention to her status as a potential Democratic presidential candidate in 2016. "Mrs. Clinton appeared alongside her husband, Bill Clinton, in a crowded ballroom here," reported the newspaper of record, "and left little doubt that she planned to reclaim the political stage she exited more than four years ago to become the nation's top diplomat."

Actually, her remarks were mainly concerned with the work she planned to do at the foundation, with a special focus on the benefits of full female participation in work, business, politics, and society—reforms that were not only morally imperative but were proved to grow economies and raise incomes. The *Times* reporter found her speech dry and excessively burdened with facts and numbers, but it also showed that, if she had evaded the question of gender as a presidential candidate in 2008, she would never make that mistake again.

———

Speaking at CGI America, Hillary had emphasized Chelsea's expanding role at the foundation, crediting her with efforts to "widen our reach to a whole new generation of young people," and hinting that she had somehow brought about CGI University, the student component of the global conference. While that suggestion wasn't accurate—CGIU long predated Chelsea's ascent—it showed how the Clintons were framing her new role. She was extending her reach into all of the initiatives and little of any consequence occurred in the foundation without input from her. Naturally, that included the selection of a new chief executive.

The Simpson Thacher review of the foundation's operations had recommended, among other things, the appointment of a full-time CEO and president. Bruce Lindsey, who had filled that role for years, had suffered a stroke late in 2011 and was ready to move to a less demanding position as board chair. Chelsea, the vice chair, had a candidate lined up to replace Lindsey, someone who shared her devotion to data streams and managerial efficiencies: a former McKinsey colleague named Eric Braverman, who had been a precocious partner in the consulting giant's Washington office.

Braverman joined the foundation as CEO in mid-July, with a mandate for sweeping reforms in line with the Simpson Thacher recommendations—a bigger and more independent board, an audit committee to oversee internal financial controls, complaints, and possible conflicts of interest; stronger management of personnel, expenses, outside employment, and CGI membership; and clearer rules and procedures for vetting of donors and their gifts to the foundation. Or so he thought.

———

Only weeks after Eric Braverman joined the Clinton Foundation, the young executive found himself on a plane to Africa. The annual trip had been scheduled for July, and he joined a motley contingent of wealthy friends, staffers, and initiative directors, including Ira Magaziner, along with actors Dakota Fanning and Jesse Eisenberg, a *Glamour* writer following Chelsea, and a camera crew dispatched by Martin Scorsese, who had agreed to produce a film about the foundation for HBO Documentaries. The potential donors included John Catsimatidis, Jr.—son of oil and grocery billionaire John Sr., a New York Republican activist—as well as several young friends of Chelsea and Marc who had made their fortunes in technology and finance.

With a large group of donors and potential donors to shepherd, the foundation's development director, Dennis Cheng, had assumed substantial responsibility for trip logistics. Cheng was ramping up his drive to build the foundation endowment, and hardly wanted to entrust his donors' care to anyone else.

Led by Clinton and Chelsea, the trip through six sweltering countries in nine days was a demanding excursion, not a pleasure jaunt. As a rule the mornings started with a very early luggage call, and the evenings could run very late, with the plane touching down at the next destination around midnight or even hours later.

The two dozen members of the "delegation," as the Clinton entourage was known, had little time to lounge around a swimming pool or shop for souvenirs. To exercise required getting to the hotel gym before 6 a.m.—where Chelsea would be on the treadmill already, running flat out. For eight full days, the hours from dawn to dusk were spent trundling across the African landscape, often in vans without air-conditioning, despite the stifling heat. The reward at day's end was dinner with the president, who would often hop from table to table, holding forth over a glass of red wine.

Early on July 30, the delegation left Kennedy Airport on a chartered Sun Country 737 to fly eighteen hours, including two fuel stops, before landing at the single-runway Lilongwe International Airport in Malawi's capital.

In Lilongwe, the country's president, Joyce Banda, accompanied Clinton, Chelsea, and the delegation to the Central Hospital, where CHAI had brought improvements in HIV testing along with inexpensive generic medicine, early diagnosis and treatment of infants, and the use of SMS technology to send test results. Waiting at the hospital was a group of AIDS patients from districts around the country, whose children had been spared the virus thanks to CHAI's assistance in preventing mother-to-child transmission. The children had come to thank Clinton, too.

From the hospital, the delegation piled into vans for a two-hour ride on rutted dirt roads out to a commercial "anchor farm" operated by the Clinton Development Initiative in the rural town of Santhe, where foundation staff worked with neighboring smallholder farmers to produce maize and soybeans with better fertilizers, cheaper seeds, cooperative marketing, and "climate smart" farming methods that conserved water and soil.

Clinton believed strongly that past Western policies had been ruinous to small farmers, worsening their poverty and driving them off the land. His foundation's projects aimed at reversing that terrible error—and as he walked through the harvested fields, Clinton boasted that the anchor farm had raised its neighbors' annual earnings more than 400 percent. As a result, the farmers said, they had better food, tin roofs on their homes, and enough money to pay their children's school fees.

Overnight they flew to Victoria Falls in Zambia, where the fauna at the Royal Livingstone Hotel included giraffes and zebra (one of which kicked Jesse Eisenberg when he wandered too close). But while Clinton took his retinue out that evening to hike around the waterfall, the day was devoted to foundation projects. The delegation traveled by van along dirt roads to a rural "health post," where CHAI staffers had trained dozens of "community health assistants" to provide basic care and treatment to thousands of local families, in a national program funded by the British Department for International Development (one of the largest CHAI donors).

That afternoon, on the hotel grounds, the Starkey Hearing Foundation staged a pop-up hearing clinic as part of its CGI commitment to give away a million hearing aids in developing countries. Bill Austin, its conservative Republican founder, had been channeling some of the hundreds of millions in annual revenue from his company, Starkey Hearing Technologies, to the charitable foundation for many years. But he told the delegation members that Clinton had twisted his arm to do more. Having donated millions of dollars to CGI, Austin, his wife, and stepson often crossed paths with Clinton in Africa during the summer.

Although he had seen this process many times, Clinton never tired of watching the emotional moment when a child—or an adult—was able to hear a sound for the first time. Under Bill Austin's careful guidance, several members of the delegation, including Clinton and Chelsea, spent two hours helping to fit local children with hearing aids. To see a boy or girl suddenly smile at the sound of another person's voice—and see that child's mother erupt in tears—was so moving for some of the delegation members that they had to turn away to conceal their own weeping.

Arriving the next morning in Dar-es-Salaam, the delegation accompanied Clinton to a CGI site in a run-down neighborhood where Barclays Bank, cooperating with CARE International, was carrying out a microfinance commitment to help woman-run small businesses with loans and financial management. The afternoon brought them to the presidential palace, where Clinton signed a memorandum of understanding with Tanzanian president Jakaya Kikwete to extend the foundation's smallholder farming program into the rural highlands, with $3 million in funding from the Netherlands government.

In a last-minute detour, Clinton brought the delegation to the U.S. embassy, which was preparing to mark the fifteenth anniversary of the suicide truck bombing that killed eleven and wounded eighty-five on August 7, 1998. That attack, coordinated with an even deadlier simultaneous truck bombing at the embassy in Nairobi, Kenya, had been the first incident that brought Osama bin Laden and al Qaeda to the attention of U.S. intelligence authorities.

Surrounded by a Marine guard, Clinton and his guests listened as U.S. ambassador Alfonso Lenhardt spoke briefly about the incident and then read the names of the victims. The former president said a few words about the bombing's impact on him and his presidency, shook hands with the ambassador and several embassy employees. Then the delegation departed.

The Clinton retinue arrived early on August 4 in Zanzibar, the legendary spice island, where CHAI was active not only in providing AIDS medications and diagnostics, but in mounting a major, multipronged attack on malaria, which still infected as many as 200 million people every year and killed nearly half a million, mostly African children, despite considerable progress in eradicating the mosquito-borne disease.

In a local stadium, thousands of cheering Zanzibaris showed up to celebrate their success in defeating malaria with a semipro soccer match that also honored the presence of Clinton and Chelsea. A kiosk manned by CHAI staff distributed free repellent-laden bednets and educational pamphlets promoting tests and treatment. After seven years of steady work on the island—and a sharp reduction in malaria diagnostics negotiated by CHAI—the incidence of infection had dropped from 25 percent to less than one percent.

During their visit to Zanzibar Clinton experienced what may have been, for him, the trip's most affecting moment.

Returning from the stadium to Stone Town in vans, the former president and his group stopped at a building called ZAPHA House, where hundreds of men, women, and children awaited them. On the Muslim island, many of the women wore colorful headscarves and waved paper signs that read "Welcome!" and "ZAPHA." The two-story building was the home of ZAPHA+, once a tiny and beleaguered AIDS advocacy organization. He had first visited their office eight years earlier when his foundation was just starting to penetrate Tanzania with medicine, diagnostics, and moral support for the pandemic's victims. He had assured its members that he would stand by them, no matter what kind of social and government hostility they faced.

No longer stigmatized and no longer scared, the handful of women he met in 2005 had been joined since then by dozens of families, proudly showing off to Clinton and Chelsea their large new headquarters, where robust counseling and educational programs as well as treatment had taken root with CHAI's assistance. The "Zanzibar People HIV/AIDS Positive" weren't only living, they were thriving—and so were their children.

To see the impact of years of his foundation's work touched the former president, as it had in many other circumstances. But as he walked into the building's sunny courtyard, something else happened.

A sturdy teenager approached Clinton, holding in his hands a big, blown-up photograph. The picture, taken in July 2005 at the old offices of ZAPHA+, showed Clinton sitting on a chair, surrounded by children and clutching two of them on his lap, a boy and a girl. Grinning at Clinton, the teenager pointed to the boy in the picture. Eight years earlier, he had been that boy with AIDS—and he had lived because of the care and medicine brought to Zanzibar by CHAI.

Clinton stood before the boy, gazing at the picture in wonder as the throng of noisy kids gawked and yelled. Smiling broadly, he embraced the young man for several seconds, and then discreetly wiped his eyes.

––––––

Engine trouble with the Sun Country 737 delayed the Clinton delegation's departure from Zanzibar until after midnight, which meant arriving in Kigali hours later. But quite a show awaited them in the morning at a primary school in the Rwandan capital, starring Chelsea Clinton, with her father as straight man.

One of the largest, most enduring, and socially valuable obligations ever undertaken at Clinton Global Initiative had occurred at its opening conference in 2005, when Procter & Gamble—with annual sales over $20 billion, the world's largest household products company—signed a commitment to provide millions of liters of clean water to communities around the world. A year earlier, working with the federal Centers for Disease Control, the company's scientists had developed a simple nontoxic chemical powder that destroyed all water-borne bacteria, viruses, and protozoa. Using a four-ounce packet, anyone could transform ten liters of foul swamp bilge into clean, potable drinking water within minutes.

So pleased was P&G management with the results of their commitment that they continued to renew it annually, working through the foundation with relief organizations on every continent. In the summer of 2013, they had purified more than seven *billion* liters of water or, as Clinton liked to say, enough for every human being on the planet. To mark the occasion, Clinton and Chelsea delivered packets to a group of schoolchildren in Kigali, while representatives of P&G and the charity WorldVision demonstrated the remarkable product.

Standing in the schoolyard, children in blue and yellow uniforms lined up around a table to watch as Chelsea dumped a packet of powder into a clear plastic bucket of dark, sludgy water. She and her father took turns stirring the bucket with a large, long-handled spoon, and she jokingly nudged him when he seemed to slack off. In five minutes, all of the dirt had precipitated to the bottom, leaving crystal-clear water. But the powder was still working to kill off whatever traces of cholera, hepatitis, or worms might lurk, so they waited another twenty minutes. Then father and daughter each took a glass and, toasting each other, drank it down. Several of the children and a few of the braver adults in Clinton's delegation tried it, too, pronouncing the taste "not too bad."

The brew at the Rwanda Coffee Company factory, an impressive foundation project designed to market the country's superior beans while raising farmer incomes, tasted considerably better. They all drank it again that evening at a dinner hosted by President Paul Kagame, who was celebrating the latest Clinton project in his country, a comprehensive feeding program created by CHAI that was designed to ensure that infants received sufficient calories and nutrients from conception to the age of two.

It was one thing to hear about new programs that had yet to produce results, but something else to see living evidence of the foundation's concepts, commitments, and projects. That same afternoon in Kigali, the delegation met doctors from top American teaching hospitals who had come to Rwanda to work with physicians at the capital's Centre Hospitalier Universitaire de Kigali, which Clinton and Chelsea (and Magaziner, since it was part of a larger CHAI project called Human Resources for Health) had launched the year before.

The delegation toured the hospital, observing resident physicians as they performed procedures on simulator dolls and received clinical instruction on patient rounds. The project was an integral part of CHAI's broad and ambitious mission in Rwanda, working with Paul Farmer's Partners in Health group to build a modern health system.

The trip's remaining days were spent in South Africa, where the delegation first arrived in the tough, economically depressed Eastern Cape city of Port Elizabeth. There they visited the Ubuntu Education Fund, an oasis of innovative services for families and children, particularly those orphaned by AIDS.

Starting out with two friends who decided to distribute pens, pencils, and other academic supplies to poor children, Ubuntu had grown over more than a decade into a model for child development, with a "cradle to career" approach emphasizing the best possible health and education services. Its success had attracted a worldwide network of donors, led by South African natives like New York investment banker Vincent Mai. The impressive new building in Port Elizabeth that housed their programs was a CGI commitment.

On their final night in Africa, Clinton and Chelsea hosted "Embrace Tomorrow," a live-streamed "conversation about the future" with eight mostly young "change-makers"—a media event cosponsored by the Clinton Foundation and the Nelson Mandela Foundation. Although Mandela himself was not well enough to attend the event at the Pretoria Fairgrounds outside the capital, his chief aide, Zelda la Grange, was present, pacing nervously and talking on her cell phone until the event was under way. Speaking before a live audience, the conversation participants could have formed a CGI panel: a foundation director, a wealthy wireless executive, a young orphaned scholar from Ubuntu, a feminist refugee leader, and the CEO of the bank with the largest customer base in Africa.

The topic was quite vague—simply "the future"—but the conversation provided a showcase for the Mandela Foundation, for Clinton, and for Chelsea, gingerly stepping out of her parents' shadow to become a bona fide public figure.

But for Clinton and Magaziner, a real event earlier that afternoon had crystallized the difficult, often frustrating work of a decade in South Africa. With the delegation they had driven north from Johannesburg, getting lost once or twice, to find a rural village called Ramotse.

An old tribal facility dating from the apartheid era, the village clinic had been upgraded with CHAI funding to provide HIV/AIDS and tuberculosis treatment. As Clinton and Chelsea finally walked up the driveway to meet a crowd of hundreds of local residents who had waited two hours to see them, dozens of children clad in zebra-striped loincloths broke into traditional songs, played drums, and danced. The South African health minister, a medical doctor named Aaron Motsoaledi, had trekked out from Pretoria, joined by a carload of national and regional officials. "Because of your help," he said, "we are able to treat three and a half times more people than we used to."

The effusive minister's declaration was fairly accurate. Under Thabo Mbeki, Mandela's successor as president, the South African government had blocked CHAI from operating in the country with the world's largest HIV-infected population for years, costing perhaps a million lives. In 2003 Mbeki had relented, but the health ministry had never fully welcomed CHAI—and by 2009, only 700,000 people were on treatment there. The situation didn't improve until a new president, Jacob Zuma, replaced Mbeki.

Following CHAI's return to Pretoria in April 2010 with a contingent of fifty advisers, the government had tripled the number of people getting treatment and expected to reach well over three million by 2015. That was possible because the number of clinics and hospitals providing testing and medication had grown since 2010 from 495 to more than 3,500. One of those facilities was the Ramotse Clinic.

Through negotiations with manufacturers of drugs and diagnostics, CHAI had achieved savings of more than $1 billion for the government's AIDS program, and brought the most sophisticated TB testing into the country as well. But above all, they had at last reversed the trajectory of the pandemic on its largest front.

On the morning of August 8, Clinton and his guests visited one last CGI commitment in Johannesburg, part of a Coca-Cola company project called 5by20 that counseled very small-scale female entrepreneurs—in this instance, a group of women who ran food stalls at the bus station. Their work looked very hard, and their appliances looked old. The women explained cheerfully how the kind ladies from Coca-Cola had taught them to know their products, know their customers, and always be friendly; the advisers had showed them how to manage their finances carefully, and even tipped them off about selling lunch combination plates.

The company had enrolled them in the 5by20 program, pledged to help five million women by 2020, because they belonged to its "value chain." That meant they sold Coke—and as the lunchtime crowd began to stream in, that was what they did.

That night, the delegation flew back to New York on the Sun Country jet, exhausted but exhilarated. Clinton had brought them to an Africa tourists never saw. He had showed them what he and his partners were trying to do there—and how they might feel if they joined him.

———

Chelsea had performed with aplomb in Africa, winning media plaudits as she moved into the spotlight next to her parents. But as with them, the press remained more interested in political ambitions than humanitarian endeavors. While she was traveling, a flurry of comical speculation over her potential future as a candidate erupted in *Politico*, CNN.com, and the *Washington Post* political blog, which published "Where Chelsea Could Run," a post closely analyzing the residency requirements for a New York City Council seat in her Manhattan district.

Lacking the desire to run for any office, she found such stories, which repeated in a continuous cycle, to be pointless and slightly frustrating. "I wish that someone wanted to talk about diarrhea and why I think we really have the chance to eradicate diarrhea, even before every country across the African continent or across the world has strong public health systems of sanitation and clean water," she said. "Yes, I

wish the mainstream media were interested in things like our growing work in diarrhea, or the work that we're doing in agriculture or the
work we're doing on HIV/AIDS and how important that is."

Her annoyance notwithstanding, most of the profiles that appeared
in the weeks and months following her sojourn in Africa were flattering—and more important, took her seriously. The story that appeared
in *Glamour* provoked the *Washington Post* media critic to write a blog
item headlined "5 Hilarious Excerpts from Glamour's Puff Piece on
Chelsea Clinton."

The positive coverage could only help, considering the harsh deadline confronted by her father, Dennis Cheng, and the foundation staff
as they raced to raise an endowment. During the fall season, they had
slated a series of big-ticket fundraising parties and events across the
country and as far afield as London. The explicit goal was to secure the
future, beyond Bill Clinton's own lifespan.

"We had to have another way to raise the funds that we need in
order to keep the lights on," explained Bruce Lindsey in a press statement. "You cannot continue to rely upon a single individual to raise all
the money you need to raise on a yearly basis. First of all, it is unbelievably grueling on President Clinton, and second of all, if anything were to
happen to him, it would end." But they needed to get it done before anyone might need to raise money for a presidential campaign, just in case.

———

The clearest signal of what another presidential candidacy would por-
tend for the Clinton Foundation arrived on August 14, when the *New
York Times* published a front-page story under an ominous headline: "Unease at Clinton Foundation over Finances and Ambitions." In
nearly three thousand words, *Times* reporters Nicholas Confessore and
Amy Chozick outlined a view of the foundation that emphasized every
embarrassing tidbit they had been able to uncover, including plenty of
anonymous gossip.

The story's opening paragraphs suggested that the foundation had
been financially mismanaged and possibly misused for personal enrichment—themes that Hillary Clinton's critics on the right would immediately amplify and exaggerate, just as they had done with the *Times*
investigation of the Whitewater land deal decades earlier.

Alluding to the Simpson Thacher report, the *Times* scolded:

> For all of its successes, the Clinton Foundation had become a sprawling concern, supervised by a rotating board of old Clinton hands, vulnerable to distraction and threatened by conflicts of interest. It ran multimillion-dollar deficits for several years, despite vast amounts of money flowing in.
>
> And concern was rising inside and outside the organization about Douglas J. Band, a onetime personal assistant to Mr. Clinton who had started a lucrative corporate consulting firm—which Mr. Clinton joined as a paid adviser—while overseeing the Clinton Global Initiative, the foundation's glitzy annual gathering of chief executives, heads of state, and celebrities.

The article didn't dwell on the successes of the foundation, but emphasized the disputes between Band and Magaziner, and their clash over management and budget issues. Evidently the notion that disagreement and anger might occur in a worldwide organization, with thousands of employees and big personalities, shocked *Times* editors (who had been irked when other publications reveled in similar scuttlebutt about the paper's executive editor Jill Abramson and her relationships with colleagues).

The *Times* also revealed that the Clinton Global Initiative had once paid to fly Natalie Portman "and her beloved Yorkie" to a CGI University gathering, first-class—"according to two former foundation employees"—and that unnamed sources also recalled how Magaziner had once reclined on a conference table when in pain from back spasms, "snapping at an employee."

More substantively, the article identified Band as the nexus of worrisome "conflicts of interest." But instead of outlining any actual conflict—meaning a specific action that benefited him while harming the foundation—the article merely listed a few Teneo clients, including Coca-Cola, UBS, and Standard Chartered Bank. Those firms had also donated money as CGI sponsors. Indeed, at first glance it would seem that Band's relationships with corporate leaders had benefited CGI and the foundation, since he had encouraged them to donate if they weren't doing so already.

How those actions had compromised the foundation or harmed anyone at all, the *Times* failed to explain. The article noted that during the 2012 CGI conference, Coca-Cola chairman Muhtar Kent "won a coveted spot on the dais with Mr. Clinton, discussing the company's partnership with another nonprofit to use its distributors to deliver medical goods to patients in Africa," as if the beverage giant had attained that glorious moment by hiring Teneo. Yet it didn't mention Coke's multiple CGI commitments, or its pathbreaking agreement with the Alliance for a Healthier Generation to slash shipments of sugary drinks to public schools—any of which would have earned its chairman a turn in the CGI spotlight.

Just as troubling as the backstairs backbiting, however, were its assertions about the Clinton Foundation's finances:

> In 2007 and 2008, the foundation also found itself competing against Mrs. Clinton's presidential campaign for donors amid a recession. Millions of dollars in contributions intended to seed an endowment were diverted to other programs, creating tension between Mr. Magaziner and Mr. Band. The foundation piled up a $40 million deficit during those two years, according to tax returns. Last year, it ran more than $8 million in the red.

In an open letter posted on the foundation's website, Clinton himself responded to those claims. The *Times* reporters, he wrote, had misunderstood how nonprofits are required to report their cash flows on the Form 990 documents that they file annually with the Internal Revenue Service.

According to the former president:

> When someone makes a multi-year commitment to the Foundation, we have to report it all in the year it was made. In 2005 and 2006, as a result of multi-year commitments, the Foundation reported a surplus of $102,800,000, though we collected nowhere near that.
>
> In later years, as the money came in to cover our budgets, we were required to report the spending but not the cash inflow. Also, if someone makes a commitment that he or she later has

to withdraw, we are required to report that as a loss, though we never had the money in the first place and didn't need it to meet our budget.

In other words, the "deficits" in 2007 and 2008 were at least partially offset by earlier commitments. Moreover, as Clinton's letter also noted, he had set aside substantial cash reserves that hedged against the financial crash and recession—leaving him able to maintain the foundation's service to HIV/AIDS patients, mothers and children, and other vulnerable groups despite a historic recession that proved devastating to many charities and businesses. If anyone understood the vicissitudes of fundraising, and how to hedge against them, surely Clinton did.

In a country that had seen stunning mismanagement, corruption, and deception at such major charities as the Red Cross and the United Way (whose late chairman William Aramony had been convicted and sent to prison for myriad abuses), the Clinton Foundation's problems were in no way scandalous. But the Clintons and their associates had long been held to a harsher standard in the national media.

Immediately, *Times* op-ed columnist Maureen Dowd showed how the Clintons' most embittered critics would interpret the paper's investigation, filing a column filled with far-fetched contentions.

"If Americans are worried about money in politics, there is no larger concern than the Clintons," she wrote, as if nobody had ever heard of the Koch brothers or the dark-money machinery operated by former White House political boss Karl Rove. Teneo was "an egregious nest of conflicts," she exclaimed excitedly, without naming any actual conflict. "We are supposed to believe," Dowd sneered, "that every dollar given to a Clinton is a dollar that improves the world." Of course that wasn't a claim the Clintons had ever made—but Dowd set an unrealistic standard for them that no political figure could meet.

———

If there was no scandal at the Clinton Foundation, its absence wouldn't discourage any would-be critic from using the term freely. As Clinton himself had noted in the past, any story featured on the *Times* front page could establish a narrative that permanently inflected other media coverage—in this case, by encouraging anonymous critics to depict Doug Band as a self-serving schemer.

Just before CGI convened its annual meeting on September 23, the *New Republic* dropped its new issue, featuring a cover story with a sensational headline: "Scandal at Clinton, Inc.: How Doug Band Drove a Wedge Through a Political Dynasty." The magazine had published maddeningly inaccurate stories designed to damage the Clintons in the distant past, and its new management seemed equally hostile.

Written by Alec MacGillis, the article was presented as investigative reporting, but the first half of its nearly nine thousand words was more of an innocuous profile, sprinkled with anonymous quotes about Band's sometimes engaging, sometimes prickly personality. It disclosed that to keep Band on staff, rather than let him wander off to a more lucrative job, Clinton had authorized Ron Burkle to engage him as an adviser and supplement his salary. It noted that Band had created CGI, and quoted Paul Begala, John Podesta, and others praising him, on the record.

MacGillis acknowledged forthrightly that "the good [the foundation] achieves is undeniable. . . . It has formed partnerships with multinationals and wealthy individuals to distribute billions of dollars all over the globe. Its many innovative projects include efforts to lower the costs of medicines in developing nations and reduce greenhouse-gas emissions in major cities."

But, he added vaguely, "it's hard to shake the sense that it's not all about saving the world. There's an undertow of transactionalism in the glittering annual dinners, the fixation on celebrity, and a certain contingent of donors whose charitable contributions and business interests occupy an uncomfortable proximity." Of course, many charities depend on gala events and endorsements by celebrities—who increasingly launch their own nonprofits, whether for commercial publicity, saintly devotion, or just a tax deduction.

No scandal there, but the story's second half included several damaging charges, starting with an anonymous quote that described Band as "a gatekeeper who charged tolls." Yet the article offered no evidence that he had ever shaken down anyone who wanted to see Clinton. It noted that at least one foundation donor, a businessman named Victor Dahdaleh, had been indicted by British authorities for allegedly paying a bribe in Bahrain (charges that were later dropped). It mentioned the *Times* coverage of Frank Giustra, without mentioning the errors uncovered by *Fortune* magazine. It revisited the Follieri affair at length.

But the nub of its complaint did not appear until near the end. According to those anonymous sources, Band and his partner, Declan Kelly, had founded Teneo on the premise that they could charge tolls for access to Clinton indefinitely, and keep raising the price. While conceding "it was only natural that Band would tap his existing network," the article emphasized "the extent to which Teneo's business model depends on [Band's] relationship with Clinton," and quoted a "longtime Clinton associate" claiming that "Band's pitch to clients was that he was 'able to fly around [with Clinton] and decide who flies around with him. . . . The whole thing is resting on his access.'"

In due course, however, that premise proved to be entirely wrong. When the *New Republic* article appeared in the fall of 2013, Band's communication with Clinton already had diminished. Raising three children in New York, he hadn't traveled with the former president for several years. With Chelsea Clinton running the foundation, his influence there was long behind him, too. And nevertheless, even though all of its corporate clients knew that Band no longer worked with Clinton and spoke with him far less often than before, Teneo grew even more quickly.

So quickly, in fact, that a year after the *New York Times* and *New Republic* articles appeared, the major private equity firm BC Partners invested hundreds of millions of dollars to acquire a minority share of the firm. By then Band and his partners had drawn up plans to develop a dozen divisions, from executive recruitment to corporate governance, business acquisitions, public relations, and strategic planning.

The firm had a sports advisory division, too, called Teneo Sports—which, in July 2014, announced the signing of its first four athlete clients: basketball superstars LeBron James, Kobe Bryant, and Michael Jordan, and the Irish golf champion Graeme McDowell. None of them had signed up with Teneo because of Bill Clinton.

————

Notwithstanding the negative media coverage that rippled out from the *New York Times* and *New Republic* articles, both Bill and Hillary

Clinton continued to collect honors and awards as well as speaking fees. That spring they had returned to Little Rock for a ceremony that marked the renaming of the city's newly renovated airport, which would be known as Bill and Hillary Clinton National Airport.

In September, the National Constitution Center in Philadelphia bestowed its Liberty Medal on Hillary, in an atmosphere where her eventual presidential candidacy seemed to be taken for granted. The Constitution Center's chair, former Florida governor Jeb Bush, quipped, "Hillary and I come from different political parties, and we disagree about a few things, but we do agree on the wisdom of the American people—especially those in Iowa and New Hampshire and South Carolina." University of Pennsylvania president Amy Gutmann spoke rapturously of "something many of us can't wait to celebrate: the first woman president of the United States." Mayor Michael Nutter, a black Democrat, bluntly predicted that first female would be Hillary. "And I assume," he added, "that she will take President Clinton along with her."

Celebrating its one hundredth anniversary in October, the Harvard School of Public Health presented its Centennial Medal to Bill Clinton, along with Dr. Jim Yong Kim, the president of the World Bank and cofounder with Paul Farmer of Partners in Health, and Gro Harlem Brundtland, the former Norwegian prime minister and director general of the World Health Organization. It was a Harvard public health expert who once had urged Magaziner to drop the idea of AIDS treatment in the developing countries. More than a decade later, the school honored Clinton for ignoring that advice. And in his remarks, he stressed the cooperation between his foundation and the school, which had recently sent doctors to train their counterparts at Rwanda's teaching hospital.

A week before Thanksgiving, Clinton returned to the White House to receive the nation's highest civilian honor, the Medal of Freedom, from Barack Obama, who also hung the medal on fifteen other distinguished Americans, including Oprah Winfrey, Gloria Steinem, Loretta Lynn, Ben Bradlee, and Ernie Banks. "This is one of my favorite events every year," said Obama. "And this year, it's a little more special because it marks the 50th anniversary of President Kennedy establishing this award." Reviewing the recipients, he spoke of Clinton last, thanking

him for his advice, "on and off the golf course . . . and, most importantly, for your life-saving work around the world, which represents the
very best in America."

Afterward, Clinton and Obama went out to Arlington Cemetery
with members of the Kennedy family to mark the upcoming fiftieth anniversary of the assassination of John F. Kennedy at the gravesite shared
with his wife, Jackie. It was a cold day but the sun was shining as the
two presidents escorted Ethel Kennedy, wife of President Kennedy's
slain brother Robert, to the gravesite and helped her to lay a wreath.

———

Wherever Clinton went, he could not escape the question of his wife's
presidential ambitions. On December 8, when Clinton Global Initiative
held its first overseas conference since 2009 in Rio de Janeiro, featuring
Brazilian president Dilma Rousseff, he agreed to an interview with Fu-
sion TV's volatile host and correspondent Jorge Ramos.

"You know, I have to ask you this question. . . . So let's just get it out
of the way. So is she running or do you know if she's running?"

"No," replied Clinton, in a tone that signaled irritation. "I don't."

"You don't know?" Ramos asked.

"No," said Clinton. "She's trying to finish her book," a memoir of her
State Department experiences. "She's gotten several projects up and
going with our foundation. And she believes and I believe that the four-
year campaign mania is a big mistake. . . . We should work on the business at hand . . ."

Taking a swipe at the *New York Times*, which had already assigned
reporters, two years before the election, to cover Hillary's campaign, or
proto-campaign, or not-yet-campaign, he continued.

"You know," Clinton said, "we have newspapers that have people
devoted to doing nothing but covering a campaign that doesn't exist.
So then they have to decide to create stories. You know, we don't need
that. We need to focus—the American people have economic and other
challenges. And our region and world have challenges. We should be
focused on those things. And that's what Hillary thinks too."

Almost instantly a volley of sarcastic comments flew out from the
Times, where reporters didn't appreciate Clinton's excursion into media
criticism or his suggestion that they were inventing stories. "If HRC

doesn't want to be covered as a likely 2016 candidate, she could just say she's not running," tweeted Nicholas Confessore, one of the authors of the *Times*'s foundation story. "Crazy idea!" responded Amy Chozick, whose byline had also graced that article—and who had been assigned to cover Hillary.

But all of the snarking and sniping in both directions was beside the point. Only days into the New Year, Maggie Haberman filed a long report in *Politico* about Hillary and the "shadow campaign on her behalf" that had been gathering momentum for at least six months. Six months earlier, according to Haberman, Hillary had listened quietly to a presentation by consultants from Dewey Square Group, where her old friend Minyon Moore worked. Her story reviewed the jockeying and prepping by a pair of super PACs, Ready for Hillary and Priorities USA, media groups, and a crew of Clinton loyalists waiting for her signal. These organizations all had at least her tacit approval.

Just below the surface, in fact, the first scouting missions and partisan skirmishes of 2016 were already occurring. In early February, a right-wing website called the *Washington Free Beacon* released a set of documents its researchers had discovered in the archives of the University of Arkansas, including notes, memos, and letters that had belonged to the late Diane Blair, one of Hillary's closest friends. There was little news, beyond Hillary's fretting over the "bimbo eruptions" of the White House years and a private reference to Monica Lewinsky as "a narcissistic loony toon."

But the story got wide circulation—there was nothing the national media relished more than revisiting the Lewinsky scandal—and showed just how early and how deeply their adversaries would dig to undermine the Clintons.

Although Clinton could hardly deny the presidential aspirations that his wife and her supporters still nurtured, he wasn't entirely wrong to question the journalistic obsession with an election that would not begin for at least another year. The nation and the world had bigger, more urgent problems that preoccupied him. And Hillary would leave her momentous decision aside for months. But there was nothing that she, he, or anyone else could do to change the media mind-set that kept his wife's future at the top of the agenda—and in fact, they and their friends had done little to discourage the endless speculation.

———

For Bill Clinton there were certainly more pressing events than a presidential election that still seemed far away—including the tenth anniversary of the opening of the Clinton Presidential Center, and the tenth annual conference of the Clinton Global Initiative, both occurring in autumn 2014.

The library anniversary promised to be a celebration of Clinton's contribution to the life and growth of his old hometown, which had seen tourism, tax revenues, and cultural life grow enormously during that decade. There would be music and barbecue, lectures, panels, tours, and at least a week of more or less related events around the city, in remembrance of that miserable rain-soaked day when the library welcomed its first guests. Bringing off the event would require much preparation, skill, and expense, but it wasn't difficult to determine what should be done.

Marking ten years of CGI was a different challenge for an event that would take place, as always, in the world media capital of New York. What was there to say about CGI after ten years? It had long since proved itself as an innovative model, helping to move the worlds of philanthropy, corporate social responsibility, and nonprofit ventures toward entrepreneurial cooperation. Indeed, it had nudged the World Economic Forum—the place where Doug Band had conceived CGI as a kind of protest—to renovate itself as a more action-oriented event. It even had inspired dozens of new events and activist discussions around the annual September meeting of the UN General Assembly, which had formerly stimulated little more than a frenzy of cocktail parties. By 2014, CGI had outlasted the unique quality that made it so significant, even if Clinton's presence as host remained a powerful draw.

But there was a deeper issue that haunted CGI. Despite all of the quarterly and annual reports from its "action networks" and diligent staff, did anyone know what the thousands of commitments, valued in tens of billions of dollars, had actually accomplished? How many of the commitment makers, praised with such enthusiasm by Clinton every September, had achieved what they pledged to do? How many had failed? And whether they succeeded or failed, did anyone know why?

In the wonkish environment of the Clinton Foundation, where

Chelsea valued data streams and measurements, and Eric Braverman brought a complementary worldview from McKinsey, these were questions to attempt to answer, not avoid. They were certain to be asked by other people when the tenth conference opened, which suggested strongly that it would be better to look for the answers first.

The upshot was a formidable attempt to collect and analyze all of the information about CGI commitments that had flowed into its offices since the first conference in 2005—a data-mining task well beyond the foundation's own capacity. The job was outsourced to Palantir Technologies, a software giant based in Palo Alto, California, that specializes in solving "big data" problems for major corporations, hedge funds, and banks. The Pentagon and several U.S. intelligence and counterterrorism agencies had used its software programs continuously since its founding in 2004.

Although Palantir's biggest shareholder was the libertarian investor Peter Thiel, its management was friendly to the Clintons and had enlisted as a CGI member years earlier. Palantir had maintained contact with the CGI staff through its own commitment to improve disaster relief with "philanthropy engineering," a method of using computer technology to more effectively harness volunteers who showed up to help victims of hurricanes, earthquakes, and similar catastrophes.

The Palantir commitments study required months of work and no small expense, yet the company performed all the work pro bono. When CGI unveiled the results at the annual conference in September, they were revealing and highly instructive.

Of nearly 2,900 commitments made between 2005 and 2013, nearly 42 percent, or 1,202, had been completed. Just below 40 percent, or 1,145, were still being executed. Only 46 commitments, or 1.6 percent, were deemed to be "stalled," and 139, or just below 5 percent, were marked as unsuccessful. Roughly 12 percent were considered "inactive," because the commitment makers had not reported to CGI for at least two years. (While the inactive commitments could be reactivated, their removal from the portfolio and metrics represented an effort to keep the data honest.)

The Palantir analysis went deeper in a search for clues to what had made some commitments successful and others fail. What the most productive commitments shared in common was a partnership model that paired a nonprofit with a corporation, as in Procter & Gamble's work on providing clean water through charities like WorldVision and ChildFund. What the failed commitments shared in nearly every instance was that they ran out of money.

Other intriguing data points were highlighted in the Palantir report. Over the years, direct monetary donations had declined rapidly as a form of commitment, while "cross-sector" collaborations between corporation and nonprofit participants had increased. The countries with the largest number of commitments were India, Kenya, and the United States (where the numbers had probably been inflated by CGI America). Some findings seemed obvious, such as the spike in commitments that occurred in Haiti following the hurricanes of 2008 and the 2010 earthquake; other spikes could be traced to a focus on particular issues, such as those oriented to helping women and girls after CGI emphasized their issues in 2009.

Clinton, Chelsea, and the CGI team felt no shame in the failures—not even the big ones, like the disappointing result of Richard Branson's promise to invest $3 billion in clean energy. Branson had spent less than a tenth of that amount. Writing in *The Guardian* a week before CGI opened, Naomi Klein had denounced the Branson commitment as a prime example of "corporate greenwashing," noting that the flamboyant billionaire himself had lately characterized it as a "gesture." Her reporting showed that even as his investments in a new green fuel languished, his aviation empire had spent hundreds of millions of dollars vastly expanding its operations—and its carbon emissions. Even if he had been entirely sincere in 2006, Branson's spectacular failure indicated that relying on "green capitalism" to save the earth might well prove disastrous.

Aside from the harsh lesson of Branson, there was much else to be learned from all the commitments that fell short, as Chelsea said in a brief video that accompanied the report's release. But the rate of reported accomplishment was impressive—a much higher average, as *Forbes* social entrepreneurship columnist Tom Watson remarked, than the survival rate for start-up ventures. Did that mean the CGI members weren't taking enough risks?

———

Having endured the fire of intense "scandal" coverage as he left the White House, and watched how that scorching heat drove away donors, speeches, and money, the negative media coverage prompted by Hillary's political profile made Bill Clinton nervous. Raising $250 million for the foundation endowment would be difficult even in a favorable media environment, but reporters didn't usually look for happy stories. Amazingly, given how much coverage CGI tended to get every year, the positive findings in the Palantir report on CGI had received little attention from American newspapers or broadcast outlets.

But when the donation figures for 2013 were added up, the summaries showed that the endowment campaign led by Dennis Cheng had performed exceptionally well. Total donations had risen from $51.5 million in 2012 to $144.4 million in 2013, according to the foundation's tax documents. The enormous increase partly reflected the consolidation of CGI back into the Bill, Hillary & Chelsea Clinton Foundation. Big donors had played a big part, with nine donors accounting for $64 million, including four who gave more than $9 million each and one who gave $15 million alone.

The spate of bad press had done little to damage the foundation or its namesakes. But as the presidential election drew nearer, their opponents on the right opened a new phase of investigation into Hillary, the foundation, and her husband, backed by millions of dollars from wealthy Republicans who were determined to defeat her, by any and every means necessary.

CHAPTER NINETEEN

In the concluding weeks of 2014, the likelihood that Hillary Clinton would again seek the Democratic presidential nomination became a certainty, although political observers had merely awaited the formality of an official announcement since September—when she and Bill Clinton showed up at their friend Tom Harkin's annual "steak fry" on a farm in Indianola, Iowa. Although the setting was picturesque and the event, in its own way, historic—as the last beef-based fundraiser hosted by the retiring Democratic senator after thirty-seven years—the presumed presidential front-runner neither confirmed nor denied her aspiration.

"It's true, I'm thinking about it," she said, still a bit coy—but then, at the end of a short speech about the travails of the middle class, she dropped a stronger hint. "It's really great to be back," she told the thousands of party activists in the crowd. "Let's not let another seven years go by."

By December, the hotly debated question in Clinton circles was when she should declare her candidacy—no later than spring 2015, was the knowing consensus among friends and former aides. Setting a date was at the top of the decisions she pondered in Chappaqua, holding daily seminars with former aides on the enormous changes in the political and media environment since 2008.

Before a new campaign could begin, the converging narratives of her political career and her husband's philanthropic activism had to be harmonized. The Clinton Foundation and all its disparate initiatives were sure to come under the harshest, most hostile, and partisan scrutiny ever as a consequence of her candidacy. To whatever extent possible, any discordant news from that quarter had to be minimized, including the management disputes that had roiled the foundation from time to time over the years.

Those disagreements had not ended with the elevation of Bruce Lindsey to board chairman and his replacement as CEO by Eric

Braverman in July 2013. While Braverman's effort to implement the recommendations of the Simpson Thacher management review had succeeded in large measure, those changes had come at a high cost to him. He had incurred the enmity of Lindsey and Magaziner, among others, who privately derided him as a "bureaucrat" who didn't understand how the organization worked.

Concerns about the foundation's direction and leadership resulted in a curious series of events leading into the election cycle. At its December 2014 meeting, the board voted to engage Simpson Thacher to conduct a follow-up review of the foundation's operations, and to hire Nygren Consulting, a California firm, to evaluate the performance of Magaziner and recommend whether and how to end CHAI's separate status, bringing it back into the foundation.

During the same meeting, the board commended Braverman by approving a salary of $395,000 for him, plus housing allowance, and an extension of his seat on the board until 2017. (The CEO's tenure had been the subject of a separate Nygren evaluation during the fall of 2014 that was never released or leaked.)

The December meeting was an ominous moment for Magaziner, who had already clashed with Braverman over the Clinton Climate Initiative. Both he and Clinton had been very excited about the possibilities for progress on renewable energy—in the absence of serious action by national and international authorities—by organizing and assisting the world's biggest cities to act together in what was called the C40.

Running the C40 scheme was complicated, very expensive, and exceeded the resources and capacity of the Clinton Foundation alone. In 2011, Magaziner lost control of the cities project when Michael Bloomberg's foundation invested tens of millions of dollars and assumed control of it after a negotiation with Bruce Lindsey that excluded him.

The Clinton Climate Initiative had continued to operate a forestry project and a project assisting small island nations in reducing their use of fossil fuels and changing to renewable energy sources. But not long after Braverman arrived, he had appointed a new director of the Climate Initiative, with support from Clinton, to displace Magaziner, who believed that the attempt to roll CHAI into the foundation represented another step in the same direction.

Within days, however, the internal debate over the fate of CHAI was overshadowed by the surprise resignation of Braverman, who evidently had grown weary of dealing with resistance and criticism he considered unfair. Whether he was pushed out or quit was never clear. On January 9, the foundation press office announced his resignation and released anodyne quotes from him and the Clintons.

"In the last few years, all the initiatives and programs have worked together to make the Clinton Foundation even stronger, and now is the right time for a new leader to take the foundation into the future," Braverman said, according to the press release. "When Eric came onboard, the foundation had been growing quickly for more than a decade," said a statement attributed to all of the Clintons. "Our individual initiatives were doing well, but Eric's leadership helped us improve our governance structure, increase coordination across the foundation and build better internal processes. We are very grateful to Eric for his leadership and these efforts."

Maura Pally, the Hillary aide overseeing her foundation projects, was named interim chief executive as the board began a search for Braverman's successor.

The consultant reviews ordered by the board were on a very tight schedule, with reports and recommendations due by February. Over Christmas and into the New Year, foundation and consulting staff had worked overtime to schedule interviews and provide documentation. The report on Magaziner echoed many of the complaints heard years earlier from Band and Lindsey, characterizing him as "disdainful" and not transparent in his dealings with the CHAI directors, especially Bill and Chelsea Clinton.

While the report also praised Magaziner as a "visionary" whose ideas had a "transformational" impact on global public health, its interviews with present and former CHAI staff included unflattering descriptions of his style as "intimidating," "abrasive," and "arrogant." It laid blame for "unhealthy" tensions between CHAI and the Clinton Foundation on him.

Magaziner regarded the Nygren report as a renewed attempt to oust him—the first since CHAI had been spun off in January 2010 and renamed the Clinton Health Access Initiative. His alarm grew when he learned that the consultants had been tasked to consider how an eventual "successor" to him might be found.

It surprised nobody that he and the CHAI managers who reported to him were determined to resist any attempt to return control of their operations to the Clinton Foundation board. Four dozen of the top managers at CHAI sent Bill Clinton a letter to that effect in late January, voicing their worries about the political and financial impact of such a change.

The Nygren and Simpson Thacher reports were delivered in a strained atmosphere at the Clinton Foundation's March board meeting. Tempers rose over the Nygren review, which Magaziner denounced as unfair. The Simpson Thacher report's findings shed more favorable light on Magaziner and CHAI, describing the initiative as well managed and noting its rapid growth, programmatic successes, and the independent audits of its finances by major donors such as the Gates Foundation. In the weeks after the March meeting, Magaziner and Clinton met privately and agreed to "let it all calm down." That agreement would hold until after the 2016 election.

In the meantime, the question of institutional authority had been resolved. With her father's encouragement, Chelsea had recruited retiring University of Miami president Donna Shalala, an old friend who had served for eight years as secretary of health and human services in the Clinton administration.

At seventy-five, the experienced Shalala didn't qualify as new blood, but she certainly knew her way around the personalities and politics of the Clintons' world—and the family trusted her. Despite controversies over staff unionization and athletics, her tenure in Miami was considered highly successful, bringing billions of dollars in new donations to the university and raising its national academic ranking in the *U.S. News & World Report* college survey from 67 to 47.

Word about Shalala had leaked to the press while board consultations on the choice were proceeding, during a Clinton Global Initiative University conference at her school in early March. A press release from the foundation confirmed the choice, noting that she wouldn't start in New York until late summer, when she was scheduled to step down from the university position she had held for fourteen years.

In announcing the appointment, Bill Clinton said, "I don't know in my long life that I've ever worked with anybody that has quite the same combination of policy knowledge and concern, political skills, a personal touch with people and a sense of innate fairness that inspires confidence across political, regional, economic, and psychological lines. She's a remarkable person."

Yet if the prospect of Donna Shalala's leadership promised stability for the foundation, Hillary Clinton's looming presidential campaign assured the opposite. A loud collision between politics and philanthropy, which had coexisted awkwardly for years, was now inevitable.

―――――

During the four years that Hillary served as secretary of state, few questions were asked about any conflict between her official responsibilities and her husband's charitable and business ventures. The arrangements reached at the outset between the Obama administration and the Clintons with respect to foundation donors, paid speeches, and restrictions on CGI seemed to have satisfied almost everyone who had expressed an ethical concern.

When the *New York Times Magazine* published a Bill Clinton profile in May 2009, the story's nearly eight thousand words discussed his proficiency at crossword puzzles and his "Oh Hell" habit, but scarcely mentioned any issue between her job and his enterprises, except to say that while some Obama White House advisers had initially worried about him, "to their surprise, [Bill] Clinton has done nothing to complicate Obama's life so far."

In the wake of Clinton's North Korea rescue mission, a few commentators had alluded to a potential problem, but only at very low volume. And later, when the foundation published its donors every year, in apparent adherence to its agreement with Obama, news stories noted, without alarm, that several of the largest were foreign governments such as Australia and Norway.

Almost nobody seemed to care, in short, despite Hillary's powerful influence on American foreign policy—and had she not been a viable candidate for president, it is possible that almost nobody ever would have cared about the donors or the speeches.

When her candidacy became more probable than possible, however, the press revived those questions—and suddenly discovered problems that nobody had noticed for four years. Months before Hillary announced that she was running for president, stories about the foundation's foreign donors began to appear again in major news outlets. The first report appeared in the *Wall Street Journal* on February 17.

Based on a search of the donor listings on the foundation website, the *Journal* found that countries including Oman, the United Arab Emirates, Saudi Arabia, Qatar, Germany, the Netherlands, and—as previously reported—Australia, Canada, and Norway had donated millions of dollars over the years. According to the *Journal*, the total in foreign donations amounted to $48 million.

All of that data, as not many observers noticed, had been posted voluntarily, since the foundation was no longer obligated to reveal any of its donors after Hillary stepped down from the State Department. The foundation had ended the limitation on foreign contributions that held while she had served—but had also continued to disclose its donors, foreign and domestic, unlike other foundations and charities.

The *Journal*'s unsurprising revelations spurred competitors to follow its lead; within two days, the McClatchy Newspapers and the *Washington Post* both published original stories on the foundation's donors, with an emphasis on donations from abroad. Each sliced the data in various directions, expanding outward from the focus on foreign governments. McClatchy found that of the 168 donors giving more than $1 million each, at least seventy were foreign individuals or entities; and of the seven top donors that had given more than $25 million, four were foreign. The *Post* indicated that of donors who had given more than $1 million, a third were foreign governments or "other entities based outside the United States."

Both stories suggested that the prevalence of foreign donations would harm Hillary politically, without regard to their humanitarian use. According to the *Post*, the foundation's foreign donors had essentially circumvented the ban on foreign contributions to political campaigns, while the McClatchy story quoted a pollster saying that her association with "big bucks" would likely alienate her from middle-class voters.

On February 20, the *New York Times* published an editorial, titled "Separate Philanthropy from Political Clout," that opened with a paean to the former president's good works. "The Clinton Foundation has become one of the world's major generators of charity, mobilizing global efforts to confront issues like health, climate change, economic development and equality for women and girls." The editorial called on Hillary to reinstate the ban on foreign contributors, "who might have matters of concern to bring before a future Clinton administration." The same could be said of domestic contributors, of course, and the *Times* didn't explore the distinction.

"No critic has alleged a specific conflict of interest," the editorial stipulated, which was true as of that moment. "The foundation, in fact, went beyond normal philanthropic bounds for transparency six years ago in instituting voluntary disclosure of donors within broad dollar ranges on its website. But this very information can feed criticism." That too was true; indeed, all of the criticism so far had been fed solely by the foundation's commitment to continued disclosure of its donors.

The editorial concluded by urging Hillary to "reassure the public that the foundation will not become a vehicle for insiders' favoritism, should she run for and win the White House. Restoring the restrictions on foreign donors would be a good way to make this point as Mrs. Clinton's widely expected campaign moves forward."

Aside from this naive recommendation—which, if enacted, would have deprived millions of people of life-saving medicine, among other needs—the editorial was fair and reasonable. But the coverage of the Clinton Foundation, its finances and its namesakes, would soon change direction, abruptly and sharply, in the newspaper of record and elsewhere.

That shift would begin on page one of the *New York Times*.

———

Late in the afternoon on Sunday, April 12, Hillary's nascent campaign released a soft-sell, two-minute video ad that featured vignettes of ordinary but diverse Americans, talking about their changing lives and their futures. Just before the end, the smiling candidate appeared on-screen to say, "I'm getting ready to do something too. I'm running for president. . . . Americans have fought their way back from tough economic times, but the deck is still stacked in favor of those at the top. Everyday Americans need a champion. And I want to be that champion."

Within the next two hours, the board members and staff of the Clinton Foundation received a personal email from Hillary, informing them that she would be resigning from the board, effective immediately, to devote her full effort to the campaign. "As I step down from that position, I know that I am leaving the Foundation in great hands," she wrote. "I am equally as excited that Chelsea will continue to lead the Foundation's mission with Bill, building upon our family's commitment to help all people live their best life story."

Beneath that cheerful message, however, both the candidate and the institution that she was leaving behind were increasingly under siege from their traditional critics in the media and on the right. In the weeks before her announcement, newspapers and airwaves had been filled with stories about her use of a personal email account—instead of an account in the State Department's state.gov domain—that questioned her motivations, probity, and adherence to laws and regulations.

Her decision to unilaterally delete thousands of emails that she deemed "private," before releasing the remainder for archiving by the federal government, had inflamed the controversy. Instantly labeled "Hillary's email scandal," it would balloon into a Justice Department investigation that haunted her campaign into the 2016 primaries and beyond.

Eventually Hillary would publicly apologize for using her private email address for government business, which violated the spirit of transparency she professed to honor. What irritated her supporters was that so many Republicans had done the same, or much worse, while escaping the censure she endured.

Several of the Republican presidential prospects—and many Republicans in Congress—had used personal email accounts for public business without drawing much or any scrutiny. And Hillary's offense scarcely compared with the Bush administration's monumental email fiasco, when millions of messages went missing from White House servers—and millions more were never recorded on those servers at all, as required under the 1978 Presidential Records Act, because dozens of White House staff were using private accounts provided by the Republican National Committee.

Among the RNC email clients had been Bush political adviser Karl Rove and his staff, who had used those accounts to communicate with the office of crooked lobbyist Jack Abramoff. Backup tapes containing all the Bush White House emails for the administration's first two years had been "recycled," which meant that messages pertaining to the 9/11 attack and the planned invasion of Iraq were gone.

Hillary had turned over 55,000 pages of emails to the State Department archivists, at their request. But similar requests to her predecessors, former secretaries of state Colin Powell and Condoleezza Rice, brought forth nothing. Powell acknowledged using a private email account for government business, but said he had not retained any of those messages. And Rice claimed not to have used email at all.

Still, media outlets and Republican politicians claimed to be shocked by Clinton's use of private email, when little or no attention had been paid to any of the Republican transgressions of that same standard.

———

Questions about foreign donations to the Clinton Foundation grew more pointed after Reuters correspondent Jonathan Allen filed a story in mid-March about CHAI's failure to report seven such contributions during her tenure at State. The countries whose donations went unreported were Australia, the United Kingdom, Papua New Guinea, Rwanda, Swaziland, Sweden, and Switzerland. Although the Clinton Foundation itself had reported donations annually as required by its agreement with the Obama administration, CHAI management had not disclosed its donors to the spinoff from the main organization in 2010—a violation that spokeswoman Maura Daley described as "an oversight."

None of the countries on the Reuters list raised any national security alarms, and the story didn't allege that the State Department had showed favoritism toward any of them. Allen also reported that the failure to list those donations meant that they had not been "vetted" by the State Department ethics officer, as promised under the 2008 agreement.

CHAI's Daley replied that the Australian, Swedish, and British donations represented increases upon prior gifts from those governments and therefore didn't require vetting. The small Swaziland and Papua New Guinea donations were passed through from other prior donors, including Australia and the Global Fund, neither of which required vetting. And the Rwanda donation was not a gift at all, but a fee for services provided by CHAI. Daley acknowledged that the Swiss donation was new and ought to have been disclosed to the State Department ethics office in advance. But altogether, the unreported donations totaled only about one percent of the organization's annual budget.

Such distinctions scarcely mattered, however, in the atmosphere of distrust that was rapidly descending over Hillary and, by extension, Bill Clinton and the foundation that bore their names. They had known for decades that even their smallest missteps would be magnified and distorted—if not by a responsible news outlet like Reuters, then by other publications, cable networks, talk radio hosts, websites, and, in the age of social media, on hundreds of thousands of Facebook and Twitter posts.

There was nothing scandalous in the funding that foreign governments—almost all of them close U.S. allies and friends like the United Kingdom, Ireland, Canada, and Norway—had provided to CHAI since 2002, beginning long before Hillary became secretary of state. (The only scandal was that Western governments hadn't started to fund AIDS treatment in the developing world years earlier.) Even Republicans who seized upon the Reuters revelations to denounce Clinton didn't claim to find a quid pro quo for any of the CHAI donations.

Still, the furor over foreign funding posed a serious problem for Hillary if not for the foundation itself. On April 15, the foundation's press office issued a statement announcing that it would accept donations from only six countries—Australia, Canada, Germany, the Netherlands, Norway, and the United Kingdom—that had historically supported its programs (and CHAI in particular) for years before her first presidential campaign. Conspicuously absent from that list were nations such as Saudi Arabia and the United Arab Emirates, whose donations to other global charities—such as Oxfam or the World Food Programme, to name only two—had never raised any questions despite their repressive policies.

The new rule would hold at least for the duration of the presidential campaign. And the foundation would also renew its suspension of any conferences scheduled abroad.

Partisan critics still found it all too easy to represent a minor error as a sinister deception, and a generous gift as an attempt to purchase influence. Improvements in transparency and appearances were not their objective. No evidence of actual wrongdoing would be necessary to create an appearance of conflict or worse, as the Clintons were about to learn once more.

———

Few American authors would dare to imagine the publicity bonanza that the editors of the *New York Times* bestowed on Peter Schweizer's *Clinton Cash: The Untold Story of How and Why Foreign Governments and Businesses Helped Make Bill and Hillary Rich.* During the weeks leading up to its publication in early May—and only days after Hillary announced her presidential candidacy—the *Times* published not one but two articles promoting and implicitly endorsing the book—which, as its title indicated, purported to expose the Clintons' enrichment by foreign interests.

It was the kind of publicity that money literally could never buy.

On April 19, the paper led its politics section with a story by Amy Chozick that described *Clinton Cash* as "the most anticipated and feared book of a presidential cycle still in its infancy." The author's background as a Republican partisan and former speechwriter for George W. Bush and Sarah Palin, wrote Chozick, would be used by Clinton supporters to discredit him as yet another in a long line of biased critics—but that might be more difficult, she added, because Schweizer "writes mainly in the voice of a neutral journalist and meticulously documents his sources . . . while leaving little doubt about his view of the Clintons."

Beyond that affirmation of his methods, Chozick reported that both the *Times* and the *Washington Post*—as well as Fox News Channel—had entered into "exclusive" deals with Schweizer to pursue "story lines" in his book. To anyone in the Clinton camp who remembered the Whitewater "scandal," which began with investigative stories in the *Times* and the *Post*, this collaboration between the two leading print outposts of the "liberal media" and hostile Republican sources looked all too familiar.

Scores of readers noticed the incongruous arrangement in Chozick's story and protested to Margaret Sullivan, the *Times* public editor. Sullivan posted a column four days later, expressing her distaste for the "exclusive" deal with Schweizer, while expressing complete faith in the paper's editors to handle such material properly.

But that same day, Sullivan's mild demurral was overshadowed as the *Times* presented the fruit of its collaboration with Schweizer on the front page of its print edition and in the top spot on its website—a 4,400-word story vaguely headlined "*Cash Flowed to Clinton Foundation Amid Russian Uranium Deal*," by investigative reporters Jo Becker and Mike McIntire, which explored the disposition of uranium mining rights in Kazakhstan and the United States by a group of Canadian investors that had once included foundation donor Frank Giustra—and that left those strategic reserves in Russian hands.

Before joining the *Times* staff, Becker had shared a Pulitzer Prize at the *Washington Post*. She also had shared a byline on the January 2008 *Times* investigation of Giustra's uranium deal in the Central Asian nation and his connections with Clinton. Whatever other motives might have inspired the paper's deal with Schweizer seven years later, the *Times* editors leapt at a chance to revisit that story—which had provoked an embarrassing public correction in *Forbes* magazine.

The April 23 story revisited the first *Times* investigation in detail, even repeating one of its most easily checked errors: the claim that Giustra and Clinton had flown together on Giustra's jet to Almaty, the Kazakh capital. (Actually, Clinton and his staff had arrived four days later on another friend's plane.)

But the new story hinted at a more serious accusation: Through a complicated series of deals, Russia had gained control of a portion of U.S. uranium reserves through a Vancouver-based firm called Uranium One, while the Canadian investors who profited had given millions to the Clinton Foundation. The Russian acquisition of those American mines had been approved by the Clinton-led State Department, while those Canadian donations "flowed."

The story noted that any such deal required the approval of "a number of United States government agencies." It mentioned that some of the story's information had been "unearthed" by Schweizer, "a former fellow at the right-leaning Hoover Institution and author of the forthcoming book *Clinton Cash*," who had "provided a preview of material in the book to the *Times*," which added its own extensive reporting.

"Whether the donations played any role in the approval of the uranium deal is unknown," the reporters acknowledged. But on the pages of the *Times*, even the suggestion that donations from Giustra or other investors influenced Hillary amplified Schweizer's theme. They also reported that Bill Clinton had received $500,000 for a speech delivered in Moscow to a bank connected with Uranium One.

The story's insinuation was bolstered by the reporters' discovery that $2.3 million from the Uranium One investors had not been disclosed on the foundation's website, but made public only in Canadian tax records. A *Times* editorial the same day complained about the "messiness" of Hillary's connection with her husband's foundation, and urged her to impose tighter restrictions on its fundraising.

The question that the *Times* failed to raise, let alone answer, is why anyone interested in the Russian uranium deal would have sought to influence the secretary of state—when her department had only one vote out of nine on the Committee on Foreign Investment in the United States that had to approve the deal.

While *Clinton Cash* attributed a "central role" to Hillary, she hadn't participated at all in the Uranium One deliberations. According to the assistant secretary of state who represented her on the panel, "Mrs. Clinton never intervened with me on any CFIUS matter." Knowledgeable observers of CFIUS believe its decisions are dominated by the Pentagon and the Treasury Department, which chairs the committee, not State. And the nine agencies on CFIUS had unanimously approved the sale of the remainder of Uranium One to the Russians in 2013, several months after Hillary had left the government. That sale also required additional approvals from the Nuclear Regulatory Commission and Canadian regulators.

In short, cultivating the Clintons would have guaranteed nothing for the Uranium One investors. They had given well over $2 million during a period of several years, but a foundation spokesman—and Giustra—insisted that Canadian and provincial tax laws forbade disclosure of their names without their specific consent.

As for Giustra, the Uranium One investors were his friends and former partners, and he was assuredly a very big Clinton donor. But he had divested all of his Uranium One stock almost three years before the Russian sale went through.

Yet somehow all those exculpatory details were ignored in the subsequent coverage on cable TV and talk radio, where Clinton's opponents talked loosely of "bribery"—often during interviews with Schweizer, whose book debuted on May 24 as the number two *Times* nonfiction bestseller and stayed on the list for several weeks.

———————

The *Times*'s promotion of Schweizer encouraged a seemingly endless series of attacks on the Clinton Foundation from almost every direction. Journalists who had paid only fleeting attention to the foundation's work over more than a decade proclaimed their concern about its finances, transparency, and efficiency.

Commentators with very little knowledge of any of the foundation's programs, still unable to distinguish the Clinton Global Initiative from the Clinton Health Access Initiative, confidently denounced the entire operation as dubious. Others glancingly recognized the good achieved by the foundation before moving on to denounce the Clintons' "greed." And media stars who had eagerly participated in Clinton Global Initiative events, broadcasting gushy interviews with Bill Clinton, suddenly voiced angry suspicions, unproven accusations, and inventive theories.

On April 27, for example, Joe Scarborough, co-host of MSNBC's *Morning Joe,* held forth about a 2010 donation to the Clinton Foundation from the government of Algeria, which had been earmarked for Haiti relief. That donation mistakenly went unreported as a pass-through, because it never accrued to the foundation balance sheet.

But to Scarborough, who had conducted a very friendly interview with Clinton from a set at CGI in September 2010, the Algerian money smacked of corruption. He had a theory, too: Algeria's government wanted to be taken off the State Department's list of nations that support terrorism.

"I think it was Algeria, maybe, that had given a donation that went unreported at a time when they wanted to be taken off of the terror list in the State Department," he mused. "They write the check, they get taken off the terror list. . . . At the same time, and then it goes unreported by the Clinton Foundation. . . . Is there a quid pro quo there? I don't know, that's really hard to tell." Scarborough continued in that vein for several minutes.

The facts were considerably less exciting. Algeria had never been on the State Department's terror list, which only included four nations; in fact, the Algerian government routinely fought terrorists within its borders and had long been a valued ally of the United States against terrorist organizations operating in North Africa.

Not at all chastened by this blunder, however, Scarborough continued to savage the Clintons the following morning when he interviewed Peter Schweizer. Having once represented a Florida congressional district, Scarborough compared the Clintons unfavorably to several former congressional colleagues and a recent governor of Virginia who all had been convicted of bribery. The proven criminal behavior of the elected officials, he insisted, "pales in comparison to [what is in] this book."

Much of the most damning material in *Clinton Cash*, however, turned out to be either factually inaccurate, melodramatically exaggerated, or both. Within weeks after publication, major media outlets reported significant errors discovered in its pages.

Time magazine debunked Schweizer's chapter on the Uranium One deal, noting that his book had mustered "little evidence" of outside influence on government decision-making, and offered "no indication of Hillary Clinton's personal involvement in, or even knowledge of, the [CFIUS] deliberations."

According to ABC News' investigative team, its "independent review of source material . . . uncovered errors in the book, including an instance where paid and unpaid speaking appearances were conflated," although "those same records supported the premise that former President Clinton accepted speaking fees from numerous companies and individuals with interests pending before the State Department." Yet ABC also found that the book "offers no proof that Hillary Clinton took any direct action to benefit the groups and interests that were paying her husband [for speeches]."

NBC News correspondent Andrea Mitchell poked gaping holes in a section that implied Hillary had promoted Boeing's multibillion-dollar sale of aircraft to Russia, in exchange for the company's $900,000 donation to the Clinton Foundation two months later.

As Mitchell pointed out, the aviation giant had donated to the foundation's Haiti projects for years, and the State Department had been promoting Boeing interests abroad long before Hillary took over. On camera, the Sunlight Foundation's Bill Allison said, "There's no—

there's no evidence that she changed the policy based on, you know, the donations to the foundation."

BuzzFeed found five major errors in a chapter on Haiti, which purported to show that Digicel entrepreneur Denis O'Brien had received a large State Department contract after arranging hundreds of thousands of dollars in speaking fees for Bill Clinton. But the dates were wrong, the State Department project had been funded mostly by the Gates Foundation, and it turned out that Clinton had delivered most of the listed speeches for free—except one that earned a donation to the foundation.

Yahoo News derided as "circumstantial" a chapter claiming that the mobile phone manufacturer Ericsson had been exempted from Iran sanctions by the State Department, after paying Clinton $750,000 to deliver a speech at a Hong Kong telecom conference. The Obama White House, not State, had made the sanctions decision.

Perhaps the ugliest distortion involved Schweizer's misuse of two truncated quotes from Clinton's own colleagues to minimize the role he had played in combating the AIDS pandemic. To suggest slyly that Clinton "may take a little more credit than he is due," the author plucked that phrase out of a much longer quote from former State Department official Princeton Lyman, who had praised Clinton effusively and felt outraged by the misrepresentation of his words.

Schweizer played a similar trick with a quote he lifted from a long statement by World Bank president Jim Yong Kim, a founder of Partners in Health. His aim was to portray Clinton as a mere "middle-man"—when in fact Kim declared the former president "absolutely one of the most important people in the global response to HIV/AIDS."

Beyond the most hostile political circles, the verdict on *Clinton Cash* was that Schweizer had failed to prove the corrupting influence of speaking fees or foundation contributions on Hillary's decisions as secretary of state. "We cannot ultimately know what goes on in their minds and ultimately prove the links between the money they took in and the benefits that subsequently accrued to themselves, their friends, and their associates," his book conceded in the end. Instead, he urged authorities with more investigative power than a mere journalist could muster to bring the Clintons to justice. But no prosecutor, and not even a Republican-led congressional committee, showed any inclination to accept that challenge.

The lengthy record of conflations, compressions, contortions, and flubs compiled by Media Matters for America, the monitoring group started by Clinton ally David Brock, ran to twenty-two detailed and footnoted citations. On May 12, Amazon informed its customers who had purchased *Clinton Cash* as a Kindle ebook that Schweizer's publisher, HarperCollins, would provide an updated edition in which "significant revisions have been made." The publisher confirmed to *Politico* that the author had made "seven or eight" corrections, while insisting that "the changes Amazon is referring to as significant are actually quite minor. We made seven [or] eight factual corrections after the first printing and fixed a technical issue regarding the endnotes." Such a "global fix," said the publisher "may have made the changes appear more extensive than they were."

One of those changes involved a press release about TD Bank and the Keystone XL pipeline that had been exposed as a hoax two years earlier.

To anyone who had perused the extensive dossier on Schweizer's past work posted by Media Matters, his bias and sloppiness would have been wholly unsurprising. In case after case, dating back as far as 1993, Media Matters found ten instances when Schweizer's reporting—almost always attacking prominent liberal Democratic elected officials such as former vice president Al Gore, House minority leader Nancy Pelosi, Senator Sheldon Whitehouse, and Representative Jim McDermott—had been found "unfair," "bogus," "inaccurate" by reputable media outlets.

If Schweizer was not the world's most competent journalist, however, he was prolific and ideologically reliable, as indicated by the tendentious titles of his previous books listed on Amazon: *Do As I Say (Not As I Do): Profiles in Liberal Hypocrisy* (Doubleday, 2005); *Architects of Ruin: How Big Government Liberals Wrecked the Global Economy—And How They Will Do It Again if No One Stops Them* (Harper, 2009); and *Makers and Takers: Why Conservatives Work Harder, Feel Happier, Have Closer Families, Take Fewer Drugs, Give More Generously, Value Honesty More, Are Less Materialistic and Envious, Whine Less . . . and Even Hug Their Children More than Liberals* (Doubleday, 2008). For several years he had written agitprop for the extreme right-wing Breitbart News websites.

For conservative funders seeking to take down the most formidable Democratic presidential contender, Schweizer offered not just audacity and experience but his own nonprofit. As president of the Government Accountability Institute in Tallahassee, Florida, he could accept millions of dollars in tax-exempt funds for research, promotion, and expenses (including his $200,000 annual salary) from foundations and individuals.

And unlike the Clintons, who had disclosed decades of tax returns and more than 300,000 foundation donors, Schweizer didn't have to reveal any of his funders.

When the Government Accountability Institute first appeared on the scene during the 2012 election cycle, the new "nonpartisan" entity almost immediately launched a series of harsh attacks on President Obama that were later determined to be inaccurate by the *Washington Post* fact-checkers. Eventually, researchers uncovered at least one important source of the money behind the "institute"—an eccentric right-wing hedge-fund executive named Robert Mercer and his daughter Rebekah, based in New York, whose family foundation had given millions of dollars to Schweizer in 2013 and 2014.

The extent of Mercer's specific support for *Clinton Cash* is not known, although it seems to have been the main project of GAI during that period. But when HarperCollins editor Adam Bellow, a friend of Schweizer, brought in the book, Schweizer alerted the publisher that GAI's wealthy supporters were prepared to spend big to promote the book. Without seeking approval from HarperCollins for ads or media outlets, the GAI ran its own *Clinton Cash* publicity campaign.

The GAI has yet to release its 990 IRS form for 2015, so any specific expenditures on advertising for *Clinton Cash* remain secret. So does the disposition of the book's advance and royalties. If Schweizer spent his nonprofit's money promoting a book whose proceeds accrued to him personally, that would appear to represent precisely the kind of self-dealing for which he had indicted the Clintons. In 2013, the organization disclosed spending more than $100,000 for advertising on the Breitbart website—a company that happened to be chaired by Stephen Bannon, who also chairs the GAI board.

———

When Schweizer set out to publicize his book, one of his first stops was Capitol Hill, where he briefed members of the Senate Foreign Relations Committee—or at least the committee's Republican members, notably Rand Paul and Marco Rubio, both already running for the Republican presidential nomination. It wasn't long before the would-be nominees started repeating the message of *Clinton Cash*.

Rand Paul had opened his campaign by tarring Hillary with Bill's sexual misconduct, clearly deciding that was the most promising way to win Republican primary votes. He mounted a cable advertising campaign in four early voting states that alluded to the foundation and email controversies. "Hillary Rodham Clinton represents the worst of the Washington machine. The arrogance of power, corruption, cover-up. Conflicts of interest," declared Paul's ads. "The Washington machine is destroying the American dream."

That thrust didn't save Paul from becoming one of the first Republicans eliminated from the primary race. Schweizer preferred Rubio, his home state senator, who most reminded him of the "optimistic" Ronald Reagan of his youth.

But the most aggressive broadsides against the Clintons and the foundation were hurled by Carly Fiorina, the former Hewlett-Packard chief and failed senatorial candidate who had once appeared on a CGI panel. During a June interview on Fox News Channel, Fiorina went out of her way to bring up one of the most destructive—and wholly false— accusations about the foundation's finances.

Asked to comment on a *New York Times* article about Marco Rubio's finances, she replied, "I wish they would do more of a story on what Bill and Hillary Clinton have been doing with their money. Or, more importantly, what they've been doing with their donors' money to the Clinton Global Initiative.

"Honestly, the question I think now for the Clintons is what else don't we know? What don't we know about your donors? What don't we know about the conflicts of interest that those donors represent?" she asked. "When Mrs. Clinton is serving as secretary of state, we are now finding out that so little of those charitable donations actually go to charitable works. They are hiring campaign staff."

As this episode showed, Fiorina didn't hesitate to stretch the truth for political gain as the primaries unfolded. The foundation had never hired any "campaign staff," an obvious falsehood. But the canard about "so little of those charitable donations" going toward charitable purposes had been repeated often enough by then to cause concern within the foundation. Fiorina may have heard it uttered by a Fox Business anchor, or read it in *Clinton, Inc.*, a 2014 book by *Weekly Standard* writer Daniel Halper. She didn't invent the slur but gave it fresh currency in the primary campaign.

The charitable explanation, so to speak, was that Fiorina had simply misunderstood how the Clinton Foundation worked. Challenged to prove her assertion, a spokesperson for her super PAC, Carly for America, referred FactCheck.org to the foundation's IRS Form 990 for 2013, which showed total revenue of $149 million—and total grant disbursements of only $9 million, or roughly 6 percent.

But of course, very little of the foundation's activity or money was spent on doling out grants. Instead, its various initiatives hired staff to pursue charitable purposes directly. Academic experts described it as an "operating foundation" or a "public charity," rather than a traditional foundation that used an endowment to write checks. Indeed, as foundation spokesman Craig Minassian explained to FactCheck's reporter, many traditional foundations, such as Gates and Rockefeller, made annual grants to the Clinton Foundation to support its programs. And the Gates Foundation, oriented toward efficiency and results, had audited Clinton Foundation programs to ensure its money was spent wisely.

Clinton critics, such as conservative commentator David Frum, carped about the foundation's spending on travel and salaries, as if a global enterprise could operate without airfares and car rentals. (Only Bill Clinton could rely on his friends' aircraft, and even he occasionally flew commercial; the foundation's two thousand other employees, including Ira Magaziner, usually flew economy class and stayed in cheap hotels.)

The critics also pointed to Charity Navigator, a rating agency that had declined to score the Clinton Foundation and placed it on a "watch list." But Charity Navigator said it was unable to rate the Clinton Foundation because its various initiatives made an unusual "business model" that didn't fit within the usual parameters. And the watch list was only meant to signal press scrutiny of the foundation, with no judgment about its probity. "A lack of a rating does not represent a positive or negative evaluation by Charity Navigator," it said.

The American Institute of Philanthropy's evaluation arm, Charity-Watch, had given the Clinton Foundation an "A" rating, based on analysis showing that 89 percent of its revenues were devoted to charitable purposes—well above the 75 percent that was standard among public charities. Daniel Borochoff, the group's president and founder, told FactCheck that Fiorina's comments had only revealed "her lack of understanding of charitable organizations," a generous interpretation of her remarks.

Before the end of 2015, the foundation had taken steps to improve its image and practices in response to negative media coverage. Frustrated as the Clintons were by what they deemed unfair criticism, appearances mattered.

In response to a series of stories in *Politico* and other outlets that raised questions about the foundation's reporting of its revenues to the IRS, Donna Shalala hired tax accountants and lawyers to review all of its 990 filings dating back to 2010. The foundation had failed to specify certain government grants on a line devoted to that category, and CHAI had made a similar error on two years of its returns in 2012 and 2013.

Correcting those mistakes—and creating a separate category for speech-related income donated by members of the Clinton family, which amounted to several million dollars—prompted the foundation to refile amended returns for those years. In statements to the press, both the foundation and CHAI described those decisions as "voluntary," since their lawyers had advised them that refiling was not required. The changes had not altered the income, expenditures, assets, or liabilities for either organization.

Several months earlier, the foundation had announced another change that had mostly been relegated to a footnote. Going forward, it would disclose the names of donors and donation ranges on a quarterly rather than an annual basis (as members of the Senate Foreign Relations Committee had suggested might be wise back when Hillary was confirmed as secretary of state).

Taken together, those changes prompted Charity Navigator to remove the Clinton Foundation from its "watch list" just before Christmas. On its website, the watchdog group explained that the foundation had "provided publicly accessible information regarding their amended tax forms for 2010, 2011, 2012, and 2013. . . . This information, along with the public memorandum submitted addressing the other issues raised in the watch list entry, meets our requirements for removal."

Coming just before the end of the year, when many Americans made final charitable donations to meet tax deadlines, the decision's timing was helpful. While several news outlets reported the change, including the *Washington Post* and CBS News, it was difficult to assess the lasting damage to the foundation's reputation.

————

The Clinton Foundation's small public relations staff struggled through the primary season to respond to the continuing drumbeat of attacks, mostly from Republicans. As Vermont senator Bernie Sanders gained surprising traction against Hillary with his left-wing, small-donor, anti-establishment challenge to her "coronation," the debate turned away from the foundation and the issue of foreign donations toward her own efforts to earn money after leaving the State Department.

Sanders exercised a surprising degree of control over the narrative of the Democratic primary. When the crusty senator declared during their first debate in October that he and the rest of the country were "sick of hearing about your damned emails," he tamped down the obsession with that topic—despite the fact that the FBI and Justice Department were conducting an investigation to determine whether anyone in the State Department, including Hillary, had violated laws relating to classified information.

The mountain populist preferred to discuss another issue: Hillary's acceptance of $750,000 in speaking fees from Goldman Sachs—the Wall Street mammoth whose conduct leading up to the 2008 recession had transformed it into a symbol for all the flaws and inequities of the American financial system.

In a refrain that would not end until she won the California primary in June 2016, the Sanders campaign demanded that Hillary release the transcripts of her Goldman speeches. Sanders only knew about those speeches—and others that had earned her almost $22 million since 2013—because unlike him, she had disclosed her income taxes. Many of those speeches had been delivered to banks and other corporate interests that had lobbied the federal government, including the State Department. The implication, repeated relentlessly by Sanders and his surrogates, was that those payments somehow shaped Clinton's policies.

When Hillary confronted her opponent, demanding that he back up his insinuations with evidence, he waved her off. He couldn't prove any wrongdoing, but she couldn't prove a negative. Her speaking fees were not out of line with the level of her celebrity, as attested by experts in the field even before she left office. She had scrupulously rejected any foreign speaking engagements in order to deflect criticism.

Like her husband, she felt such confidence in her own probity that she was unable to imagine how others might view her acceptance of enormous sums of money from special interests. She also seemed unable to comprehend how adversaries on the left and right would use her sudden wealth to alienate her from working families still suffering the financial effects of the recession. Her failure to anticipate the appearance of excessive "buck-raking," especially from her widely despised friends on Wall Street, relentlessly dragged down the public approval ratings that had once soared.

Yet despite Sanders's spirited challenge, Hillary persevered through the primaries, defeating him in the biggest states and racking up large majorities in the popular vote and delegate count. Within the Democratic Party, which the Vermont independent only joined to run for president, she remained highly popular.

So did her husband—but in organizing the 2016 campaign, her managers were careful to use Clinton sparingly, avoiding any repetition of the 2008 South Carolina fiasco. The question was how to deploy him to the campaign's best advantage, without allowing him to become a distraction.

Looking toward his seventieth birthday in August, a few weeks after the Democratic convention, Clinton had better and worse days. Reporters covering his campaign appearances would sometimes notice his hands quivering, or describe him as looking frail and elderly; at other times, he seemed as robust and forceful as ever.

Even more than in 2008, his presidential legacy was a double-edged sword. To many voters, he was still the symbol of prosperity and peace. Yet what had once been deemed important legislative achievements, such as the North American Free Trade Agreement and the 1994 omnibus crime bill, had become political liabilities in a new era.

Those laws were routinely denounced not only by Sanders, who excoriated NAFTA in every speech (and tried to ignore his own vote for the crime bill as a House member), but by new movements like Black Lives Matter, whose rhetoric blamed Clinton for the excessive incarceration of young black men. He had to listen—and agree, in part—as his wife carefully distanced herself from aspects of his administration.

On a campaign trip to Philadelphia in early April, Clinton was forced to cope with the new political environment. At a community center on the city's outskirts, in a largely African American neighborhood, he headlined a rally for Hillary that included local officials, the city's former mayor, and former governor Ed Rendell, a longtime friend and ally. More than six hundred excited residents had crowded into the center's gymnasium to hear him, waving Hillary signs and chanting her name as he took the podium.

"Before I came in here," he said, after the other officials had spoken, "all the kids came out from school and started waving at me, which put me in a good mood—and reminded me that elections are about the future!" He launched into an energetic defense of Hillary as "the most qualified candidate, with the best ideas" for creating jobs, reducing the cost of higher education, and removing the barriers that kept so many Americans from realizing their potential. She had been endorsed by most labor unions, the Congressional Black Caucus, Planned Parenthood, and the American Nurses Association not because she or they were "establishment," but because she would "show up for work" as president, to "stand and deliver."

He knew that Americans had been suffering, despite the progress won by President Obama, and he warned against an embittered vote. "Too long a sacrifice can make a stone of the heart," he said, quoting Yeats, then paused. "Don't let it make a stone of the head."

As Clinton continued to argue for his wife, a murmur arose from the center of the crowd and then grew louder. "Hillary is a murderer!" screamed a middle-aged woman in dreadlocks, as she and her male companion began to wave homemade signs marked with that strange slogan. "Hillary is a murderer!" Then she yelled, "Hillary called black youth super-predators," a reference to a 1996 speech in which she had used that phrase to describe the most violent young criminals—a statement for which she had apologized.

When others in the crowd tried to calm the woman, she refused to stop screaming until she briefly ran out of breath, shouting over Clinton. But even as he grew frustrated and his face reddened, he told security not to remove her.

"I love protesters," he said. "I like protesters, but the ones that won't let you answer are afraid of the truth. That's a simple rule." Responding to criticism of the crime bill, he continued, "I talked to a lot of African American groups. They thought black lives mattered; they said take this bill because our kids are being shot in the street by gangs. We had 13-year-old kids planning their own funerals." He wagged a finger at the woman and her companion, who continued to wave his "Hillary Is A Murderer" sign.

"I don't know how you would characterize the gang leaders who got 13-year-old kids hopped up on crack, and sent them out in the streets to murder other African American children. Maybe you thought they were good citizens—she didn't."

After the rally ended, Clinton thought he had handled the situation well. "I get that kind of thing every week now," he said. But while those situations rarely drew much coverage, the Philadelphia confrontation became a national story, sparking outrage in the Black Lives Matter movement (although the woman who confronted Clinton was not affiliated with any group). The next day, Clinton said he regretted the confrontation.

Whatever the fleeting cost of that incident, Clinton had quietly performed yeoman service to his wife's campaign earlier the same day. At Philadelphia's Convention Center, he had enjoyed an effusive welcome by the nation's African Methodist Episcopal bishops, who were celebrating their church's bicentennial in its birthplace. These black religious leaders, mostly but not all men, included some of Clinton's oldest friends from Arkansas and elsewhere. They threw their arms around him, whispered in his ear, laughed uproariously with him. He had been invited to make the case for Hillary, which he proceeded to do with gusto as he took the auditorium stage.

Recalling her undercover investigation of segregated academies in

Alabama as a young law student, her years at the Children's Defense Fund with Marian Wright Edelman, and her work to pass the Children's Health Insurance Program as first lady, he invoked Scripture. "I will show you my faith by my works," he said. "It's about making change."

He spoke about Hillary's plans and proposals as always, but that didn't seem altogether necessary. He had showed respect, he had laid on hands, and—quoting a familiar trope from Isaiah 6:8—he had concluded with a peroration: "Whom shall I send? She has said, send me."

They would send her, and indeed already had sent her millions of votes from their church pews—a substantial part of the massive minority support that had won her the Democratic nomination and promised to win her the presidency. And they had done so, in no small part, out of enduring love for her husband.

———

In late June, Bill Clinton made the kind of mistake that a former law professor—not to mention a former president—ought to have avoided instinctively. While his plane was parked on the tarmac at Phoenix International Airport, Clinton had learned that Attorney General Loretta Lynch and her husband were in a government plane parked nearby. Merely by walking over to her aircraft, uninvited, to engage Lynch and her husband in social chatter about their grandchildren and other anodyne topics, he had set off an explosion of indignant questions about the integrity of the Justice Department's email investigation. Republicans darkly warned that this innocent encounter proved that the case against Hillary, which they had predicted for months would result in her indictment, had been fixed at the highest levels.

Lynch apologized publicly and promised to follow whatever recommendation might come from the FBI and prosecutors handling the case. Eight days later, on July 5, FBI director James Comey announced that despite Hillary's "extremely careless" treatment of highly sensitive information, his agents had found no basis to indict her—after an extensive probe that had concluded on July 2 with a three-and-a-half hour "voluntary" interview of Hillary herself.

Long before Comey's decision, however, hostile media coverage had focused once more on her husband. Donald Trump, who had clinched the Republican nomination in an extraordinary campaign littered with offensive, racist, and xenophobic language, again directed his fire not only at "Crooked Hillary," but at Clinton, the erstwhile friend he attacked in nearly every speech.

This had been Trump's plan from the beginning. Lurking in his political circle for over a decade was Roger J. Stone, the former Nixon aide and consultant who unabashedly reveled in his notoriety as a perpetrator of dirty tricks and unhinged rhetoric. The conspiracy-minded Stone had spent months locating women whose stories of sexual encounters with Clinton—including Juanita Broaddrick, who had accused him of assaulting her in 1998—and Trump himself had used the word "rape" to defame him at least once.

Among Stone's contributions was the reintroduction of Kathleen Willey, a Virginia woman who had once worked at the White House and, in 1998, accused Clinton of accosting and forcefully kissing her there. The independent counsel had immunized her as a witness in the Lewinsky case, then immunized her again when FBI investigators found that she had lied to them. Over the years since then, Willey had lodged various improbable accusations against the Clintons and their associates, including a plot to murder her cat.

On a right-wing talk radio show, Stone said he had established a GoFundMe account for contributions to help pay off Willey's mortgage, "so she can hit the road and start speaking out on Hillary." He said that Trump himself had donated to help Willey, an assertion denied by Trump and later withdrawn by Stone.

Trump's plotting with Stone and his ugly descriptions of the Clintons belied his copiously documented, sometimes obsequious efforts to befriend them—with donations to the foundation and to Hillary's campaigns, with free membership at his golf courses for Bill, and with the praise he had lavished on both of them in previous interviews. He and Clinton had played in foursomes together occasionally at Trump National, his club in northern Westchester, where—until 2016—signed photographs of the former president adorned the clubhouse walls.

But that was then—and now Trump and both Clintons armored themselves for what promised to be the most viciously personal presidential contest of modern times.

———

The direction and tenor of 2016 campaign coverage began to shift in the weeks after Trump and Hillary clinched the respective nominations of their parties. In the mainstream media, editors and producers appeared to realize how shallow and pointless much of the previous year's coverage of Trump had been, allowing a demagogic and perhaps very dangerous candidate to win the support of a Republican electorate that knew very little about the seamier aspects of his career.

Major news outlets began to investigate Trump in earnest, applying some of the same scrutiny to his dubious associations, business practices, philanthropic donations, and character that had been focused on Hillary for years. Some of the country's best investigative journalists—including several who had looked very hard at the Clintons—probed his company's connections with organized crime figures, his misogynist attitude toward women, his multiple bankruptcies, and his thin record of charitable giving for someone who claimed to be one of the richest men in America. The results were not pleasing to the developer turned TV personality, as he repeatedly maligned reporters and outlets that displeased him—and even banned *Washington Post* reporters from his campaign events.

Having long complained about Hillary's overreaction to negative coverage, many journalists gained a fresh perspective on her vexed relationship with the press. She had never taunted or banished reporters covering her campaigns.

The shift in media focus toward the vulnerabilities of the presumptive Republican nominee in early May hardly exempted Bill Clinton or the Clinton Foundation from hostile coverage, especially not in conservative and right-wing outlets. On May 12, the *Wall Street Journal* published a story headlined "Clinton Charity Aided Clinton Friends," which explored the names and relationships behind a $2 million CGI commitment that had been made more than five years earlier.

The parties involved were Kim Samuel, a Canadian investor and philanthropist who had become a CGI member years earlier, and a group of Clinton friends and donors—including financial author Andrew Tobias and souvenir marketer Mark Weiner—who together owned a home energy conservation firm in Nebraska called Energy Pioneer Solutions, Inc.

At the CGI meeting in September 2010, Samuel had made a commitment to invest $2 million in the conservation firm, a small business that insulated private houses and allowed the homeowners to pay for the retrofit in their utility bills over time.

The issue raised by the complicated *Journal* story, written by James V. Grimaldi—a reporter who had shared a Pulitzer for his reporting on the Jack Abramoff lobbying scandal in 2006—was whether CGI had abused its tax status by assisting a for-profit enterprise. To make that point it cited a section of the IRS website stating that tax-exempt charitable institutions "must not be organized or operated for the benefit of private interests."

But the reaction of tax and philanthropy experts to this attempted indictment was swift, unfavorable, and, for the Clinton Foundation, entirely exculpatory.

The next day, *Inside Philanthropy* editor David Callahan posted a response on his publication's website titled "Hit Job: A Closer Look at the WSJ's Clueless Attack on the Clinton Foundation." In sardonic tones, Callahan pointed out that "impact investing" in energy conservation was entirely in keeping with the foundation's stated purposes; that such philanthropic investments, especially in the energy sector, were increasingly common; and that CGI had shepherded the same kind of commitments on many occasions before and since.

"The former president and Clinton Foundation did a wise thing here—albeit without a keen enough eye toward how a Rupert Murdoch–owned newspaper might work with this material when Hillary made a White House run," wrote Callahan.

Notre Dame law professor Lloyd Mayer, a specialist in nonprofit tax law, commented that CGI had "only facilitated an investment by private parties in a company with a mission that matched the Clinton Foundation's charitable purposes," with an "incidental benefit" to third parties that was "permitted legally." Literally scores of easily contacted sources, from lawyers and academics to foundation executives, could have explained these commonplace facts.

So Grimaldi's complicated story, which he had pursued for a year, was no story at all. But CGI's alleged tax violation was essentially an excuse to publish the name and picture of one of the company's owners, Julie Tauber McMahon—a blond, divorced Chappaqua resident and friend of Clinton who had been identified as his "ex-mistress" by the

National Enquirer and other tabloids on several occasions since 2008. She owned 29 percent of Energy Pioneer Solutions.

Clinton always denied an affair with McMahon, and she called him "a family friend," but that didn't discourage shrieking tabloid coverage for a couple of days. On the front page of Murdoch's *New York Post* ran the headline "Blond Bombshell: Bubba Steered Charity $$ to 'Friend,'" with a story inside reporting wrongly that the Clinton Foundation had given $2 million to Energy Pioneers.

And Trump played his part, calling in to the *Fox and Friends* morning show on Murdoch's news channel to offer his view. "It's a bombshell. There's no doubt about it," he said. "It's a rough story and a lot of people have been talking about it for years."

Pursuing negative allegations about Clinton—accurate or not—also allowed the right-wing media to soften the impact of the most troubling stories about Trump. The saga of "Trump University," an expensive nondegree study course that had allegedly defrauded many gullible students, while earning millions for Trump, was inflicting political damage as it headed toward a civil fraud trial in federal court.

Rather than defend the indefensible, the *New York Post* and Fox News Channel seized on another trope from *Clinton Cash* that they dubbed "Clinton U." In 2010, Clinton had signed up as the honorary chancellor for Laureate Education, an international for-profit higher education company. Its founder and chairman, Douglas Becker, paid Clinton $3.5 million a year to accept that title and deliver several speeches a year to students at its far-flung schools in Asia, South America, and the Middle East.

Becker was also the unpaid chair of an independent nonprofit called the International Youth Federation, which had no financial relationship with his company—and which had received millions of dollars in education grants from the State Department, dating back to the Bush administration. In the tabloid press and right-wing Internet sites, these relationships were compressed and distorted into claims that Hillary had steered $55 million to Becker's company.

Trump seized on *Clinton Cash* and the insinuations in the Murdoch media to claim that Hillary had "laundered money to Bill Clinton through Laureate Education. . . . Clinton's State Department provided $55.2 million in grants to Laureate Education. . . . Laureate thanked Bill for providing unbelievable access to the Secretary of State by paying him off $16.5 million."

Not a line of those accusations was true, as the *Washington Post* established with a few phone calls. Hillary had never done any favors for Laureate, which had obtained no U.S. government contracts, and Clinton had disengaged from the education company when his contract ended in 2015.

By then Trump had uttered so many falsehoods, about himself and others, that he possessed little credibility on any subject, including Bill and Hillary Clinton, even among a press corps that rarely hesitated to rough them up.

Citing *Clinton Cash* had not bolstered him at all—and may well have undermined Schweizer, who saw his book disparaged as "widely discredited" by reputable media in the wake of Trump's speech. Such skepticism did little to discourage Schweizer, who had used a fresh infusion of cash to turn his book into a movie whose American premiere was scheduled for Philadelphia, on the eve of the Democratic convention.

At last he dropped all nonpartisan pretenses, telling an interviewer, "The key is to engage voters. If you look at what's motivating Trump and Sanders fans, it's disgust with cronyism and corruption in Washington." He had produced the movie with Stephen Bannon, chairman of the sedulously pro-Trump website Breitbart News.

So Clinton and his foundation would remain primary targets for the Trump campaign, the Murdoch media, and the far right. So much had changed since the Clintons had left the White House—and so little.

———

Within the noise and turbulence of a presidential election, even as the possibility of profound change emerged on the horizon, Clinton might still reflect on what his post-presidency had meant to him and the world. He had always relied upon his ability to insulate himself mentally from crisis, to look beyond obstacles and see ahead, to analyze and synthesize, to think.

If he looked back, and asked what he had done, he would surely answer, "Not enough." He had helped to rescue people from AIDS, malaria, tuberculosis, diarrhea; he had helped American children change their diets to stave off obesity and diabetes; he had helped to rebuild Gujarat, Rwanda, Banda Aceh, New Orleans, Haiti, and many other forgotten places; he had helped to improve the lives of human beings everywhere, through the thousands of commitments and investments sponsored by the Clinton Global Initiative; and he had helped Barack Obama win re-election as president, despite their personal frictions, preventing a Republican political hegemony that he believed would be disastrous for his country and the planet. He had done that and much more, and yet he would never believe that he had done enough.

But if he looked ahead, he might have to consider how to sequester, shed, and spin off much of what he had built in the course of those achievements, to protect the integrity and image of Hillary Clinton's historic presidency.

Weeks before she was to be nominated, the former president, his daughter, Donna Shalala, and top staff had met to begin considering what should become of the Bill, Hillary and Chelsea Clinton Foundation following a November election victory. No decisions had to be reached yet, of course, but there were several likely possibilities. The Clinton Global Initiative could declare victory in its original mission to reshape philanthropy, set its action networks free, and turn its archives and databases over to a university library, or perhaps the Clinton School for Public Service. The Clinton Health Access Initiative could and almost certainly should continue, either independently or under the auspices of a major foundation, nonprofit, or international organization. The Alliance for a Healthier Generation might proceed as a subsidiary of the American Heart Association. Other foundations that shared the missions of the remaining initiatives, such as the climate effort and the Too Small to Fail early childhood program, might adopt them—or not.

Someday, the creative ideas generated by the Clinton Foundation—along with the dedicated people who had conceived and tried to implement them—just might find their way into a smart government seeking fresh solutions to festering problems. Whether that ever were to happen or not, the repetitive collisions between politics and philanthropy would end, perhaps in a synthesis yet to be conceived.

And Bill Clinton could wake up in the White House, on the morning after Hillary's dizzying inauguration, the first day of his life as first gentleman, starting a new job that nobody yet knew how to do.

It would be Saturday, January 21, 2017.

At least someone would bring the coffee.

AFTERWORD

Only in the final week of the 2016 presidential campaign did Hillary Rodham Clinton's husband join the bandwagon of pollsters, political science professors, journalists, meta-analysts, and practicing politicians who proclaimed with varying degrees of confidence that—overcoming all the stumbles, pratfalls, traps, ambuscades, and conspiracies—she would be elected America's first female president on November 8. By then, Bill Clinton even allowed himself to discuss future White House staffing with John Podesta, his own former chief of staff and the campaign's chairman.

Until then, Clinton had quietly (and sometimes not so quietly) warned the Hillary campaign staff and others that the numbers and appearances were deceptive, that the voters were in an angry and potentially destructive mood, and that he sensed a populist upheaval threatening her seemingly certain victory.

"We're losing," he had said more than once, dismissing all the favorable polls. He had said it directly to campaign manager Robby Mook, who plainly believed that Clinton's renowned political intuition was an outdated instrument, and that the campaign should be guided entirely by a model based on "the analytics": a daily, granular stream of geographical and voter data that flowed from a closely guarded computerized system. An algorithm, nicknamed "Ada" after a nineteenth-century female British mathematician, generated the analytics, which virtually dictated the campaign's allocation of resources and personnel as well as its calendar of events.

Following Ada, for instance, meant that the prodigiously frugal Mook spent very little on traditional items like yard signs, bumper stickers, and political literature. In many suburban and rural districts, that meant only the Trump campaign was visible.

From all outward appearances, Mook had brushed aside the former president's concerns, vague as they must have sounded to him. Clinton would say that he was worried by the British vote to leave the European

Union, as a signal of deep discontent in the Western democracies, even though most American voters probably still had no idea what "Brexit" meant. He would fret over the bitter and hostile atmosphere in the country, and the absence of any positive message that could break through. He felt the campaign was humoring him, not listening to his warnings.

The Brooklyn headquarters had responded to the former president by dispatching him to what one aide called "bullshit events," sometimes in obscure locations. Ironically enough, he was used to less advantage in his wife's 2016 race than in Barack Obama's 2012 reelection campaign, when he had arguably played a central role in persuading working-class voters in Pennsylvania, Florida, and Ohio to line up again behind the African American president. Evidently Ada told the campaign not to expend too much effort in those communities.

Those around Clinton heard his outbursts of frustration, not only with Hillary's staff but with media coverage of her and the campaign. Cynical as he had become over the years about the Washington press corps' attitude toward him and his wife, he was still astonished by their overwhelming obsession with her emails and their failure, until very late in the season, to deliver any substantive illumination of Trump's inauspicious history in business, charity, and politics, let alone the absolute vacuum of policy he represented. (Much of that examination would only come after the election.)

What had underlined that imbalance in coverage—and emphasized how Hillary's "damned emails" overshadowed her campaign—was the stunning letter sent by FBI director James Comey on October 28 to the chairs and ranking members of eight House and Senate committees, informing them that he needed to "supplement" his earlier testimony about his agency's Clinton email probe. Working on an "unrelated case," he wrote, FBI agents had found additional emails "that appear to be pertinent to this investigation." (Those emails were discovered on a laptop computer owned by Huma Abedin's husband, Anthony Weiner, then under federal investigation for sending obscene electronic messages to a fifteen-year-old girl, although Comey's letter didn't reveal the emails' provenance.)

While Comey carefully noted that the FBI could not determine whether any of the newly discovered emails were "significant," that didn't discourage Rep. Jason Chaffetz, chair of the House Oversight Committee, who instantly issued an excited tweet: "Case reopened." The Utah Republican set off a sustained roar of hyperbole, with the tone set by Republican National Committee chair Reince Priebus, who claimed, "This stunning development raises serious questions about what records have not been turned over . . . and whether they show intent to violate the law"—despite the absence of any such negative inferences in Comey's letter.

Trump himself praised the FBI and the Justice Department as "willing to have the courage to right the horrible mistake that they made" in clearing Hillary. "It is everybody's hope that it is about to be corrected." Yet Comey had said nothing about reversing his July decision against prosecuting Hillary Clinton or anyone else in the email probe. Nor would he reverse that decision after his agency's analysis of the emails on the Weiner laptop, none of which were actually "new." On November 6, two days before the election, the FBI director sent a second letter to Congress: "Based on our review, we have not changed our conclusions."

By then the momentum had shifted decisively. And while many factors arguably affected the outcome, post-election polling analysis showed that her campaign never fully recovered from Comey's October 28 letter to Congress.

———

On Election Night, the Clinton family assembled on the nineteenth floor of the Peninsula Hotel in midtown Manhattan, just one block south of Trump Tower. Hillary's top aides, including Mook, Huma Abedin, and campaign chair John Podesta, were ensconced in rooms on the same floor, adjoining Bill and Hillary's very large suite. The former president parked himself on a big couch in the living room, opposite the television, and remained rooted there for most of the night, making telephone calls to his own network of longtime campaign aides and friends in key states, sometimes chewing on an unlit cigar.

The Clintons had come up to the hotel in a jubilant mood after an early dinner at Eataly, Mario Batali's market and restaurant complex. And they weren't alone in anticipating victory. The usually parsimonious Mook, renowned within the campaign for his steadfast refusal to waste money on luxuries like edible food, had ordered up an enormous, lavish buffet.

The campaign manager and his principal aide Elan Kriegel hovered, large iPads in hand, ready to receive early voting returns from Florida and able to focus on numbers from any district with the slightest touch. They had all arrived at the hotel in a mood of cautious optimism. But when the data began to arrive—meaning tallies of actual votes—those screens revealed a picture that grew darker with each passing hour. A suffocating pall of gloom slowly suffused the Clinton suite, while both the candidate and her husband seemed to go numb. The Sunshine State was the first crucial target to fall to Donald Trump at around 9:30 p.m. Eastern Time, followed by North Carolina, and then the Midwestern "blue wall" of Michigan and Wisconsin; the hours passed torturously until around 1 a.m., when Pennsylvania went down, eking out the Republican's astonishingly narrow Electoral College majority.

The Clintons and their aides, some of whom had toiled by their side for decades, faced an unthinkable conclusion of the political saga that had begun in Arkansas more than a quarter century ago. There was no shrieking, no bellowing, no hurling of objects nor angry recriminations. There were only empty eyes and stunned murmuring. When Bill Clinton realized that his wife was losing, he thought again of Brexit, the bellwether that had worried him for months.

Hillary Clinton at first hesitated to concede Trump's hairbreadth triumph, and many of her closest, longest-serving associates were even more resistant—understandably so, since she was well ahead in the popular vote, where she would ultimately notch a 2 percent margin over her adversary. But in this contest, her three-million-vote advantage counted far less than the roughly 77,000 votes that had bagged three critical states for him.

Finally, at the urging of President Obama, in recognition of her own duty to validate the democratic process and the peaceful transfer of authority, she took the telephone from Abedin, who had contacted Trump's entourage, and when he came on the line, said a phrase she had never expected to utter: "Congratulations, Donald."

———

Bill Clinton's first appearance in the spotlight after Election Day came on December 3, when he went to Washington for the Kennedy Center Honors. Hosted by Stephen Colbert, with both Barack and Michelle

Obama present, the annual lifetime achievement awards ceremony served as a public farewell to the departing First Family, who received a lengthy standing ovation as it began. This was a friendly crowd for Clinton, too, who counted many friends among the actors, musicians, and entertainers in the audience.

The former president had come to praise James Taylor, one of the evening's honorees and an old friend. "His influence in our lives goes way beyond his contributions to the American songbook," Clinton said. "His songs and lyrics have become the seams in the fabric of our national life." He recalled an evening during his presidency when they had sailed together off Martha's Vineyard, and how the singer had taken down the sails to perform an intimate concert under the stars. "Every single summer since I have thought about that night," he said.

Backstage he ran into Sean Penn, another longtime friend who was there to pay homage to honoree Al Pacino. A dedicated social activist who persistently devotes time as well as money to rebuilding devastated communities, Penn had gotten to know Clinton well in Haiti. In fact, Clinton had chosen Penn's own successful J/P Haitian Relief Organization, supported by his friends and colleagues in Hollywood, to continue the Clinton Foundation's programs in the island nation (with support from Denis O'Brien's Digicel Foundation).

Now the actor looked the politician in the eye and growled, "I will never speak to you again if I ever hear you express any doubt that Comey cost you this election."

Clinton laughed ruefully. "What's *your* story?" he asked. Nearly everyone he met needed to vent about Hillary's loss and Trump's victory, to discharge the lingering anger and growing worry.

Penn told him about family members who had been ready to vote for Hillary until they learned about the Comey letter—and read the online "news" articles predicting that she would soon be sent to prison.

Having heard scores of stories like that from friends and acquaintances across the country, Clinton scarcely needed persuading. For many months after the 2016 election, he could talk about little else except the election—and how it had been lost—to anyone who would listen.

No longer dwelling on the defects of his wife's campaign, which had preoccupied and often enraged him during the election cycle, he focused on the singular event that he believed had turned off potential Hillary voters—and how press coverage had laid the groundwork for that moment. Without the extraordinary intervention of the FBI director in reviving the email issue in late October, he believed, Hillary would have won. In the end, nothing else had mattered nearly as much.

Being Clinton, he framed that simple assertion against a more complex backdrop. Despite Trump's obvious defects as a candidate, he had always feared the race would be close, if only because millions of voters were seizing the chance to express their alienation from elites and their fear of economic and cultural change. And that alienation had been stoked by imbalanced media coverage of Hillary, which trumpeted the email investigation far out of proportion to its substance—while glossing over the most troubling aspects of Trump's background, and almost wholly ignoring the real issues that divided the candidates and parties.

When the Shorenstein Center at Harvard's Kennedy School of Government released a post-election study of campaign reporting by major newspapers and television networks, titled *News Coverage of the 2016 Election: How the Press Failed the Voters,* Clinton wasn't surprised by its findings: Hillary's "scandals" had received four times as much attention as Trump's mistreatment of women, and sixteen times as much attention as her most heavily covered policy position (namely, her difficult straddling on international trade).

The Shorenstein study reaffirmed Clinton's complaint about the failure of the press to fairly evaluate the candidates' records. Amplified by the relentlessly negative coverage of both Trump and Hillary, that failure encouraged voters to assume a "false equivalency" between them. In the study's concluding discussion of the worst deficiencies in campaign reportage, its authors cited a salient example: "When journalists can't, or won't, distinguish between allegations directed at the Trump Foundation and those directed at the Clinton Foundation, there's something seriously amiss."

To Clinton, business considerations seemed to have dictated not only coverage of Hillary's email "scandal," but also the obsessive, promotional attention lavished on Trump, who received hundreds of hours of free advertising. The drive to win ratings and revenues, overshadowing any commitment to public service journalism, had served voters badly from the beginning.

For media executives, particularly in the cable news industry, a close election translated into millions of dollars. If that meant promoting "fake news" about Hillary, that was nothing new in mainstream media treatment of the Clintons, who had been targeted successfully by ideological purveyors of fake news ever since the fabrication of the Whitewater affair in 1992.

What made 2016 different was the role of the Kremlin in promoting a toxic mixture of stolen information and disinformation—and the susceptibility of American media outlets to that scheme. In their relentlessly negative approach to Hillary's candidacy, he felt, Washington's political press corps had proved to be easily manipulated.

But as the full story of the election unfolded, and Clinton absorbed every point of data and analysis, he was increasingly persuaded that the Comey letter had killed her chances. The most dispassionate polling analysts, such as Nate Silver of FiveThiryEight.com, amassed numbers that showed the sudden drop in Hillary's support after October 28. There was no other plausible explanation, Silver argued, for that precipitous plunge.

Perhaps even more persuasive was a report from Engagement Labs that Clinton read shortly after his encounter with Sean Penn. An innovative Canadian market research firm, Engagement conducts daily online surveys for clients like AT&T, Google, Charles Schwab, American Express, and Toyota, tracking brand position by word-of-mouth conversations between consumers. Since 2008, Engagement has supplemented its brand research with a political survey, measuring public attitudes toward presidential candidates. The firm's chief research officer, Brad Fay, explained what they found during the final week before Election Day 2016:

> While both candidates were always firmly in negative territory, Clinton nevertheless enjoyed a persistent lead over Trump that opened up after the first debate and expanded in the immediate aftermath of the infamous audio recording of Billy Bush and Donald Trump.
>
> But there was a sudden change in the net sentiment results that follows [sic] immediately after FBI Director James Comey released his letter about a renewed investigation of Clinton emails to lead-

ers of Congress on October 28. Immediately afterwards, there was a 17-point drop in net sentiment for Clinton, and an 11-point rise for Trump, enough for the two candidates to switch places in the rankings, with Clinton in more negative territory than Trump. At a time when opinion polling shows perhaps a two-point decline in the margin for Clinton, this conversation data suggests a 28-point change in the word of mouth "standings." The change in word of mouth momentum was stunning, and much greater than the traditional opinion polling revealed.

Based on this finding, it is our conclusion that the Comey letter, 11 days before the election, was the precipitating event behind Clinton's loss, despite the letter being effectively retracted less than a week later. In such a close election, there may have been dozens of factors whose absence would have reversed the outcome, in particular the influence campaign of the Russian government as detailed by US intelligence services. But the sudden change in the political conversation after the Comey letter suggest [sic] it was the single, most indispensable factor in the surprise election result.

If Comey's actions determined the result, those "dozens of factors" had caused substantial collateral damage, particularly to the Clinton Foundation, which had endured a steep, undeserved loss of stature among citizens who never fully understood its aims or its achievements. As the Shorenstein study indicated, the stain on the foundation's reputation was largely owed to a torrent of inaccurate, sloppy, and sometimes malicious journalism that overwhelmed Clinton and his foundation's staff.

To rebut the falsehoods and exaggerations would have required a large-scale advertising and public relations effort, at a potential cost of millions of dollars. The former president had felt constrained by law from expending foundation resources on a media campaign to refute lies emanating from the far right (and echoed in the mainstream media). Those same critics—and perhaps the IRS or the Federal Election Commission—would have denounced any such spending as an unlawful contribution by a tax-exempt organization to Hillary's presidential campaign. The foundation's lawyers had advised against it.

The propaganda blitz against the foundation—long planned by Breitbart chair Steve Bannon—had certainly affected the election's outcome as well. While Clinton felt that the *New York Times* and other mainstream outlets had ceased attacking the foundation well before Election Day, the themes established in 2015 by *Clinton Cash* and its early promotion by the *Times* had inflicted irreparable damage on Hillary's campaign.

The proof arrived in August 2017, when media experts at Harvard and MIT released an exhaustive report that compiled and analyzed online media coverage and its impact on the presidential campaign. Its principal finding was that reporting on Hillary "primarily focused on the various scandals related to the Clinton Foundation and emails" but that in reporting on Trump, "major substantive issues were prominent," including the Republican's central issue of immigration. Voters didn't know what Hillary stood for because the press refused to tell them.

Titled *Partisanship, Propaganda, and Disinformation: Online Media and the 2016 U.S. Presidential Election*, their study included a special section on the irresponsible and misleading coverage of the Clinton Foundation. Beyond debunking the flood of grossly inaccurate, bigoted, and invented "scandal" pieces produced by far-right and conspiracy-mongering websites, the Harvard study's authors dissected "investigative" reports on the foundation produced by three of the nation's most respected news outlets: the Associated Press, the *Washington Post*, and the *New York Times*. In all three instances, those influential articles had omitted or buried vital exculpatory facts that proved the foundation and the Clintons had breached no ethical boundary.

But the study went still further, tracing the ways that biased negative coverage in the mainstream media had enabled the smear campaign by Hillary's right-wing opponents (and their Russian allies). Considered in total, the attacks on the foundation represented "a classic instance of a disinformation and propaganda campaign mediated through a network of allied media sources." Sites with higher visibility, such as Fox News and Bannon's Breitbart News, where *Clinton Cash* originated, linked to lower-ranked sites that endlessly repeated and supported false accusations. What made the smear so broadly effective, however, was the support lent by reputable sources like the AP, the *Times*, and the *Post*.

The key to Bannon's successful disinformation campaign against the Clinton Foundation, according to the Harvard study, was "to set the agenda for the mainstream press and then rely on that press coverage as an external source of validation and accreditation."

Rather than debunking groundless charges of corruption and tracing them to their sources, the most respected news organizations in the country placed their reputations behind a partisan distortion of the truth. As much as James Comey or Robby Mook, those journalists are responsible for the Trump presidency.

———

Long after the election, Bill and Hillary Clinton—and the Clinton Foundation—continued to draw attention from the media and the Republican right, seemingly unable to relinquish those perennial objects of fascination. Even in the shadow of Donald Trump's stumbling assumption of power, even with Hillary vanquished and exiled, the Clintons remained irresistible. And so did the impulse to invent narratives that might somehow diminish them.

During the week before Trump's inauguration on January 20—a joyless ceremony dutifully attended by both Clintons—the New York State Labor Department issued a pro forma announcement that the Clinton Global Initiative would lay off twenty-two employees during the coming fiscal quarter. Media outlets, especially on the far right, headlined this routine bureaucratic bulletin as proof that the election defeat had forced Bill Clinton to shut down his signature philanthropic project because—as one pro-Trump website put it—"nobody pays bribes to people unable to deliver favors."

All the gloating obituaries ignored a basic fact: Clinton and his key advisers had decided to close out CGI's annual September conference—and issued a press release confirming that decision—well before the election, when they believed Hillary would win. The Labor Department's layoff notice in January reflected nothing except the foundation's decision to keep dozens of CGI employees on its payroll for up to six months while they looked for new jobs. To describe that compassionate policy as a mark of disgrace or defeat was a misrepresentation typical of the foundation's partisan critics.

Around the same time, reports popped up in the Murdoch-owned media and other right-wing outlets, crowing over the reported withdrawal of funding by the Australian and Norwegian governments. Again, the stories insinuated that without White House pay-for-play, foreign governments would no longer support the foundation's work. And again, that insinuation could only be sustained by exaggerations and falsehoods. Having donated tens of millions of dollars to Clinton's AIDS projects from the very beginning—long before Hillary became secretary of state or ran for president —the Norwegians had withdrawn none of their committed funding. As for the Australians, a change in government there, rather than the U.S. election result, had cooled the relationship with Clinton. An Australian-funded project helping farmers in Kenya to cope with climate change was transferred to the Kenyan government, as originally planned. And shortly after the election, the German government renewed its support for a series of foundation-sponsored health clinics in Malawi.

If the foundation raised less money in 2016 than in previous years, that was unsurprising—and unrelated to the election, except in the sense that some individual friends had given more to Hillary's campaign and less to the foundation. But the foundation's major donors would continue to support its work.

Two weeks after Trump's inauguration, Clinton responded forcefully to the attacks on the foundation in a letter he issued with its 2016 annual report. "The attacks on our efforts have not come from people and organizations who understand or care about the work we do," he wrote. "By contrast, those who do understand have a very different view of what we do and how we do it." He pointedly noted that the nation's three main charity review groups—which provide a detailed examination of governance, financial health, transparency, and accountability, "have given us high ratings."

Those nonpartisan assessments were in fact uniformly positive: a "Four Stars" rating from Charity Navigator, an "A" rating from Charity Watch, and a "Platinum" rating for transparency from GuideStar. Clinton went on to pledge that most of the foundation's initiatives, aside from CGI, will continue—notably including the Clinton Health Access Initiative, whose programs have saved the lives of millions of HIV/AIDS patients across the world.

On the same evening that Clinton's letter was released along with the foundation's 2016 annual report, the *New York Times* ran a speculative story about its uncertain prospects. "Many believe the foundation's future will depend on Mr. Clinton, now 70, always its driving force," the *Times* observed.

The paper of record also noted in passing that Hillary's political opponents had "pounded" the foundation with accusations of conflict and self-dealing during the presidential campaign. While acknowledging that "no evidence emerged of a quid pro quo while Mrs. Clinton served as secretary of state," nevertheless "the overlapping interests of foreign donors to the foundation and official international affairs dogged her candidacy."

Barely two months later, as if responding to concerns about his ongoing commitment, the foundation announced Clinton's appointment as board chair, while former chair Bruce Lindsey stepped aside, remaining on the board and serving as "counselor" to Clinton. Chelsea continued as vice chair. Donna Shalala would return to the University of Florida, replaced by acting chief executive Kevin Thurm, her longtime deputy. In a statement to the foundation supporters and staff, Clinton said, "This has been my life for the last 16 years and I want to send a clear signal that we're serious about continuing our work which, I believe, is now more important than ever."

———

However important, that work would continue in a different style. The aging Clinton had hosted the last of the big, glitzy September conferences that featured heads of state, celebrities, academics, activists, donors, and nonprofit entrepreneurs packed into Manhattan's midtown Sheraton Centre. But he was undoubtedly determined to continue CGI—and the work of the Clinton Foundation—in other forms and venues.

Hundreds of idealistic college students pursuing social and environmental projects would keep meeting every year under the banner of CGI University, with costs subsidized by the foundation. Even as the misleading death notices appeared, the next CGIU conference already had been confirmed for October 2017 at Northeastern University in Boston. Clinton also hoped to revive CGI America, the domestic offshoot inaugurated in the wake of the 2008 recession—which by 2016 had completed a successful commitment by major union pension funds that plowed $14.5 billion into infrastructure projects.

The Clinton Health Matters Initiative would continue to address a promise Trump failed to fulfill: ameliorating the epidemic of opioid addiction that had cost more than 47,000 lives in working-class and rural communities. Under agreements with the manufacturers of Naloxone, a drug that can save lives by reversing opioid overdoses, the initiative would oversee distribution of Naloxone kits free or at low cost to every high school and college in the country—and train health aides in using them. The foundation's programs fostering early childhood education and fighting childhood obesity would likewise continue in many of those same communities.

In Africa, Asia, and Latin America, the Clinton Development Initiative would bolster the incomes, education, and health of hundreds of thousands of the world's poorest farmers and their families. Like the Haiti Action Network, the Clinton Giustra Enterprise Partnership would gradually spin off into a separate Canadian charity under the aegis of Frank Giustra.

Perhaps most important, the Clinton Health Access Initiative—with a budget well over $150 million that represented more than half of the foundation's total annual revenues—had weathered both internal and external stresses. Under a new independent board, the flagship program would persist in its lifesaving work.

For years, CHAI's chief executive Ira Magaziner had worried about the impact of another Hillary presidential campaign on the foundation. As the election cycle began in 2015 he had seen many of his fears fulfilled, exacerbating his tense relationship with the Clintons. While they had reached a truce of sorts during that period, the relentless negative publicity about the foundation had increased pressure on CHAI's largest donors to justify their continued support. The result was a wave of audits and assessments—totaling seventy-two before the end of 2016—by government development authorities, international charities, and U.S. and foreign foundations that combed through CHAI programs and finances.

Auditors and consultants invariably find grounds for improvement, but CHAI passed the dozens of inspections without sustaining any damage. The IKEA Foundation conducted a major evaluation and, in June 2017, announced two new CHAI grants worth nearly $17 million to reduce child mortality in Kenya and India. Indeed, according to Magaziner, none of the agencies and foundations that examined CHAI's programs found any reason to curtail their support.

To help resolve the long-standing difficulties between Magaziner and the Clintons, the CHAI board reorganized itself in March 2017. Its board grew to fifteen, with distinguished new members including Gro Harlem Brundtland, the former Norwegian prime minister and World Health Organization director-general, and former UNICEF chief Ann Veneman. Tadataka "Tachi" Yamada, the president of global health programs at the Gates Foundation, was elected board chair. As for Magaziner, approaching his seventieth birthday in November 2017, he gave up his own seat on the board and accepted an ex officio seat, agreeing to remain as CEO until the appointment of a successor sometime during the coming years.

Beyond the scuffling and shuffling at the top, CHAI's staff and volunteers maintained the innovative humanitarian spirit that had animated its work since 2002, when the AIDS project notched its first small victory in the Bahamas. While its HIV/AIDS program continued to provide access to medication and services for millions of people around the world, its remit had long since expanded to include programs fighting malaria, training health workers, and improving maternal and child health. Early in 2017, CHAI announced a new project to bring down the cost of cancer medication in the developing world, where pharmaceutical prices bar treatment for millions of patients.

None of the alleged "scandals" promoted by the Clintons' adversaries—or the media that enabled them—appeared to have affected the real capacity of the Clinton Foundation. Hundreds of organizations of every kind and every size, from the Bill and Melinda Gates Foundation and the George H. W. Bush Presidential Library Foundation to the Nature Conservancy and the National Association of School Nurses, across America and around the world, showed no signs of backing away from the foundation—or any reluctance to identify with its work.

———

Elections have consequences, and sometimes those consequences are deadly. For Bill Clinton, the outcome of the 2016 election posed a threat not only to the most significant aspect of his post-presidential legacy, but to the lives of millions of people across the world who have survived because of his foundation's work.

It was not difficult to foresee that the incompetence, xenophobia, malice, and plain stupidity of a Trump administration might well augur major reductions in U.S. foreign aid programs such as the President's Emergency Plan for AIDS Relief (PEPFAR). Surveys have consistently shown that many Americans, including no doubt many Trump supporters, are poorly informed about the cost and the benefits of foreign assistance—for example, in containing pandemic diseases like HIV/AIDS and Ebola. Neither Trump himself nor any of his close associates have ever appeared to understand those issues.

Within days after the election, Clinton called George W. Bush, who had started PEPFAR as president and, at Clinton's urging, then built an alliance with CHAI, the Global Fund, and other multilateral organizations to bring medical care to millions. He warned his successor that they should expect Trump to defund PEPFAR. "You better get in gear," he said. Evidently Bush agreed, and the two former presidents spent many hours in the months that followed, quietly lobbying to save the program after Trump—as predicted—proposed sharp cuts.

Clinton knew that the argument for fully funding PEPFAR was as powerful as ever. After more than a decade of effort, the U.S. government's own surveys showed clear evidence that the most afflicted countries were curtailing the spread of HIV/AIDS, malaria, and tuberculosis. Despite the lack of a vaccine or a cure, the number of AIDS deaths had been halved since 2005. With continued spending and applied research, a dawn without new infections was just over the horizon. It would be far worse than mere irony if Hillary's political defeat ended that progress and revived the pandemic.

Although Democrats in Congress successfully maneuvered to kill Trump's 2017 budget, the White House wasn't discouraged or dissuaded. Trump's 2018 budget proposed nearly a billion-dollar decrease in PEPFAR spending. But as the president's popularity plunged, congressional Republicans became more willing to defy him—and perhaps to fulfill the promise they had ratified when Bush began the program. In its 2018 budget markup, the House Appropriations Committee brushed aside the Trump request and maintained full funding for PEPFAR.

Yet Clinton had no illusions that the struggle would end there. At the end of June 2017, speaking before a Washington gathering of international nonprofit leaders, he described the Trump ascendancy as "a perfectly predictable period of reaction" and urged them "not to be weary, not to grow discouraged."

———

Until Election Day, Clinton had believed he might soon be living in the White House again, this time as the First Gentleman. But that reverie ended with Hillary's loss, and suddenly his own work took on a different dimension. For half a century his life in politics had defined him, lifting him to the presidency and then shaping his post-presidential career. Now for the first time he had entered a new chapter with no political ambitions or motives.

At seventy-one years old Bill Clinton wasn't weary—and he wasn't finished yet.

AUTHOR'S NOTE

The idea that eventually turned into this book first emerged from a profile of President Bill Clinton that I wrote for *Esquire* magazine more than ten years ago, at a time when he was still developing the philanthropic initiatives that have since become so well established. On that assignment, traveling through Africa and talking with him, I began to understand the scope of his aspirations.

Fewer than twenty ex-presidents have lived more than fifteen years beyond the end of their political careers, and of those even fewer sought to continue their public service in a meaningful way, although that has changed in recent decades. For those whose presidencies were controversial, the urge to serve often seems to be stronger.

Life after the presidency is a fascinating aspect of American history that Clinton has studied closely, tracing the abolitionist crusade of John Quincy Adams; the worldwide travels, scientific expeditions, journalistic triumphs, and political misadventures of Theodore Roosevelt; the postwar European relief projects of Herbert Hoover; and of course the humanitarian, diplomatic, and literary endeavors of Jimmy Carter, who retired from office more than thirty-five years ago—and is a man whom Clinton admires greatly, despite their clashing personalities and attitudes. The forty-second president has followed his own course, for better and occasionally for worse, one very different from each of those worthy predecessors yet with echoes of all of them.

In my effort to tell the story of Clinton's post-presidency, I was very fortunate that he and his staff agreed to cooperate with me. They have done so over the past several years, at no small cost in time and trouble, as did Hillary and Chelsea Clinton, and many of the Clintons' associates and friends. It is a sprawling, complicated epic with numerous narrative lines. I could never have found a path through it without their thoughtful and diligent assistance.

This is not an official account, nor did the former president approve its text. But most of the reporting in these pages is based on interviews with him, his present and former aides, and others who were involved in his endeavors. I have also traveled extensively with him in the United States and abroad, including two additional trips to Africa. And I have had substantial access to Clinton Foundation documents, some of which are quoted, dating back to the organization's earliest days.

Where I have relied on other sources, including news reports and broadcast transcripts, those are generally noted. Aside from Clinton's own works—*My Life* (Alfred A. Knopf, 2004); *Giving: How Each of Us Can Change the World* (Alfred A. Knopf, 2007); and *Back to Work: Why We Need Smart Government for a Strong Economy* (Alfred A. Knopf, 2011)—several books proved particularly valuable:

AIDS Drugs for All: Social Movements and Market Transformations, by Ethan B. Kapstein and Joshua W. Busby (Cambridge University Press, 2013).

All the Best: My Life in Letters and Other Writings, by George H. W. Bush (Simon & Schuster, 2013).

The Asian Tsunami: Aid and Reconstruction After a Disaster, by Sisira Jayasuriya and Peter McCawley (Edward Elgar, 2011).

The Big Truck That Went By: How the World Came to Save Haiti and Left Behind a Disaster, by Jonathan M. Katz (St. Martin's Press, 2013).

The Center Holds: Obama and His Enemies, by Jonathan Alter (Simon & Schuster, 2013).

Clinton in Exile: A President Out of the White House, by Carol Felsenthal (William Morrow, 2008).

Game Change: Obama and the Clintons, McCain and Palin, and the Race of a Lifetime, by John Heilemann and Mark Halperin (HarperCollins, 2010).

Haiti After the Earthquake, by Paul Farmer (PublicAffairs, 2011).

Hard Choices: A Memoir, by Hillary Rodham Clinton (Simon & Schuster, 2014).

Infections and Inequalities: The Modern Plagues, by Paul Farmer (University of California Press, 1999).

Katrina: After the Flood, by Gary Rivlin (Simon & Schuster, 2015).

The King of Oil: The Secret Lives of Marc Rich, by Daniel Ammann (St. Martin's Press, 2009).

Power in Numbers: UNITAID, Innovative Financing, and the Quest for Massive Good, by Philippe Douste-Blazy and Daniel Altman (PublicAffairs, 2010).

Somewhere Inside: One Sister's Captivity in North Korea and the Other's Fight to Bring Her Home, by Laura Ling and Lisa Ling (HarperCollins, 2010).

The Southern Tiger: Chile's Fight for a Democratic and Prosperous Future, by Ricardo Lagos with Blake Hounshell and Elizabeth Dickinson (St. Martin's Press, 2012).

ACKNOWLEDGMENTS

To write a book about Bill Clinton, as I know from past experience, is to invite pointed criticism and even angry denunciation. So be it. But I must express my gratitude to everyone who lent their kind assistance to me over the long gestation of this project, without implicating anyone else in my errors or opinions. The credit is to be shared, but the blame is all mine.

Alice Mayhew, my justly renowned editor, proved her patience and kindness as well as her wisdom many times over. I also owe much to assistant editor Stuart Roberts for managing this process so skillfully, and great appreciation to production editor Lisa Healy, executive art director Jackie Seow, designer Paul Dippolito, copy editor Fred Chase, proofreader Mara Lurie, managing editor Kristen Lemire, publicist Leah Johanson, and marketer Stephen Bedford. Elisa M. Rivlin's legal review improved the text. I also want to thank Simon & Schuster's president and publisher Jonathan Karp and associate publisher Richard Rhorer.

I continue to be among the fortunate clients of the Wylie Agency, where Jeffrey Posternak and Andrew Wylie offer encouragement and friendship as well as the best professional advice.

Very special appreciation is due for the generous support of Brian Snyder, Cecilia and Seward Johnson, and Bernard Schwartz, and for the counsel of Jill Straus and Susan Torricelli. My profound thanks as well to John Podesta and Debbie Fine for fellowship support from the Center for American Progress, and New York University's Center on Law and Security, where former executive director Karen Greenberg and her staff were enormously helpful.

President Clinton agreed to participate in this project, spending many hours in conversation with me about his ideas and work. Secretary Hillary Rodham Clinton and Chelsea Clinton kindly found time for interviews. I also appreciate the guidance of Nick Merrill, Cheryl Mills, Tamera Luzzatto, and Philippe Reines.

Not everyone who provided interviews or insights can be named here, but I owe the most sincere thanks to Douglas J. Band and Justin Cooper, as well as Jonathan Alter, Bill Babiskin, Ehud Barak, Bradley Beychok, David Brock, Ellen Chesler, Sandra Cress, Adrienne Elrod, Michael Feldman, Matt Gertz, Frank Giustra, Don Hazen, Harold Ickes, Pranay Gupte, Zelda LaGrange, Gene Lyons, Edwin Macharia, Terry McAuliffe, Matt McKenna, Eric Nonacs, John Podesta, George Polk, James Stewart Polshek, Jonathan Powell, Christopher Ruddy, Martin Rosenblatt, Douglas Schoen, Jake Siewert, Strobe Talbott, Karen Tramontano, Casey Wasserman, and Ted Widmer.

I am similarly indebted to Valerie Alexander, Ilya Aspis, Dr. Roger Band, Corey Ganssley, Jon Davidson, Amitabh Desai, Marc Dunkelman, Tina Flournoy, Robert Harrison, Ed Hughes, Amed Khan, Barbara Kinney, Terry Krinvic, Bruce Lindsey, Ira Magaziner, Kelly McCrystal, Walker Morris, Mary Morrison, Craig Minassian, Hannah Richert, David Ripin, Helen Robinson, Stephanie S. Streett, Angel Urena, Chris Wayne, Ed Wood, Clyde Williams, and Maggie Williams.

The Secret Service agents who protected President Clinton were required to put up with me on more than one long trip. I appreciate the patience and assistance of Dave Watson, Ralph Sozio, Mike Lee, Joe Russo, Jeff Irvine, Edna Perry, Will Dinkins, and all their dedicated colleagues.

The astute, diligent, and resourceful Emily Martin met my research needs capably and cheerfully, producing copious source material on very short deadlines. Sonia Houmis and her colleagues at TruTranscripts in New York transcribed interviews rapidly and superbly, as always.

The Writers Room provided a comfortable, quiet space to work and a friendly atmosphere enhanced by executive director Donna Brodie, Liz Sheman, and Vilma Torres.

It is difficult to express my lasting gratitude to the exceptional physicians who made my work possible, notably Dr. Thomas MacGillivray, Dr. Joseph M. Garasic, Dr. Faith Frable, and Dr. Allan Schwartz and his assistant, Trudi Santobello. I prefer not to imagine what would have happened without them.

The inspiration for this book began with a profile of President Bill Clinton that I wrote for *Esquire* in 2005. I still feel grateful for that assignment and the marvelous experience of working with David Grainger and Mark Warren, both outstanding editors.

The leadership and staff of The Nation Institute and the Investigative Fund could not have been more sympathetic, patient, and cooperative. I am especially grateful to executive director Taya Kitman and my longtime colleague Esther Kaplan, as well as Sarah Blustain, Kristine Bruch, Annelise Whitley, Eli Clifton, Kelly Virella, Hendrik Hertzberg, Roz Hunter, and all of my colleagues there.

I also depended on the undaunted staff at *The National Memo*, including publisher Elizabeth Wagley and all those who sustained our newsletter and website whenever I had to direct my attention elsewhere, in particular Matt Shuham, Eric Kleefeld, Sam Reisman, Henry Decker, Avi Zenilman, and Harold Itzkowitz.

I cannot imagine at all how I would have completed this book without the warm support of our friends who gave me so much in so many different ways. Dr. Gail Furman, Mary Pat Bonner, Joan Bingham, Sidney and Jackie Blumenthal, Arki Busson, Philippe Dennery, Karen Greenberg, James Hamilton, Stephen Jones, Rory Kennedy and Mark Bailey, Gina MacArthur, John Sexton, Uma Thurman, and Eugenie Voorhees were among those who stepped up when things got rough.

Our amazing family lifted me up in those dark moments too, especially Symmie and John Newhouse, Ann and Graham Gund, Jean and John R. Wagley, Sr., Dr. Barbara Landreth, Julie Conason and Geoff Bryant, and Rose Masinambow.

And above all, I owe everything to my wife, Elizabeth, and our children Eleanor and Edward, who light up my world every day.

INDEX